WITHDRAWN
HARVARD LIBRARY
WITHDRAWN

The Evolution of a Quaker Community

THE EVOLUTION OF A QUAKER COMMUNITY
Middletown Meeting, Bucks County, Pennsylvania
1750-1850

Martha Paxson Grundy

The Edwin Mellen Press
Lewiston•Queenston•Lampeter

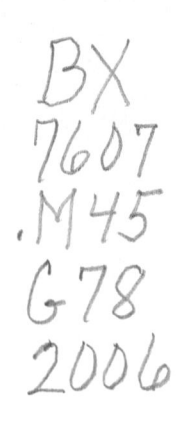

Library of Congress Cataloging-in-Publication Data

Grundy, Martha Paxson.
　The evolution of a Quaker community : Middletown meeting, Bucks County, Pennsylvania 1750-1850 / by Martha Paxson Grundy.
　　p. cm.
　Includes bibliographical references and index.
　ISBN-13: 978-0-7734-5568-9
　ISBN-10: 0-7734-5568-X
　I. Title.

hors série.

A CIP catalog record for this book is available from the British Library.

Copyright © 2006 Martha Paxson Grundy

All rights reserved. For information contact

<table>
<tr><td>The Edwin Mellen Press
Box 450
Lewiston, New York
USA 14092-0450</td><td>The Edwin Mellen Press
Box 67
Queenston, Ontario
CANADA L0S 1L0</td></tr>
</table>

The Edwin Mellen Press, Ltd.
Lampeter, Ceredigion, Wales
UNITED KINGDOM SA48 8LT

Printed in the United States of America

for Ken:

to say why would take a book

TABLE OF CONTENTS

NOTE ON MIDDLETOWN MEETING HOUSE..i
LIST OF FIGURES...iii
LIST OF TABLES..v
PREFACE by Professor Thomas D. Hamm..vii
ACKNOWLEDGEMENTS...ix
CHAPTER 1: INTRODUCTION..1
    Approach: Faith Development as an Analytical Tool.............................4
    Method..10
    Sources...11
    The Data Set...15
CHAPTER 2: SETTING THE SCENE...17
    The Religious Society of Friends...17
    Establishment of Pennsylvania..21
    Middletown Monthly Meeting in the 1750s.......................................26
CHAPTER 3: TIGHTENING THE DISCIPLINE..37
    Reform and Philadelphia Yearly Meeting...39
    Reform and Middletown Meeting...43
CHAPTER 4: ANTISLAVERY..57
    Middletown Meeting's Response...58
    Family Responses..62
    Pennsylvania and Slavery...70

    Racism..73
CHAPTER 5: WAR...77
    Philadelphia and Bucks County Prepare for War.............................78
    The Cost of Upholding the Peace Testimony....................................83
    Middletown Meeting Families Face War..90
CHAPTER 6: CHANGING ECONOMIC VIEWS................................101
    Business Failure...104
    The Farmers' National Bank of Bucks County...............................109
    Inventions and Improvements..111
    Speculation..115
CHAPTER 7: EVANGELICALISM...119
    Evidence for Evangelicalism in Middletown....................................125
CHAPTER 8: SEPARATION..131
    The Scholarly Trail...132
    The Separation in Philadelphia Yearly Meeting...............................135
    The Separation in Middletown Meeting..136
    Who Went Which Way, and Why...141
CHAPTER 9: POLITICS, REFORM, AND FURTHER ACCOMMO-
    DATION..163
    Jacksonian Democracy and Middletown Friends.............................165
    Reform Movements..176
    Non-Reform Secular Organizations...192
CHAPTER 10: DATA SET, MEETINGS, AND TOWNSHIP IN 1850.............201
    The Data Set Families and Middletown Meetings...........................201
    Economic Profile..209
    Political Profile...216
CHAPTER 11: CONCLUSIONS...223
    Family Patterns...225
    Another Look at the 1827 Separation..225
    Faith Development as an Analytical Tool...228
APPENDIX 1: DEMOGRAPHICS OF THE DATA SET AND MEETING.....231

APPENDIX 2: MIDDLETOWN MEETING ADULT MEMBERS, 1750.........235
APPENDIX 3: MIDDLETOWN TOWNSHIP 1757 TAX LIST........................239
   Single Men..241
APPENDIX 4: MEMBERS OF MIDDLETOWN MONTHLY MEET-
   INGS, 1850..243
   Bristol Preparative Meeting (Hicksite)..243
   Middletown Preparative Meeting (Hicksite)..245
   Middletown Monthly Meeting (Orthodox)...247
APPENDIX 5: GENEALOLGY CHARTS OF THE DATA SET FAMILIES. .249
   Allen..252
   Blakey...254
   Comfort...256
   Croasdale..258
   Gillam...260
   Jenks...262
   Kirkbride...264
   Linton..266
   Longshore...268
   Mitchell...270
   Paxson...272
   Richardson..276
   Stackhouse..278
   Watson..282
   Wildman...284
   Wilson...286
   Woolston...288
ABBREVIATIONS..290
NOTES..291
   Notes for Chapter 1: Introduction...291
   Notes for Chapter 2: Setting the Scene...293
   Notes for Chapter 3:Tightening the Discipline..296

Notes for Chapter 4: Antislavery..299
Notes for Chapter 5: War..303
Notes for Chapter 6: Changing Economic Views..306
Notes for Chapter 7: Evangelicalism...309
Notes for Chapter 8: Separation..311
Notes for Chapter 9: Politics, Reform, and Further Accommodation.............312
Notes for Chapter 10: Data Set, Meetings, and Township in 1850.................317
Notes for Chapter 11: Conclusion..318
Notes for Appendix 1: Demographics of the Data Set and Meeting...............318
Notes for Appendix 5: Genealogy Charts of Data Set Families.....................319
BIBLIOGRAPHY..321
INDEX..345

NOTE ON MIDDLETOWN MEETING HOUSE

The meeting house pictured on the front cover was built in 1793. It is the third house built by the meeting. Thirty silver maples were planted on the grounds in 1851. As some of them have grown large enough to obscure the building, the artist took the liberty of removing one from the painting. On April 9, 1962 the sheds which in early generations had sheltered horses, burned. Friends used the opportunity to replace them two years later with new stone First Day School rooms, that are to the right, out of sight in the illustration. In 1966 a garage was added and the drive was black-topped. In 1969 the meeting house was connected to the town sewer system.

The cemetery, where many of the individuals mentioned in this book were buried, lies behind the meeting house.

The meeting house is still in regular use by Middletown Meeting. It is located at 453 West Maple Avenue, Langhorne, Pennsylvania.

LIST OF FIGURES

FIGURE 1: Bucks County with Meeting Locations and Township Boundaries...25

FIGURE 2: Middletown Monthly Meeting Discipline Cases, 1740-1776..............43

FIGURE 3: Number of Discipline Cases by Type..44

FIGURE 4: Frequency of Offenses by Type, Data Set families, 1750-1787 and 1788-1850..45

FIGURE 5: Simplified Jenks Family Chart Showing Hicksite and Orthodox Affiliation...155

FIGURE 6: 1828 Presidential Election Returns in Bucks County by Township..220

LIST OF TABLES

TABLE 1: Average Tax Valuation for Middletown Township Quakers, Possible Quakers, and Non-Quakers, 1757...28

TABLE 2: Mean Tax Valuation for Data Set and Other Friends in Middletown Meeting, 1757..28

TABLE 3: Comparison of 1757 Tax Valuation with Estate Inventories of Four Data Set Heads of Household, 1757-1767...29

TABLE 4: Relative Income, Meeting Activity of Parents, and Disciplining of Children, Third Quarter 18th Century, Among Data Set Families............52

TABLE 5: 1785 Tax Valuation and Children Disowned, Among Data Set Men..97

TABLE 6: Taxable Wealth, Middletown Hicksite and Orthodox Data Set Families, with Constant Dollar Values, 1820, and 1830...............................142

TABLE 7: Percentage Change in Tax Valuation 1820 and 1830, Hicksite and Orthodox Data Set Families...143

TABLE 8: Household Size, Cattle Owned, Cattle Producing Potential Marketable Surplus Dairy Products, for Hicksite Data Set Men Resident in Middletown Twp...144

TABLE 9: Household Size, Cattle Owned, Cattle Producing Potential Marketable Surplus Dairy Products, Among Orthodox Data Set Husbands and Widows Resident in Middletown and Bensalem Townships...145

TABLE 10: Data Set Men whose Names Appeared in Bucks County
Newspapers as Involved in Political Activities, 1822-1850..........................168

TABLE 11: Philadelphia Yearly Meeting Actions Against Alcohol Use
and Abuse..182

TABLE 12: Residence of Blacks and Mulattoes in Quaker and Non-
Quaker Households, Middletown Township, 1850.......................................187

TABLE 13: Data Set Family Members of the Attleborough Protective
Company with Hicksite/Orthodox Affiliation, 1839-1851............................196

TABLE 14: Place of Birth of Inhabitants of Middletown Township and
With Whom They Lived in 1850..197

TABLE 15: Number of Tasks Assigned to Each Man per Year, Middletown Orthodox Men's Meeting, Ninth Month, 1827 through
Twelfth Month, 1850..204

TABLE 16: Occupations of Quaker and Non-Quaker Male Heads of
Household in Middletown and Bensalem Townships, as Listed in
the 1850 Census...210

TABLE 17: Most and Least Valuable Real Estate Holdings in Middletown Town-ship in 1850, with Age of Owner and Quaker Affiliation........211

TABLE 18: Value of Real Estate Owned by Quakers and Non-Quakers in
Middletown Township, 1850, Compared with Bensalem Township............212

TABLE 19: Comparison of Taxable Wealth Among Data Set and non-Data
Set, Hicksite and Orthodox, Members of the two Middletown Monthly
Meetings, 1850...214

TABLE 20: Comparative Numbers of Data Set, Hicksite, and Orthodox
Friends Who Were Residents of Middletown Township in 1850................232

TABLE 21: Comparison of Fertility between Middletown Township
Quakers and Non-Quakers in 1850 with 102 Rural Northern
Townships from New Hampshire to Kansas in 1860...................................233

TABLE 22: Heads of Household by Gender and Quaker Membership,
Middle-town Township, 1850..234

PREFACE

In this work, Martha Paxson Grundy gives us an unparalleled glimpse into the evolution of a Quaker community. For a generation now, community studies have been a staple of American historiography, testing broad theories about economic change or political conflict or gender roles through intensive, focused study of a particular locale. Such studies have revolutionized our understanding of colonial America, the western frontier, and the dynamics of slave communities, to name but a few examples.

Studies of Quaker communities, however, have been rare. At first glance, this is difficult to understand. Certainly Friends meetings, with their carefully recorded records of births, deaths, and marriages, and minutes of both men's and women's business meetings, offer a mass of relevant material to rival the New England town records that have been the foundation for so many dissertations. And certainly one can make an argument that colonies with strong Quaker influences, particularly Pennsylvania, better foreshadow the future direction of the United States than New England or the plantation South. For the most part, however, scholars have not seen Quaker communities as likely to answer the questions that most concern them.

This work raises questions that are of interest to scholars both of Quakerism and of broader American history. It does so with careful attention to detail, made possible by a wealth of documentation, and with an eye for larger questions of interpretation.

Grundy's century, from 1750 to 1850, was a crucial one for Quakerism. It saw three seminal changes: the tightening of the Discipline that heightened Friends' sense of themselves as a "peculiar people" between 1750 and 1780; the Hicksite Separation of 1827-1828 that created a rift in Quakerism that remains to this day; and the Quaker repudiation of slavery, which began with Friends freeing their slaves and ended with bitter controversy over how radical Friends should be in opposing the institution. The experience of Friends in Middletown Meeting in Pennsylvania sheds light on all of these matters that historians of Quakerism will need to take into account.

More broadly, however, Grundy asks a question that will interest all religious and intellectual historians–how do we explain the choices that members of a particular religious community made? Why did some Friends accept a tightened Discipline while others chose to leave the Society? Why did some side with the Orthodox and others with the Hicksites in the 1820s? Why did some embrace a plethora of radical reforms in the 1830s and 1840s while others, however sympathetic they were to peace and temperance and antislavery, remained aloof or even condemned them? Grundy's work is a caution against finding causes in factors that we can quantify on the basis of surviving records, such as wealth or class, and instead reminds us of the primacy of that element of individual choice, conditioned by a variety of factors that we cannot always reclaim.

Professor Thomas D. Hamm
History Department
Earlham College
Richmond, Indiana

ACKNOWLEDGEMENTS

The early research for this study was done in the 1980s, and many of the librarians who were so helpful then are no longer at those posts. Nevertheless it seems important to mention a few of their names, to let them know I still appreciate their friendly interest in my project and their unfailing cooperation. My special thanks to Elisabeth Potts Brown of the Quaker Collection at Haverford College, Albert Fowler at the Friends Historical Library at Swarthmore College, and Angel Conran of the Spruance Library of the Bucks County Historical Society. Then there were those who cheerfully put me up in their homes while I delved day after day in various archives. Fred and Eileen Roedel in Doylestown were especially hospitable.

My thanks to the History Department at Case Western Reserve University. They taught me a great deal of what I've learned about how to research and write history. My lapses are not to laid at their feet.

This study has been informed by my own experience among Friends. The interaction between past and present heightens my understanding of both. Although I am no longer involved with some of these groups, I want to acknowledge my debt to them for what they taught me in the 1980s and early 1990s: Cleveland Monthly Meeting, Lake Erie Yearly Meeting, Salem Quarterly Meeting, and Ohio Yearly Meeting (Conservative), as well as the Religious Education Committee and the Advisory, Executive, and Central Committees of Friends General Conference.

My thanks go to Middletown Monthly Meeting (Bucks Quarter) which permitted me to make a microfilm copy of their minutes to use in Cleveland for the preparation of a substantive index of the Women's Minutes, 1683-1893. This was invaluable for analyzing what went on in the meeting and in its families from the colonial through the antebellum years. I am grateful to Christopher Densmore, curator of the Friends Historical Library, for permission to quote from original records of Philadelphia Yearly Meeting and Middletown Monthly Meeting and their subordinate meetings. These records are in the Friends Historical Library at Swarthmore College and the Quaker Collection at Haverford College. Many of the records are on microfilm and available at both locations. Permission has generously been granted to quote from either, and the library that I list in any given note is often dependent on where I was researching that particular day.

My thanks to Ben Pink Dandelion for his persistent encouragement to offer this book to Edwin Mellen's Quaker Studies series, and especially to Tom Hamm for graciously agreeing to write the Preface.

Finally, this book would never have been written without the encouragement of Ken–not the first time around, and certainly not now. Will, Bonny, Tom, and Dave have more confidence in my computer skills than I do, when Will encouraged me to get in over my head using OpenOffice.org to format, "type set", and print out the manuscript. Their unfailingly cheerful assistance got me through many an impasse. I am grateful for permission from the artist, Anne E. G. Nydam, to use the watercolor painting of Middletown Meeting house for the front cover. She has also given permission to use the photograph on the back cover. She and a pair of the world's more adorable grandtwins, Trintje and Peter, have the ability to sooth the most frustrated non-geek grandmother.

Cleveland Heights
January 2006

INTRODUCTION

It has been said that to come close to God is to change. It is also true that coming closer to God means moving farther from the center of the dominant culture. Most spiritual leaders, saints, and holy ones live on the margins of society. The first Friends in the seventeenth century experienced this and knew it to be true. Because of their own developing relationship with God, their priorities were different from those of most of their non-Quaker neighbors. They envisioned themselves as if living in God's Commonwealth, tiny outposts of which were springing up throughout England. Their attitude toward the culture in which they lived was summed up in the familiar Quaker admonition to be in the world but not of it. This meant that they were not to withdraw into hermitages or cloistered communities. They were to participate in the economic and political world in which they found themselves. But they were to play by different rules. Their ultimate allegiance was to God, and the social, economic, and political rules they sought to obey were those in conformity with God's realm.[1]

In the century after Quakerism burst upon the English scene its radical exuberance was replaced with sober steadiness. Quakers founded Pennsylvania as a "holy experiment" and they prospered. Eventually, wealthy Quakers came to uphold the status quo rather than to challenge it. They were no longer dissenters living at the margins, and their radical critique of the "world" became muted.[2]

In the mid-eighteenth century Philadelphia Yearly Meeting underwent a reform movement which left it smaller but more homogeneous in terms of outward conformity to Quaker testimonies regarding marriage, plainness in speech and dress, slavery, military activity, and office holding. Historian Jack Marietta describes the process of deliberately choosing to weed out members who did not behave in ways which upheld the group's testimonies as an effort to maintain—or regain—a Society in which religion would color all areas of a member's life.[3] In a way, reform can be seen as an effort to reclaim the radical community of the seventeenth century that had been forged on the fringe of society through suffering for the sake of conscience. Then, having been transformed, they witnessed with a holy zeal to God's order as they had come to understand it.

The insight that religion should suffuse all of life and not be segregated to a single compartment relevant only on Sunday morning, meant that there were Quaker expectations of behavior in a wide spectrum of situations. These included, among others, business affairs, patterns of speech and dress, entertainment and leisure time activities, family relationships, the status of women, and marriage practices. There were also clear expectations of behavior in unusual situations arising out of slave-holding or war. When someone wanted to join early Friends, he or she was not questioned about beliefs or articles of faith. Instead Friends looked at his or her behavior to see if it witnessed to Friends' testimonies. Friends assumed a congruence between inward spiritual condition and outward behavior. They accepted the Biblical admonition, "the tree is known by its fruit." [Matt. 12:33b, NRSV]

In 1750 Quakers held political, economic, and social power in colonial Pennsylvania. There are many studies of how they withdrew from provincial political offices at the time of the Great War for Empire, known locally as the French and Indian War. Their unpopular neutral and pacifist stand during the American Revolution further undermined their economic and social position. These two wars brought great changes to the position of Quakers within Pennsylvania. They became marginalized in their own land. Individual Friends were forced to make choices between the requirements of their religion and the pushes and pulls from non-Quaker society. After the new American republic was established and Quakers felt free to accept it as the duly instituted government, they tended to be dropped from the view of most historians.[4] However, in the last few decades a new interest, especially in women's history, has led to a resurgence in scholarly study of Friends.

American life is not static. At the end of the eighteenth and into the nineteenth century there were tremendous changes. Of course these did not affect all people equally. Some changes were embraced enthusiastically by some people, others were resisted with great vigor. Most individuals picked and chose where to draw the line between what to accept and what to reject. What were some of these changes? A quick list would include the expanding scope of market capitalism in the form of banking, internal improvement schemes, industrialization, speculative ventures, increased importance of market farming, and geographical mobility. There was a shift from the subsistence family farming culture of rough equality, mutual dependence, and patriarchy to a market economy which commodified goods, labor, and relationships, while increasing individual self-reliance and economic inequality. Evangelicalism swept through protestant denominations, clashing with Enlightenment deism and Unitarian and Universalist humanism. Its underlying dynamic of seeking purity resonated with the Religious Society of Friends, but was at odds with the unique Quaker understandings of scripture and the Inward Christ. Reform movements and voluntary associations arose to tackle such problems as slavery, alcohol, illiteracy, and crime that had previously been the purview of church or state.

For its first hundred years the Religious Society of Friends had been remarkably unified in faith and practice. A constant stream of men and women travelling in the ministry among meetings and Friends' families on both sides of the Atlantic shared spiritual experiences and built a sense of community.[5] But in 1827 a growing divergence over theology, ecclesiology, and personalities, combined with socio-economic tensions within the larger polity of the young United States, erupted into a separation in Philadelphia Yearly Meeting between so-called Hicksite and Orthodox factions. This Separation rippled out to other yearly meetings, and with succeeding schisms has colored succeeding Quaker activities.

This study examines the choices rural Quaker individuals made within the context of their families and religious community between the expectations of their faith and the multiplicity of new options offered by the culture outside their Society. Between 1750 and 1850 there were two major crises within Philadelphia Yearly Meeting, and to a certain extent within all North American Quakerism. The first involved the reform movement of the 1750s through the Revolution (Chapters 3, 4, and 5), the second involved the Separation in 1827 (Chapter 8).

Friends also faced a series of crises of a different sort. These were quiet crises, without sharply defined points demanding clear choices. Although their magnitude may have been almost imperceptible to those living through them from day to day, they are more obvious looking back over time. These quiet crises included the shift from the "fair price" concept of the colonial world to the market capitalism of the nineteenth century (Chapter 6). Another was the transition from the religious world of the seventeenth century to the Enlightenment of the eighteenth and then to the evangelicalism of the nineteenth (Chapter 7). In some respects Friends had a harder time dealing with these invisible crises than they did with the difficult but specific demands laid on them during the American Revolution or decision of the Religious Society of Friends to free itself of slave holding.

Approach: Faith Development as an Analytical Tool

This book uses two different ways of trying to understand the choices Friends made. One is a relatively new technique for historians, the concept of faith development as an analytical tool. This is useful in two ways: to shed light on the motivation of an individual in a specific situation, and in what seems like quite a different use, to help understand some of the underlying dynamic of broad movements within the institution of the Religious Society of Friends. Secondly, this study looks at Quaker families, as nuclear units and over time, to search for patterns of orientation toward the meeting, toward political activity, or toward economic activity. Taking the original Quaker assumption that one's outward life reflects one's inner, spiritual life, we can make the bold attempt through studying the record of their outward lives to draw some conclusions about their spiritual lives. Thus circling around again to concepts of faith development.

Max Weber identified two kinds of prophetic religion. Although he was dealing with all religions, and he used the categories somewhat differently than I do, they are still useful. The "emissary" type is concerned with outward conformity to a set of rules, and is deeply involved with the enforcement of those rules on others. The "exemplary" type is mystical, and more concerned with the inward demands made by religion on the individual's own behavior. Quakerism he labels "emissary", while noting that it also contained "very strong contemplative elements".[6] Historian Jean Soderlund has shown that the "emissary" type of Friend was interested in the enforcement of the discipline within the Society of Friends, while the "exemplary" type was concerned with applying to outward life the spiritual truths that had been gained inwardly. In her study of reform and antislavery within Philadelphia Yearly Meeting, she found the "emissary" type was concerned with marriage procedures and plainness of speech and apparel, while the "exemplary" type was interested in the manumission of slaves and their well-being. The former could be categorized as tending to be more concerned with the tribal identity of the Society of Friends or with religion seen as a necessary mechanism for controlling behavior, while the latter saw religion in terms of response to a divine imperative to love one another.[7]

John Auping makes a division between "intrinsic" and "extrinsic" religion. After reviewing theories about religion, the abolition of slavery, and capitalism, he concluded that intrinsic Christianity "makes market consciousness connect with compassion in an effort to limit by law the workings of the market, but no more than is necessary to prevent or correct social injustice." Extrinsic Christianity, he found, compartmentalized thinking to "let the freedom of stronger actors to exploit the weaker ones go unchecked."[8] It would seem that "emissary" Friends might have some commonalities with Auping's "intrinsic" group, in their dependence on laws, and what might be perceived as choosing the minimum that had to be done to satisfy conscience while not overly inconveniencing business. In time Friends were persuaded to eschew his "extrinsic" category, at least in regard to slave-holding by Friends, if they wanted to remain members of their meetings.

Another tool for studying the differences reflected in these two ways of looking at the dynamics of Quakerism (or other religious groups) is the concept of faith development. Sigmund Freud has taught us to think in terms of stages of psychological growth: oral, anal, oedipal, latent, etc. Arnold Gesell and Frances Ilg gave a generation of mothers conceptual tools for observing the physical growth stages of children. Educationists talk about levels or stages of cognitive development. Some theologians have discovered that similarly there are stages in the development of an individual's religious faith.[9] Now efforts are being made by Ken Wilber, Don Beck, and others to pull all these ideas of levels and stages of development in four quite different areas into one grand integral theory.[10]

In terms of developmental stages, Erik Erikson is probably the scholar most familiar to historians. Theologian James W. Fowler has constructed a schema of six levels of faith development. Quaker historian Howard Brinton has identified the common stages through which Quaker ministers progressed, as revealed in their journals. For the purposes of this study, however, the simplified and popularized concepts of M. Scott Peck are more useful because they fit the experience of ordinary Friends who did not become ministers, and because they help explain some of the tensions during times of change within the Religious Society of Friends as an institution.[11]

Peck sketches four levels in the development of faith. They are simplistic, and therefore rarely explain completely a specific individual's spiritual journey. But as a crude diagram of the way we develop, it is at least as useful as Freud's diagram of psychological growth, or Gesell and Ilg's description of the physical development of a child. Peck's levels mesh rather nicely with the spiral of development levels or memes described by Ken Wilber, Don Beck, and Chris Cowan.

Peck's first, beginning level is chaos, or the self-centeredness of a child or an amoral adult. This would be the "beige" first level meme of spiral development theory. The second level, which Peck calls formal or institutional, is characterized by attachment to the forms (as opposed to the spirit) of religion, and a vision of God as "almost entirely that of an external, transcendent Being". It is the normal progression for a healthy child in a religiously-aware home. One can move into this second level either by accepting the rules and mores of one's family and church, or through a "born again" conversion experience. In either event one supports and upholds the institutionalized church. This would roughly approximate the fourth, blue meme of Wilber *et al*. Peck's third level is epitomized by the Enlightenment's skepticism, individualism, and an urge to reform the world through human action. Wilber names this the sixth or green meme. However, Wilber's analysis is much more tuned to the late twentieth century than to the dynamics and issues of the nineteenth.[12] Peck's fourth level, and Wilber's second tier, the mystic or communal, are aware of the underlying connectedness of all life. One moves into this stage through a gradual disillusionment with skepticism and rationality, and a rediscovery, at a far deeper level, of the spiritual truths embraced as level twos. At this level one knows one cannot do justice and seek peace in one's own strength; one experiences the walk with God, grows in it, and finds there the instruction and the empowerment to live as if in God's Commonwealth, in the midst of the very human world.[13]

Any individual at a given time will be predominately at one level. But on some issues one may revert to an earlier level, as one may also do at a particularly stressful time. These levels are approximations, useful for increasing understanding, but not so precise that we should expect them to fit all individuals and all situations. In a way the term "level" or "stage" is a misnomer. They are not plateaus where nothing happens, even though many people may remain for a good part of their lives at a given level. It is, perhaps, more useful to think of one's spiritual life as a journey, with a series of milestones along the way. Level two, for example, might run from milestone 3 to milestone 7. In other words, there are gradations and growth within each level. However, growth is not linear. It circles around, doubles back, and revisits old issues again and again, but at increasing depth. The richness and subtlety of these possibilities will not be used in this study. Let the reader be warned that I am just using the basic concept of faith development as a tool for increasing general understanding of specific historical incidents and trends, not as the finely honed instrument it can be for other purposes.

Seeing Weber's "emissaries" in terms of Wilber's blue meme or Peck's stage two, and his "exemplary" in terms of Wilber's second tier or Peck's fourth level, opens new understandings of the crises in this study. Individuals can be mired at one level or can change over time. Even though people at level two and level four use the same words, and follow the same rules, they have different understandings of their meanings. They tend to puzzle and eventually aggravate each other. People at adjacent levels, for example level two and level three (Wilber's blue and green memes), tend to see each other as just plain wrong.

The use of levels of faith development as a tool of analysis does not mean that we categorize every individual. That is a perilous and unsatisfactory undertaking. However, this tool is helpful to analyze specific behavior in a given situation, and to help understand the dynamics within a larger movement in history.

There is one other dimension that we need to consider, and that is the degree of passion or indifference an individual feels toward his or her religious life. This cuts across the levels of faith development that we have been describing. A passionate level two, for instance, will be very active in watching over the purity of the church, or reaching out to bring salvation to others. An indifferent level two may drop out altogether, or be a Christmas and Easter attender. Among Friends in the period under study, someone approaching the indifferent end of the scale would probably prefer disownment to changing a specific behavior, all other things being equal (and they rarely were). A passionate level three would be very involved in social actions designed to bring about a more just world. An indifferent level three would assume that religious questions are a silly waste of time, and would get on about what he or she considers to be the "real" business of life.

The traditional academic approach to study people who define themselves in terms of religion has been to apply a skeptical third level, orange or green meme, "outsider" analysis. As Howard Brinton observed, such academicians "tend to neglect what might be called its inner side."[14] The assumption is that by avoiding the subjective "inner side", their history will be unbiased. But many historians realize that there is no truly unbiased history. They argue that it is important to acknowledge our biases, so the reader is forewarned. Therefore, be aware that this study attempts to come at its subjects from the "inside", by giving credence to the spiritual life by which these people defined themselves.

Anthropologists and ethnologists of ritual and religion have examined the issue of the "insider/outsider problem". For well over the first half of the twentieth century they assumed the detached, scientific objectivity was both possible and desirable. They observed and commented on the exotic "other". More recent work dismantles this dichotomy, particularly as anthropologists have turned to study groups of which they are themselves members.[15] Historians who tried to be objective wrote as "outsiders" about the individuals or groups who defined themselves in terms of religion. The result tended to be a stance of superiority towards the ignorance and superstition of the objects of their studies. This is changing, as historians increasingly acknowledge the importance of faith as an element in interpreting history, and give credence to it.[16] As a Friend myself, who has participated at local, regional, and national levels, I have been aware of the duet between past and present, between what I study and what I experience. Examination of seventeenth and eighteenth century Quaker experience has informed—and been informed by—my own interactions with the faith and practice of Friends over the past half century.

Broadly speaking, this study looks at how a group of Friends grappled with the disjunctions between the requirements of their faith and the demands and opportunities of the world beyond their Religious Society. As this outside world changed between 1750 and 1850, Friends' understanding of it and their relationship to it also changed. In 1750 Friends tended to see their community as separate from the rest of the world. This was a world to be interacted with on the political or economic level, but less so on a social level, and only very sparingly as a source of spiritual ideas.[17] By 1850 the unity of the Society of Friends had been shattered, and different fragments perceived various parts of the outside world in conflicting ways. Orthodox Friends looked on evangelical Protestants as fellow Christians with whom they shared a great deal, including a fear and loathing of "infidels" and Hicksites. Some of the so-called Hicksites favored Unitarians and theologically-liberal Christians, while the majority were still essentially quietist. Conservative Friends in both branches still tried to "hedge out" the non-Quaker world. That world became increasingly complex and diverse as the nineteenth century progressed, and parts of it reached deeper and deeper into individual Quaker lives. But Friends were not in unity as to which parts to absorb. Over time as the line became increasingly blurred which separated Quaker understandings of their own faith and practice from those of non-Friends of a variety of persuasions, the lines grew sharper which separated the Quaker branches from each other.

Method

The approach of this study has been to select a group of families and search a variety of records for evidence of their behavior in a wide range of situations. From behavior we can infer choices. If patterns emerge, we can draw conclusions about how this group of people, at least, dealt with the changes and crises between 1750 and 1850.

Quakerism has no written creed. It did not, originally, subject its members to a test of theological orthodoxy. Instead it expected that the life of each Friend would bear the fruits of the "measure" of his or her inward condition. Therefore, they disciplined members for outward behavior. This characteristic of "letting their lives speak" invites the historian to use the same method of noticing outward behavior and inferring inner spiritual condition from it.

Since the family was the core unit for Quakers in this period, this study examines the families which had members of one rural Quaker meeting for the hundred years under discussion. Those who stayed were a distinctive group, and cannot be assumed to be typical of all Quakers. However, if the Quaker community and the family were important then one must study the roughly four generations of people who were part of that community and those families. Comparisons will be made with those who left the meeting membership and/or the area, when they can be traced and if it helps our understanding.

This book is concerned with how individual Friends, within the context of their families and facing the changing political, economic, religious, and social events and movements of this period, defined and lived their religion. The concept of faith development can help us understand individuals in specific situations, or general movements. But it is not a particularly useful tool for studying the dynamics of families, which are groups of people. *Individuals* undergo spiritual growth; families can share experiences and provide the nurture and atmosphere which can encourage such growth. But each person must go through the process within himself or herself.

The seventeen surname families that had members in Middletown Monthly Meeting in Bucks County, Pennsylvania for the entire one hundred years from 1750 to 1850 form the basis of this study. While there probably does not exist such a thing as a typical meeting, Middletown was not extraordinary. There were no widely famous weighty Quakers, no stellar political figures, no extremely wealthy families. Therefore, it is a good meeting to study if one is attempting to look at ordinary Quakers and their families. The meeting was not in the forefront of the reform movement nor did it mount a consistent rear guard action against change. The monthly meeting was set off in 1683, so by the time this study begins it was well established, with many of the families already in their second or third generation of participation.

Sources

The main sources of information on individual Quakers are the Middletown Monthly Meeting records.[18] These include minutes for the men's and the women's meetings for business (or discipline, as they were sometimes called). There are lists of births and deaths, and copies of marriage certificates and certificates of removal. There are copies of the papers written to publicly explain in what way an individual's behavior had been inconsistent with Friends' principles resulting in that person no longer being "owned" as a member. Finally, there are copies of papers written by penitent men and women acknowledging their inconsistencies, repenting of them, and asking to come again under the care of Friends. This wealth of records yields information for reconstituting families, and for tracking movements into or out of the geographic area served by Middletown Meeting. Although Quaker records are justly famous, particularly in comparison to those of other churches, they are not perfect. There are inevitably gaps caused by an absent-minded recorder, lost pages or books, faded ink, or indecipherable handwriting.

In addition to the genealogical data available, Friends' records also yield information on who was active in the meeting and in what ways. Since Friends had no paid clergy, everything that had to be done officially in the way of pastoral care or financial and "housekeeping" activities was delegated to small committees appointed by the monthly meeting. The minutes record who was named to which committees. The substantive index of the women's minutes (1683-1893) has provided an invaluable tool. The same type of data has been compiled for 1750-1850 from the men's minutes.

There are two additional Quaker sources: memorials and journals. Both were published to illustrate Friends' faith as practiced by exemplary Friends. There is a memorial to Grace Croasdale of Middletown Meeting. The journal of Middletown minister William Blakey was printed in *Friends' Miscellany*.[19]

Data from Quaker sources is augmented with secular records. For the colonial and revolutionary periods the *Colonial Records* and *Pennsylvania Archives* yield names of county and provincial officeholders. There are minutes of the Provincial Council and Assembly, although due to the influence of Friends' ways of doing business they lack, for example, roll call votes. For the Revolutionary War period, the *Archives* provide minutes of the "Committees of Safety," names of those called up into the various companies of militia, and fines levied against those who refused to serve. There are also records of those arrested for collaboration with the British, and of those whose estates were distrained and sold.

Tax records yield data on comparative wealth, but they must be used with caution.[20] They are incomplete, and the currency varied in type and value.

Friends put a high value on "good order" and an orderly thing in one's personal life was to leave a proper will.[21] Again, historians must deal with incomplete records. Not everyone made a will, especially women who died before their husbands. The records, which might consist of wills, estate inventories, and various administration papers, are useful for family reconstitution and comparative wealth. Over the hundred year period they document the increasing number and variety of farm equipment, household furnishings, books, and other things which people owned. They also show the economic network: to whom the deceased owed money and to whom he or she lent money. In the nineteenth century estates increasingly contained "paper": bonds, bank shares, stock, and notes of various kinds.

The United States census is another source of data, although of limited use before 1850, the end point of this study. Each census became more detailed after the first in 1790. In that one, only heads of household were named, with numbers in a few age and gender groups for each household, without indicating which returns were for which township within a given county. In 1850 every person's name and age, and usually their occupations, were recorded for the first time.

Colonial newspapers are not much help for this study. They tended to reproduce news from other places, with only the Philadelphia advertisements occasionally shedding light on the actions of a Bucks County individual. In 1804 a newspaper was first published in Bucks County, but it followed the usual practice of reprinting external news and literary items. It was assumed that local people already knew local news. After the War of 1812 local newspapers proliferated, each having an identifiable political bias. Then it becomes very useful to read them, seeing who put their notices of family events in which papers: people tended to put them in the paper which reflected their political views. It was not until 1843 that a Bucks County newspaper began to print sizable amounts of Bucks County news. Unfortunately, only the *Bucks County Intelligencer* (and its many name permutations) has been indexed, and that only for births, marriages, and deaths. Also, there is the familiar scholarly problem of incomplete runs of local papers, as well as very short publishing lives for most of them.[22]

After the Separation in 1827 several Orthodox Friends in Philadelphia began publishing *The Friend*, "to defend and uphold the great principles, both in theory and practice, which the Society of Friends, from their rise to the present time, have professed and maintained. But . . . to avoid, as far as practicable, all controversial discussions, more particularly on questions which lead to no important practical result."[23] Hicksite Friends did not begin publication of the *Friends Intelligencer* until 1844. The Orthodox split into Gurneyite and Wilburite groups was reflected in *The Friends Review* (Gurneyite) which began publication in 1847. Birth, marriage, and death notices in specific journals indicate the sectarian sympathies of individual Friends. Occasionally obituaries yield personal data, although usually they were clothed in platitudes.

Finally, a word is needed about the secondary sources. There are two main types for a study of this kind. One is academic and the other is amateur or informal. A good deal of recent scholarly work is helpful for one or another aspect of this paper. These studies will be discussed in more detail throughout as historiographical questions arise.

Older amateur histories sometimes blend over into primary sources because of the personal knowledge of their authors. Many take the form of local or family histories. The golden age of local history was the end of the nineteenth and beginning of the twentieth centuries. There are three such histories of Bucks County, two of Bristol and one of Byberry.[24] They are an historian's dream and nightmare, and must be used with care. They are anecdotal, undocumented, unindexed, and often borrow from each other. Their underlying purpose seems to have been to celebrate the solid, well-established families, ignoring the newcomers, often of different ethnic backgrounds. Family histories run the gamut from large volumes extensively documented, through articles in the many genealogical magazines, to handwritten gossipy, anecdotal accounts in the files of the Bucks County Historical Society (BCHS) or one of the other historical libraries. Increasing amounts of genealogical material on the web must be used with care for it often is undocumented and websites copy from each other as if repeating something often enough will make it true. The publications of the Historical Society of Pennsylvania (HSP), the Friends Historical Association (FHA), and the Bucks County Historical Society follow the pattern of amateur historiography in their early years, while recent material is done in a much more scholarly style.

The Data Set

The purpose of this study is to ascertain the choices Friends made, within the context of their families, between the requirements of membership in the Religious Society of Friends and the expectations of the dominant culture. It examines the seventeen surname families that included members of Middletown Monthly Meeting for the entire hundred years from 1750 and 1850. These families were: Allen, Blakey, Comfort, Croasdale, Gillam, Jenks, Kirkbride, Linton, Longshore, Mitchell, Paxson, Richardson, Stackhouse, Watson, Wildman, Wilson, and Woolston.[25]

The data set is comprised of 624 adult men and women of these seventeen natal surnames who had not died by 1750, and were born by 1829. Along with married members who remained in the meeting, the set also includes people who left the area, who left the Religious Society of Friends, who died as young adults, and who did not marry. It does not include the children of those who left the area or the meeting. Nor do the statistics include wives from non-data set families who married data set men, although some of these are mentioned in the text.

Chapter 3 compares the data set Friends with the rest of Middletown Meeting in the mid-eighteenth century, while Chapter 10 repeats the comparison for the mid-nineteenth century. Appendix 1 provides a more detailed comparison of the demographics of the data set, Middletown meeting as a whole, and the general population.

SETTING THE SCENE

The Religious Society of Friends

The Religious Society of Friends rose out of the turmoil and questioning of the English Civil War in the mid-seventeenth century.[1] Quakers, as they were derisively called, preached a radical "primitive Christianity". They directed people to the Light of Christ within each of them which would not only show them their sin, but also direct them to their Saviour. It would teach them how to obey him, and would empower them to do so. Friends believed that religion permeated all of life, and therefore everything they did was accountable to God and should be open and transparent, a shining witness to God's Kingdom.

Faith and Practice

Out of their personal experience of the transforming power and love of God, which drew them away from the dominant culture of their day and into unity with others who were trying to live a more Christ-centered life, grew a set of testimonies and practices which differentiated Friends from their neighbors. Two such testimonies were the refusal of "hat honor" and the use of plain language. The social conventions of the time called for elaborate gestures of deference, and the use of the second person plural when addressing a social superior. But Friends understood that all are equal in God's sight, and refused to accord some people special honor because of their wealth, rank, or social position. Friends realized that by being humbled themselves they had been able to experience God, and they wanted to encourage other people to experience that productive humility, too.[2] Another testimony involved the refusal to swear an oath. Friends demanded of themselves a single standard of truth at all times, rejecting the idea that only when they swore were they bound to accuracy. Other testimonies involved setting a just price rather than bargaining for merchandise, renunciation of violence and war, refusal to pay tithes or attend services of the established church, and elimination of the lace, trims, and fashionable excesses of clothing. Their understanding of the place of women and of the spiritual equality of all people and their economic views, as well as their theology, were revolutionary in implication, and threatening to the established order. Friends were persecuted during the Commonwealth and even more so after the Restoration. The Act of Toleration brought relief from most of the harshest measures. But a hundred years later a few Friends still perished in English gaols for refusing to pay tithes.

In the eighteenth century Quakerism entered a period of quietism. As persecution diminished in the British Isles, and the testimonies for honesty in the market place led to prosperity and respect for Quakers, there grew a reluctance to carry on aggressive work for fundamental change in the world.[3] The exhaustion following the religious excesses of the seventeenth century, and the rise of deism with its tendency to emphasize morality over theology, spilled over from the larger society to affect Quakers. Friends adopted distinctive patterns of speech and dress to hedge themselves off from the rest of society as a peculiar people.

Theologically, quietism called Friends to empty themselves of their own self-will and ideas so that the Holy Spirit might speak through them, as through a hollow tube. But as Quaker historian Douglas V. Steere notes, the inward turning was not just passive. At its best it blended with social outreach to create an active witness to changing the world.[4] The quintessential quietist, of course, was the activist John Woolman.

Quaker historians like William C. Braithwaite have seen quietism as declension. Towards the end of the twentieth century historians began reinterpreting Braithwaite's declension model of the eighteenth century's quietism. They suggest that the energy released by the spiritual fervor of the seventeenth century did not die into a negative quietism in the eighteenth. Instead it was transmuted into a new culture which flowered in the Delaware Valley. Barry Levy points to the importance of child rearing and the new concepts of intra-family relations that Friends developed. We can revisit Thomas Clarkson's description of Quaker culture as seen at the close of the eighteenth century. William Taber shows how quietism blossomed in rural Ohio in the nineteenth century.[5] Recent scholarly attention to female Friends has resulted in reprinting and studying the writings and work of many eighteenth-century women that demonstrate the vigorous activity–inward and outward–of these Friends ministers.[6]

Organization

Since the 1660s the Religious Society of Friends has been structured in a way intended both to guard against individual excesses and to allow for new revelation to break forth. It has concentric circles or levels of corporate groupings while mostly managing to avoid giving hierarchical powers to individual offices.

Local groups were settled into preparative meetings, which prepared items of business for the monthly meeting. The monthly meeting, constituting one or more preparative meetings, was responsible for the financial, pastoral, and spiritual care and business of local Friends. There was no paid clergy or staff. Both meetings for worship and meetings for business were held in the expectation that Christ would be present to lead his people. Consequently the only officer at a business meeting was a clerk to order the agenda and minute any decisions. Decisions were not made by voting but by corporate discernment of what God wanted the group to do.[7] Actions were carried out by committees appointed at the time for the specific purpose. In the late eighteenth century a few committees became more permanent as members were appointed for a year to deal with ongoing concerns such as caring for freed slaves or "necessitous" Friends.

A group of monthly meetings in a given geographical area, often a county, sent representatives four times a year to a quarterly meeting. There they dealt with business concerning the entire area, helped a monthly meeting with a particularly difficult problem, worshipped together, shared experiences, cemented ties, and socialized. Representatives from all the quarterly meetings in a larger area gathered annually at a yearly meeting—which was an event as well as an organization. There were six yearly meetings in the thirteen colonies. The yearly meeting was the final disciplinary authority for Friends within its verge. They were auto-nomous in theory but in close communication with each other, and in practice the yearly meetings in the colonies deferred to London Yearly Meeting.[8]

This system of meetings was made up entirely of men. Friends recognized that God could also speak through women, but that the culture of the time made it very difficult for a woman to exercise her gifts in a mixed group. Therefore a whole parallel system of preparative, monthly, quarterly, and yearly meetings was established for women.[9] Women clerked their meetings, handled their own finances, disciplined their members, gave material and spiritual assistance to Friends in need, but did not deal with matters which also touched the men. They were separate but not quite equal. In matters concerning the whole meeting, the women acted only with the concurrence or approval of the men. However, in comparison to the position of women in any other English church of the time, Quaker women were free to develop and use their God-given talents.

In addition to the men's and women's hierarchy of meetings, there were preparative, monthly, quarterly, and yearly "select" meetings for ministers and elders. Later these also included overseers. Ministers were men and women who were recognized as having a divine gift of vocal ministry in meetings for worship. Elders were those who were recognized as having the gifts of encouraging and guiding the ministers, being gifted with discernment, and having a particular care of and concern for the spiritual life of the entire meeting. Overseers were charged with the pastoral care of members. These Friends met together for worship, to clarify their own discernment, and to nurture the ministry and spiritual health of their meetings. Gender discrimination in the select meetings, of which the clerk was invariably male, was relatively subtle and subject to influence by strong personalities, female as well as male.

This organization was intended to provide sufficient structure to encourage Friends to live upright God-centered lives while providing an orderly way to test any new revelation. Quakers felt clear about what behavior could be expected to flow from a life centered in God. By the mid-eighteenth century these expectations had been codified in a series of Advices and Queries. The Advices were pithy distillations of corporate wisdom, usually culled from minutes or epistles. The Queries were questions to be answered by the local group about its practice. The responses from local meetings were passed up to quarterly and on to yearly meetings. The locally-held manuscript *Books of Discipline* were subject to revision as new insights, understandings, and expectations arose, worked their way to the attention of the yearly meeting, and, after approval, were sent back to the local meetings for official inclusion. The system, then, included both conservative maintenance of traditions and a process whereby new directions could be taken to meet changing conditions and new revelations.

Establishment of Pennsylvania

The wealthy young courtier William Penn (1644-1718) became convinced of Friends' Truth and actively involved himself in their growing Religious Society. He combined a deep Quaker spirituality with a political desire to change the repressive British laws which were battering Quaker family and civil life. In the 1670s he worked with others to write a constitution for West Jersey which allowed broad religious and other freedoms.

In 1681 Penn obtained a charter for a proprietary in the new world in exchange for debts Charles II owed to his father, Admiral Sir William Penn, for whom the new colony was named. Here Penn was able to put into practice his religious views mixed with some of the radical political ideas he shared with John Locke, Algernon Sydney, and others. Penn's Frame of Government guaranteed freedom of religion (although it kept some restrictions on non-Christians), greatly reduced corporal and capital punishments, provided for no militia and only a small police force, and made allowances for affirmations instead of oaths.[10] It provided a venue in the Delaware Valley where a quiet Quaker subculture centered in the home and meeting could develop and flourish. Others, particularly pietists of various denominations from the Rhine Valley, were invited to settle in the new colony. Their distinctive set of values and lifestyles, combined with Penn's liberal government and a geography which encouraged mixed agriculture, gave Pennsylvania a unique flavor.[11]

If the south can be characterized by the machismo Bertram Wyatt-Brown identifies as "southern honor", or the love of display studied by Rhys Isaac, then Quaker Pennsylvania was plain, sober, and concerned with earning a decent, honest living, with devoting time to activities involving the meeting and the family, with eschewing vain and frivolous activities and possessions.[12] It differed from New England (excepting, perhaps, Rhode Island where considerable numbers of Quakers had settled by mid-century) in several significant respects.[13] Pennsylvania Quakers understood that the Native Americans were the original land-owners, that they were beloved by God and capable of loving the divine, and that the way to relate to them was the same way one should relate to any human being: with honesty, goodwill, and peace. However, it is doubtful Friends comprehended the devastating, genocidal impact that smallpox and European encroachment on their land had on Native Americans and their culture.[14] These same principles colored their relations with their non-Quaker European neighbors. That is not to say that no individual Friend profited unfairly from the fur trade, or despised his neighbors, or tried to control the political and economic destiny of the colony for his own ends. The province as a whole tended to reflect the enlightened and humane conduct of Friends, even though it was being slowly modified by pecuniary motives and political compromises, as well as by a large influx of non-Friends.[15]

Earlier Quaker settlers in West Jersey had established Friends meetings in the 1670s. So Penn's colonists found a yearly meeting already gathered in Burlington. The rapid growth of Philadelphia led to the yearly meeting assembling alternately in the two towns until 1760, by which time Burlington had become so overshadowed that Philadelphia became the sole venue. By the middle of the eighteenth century Philadelphia Yearly Meeting encompassed meetings in Pennsylvania, Delaware, eastern Maryland, and most of New Jersey.

At the midpoint of the eighteenth century things seemed to be going well for William Penn's Holy Experiment. Although some historians have looked at the fractious relations among the Assembly, Council, and Governor General, and at the political divisions drawn on ethnic and religious lines, historian Alan Tully saw the colony as remarkably amicable.[16] Certainly it was prosperous. Philadelphia Quakers, with their sober business sense, directed the affairs of the province with steady hands and set the tone for much of the culture of the colony, or at least its three eastern counties where Friends were concentrated.[17]

Bucks County

Bucks County, one of the three original counties laid out by William Penn's surveyors, nestles in the bend of the Delaware River, northeast of Philadelphia. The lower half of the county is roughly divided in half lengthwise by the Neshaminy Creek. The colonists found good soil, abundant streams, and adequate water from shallow wells.[18]

In Third month 1683 a monthly meeting was established on the Pennsylvania side of the Delaware near the falls.[19] Four months later newly established Bucks Quarterly Meeting (which consisted of that single monthly meeting) authorized the setting off of a second monthly meeting to be held "about Neshamina". In 1706 the meeting's name was changed to Middletown to conform with the Township. As the county became more thickly settled additional monthly meetings were set off at Buckingham (1720) and Wrightstown (1734). Friends in Bristol belonged to Falls Meeting until 1788 when they formed a preparative meeting under Middletown. It was not until 1873 that Bristol became a monthly meeting in its own right. Newtown Friends were a part of Middletown until 1815 when they became an indulged meeting (i.e. held their own meetings for worship but not for business) and then two years later became a preparative meeting under Wrightstown. Makefield, an indulged meeting under Falls in 1750, became a preparative meeting in 1790, and joined with Newtown to form a monthly meeting in 1820. Friends who lived in Southampton and Bensalem were members of Byberry, Bristol, or Middletown Meetings.[20] See Figure 1. There do not appear to have been rigid boundaries between meetings, but generally Friends attended the nearest one. The changes in the status and composition of the various meetings within Bucks Quarter seem to have been made with careful deliberation and regard for geography and the spiritual health and financial viability of the individual meetings.[21] They do not seem to have been caused by partisan tensions.

The Quaker immigrants established Bucks County. Land was surveyed and taken up by settlers and some absentee landlords. Roads were marked. A few mills were built. In 1692 the first five townships were officially laid out: Bensalem, Bristol, Falls, Makefield, and Middletown.[22]

The predominately English Quaker settlers followed the Delaware and the Neshaminy, filling in the peninsula of land between the two rivers. The first five townships, plus Newtown, Wrightstown, Buckingham, Solebury, Plumstead, and isolated Richland, had significant Quaker populations. The Dutch concentrated in Northampton, Southampton, Bensalem, and Bristol Borough. Welsh Baptists from Gwynedd and North Wales moved into Warrington and Bedminster townships. Germans moved north and east, through what would become Montgomery County, to the upper and western townships of Bucks. Scotch-Irish Presbyterians followed the Quakers up the rivers, then went farther and established themselves in Tinicum, Bedminster, and parts of Plumstead and Warwick. French Huguenots lived in Bristol Borough, Bensalem, and Southampton. But that is just a broad outline of ethnic movements. Each township had a mixture of peoples. The budding commercial port of Bristol Borough and the townships on the central western border were particularly heterogeneous.[23]

By the middle of the eighteenth century Bucks County was well established. The lower half was less than half Quaker, with substantial numbers of Dutch Reformed from New York, Presbyterians, Baptists descended from Keithian Quakers who had broken off in the schism of the 1690s, and numbers of people who belonged to no organized church.[24] The upper part of the County had

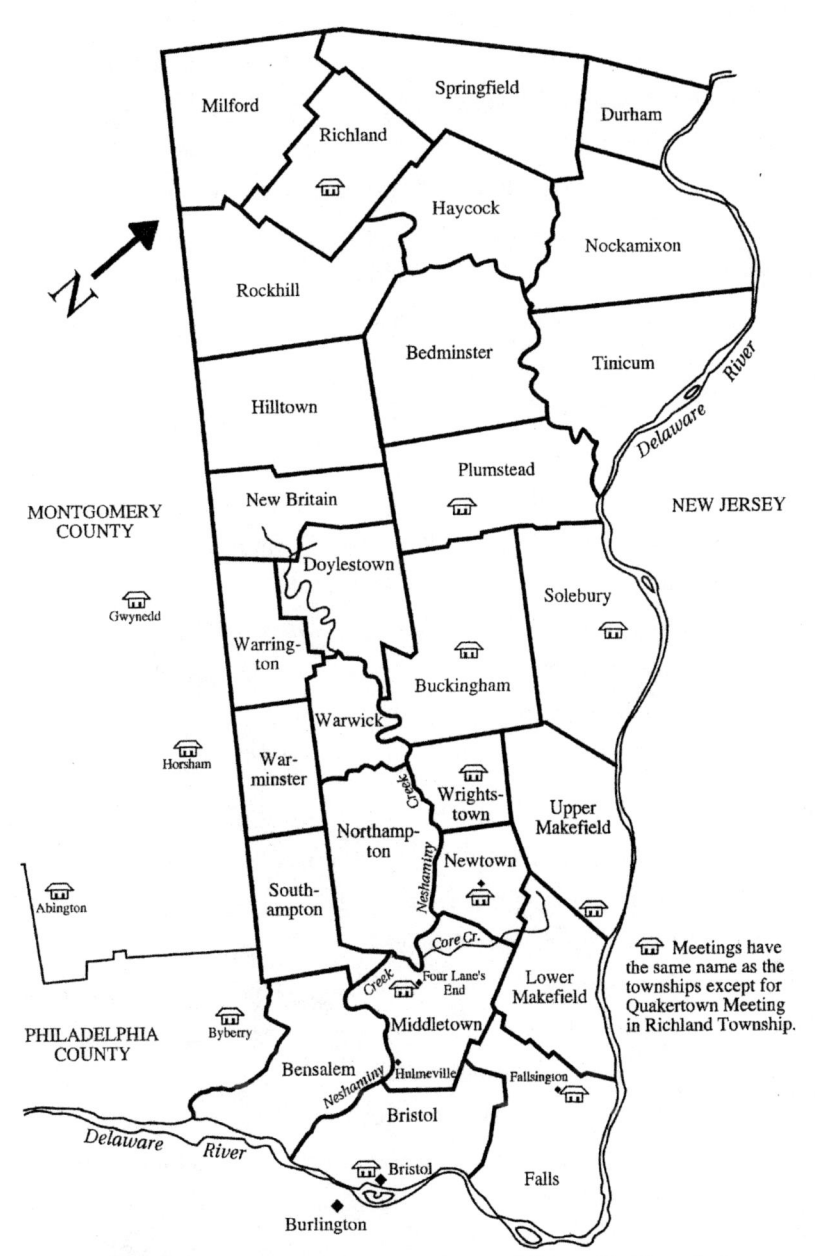

Fig. 1: Bucks County with Meeting Locations and Township Boundaries
  Note: Townships as in 1746-1890, including Haycock established in 1763, Durham in 1775, and Doylestown in 1818.

a large proportion of Germans ("Pennsylvania Dutch") of a variety of denominations, and Scotch-Irish Presbyterians. Farming was the predominant occupation. By mid-century Pennsylvania farms were producing enough wheat and other products to feed Philadelphia and support a thriving export business. In addition to agriculture, Bucks County had iron forges in the northern corner at Durham, lime burning south of that, mills clustered along the Neshaminy and the little creeks emptying into the Delaware, at least three ferries over the River, and numerous taverns and public houses. Bristol had a fair.

Middletown Monthly Meeting in the 1750s

In June 1750 Middletown Monthly Meeting had about 102 men, 101 women, and 175 children for a total of 378 members.[25] In order to study specific families over time, the focus must be narrowed from the entire meeting to the seventeen surname families that had members in it for 100 years. Before we focus on the data set families, however, we need to know how they resembled or differed economically and politically from the rest of the meeting.

Economic Profile

To obtain a more complete picture of the Friends' community in Middletown we will look first at economic factors. The Second month 1757 Middletown Township tax for the "releaf of the poor" can be used to indicate relative wealth.[26] Colonial records were rarely complete so this list must not be assumed to be an accurate census. In addition to other gaps, poor people, obviously, were excluded. It was not even a completely accurate picture of the comparatively wealthy. Lucy Simler has shown from her work with Chester County tax lists that the people who appeared on them were those using the land, not necessarily the owners. A wealthy widow, for example, who rented her land to others, may appear much poorer than she actually was. A renter may appear more wealthy than he was in reality.[27]

There is another difficulty in using the tax records. The assessments were made in Pennsylvania currency. But over the one hundred years of this study the use of that, British sterling, continental currency, and United States dollars, with the effects of inflation, especially during the Revolution, makes comparison of wealth over time very difficult. Fortunately, the carefully researched and constructed tables of Anne Bezanson and others make it possible to convert monetary amounts into "constant dollars". Pounds, shillings and pence are first converted into dollars at the rate of seven shillings and six pence to the dollar. One dollar of Pennsylvania currency equals ninety pence. Then the value of such dollars in terms of commodity prices for a given year is translated into constant dollars (C$) based on the geometric average of monthly prices of twenty commodities sold in Philadelphia between 1721 and 1825. For 1757, for example, the average is 62.50, so in that year six shillings equal C$1.28.[28] The resulting constant dollar figures correlate with any other "C$" financial amounts used in this book.

The 1757 tax duplicate listed eighty-seven male heads of household in the township of whom thirty six were known Friends, one was recently disowned, twelve were probable Friends, and thirty eight were known not to be Quakers (see Appendix 3). It is immediately obvious that known Quakers as a group tended to be more wealthy than their non-Quaker neighbors. See Table 1. The mean constant dollar tax valuation for all taxable male heads of household in the township was C$82.43. For Quakers it was C$103.51 and for known non-Quakers it was only C$69.50. If all the unknown/possible Quakers were averaged with the known Quakers, the group would still be more wealthy than the known non-Quakers: C$93.67 compared to C$69.50. The two wealthiest men, Joseph Richardson and Joseph Wright, both assessed on C$322.67 were Quakers, as were the next two, William Paxson and John Praul, assessed on C$215.10. The fifth wealthiest, on C$193.60, was the richest non-Quaker, Stephen Williams. Among the poorest heads of household, eighteen were assessed on C$25.80. Three (16%) of them were known Quakers; eleven (61%) were known non-Quakers. All single men were taxed on an assesment of 6 shillings (C$1.28). As there were eighteen non-Quaker and only four known Quaker single men, the addition of these men further skews the wealth towards Quakers: C$47.57 for non-Quakers and roughly double that, C$93.29 for Quakers. The poor who were receiving relief, and those below the tax limit but above destitution, were not included on the tax duplicate.

TABLE 1: Average Tax Valuation for Middletown Township Quakers, Possible Quakers, and Non-Quakers, 1757

	\multicolumn{2}{c}{Quakers}	\multicolumn{2}{c}{Possible Quakers}	\multicolumn{2}{c}{Non-Quakers}	\multicolumn{2}{c}{Total}
	N	Constant $	N	Constant $	N	Constant $	N	Constant $
Heads of Household	36	C$103.51	12	C$64.12	39	C$69.50	87	C$82.43
Single Men	4		6	1.28	20	1.28	30	1.28
Total	40	93.29	18	43.17	59	46.37	117	61.62

SOURCE: 1757 Tax "for the Releaf of the Poor", Middletown Township, Spruance Library, BCHS.

NOTE: Robert Longshore, disowned in 1740, is counted as a non-Quaker, as are two single men, disowned in 1751 and 1755.

Table 2 compares the seventeen surname families with the meeting as a whole. Out of the thirty-six known Quaker men on the tax duplicate, twenty three (plus one recently disowned), were in the data set. The average valuation of the twenty three was C$110. All four known Quaker single men, plus two recently disowned, were also in the data set. Adding in these four men changes the data set's average to C$93.89. So without the single men the data set men were slightly wealthier than the average of all Quakers; with the single men they were virtually identical.[29]

TABLE 2: Mean Tax Valuation for Data Set and Other Friends in Middletown Meeting, 1757

	\multicolumn{2}{c}{Data Set}	\multicolumn{2}{c}{Non-Data Set Friends}	\multicolumn{2}{c}{Total Friends}
	N	Constant $	N	Constant $	N	Constant $
Heads of Household	23	C$110.00	13	C$91.87	36	C$103.51
Single Men	4	1.28	0	1.28	4	1.28
Total	27	93.89	13	91.87	40	93.24

SOURCE: 1757 Tax Records, Middletown Township, Spruance Library, BCHS.

The tax assessments were made, usually, on real estate and numbers of horses, cattle, servants, or other specified items. At the death of a person who owned property, an inventory was usually made of his (or more rarely her) personal property and outstanding debts and loans. It is interesting to compare estate inventories with the tax record to see if individuals had roughly the same relative wealth measured by the two different standards.

Four men from the seventeen families died within ten years after the 1757 tax, and had their estates probated. Unfortunately, they demonstrate the frustrations of incomplete data too often found in eighteenth-century research.[30] See Table 3. In this very small sample, not one man has the same rank order under the two methods of valuation.[31] These four men are sufficient warning not to depend exclusively on a single method of assessing comparative wealth.

TABLE 3: Comparison of 1757 Tax Valuation with Estate Inventories of Four Data Set Heads of Household, 1757-1767

Name	Estate Value			1757 Tax Valuation		
	Pa. Currency	Const. $	Rank	Pa. Currency	Const. $	Rank
John Watson 1703-1764	£353.11.6	C$1382.50	1	£30.5.0	C$129.07	2
Stephen Wilson 1694-1761	323.11.7	C$1241.55	2	12.0.0*	C$103.25	4
William Paxson 1712-1767	322.15.10	C$1207.12	3	50.8.4	C$215.10	1
Euclydus Longshore d. 1764	98.18.12	C$386.90	4	26.4.4	C$111.86	3

SOURCE: 1757 Middletown Township Tax records, BCHS; Probate records, Bucks County Court House, Doylestown, Penna.
* also listed with an "estate" valued at £12.4.0, meaning land he was renting from another. He was taxed on the value of both parcels.

Nearly every man in Middletown township was a farmer, although many had a secondary occupation such as shoemaker or carpenter.[32] Joseph Richardson, one of the two wealthiest men in 1757, had opened a store in the 1730s at Four Lanes' End, as the hamlet in Middletown Township was then called. This was the only store between Durham, with iron works in the north of Bucks County, and Bristol, the port on the Delaware in the south. He did very well, trading imported goods for local commodities, lending money, investing in land and slaves to work it. Thomas Jenks owned a fulling mill on Core Creek, a tributary of the Neshaminy. Richard Mitchell had a grist mill further up the Neshaminy in Wrightstown. His brother Henry (died 1726) had been one of the original partners who built a flour mill in Hulmeville, Middletown Township.[33] This little industrial complex was increased with the addition of a plaster mill, then subsequently a woolen mill. Jesse Comfort built a mill in the early 1730s at Bridgetown, between Newtown and Four Lanes' End. In 1749 non-Quaker Stephen Williams became the owner of a flour mill. He also had a wharf and storehouse on the Neshaminy.[34] But many of the wealthier men in the area were mainly farmers, like William Paxson, Stephen Comfort, and Isaac Stackhouse. When a man accumulated surplus cash, he tended to use it either to purchase additional land or to lend to his neighbors in the form of bonds or notes. So any relatively wealthy man was not only a farmer, but also to some degree a banker and a real estate speculator.

Towards the other end of the economic scale were relatively poor farmers like Thomas Longshore, assessed on C$25.80, James Stackhouse (disowned Tenth month 1758) on C$34.51, and Samuel Woolston assessed on C$52.27.[35] Then there were men like Lucas Gillam, David Wilson, and Benjamin Linton. Gillam, an orphan, had been apprenticed to a cooper. He purchased a farm in 1751, three years after he was married. The records are unclear whether he maintained himself more from coopering than from farming, but in 1757 he was assessed on C$52.27. Wilson, a mason, was assessed on C$25.80. Linton, a weaver, did not appear in the tax record at all. At both ends of the economic scale there were men who earned their living from farming, from trades, or from a combination. Quakers could be found along the entire economic spectrum.

By and large the community was based on agriculture, with the secondary industries and services needed to sustain a rural economy. Quakers figured prominently in the local economy, with members of the seventeen families slightly ahead of the other members of Middletown Meeting in terms of wealth. This is probably because most of them were already well established and into their second or third generation in the area.

Political Profile

Quakers also figured prominently in the political scene in Bucks County at mid-century. By that time there were a number of county and township offices, as well as eight representatives elected to the Provincial Assembly. Three county commissioners (limited to single, staggered three-year terms) and six county assessors were elected directly.[36] These nine men appointed the county treasurer. The sheriff and coroner were appointed by the governor from among the two highest vote-getters for each office. In the absence of gubernatorial action, the man with the largest number of votes took office. The sheriff could serve no more than three consecutive one-year terms. The governor appointed one man to serve the multiple functions of clerk of court, prothonotary, recorder of deeds, and registrar of wills. The governor also appointed the sealer of weights and measures. William Watson was so appointed in 1731, but no reference is made in the *Pennsylvania Archives* to possible successors. The governor also appointed eighteen justices of the peace. They in turn appointed one or more overseers of the poor for each township from names supplied by the outgoing overseers, appointed overseers of the highways for the county (until 1762), and chose a constable for each township from among the two highest vote-getters. One of the constables' many jobs was to prepare the tax assessments. After 1758 township assessors were elected to do that. The Provincial Assembly appointed the collector of excise. With this variety of paths for attaining public office, it is difficult to draw conclusions about men who held office except that they all wanted or were willing to serve. It has been impossible to find the names of all of them, let alone their religious affiliation.

Eight men from Bucks County were elected to the Provincial Assembly. In 1750 they included four known Quakers, three probable Quakers, and one Dutch Reformed/Presbyterian. Of the three elected County Commissioners in 1750, two were Friends and one was a Baptist.

In 1750 there were six appointed county offices held by four known Quakers, one probable Quaker, and one Baptist. For the entire County there were eighteen justices of the peace plus the chief burgess of Bristol. These men seem to have been appointed on a geographical basis, so it would be expected that those from the upper half of the county would reflect their predominately non-Quaker constituency. Seven of the justices appointed June 30, 1749, were Quakers and one was Anglican. I have not found the religious affiliation of the rest. The single Bucks County member of the Governor's Council was Lawrence Growden, a wealthy Quaker who had a plantation in Trevose, Bensalem township. He also served as Prothonotary from 1742 to 1770.

Quakers were concentrated in the lower and eastern townships. The other townships had very few Friends. Yet even in the townships with the heaviest Quaker concentrations, they were probably slightly less than half the population. Considering that the county was relatively evenly populated with no large towns, the proportion of Quakers for the whole county would have been perhaps 20% to 30%. Yet Friends dominated all the political offices except the geographically-named justices of the peace.

Among the seventeen surname families, two men held public office in 1750. John Watson, Jr. (d. 1764) was county commissioner in 1747 and treasurer from 1750 to 1757. John Woolston was elected county commissioner in 1748 and a member of the Provincial Assembly from 1749-1751. After that he served as collector of excise from 1751 to 1756. County-wide office holders for several years on either side of 1750 include William Paxson, county commissioner in 1751, and Joseph Watson the following year, followed by non-data set Quakers. Timothy Stackhouse of Bristol was county sheriff for 1757-1758. In addition three brothers of Middletown Friends held office: Mahlon Kirkbride of Lower Makefield was an Assemblyman and justice of the peace, Mark Watson (d. 1749) was a justice from Falls, and Richard Mitchell was a justice from Wrightstown.

In addition to the county-wide offices there were the chief burgess, burgesses, five councilmen, and assessors of Bristol Borough, and the various township officials mentioned above. There does not seem to be an organized list of any except the burgesses. Names were gleaned from miscellaneous county papers and a variety of secondary sources.[37] The following list cannot be assumed to be complete. More men seemed to serve shorter terms in the local offices, resulting in greater sharing of the experiences of self-government. If we look at a few years on either side of 1750, we find the following members of data set families serving in public office: William Paxson, overseer of the poor for Middletown in 1742; John Allen, the same for Bristol in 1753; Isaac Stackhouse, overseer of the highways for Middletown in 1755; and Thomas Paxson, assessor for Middletown in 1748 and 1749. With such an unsystematic list of township office-holders it is impossible to state whether data set men were more heavily represented than other Friends. But it does appear that Quakers as a group were over represented in public office.

The Seventeen Families and Middletown Meeting

At mid-century the seventeen surname families constituted a little under half the members of Middletown Meeting. See Appendix 1 for additional demographic details. Among the long-time, weighty Friends, fifty years or older, were John Stackhouse (b. 1670); William Croasdale (b. 1690); his brother Jeremiah Croasdale (b. 1694) who died in 1749; David Wilson (b. 1691); his brother Stephen (b. 1694) who lived away from Middletown from 1741 to 1752; Joseph Linton, whose birth and death dates are unknown but who married in 1727 and probably died just before 1750; Grace (Stackhouse) Wilson[38] (b. 1697); Alice (Stackhouse) Longshore (b. 1699); and Thomas Jenks (b. 1700).

The next generation, men and women in their thirties and forties who would become very active in the meeting, were infrequently named to positions of responsibility at mid-century. Appearance in the ministry, however, was not tied to age. John Stackhouse had been recommended as a minister in 1727 at the age of 57. But Stephen Comfort (b. 1721) was recommended when he was only 26.

Participation

Noting the individuals who were especially active within the monthly meeting does not give a complete picture. The underlying theory of Quaker practice assumed that abilities would not be evenly dispersed, but that these gifts might appear in any member of the group. There has not been much research on the breadth of participation in the business functions of the meeting in this period. Within the first century of Quakerism there were two contradictory thrusts. One was the democratic radicalism of the first decade. The second was the limited number of Friends actually involved in the business of running the Society. This had its roots in the impossibility of everyone participating in the various levels of decision making because of economic constraints, because of newness to Quaker process by recent converts, because of imprisonment, or because of uneven ability and interest. In seventeenth-century England all members did not attend monthly meetings for business. It is difficult to document when that pattern changed in Pennsylvania, but eventually all adult members were expected to participate.

A close examination of the seventeen surname families shows that a majority of individuals who were twenty-five years or older in 1750 and who lived a considerable portion of their adult lives in Middletown Meeting, did participate in the meeting for business. A count of the times individuals were assigned to a committee during the time they were members in Middletown (that is, not tracing them in the minutes of meetings to which they might have removed) reveals that twenty-six men and women (54.2%) were very active, with over twenty assignments each; five (10.4%) were less active; seventeen (35.4%) never carried out a task for the meeting. Of those never receiving an assignment, two were disowned in 1751 and therefore should be eliminated. An additional four who would have fallen within the sample were disowned before 1750. So 32.6% of the forty-six Friends stands as the baseline figure of data set members who were not involved in the ongoing business of the meeting in the middle of the eighteenth century. We will see if this percentage has increased or decreased a hundred years later.

The minutes are silent about the fifteen non-participating individuals. They included ten men and five women from ten data set families. We do not know if they were present but declined appointment to a committee, or if the meeting considered them incompetent for one reason or another and therefore failed to assign them any tasks. They could have been habitually absent. We can assume that they did attend meetings for worship. If not, it would have been minuted that a few Friends were delegated to meet with them. The most likely explanation is a combination of all the above with a generous dose of lack of interest. These were the grandchildren and great grandchildren of those whose lives were radically altered by their convincement in the pentecostal days of the mid-seventeenth century. They themselves may have never experienced the life-changing reality of the presence of the Inward Christ.

Meeting activity tended to cluster in about half the data set families. But at least one member of each of the remaining families was occasionally asked to serve on a committee. The result was that although the responsibility for the functioning of the meeting was not evenly shared, it was widely shared among the family groups as well as among individuals.

Discipline

Individuals whose actions Friends felt required discipline were not evenly found throughout the seventeen families. In the decade from First month 1745 through Twelfth month 1754 there were twelve cases of discipline in the men's and women's meetings involving data set members. Half involved a breach of sexual norms or marriage procedures, two involved drinking, and the remaining four were a variety of miscellaneous offenses. Five disownments resulted.

There were thirty-six discipline cases among the Friends who were not part of the seventeen surname families.[39] Twenty were for sexual or marriage procedure deviations, eight for drinking (sometimes with additional offenses), and the remaining eight were for various other offenses. Seventeen of the thirty six were disowned. There were only one third the number of discipline cases against members of the data set families even though they were 44% of the meeting. These issues will be taken up in the next chapter. A tentative hypothesis suggests that being part of a well-established meeting family tended to curb the temptation to step beyond the bounds of acceptable behavior. An alternate hypothesis is that these families, because they had less deviance, were the ones which remained within the meeting for the next hundred years. A third hypothesis is that the meeting overlooked the deviance of individuals in these families.

To summarize, the bulk of the meeting's work was carried on by men and women over fifty years of age: those who had the time as well as the experience to deal with sometimes delicate or thorny problems. A relatively large number of Friends were involved in the meeting's business, but they did not share the burdens equally. Finally, a fairly large number of individuals were felt by the meeting to need disciplining, roughly half for sexual or marriage offenses and one sixth for drinking. About a third of the discipline cases resulted in disownments. The only significant difference between the data set and the rest of the meeting was the lower percentage of discipline cases in the families that would stay in the meeting for the next century.

The seventeen data set families are not a representative sample of Middletown Monthly Meeting in the technical meaning of the term. They were not selected for that purpose. But they do mirror most of the characteristics of meeting members. They had comparable average wealth. Some of them were involved in politics. Some were very involved with the ongoing business of the meeting. By definition of the way they were selected, they were more permanently settled than others in the meeting.

With this examination of the seventeen families and Middletown Meeting, we are now ready to turn to the specific problems which presented them with choices in the three decades following 1755. There were three interrelated issues, one or more of which had a direct impact on virtually every Quaker family. The upheavals came both from within the Society of Friends and from outside forces beyond their control. They presented sharply defined crisis points at which individual Friends were forced to choose between the dictates of their faith and the demands of the dominant culture. Chapter 3 examines the Quaker reform movement. Chapters 4 and 5 look at slavery and war.

CHAPTER 3: TIGHTENING THE DISCIPLINE

Perhaps it is inevitable that the bright flames of radicalizing new spiritual truths in time die down to ash and dull ember with only here and there a bright hot spark. It is not surprising, therefore, that one hundred years after the early Friends began proclaiming a relationship with Christ which, in effect, turned the world upside down, the Religious Society of Friends had become, in the eyes of observers, mildly eccentric rather than dangerously radical. Some have blamed the institution of membership in the Society of Friends by right of birth, which London Yearly Meeting acknowledged in 1737, as marking the point of decline in which there would always be a certain number of unconvinced among the members.[1] With the end of persecution in England, and the concentration of Friends, by necessity, in commerce and industry, came a caution born of increasing wealth and new-found respectability.[2]

Early Friends had undergone a spiritual rite of passage when they declared themselves Children of the Light. Adopting the distinctive Friends' witness of behavior, speech, and dress meant accepting the suffering of derision, persecution, and potential violence. This intense, transformative experience bonded early Friends into a dissenting, marginalized community. In the eighteenth century as Friends became respectable and prosperous this liminality was seriously eroded.[3]

In Pennsylvania, especially in Philadelphia, the wealthy men who controlled the political and commercial life of the colony also held positions of influence within Philadelphia Yearly Meeting. The ends of these three interests were not always compatible, and thus spiritual concerns might be sacrificed to political or economic expediency. It was a situation which Penn had built into the Holy Experiment, but the results in the eighteenth century were probably different from what Friends had envisioned in the seventeenth.[4]

The eighteenth century saw an increasing divergence between the mindset and values required for success in the secular world of growing rationalism and materialism, and the Quaker ethic which emphasized "love, righteousness, humility, self-denial, self-suffering, and devotion to God." As historian David Robert Kobrin spelled out in detail, these concepts were incompatible with and essentially alien to the intellectual tone of the Revolutionary generation.[5] Non-Quakers viewed traditional Friends' faith and practice as increasingly irrelevant. Many Friends, especially wealthy Philadelphians, found themselves drawn toward the intellectual, economic, and political world inhabited by their non-Quaker neighbors and business associates. More traditional Friends, especially from rural meetings, were disturbed by the increasing "worldliness" they observed within the Society.[6] Individual Quakers varied considerably because each had to make the small, day-to-day decisions which added up to a life oriented toward obedience to God's will or toward self-will. Myriad unrecorded choices ranged from the sublime through compromise to self-centered. The great majority of very human individual Quakers fell somewhere in the compromise zone between the extremes.

Some Friends cried out against this loss of spiritual power in their present comfortable circumstances. They felt the same desire for spiritual purity that was at the root of the Great Awakening. Friends commented very little on the Awakening, seemingly untouched by what they saw as excesses of "enthusiasm" and insincerity. Historian Maria Mazzenga has shown that Friends nevertheless shared a common religious discourse with this larger pietistic movement. They shared a similar vocabulary while attributing different meanings to various terms. Friends were able to articulate the characteristics of Quakerism that differentiated it from the Calvinism of the Awakening.[7]

While a number of Quaker ministers, in particular, were working to reform their Religious Society, they varied in their understanding of what was wrong and what was needed to restore the primitive purity of the church. All the reformers were devoted to the same objectives: the service of God, the revitalization of the Society of Friends, and the preservation of Quaker culture. But they interpreted these goals in different ways.[8]

The concept of faith development can help us understand some of the underlying dynamic of dissension over reform. Friends characterized by the second level of formal, or institutional, understanding, tended to emphasize the importance of strict adherence to rules. They believed that tight enforcement of the discipline would result in a revitalized Society. Friends at a more mature fourth level tended to emphasize the importance of inner transformation. As they had experienced the work of the Holy Spirit within themselves, they had discovered it moved their outward lives into closer conformity with the testimonies of Friends. Therefore, level-four Friends also spoke of increased faithfulness to the testimonies. But they understood this would come as the result of realigning the inward life toward God. Both groups looked superficially the same. Both hoped Friends would increasingly conform, in their outward lives, to traditional Friends' disciplines. But the inward dynamic was understood differently by the two groups.

Reform and Philadelphia Yearly Meeting

The reformers controlled most of the important leadership positions in Philadelphia Yearly Meeting. Their indefatigable technique was the same as that of the first generation of Friends: travelling in the ministry. They visited other yearly meetings up and down the coast and across the ocean; they visited quarterly and monthly meetings; they visited select meetings for ministers and elders; and they visited individuals and families. Their message was a prophetic call to return to the strait and narrow path.[9] Their approaches varied from the wise and gentle invitation to wholeness of John Woolman, Anthony Benezet, Daniel Stanton, or David Ferris, to the persistent demand to change specific outward behaviors regarding such things as plain dress, speech, and marriage procedures, made by John Churchman, Samuel Fothergill, Catherine (Payton) Phillips, or Thomas Chalkley.[10]

In the absence of journals or other personal records, the internal impact which the reformers made on individual Quaker souls and psyches cannot be ascertained by an historian. However, the external impact is clearly visible through the disciplinary actions taken by each meeting. Jack Marietta's study of the discipline cases of nearly all Pennsylvania monthly meetings from 1682 to 1776 shows the practical result of the efforts by reformers to tighten the discipline: a large increase in disownments and thereby a shrinking of the membership rolls. It also supplies a background against which we can place a more detailed examination of Middletown Meeting.

It is necessary to understand what Quakers meant by disownment. It was not excommunication in the sense of some denominations which claim either to control or have access to knowledge about a person's ultimate destination of heaven or hell. Membership in the Religious Society of Friends did not mean one was guaranteed salvation, and disownment did not mean one was damned. From the early days of persecution the Society was concerned about publicly upholding a witness through the daily lives of all its members. Friends understood themselves to be a demonstration model, as it were, of Christ's kingdom blossoming here on earth. Therefore all who called themselves Friends were expected to live in such a way that their day-to-day life witnessed to Christ's way. For example, since Friends refused to swear oaths it was of crucial importance that all Friends be of exemplary honesty in all their dealings. If a Friend was found to be dishonest, he brought reproof (and physical danger) on other Quakers, and therefore the Society could not "own" him as a member. The meeting publicly disassociated itself from him until such time as he acknowledged and repented his transgressions and brought his actions once more into consistency with Friends' testimonies.[11]

Friends refused, for a number of reasons, to participate in the marriage ceremonies of the established church. Therefore it was important that they carefully follow their own quasi-legal procedures. When Quaker couples married contrary to Friendly rules, the meeting had to make a public statement disassociating itself from them. Even in Pennsylvania, where the laws were framed to make allowances for Friendly scruples, Quakers adhered to the same testimonies and procedures as Friends elsewhere. Such a high value was placed on the Quaker family that Friends felt it imperative that both parents be members in order to bring up their children in the faith and practice of the Society of Friends. Therefore a Friend was disowned for marrying a non-Quaker.[12]

Disownment, as practiced by Friends, was a public witness that an individual had transgressed the testimonies and practices of the Religious Society of Friends, and therefore could no longer be considered a member. This did not mean he or she was ostracized. A disowned person could continue to attend meetings for worship and participate in the Quaker subculture. He or she could not participate in making decisions for the meeting, and any children born after their parents' disownment would not be considered members unless they applied for membership.[13]

Not all infractions of Quaker rules were brought to the attention of the monthly meeting, let alone resulting in disownment. But if a transgression progressed to the point where the matter was brought before the meeting, it appeared in the minutes, and historians have access to it. All such infractions are referred to in this study as discipline cases, whether or not they resulted in disownment.

Marietta found that of all the variations among meetings and regions, or between genders, the most obvious difference in discipline cases occurred before the reformation of the 1750s and during it.[14] In the first three decades of Quaker settlement in Pennsylvania, there was very little delinquency among Friends, no matter how it is defined. In the second three decades, the number of discipline cases steadily rose. As offenses tended to cluster around age-related acts, (see below) the statistics corroborate the picture of a generation which was content to loosen its devotion to Quaker testimonies. In the following decade (ca. 1745-1755) the increase accelerated. The reformers (both level-two and level-four) made their strength felt at the yearly meeting sessions of 1755. To further their goal of revitalizing the Religious Society of Friends the discipline was revised, with the addition of a clause directing elders, overseers, and others to work zealously to "repair the breaches" and thus restore "the primitive beauty and purity" of the Society. A committee of thirty-one Friends was appointed to visit all the quarterly and monthly meetings to see that the discipline was being upheld. Queries were developed for each monthly meeting to consider regularly. Each meeting was to send written answers to every quarterly meeting. In 1756 discipline cases mushroomed. They remained relatively high for the next three decades.[15]

Except for discipline cases involving slavery and war, with which we shall deal in later chapters, the offenses within local meetings of Philadelphia Yearly Meeting tended to be the same kinds of things they had always been. Marietta grouped offenses into three categories: sectarian (including marriage), sexual, and those involving other people as victims. From about 1725 to 1775 the last category, which involved actions prohibited by law such as debt, assault, larceny, slander, and fraud, remained at about 10-12% of each year's cases. During that time, sexual offenses, which involved mostly fornication with fiancé(e), or occasionally with someone else, were approximately 13-15% of each year's total cases.[16] The largest group of offenses was sectarian, that is, those which resulted when individuals did not live in ways that reflected the upright, God-centered lives Friends expected of anyone professing membership with them. Instead they indulged in acts that, while not considered illegal by non-Friends, did not testify to the inward work and power of Christ that Friends hoped to witness to the world. The prohibitions included such things as marriage outside of Friendly procedures, attending such an "irregular" marriage, drunkenness, inattendance at ("neglect" of) meetings for worship, profanity, quarreling, gambling, "loose conduct", or "disorderly walking". If marriage offenses were separated out of the sectarian category, each of the two new groups (marriage and the remaining sectarian offenses) was still far larger than Marietta's other two groups of offenses.

Monthly meetings in Bucks Quarter tended to have the most lenient policy towards offenders. They tended to have fewer disownments and more pardons than Philadelphia Quarter, and considerably fewer than Chester Quarter.[17]

With this summary of the general outline of the Quaker Reform, we will turn to Middletown Meeting to try to determine how individual Friends and their families behaved when asked to participate in reform.

Reform and Middletown Meeting

The pattern of discipline within Middletown Monthly Meeting mirrored what Marietta found for Philadelphia Yearly Meeting as a whole, although it was not until 1757, two years after the yearly meeting had revised the discipline, that Middletown's annual number of cases jumped into double digits, and even then they were uneven.[18] See Figure 2. Discipline cases against data set members roughly paralleled those against all members of the meeting.

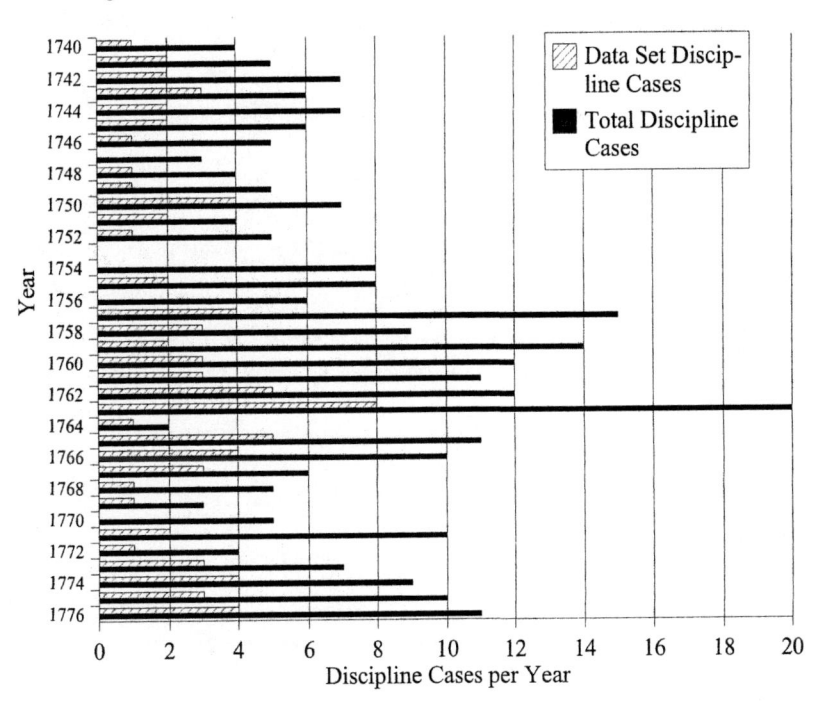

Fig. 2: Middletown Monthly Meeting Discipline Cases, 1740-1776

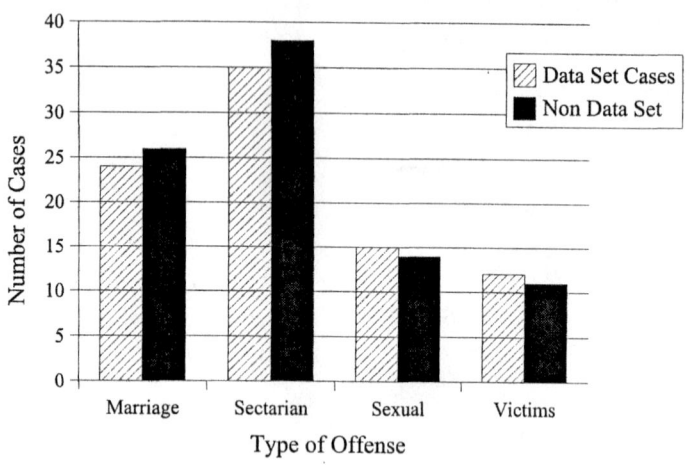

Fig. 3: Number of Discipline Cases by Type, 1750-1766

Using Marietta's four broad categories, the data set families display the same general patterns as Philadelphia Yearly Meeting, and as Middletown Meeting as a whole. See Figure 3. These patterns held true not only for the reform period, but for the entire century.

A breakdown of the four large groups of offenses into the forty-four different categories by which Marietta originally coded them (Middletown data set members were guilty of only twenty-two types), further shows the high proportion of marriage offenses. The next most common transgressions involved the misuse of alcohol, military activity, unchastity before marriage with the person later married, fornication, and debt. Drinking, military activity, and fornication might all be interpreted as actions resulting when one is not concentrating on orienting one's life toward God. See Figure 4. The relative numbers parallel those of the larger body of Friends.

Official Meeting Response

Middletown Meeting had no members who were highly visible early supporters of reform or who were recognized as part of the informal network within the yearly meeting working to revitalize the Society of Friends. That is not to say

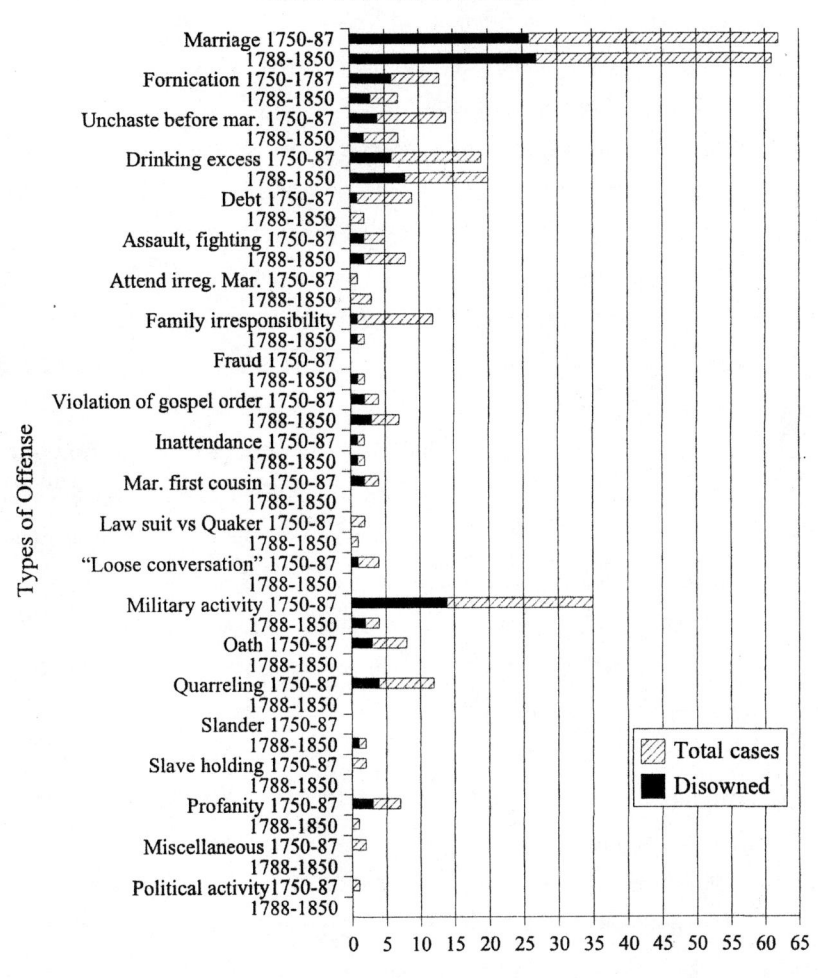

Fig. 4: Frequency of Offenses by Type, Data Set Families,
1750-1787 and 1788-1850

Total Number of Cases and Number Disowned

there were no Friends who were sympathetic to the need for reform, or agreed with its general direction. But when the advice from Philadelphia was received there was no great enthusiasm to follow through to comply with tightening the discipline. Eventually, however, Middletown Friends did fall into line.

Printed extracts from the men's and women's yearly meeting minutes routinely were forwarded to each quarterly meeting, which sent copies to the monthly meetings. At that point local Friends had to deal with any issues raised at the yearly meeting. The dynamic initiatives of the 1755 yearly meeting were sloughed over briefly in the Middletown men's minutes of Twelfth month, as a reminder to send in the contributions, to "revive the Practice of visiting Families &c with divers other Matters which the Clerk is desired to transcribe at Large for the Use of this Meeting."[19] Of all the issues raised by the yearly meeting, Middletown chose to consider the one with which it presumably felt most comfortable. The next month, the "practice of visiting families coming under the solid consideration of this meeting and Friends apprehending that a Revival thereof might be of good Use at this Time," four men were appointed to this service "in company with such of the women Friends as they may appoint." William Croasdale, James Thackray, Stephen Comfort, and Stephen Wilson served with Grace Croasdale, Sarah Cary, Mary Shaw, and Ann Mary Biles. Eight months later the Friends reported that "they have pretty generally performed that Service, and that they had good satisfaction therein." When the yearly meeting brought it up again in 1757, Middletown minuted that it "being solidly thought of and spoken to in this meeting, Friends appear to have good Unity with the Practice".[20]

However, visiting families was not all the yearly meeting was asking. Middletown men appeared somewhat ambivalent about other aspects of tightening the discipline at the expense of a presumably comfortable status quo. Several examples will illustrate.

In Third month 1757 a Friend was "dealt with" for quarreling and fighting in a public place. He was present at monthly meeting and said he was sorry. In the past Friends might have been satisfied with this. But the Clerk, perhaps ruefully, minuted that "as the Discipline requires that Disorders of such a Nature should be condemned in Writing, Joseph is required to bring a few Lines to next Meeting for yt Purpose." Nearly identical wording appeared two years later in a similar incident involving Joshua Stackhouse. In an ongoing case of debt owed by Samuel Woolston, the meeting finally decided that its hand was forced, and

Samuel was told "that unless he satisfied" his creditor "before next Meeting, Friends will be obliged to deal with him as a disorderly Person."

Finally, in a difficult case referred to the men by the women's meeting, the men decided that Ann should be disowned for "keeping company with another woman's husband". She appealed to the quarterly meeting, as was her right, and was upheld. The men rather grumpily minuted that the report from quarterly meeting "appears somewhat unintelligible: But as it seems intended that the Care and Labour of the Meeting in that Case may thereby tend to the Discouragement of a Religious Exercise of our Discipline, we are inclined to appeal their Judgment to the next Yearly Meeting". After considering it further the next month, Middletown men "unanimously agree" to do so. The unanimous nature of the decision was again mentioned just before the yearly meeting sessions were held. What started as a not untypical "difficult" case became an opportunity for the local meeting to tweak the noses of those urging increased strictness by claiming the reversal of their decision would weaken their ability to further exercise discipline. The conclusion of the case was that the yearly meeting upheld Middletown but, as the latter minuted it, "as some Expressions in our said Testimony did not sit easy on some of their Minds, they unanimously agreed on another Form, which they . . . recommended . . . in Lieu of that which we had prepared." The local meeting accepted the new wording, and Ann was disowned.[21]

One issue that Middletown Friends had trouble with was the prohibition against the marriage of first cousins. In 1739 the yearly meeting had warned Friends to testify against intermarriage between first cousins. In 1753 this was enlarged to prohibit marriage with the first cousin of a deceased spouse. Middletown Friends were very "uneasy" with this, and asked Bucks Quarterly Meeting to send it back to the yearly meeting for further consideration. After a long and tedious debate, which tended to divide Friends, the yearly meeting upheld the prohibition. Middletown Friends were still unhappy. They did not see the need for such a rule, but some of them did not want to subject the yearly meeting to another divisive session. Middletown reported to Bucks Quarter, however, that "the greater part" of the meeting did want the matter sent back to the yearly meeting.

The quarterly meeting conveyed to the yearly meeting its uneasiness that such a prohibition could lead to a loss of love amongst brethren, and break the Christian fellowship. "Dynastic" marriages among wealthy British Quaker kin were increasingly common. It was very unusual for the Atlantic Quaker community to be divided on a policy issue.[22] Over the years there had been several marriages of this type among Middletown Friends, making the issue a highly personal one. Before the reform, Thomas Paxson and his second cousin Ann Paxson had to acknowledge and condemn their "outgoing" in marriage with each other (1737), as did David Wilson and his cousin Elizabeth Stackhouse (1745). After the reform, Samuel Allen and his first cousin Sarah Allen were disowned (1773), as were first cousins Hannah Croasdale and Jonathan Croasdale (1787). Middletown Friends went along with the yearly meeting, even while minuting the distress of some of their members.[23]

The Middletown women's minutes appear almost oblivious to the reform movement, except for an increase in discipline cases. The first report of the 1755 yearly meeting said that visiting families was recommended, and the collection of funds was to be continued. The next quarterly meeting report added that the queries should be read and answered. The following quarterly meeting report specified that the answers were to be in writing. From then on Middletown women regularly read and answered the queries. In 1757 the women appointed four Friends to visit families in company with the appointed men, as mentioned above. The following year women minuted the exhortation to encourage children to attend meetings for worship. It was not until 1763 that the local meeting was again asked to appoint Friends to visit those who were negligent in attending meetings. Four years later the women were advised to add to the number of elders; two years after that they were reminded to use the ancient practice of certificates when a Friend removed to another locale. But these were pretty minor items sent down from the quarterly meeting. It is tempting to hypothesize that under the spiritual leadership of Grace Croasdale (d. 1769), her daughter Mercy Comfort, and daughter-in-law Margery (Hayhurst), the Middletown Women's Meeting was more interested in the inner relationship with God than with enforcing the letter of the law. This would fit the pattern Jean Soderlund found in Shrewsbury Meeting.[24] It could indicate a fourth level of faith development.

It wasn't until the mid-1770s that Middletown women were finally caught up in the impulse to tighten all the particular aspects of outward behavior that served to separate them from their non-Quaker neighbors. Regarding advice from the women's yearly meeting, Middletown minuted the recommendation

> to Parents and Heads of Families to deeply attend to the Reproofs of Instruction in their own Minds, which is the Way to Life and Peace; And endeavor to educate their Youth in the Way of Purity and Plainness . . . in order that a Reformation may be come to, in Regard to the wakeful Attendance of our religious Meetings, Plainness of Speech, Behaviour, and Apparel, and Household Furniture. As also the sorrowful Deficiency in the Education of the Youth, with other Deficiencies mentioned in the Answers to the Queries.[25]

This minute illustrates a blend of the two strands of reform. The first part points to the necessity for inward work. The second part emphasizes the outward rules to which Friends were called to conform.

Family Patterns

Among the ministers in Middletown Meeting in the 1750s was Grace Croasdale, widow of Jeremiah and daughter of Robert and Grace (Pearson) Heaton. She had married young and had borne nine children. "As she advanced in years, she grew in religion, and became very serviceable in divers stations in the church." She first appeared in the ministry about 1745, at the age of 42. Her vocal ministry was "edifying, exhorting all to the true love and fear of God, and a humble attention to the divine principle of truth in themselves; adorning her doctrine by a life and conversation answerable thereto." As her family took decreasing amounts of her time, she became more active in visiting families within her own and other meetings. She was thought particularly well suited to this service, and was described as "a peaceable kind neighbor, a visitor and sympathizer with the sick and afflicted whether in body or mind".[26] Grace's daughter Mercy served as clerk of the women's meeting in 1754, and later became an elder. Another daughter, Ann, wife of John Hampton, was recorded as a minister in 1778.

Another minister was Stephen Comfort. He had moved to Middletown from Wrightstown in 1743, and married Grace Croasdale's daughter Mercy the following year. Stephen was recommended as a minister in 1747, at the age of twenty six. He was described as having "an open and cheerful disposition".[27] When Stephen accompanied the older, more experienced minister Abraham Griffith on a religious visit to Long Island in 1752, the meeting minuted that he was "a young man of a sober and religious conversation and his little appearance in the ministry amongst us is very well accepted . . . ."[28]

There were clear patterns within some families. We would expect that because of the Quaker subculture's emphasis on the family, the children of "weighty" Friends like Stephen and Mercy (Croasdale) Comfort would be exemplary. Their ten children, of whom nine reached adulthood, and eight married, were too young when the reform began to have run afoul of Quaker expectations.

A more telling example is the family of William and Jael (Bickerdike) Blakey. Both parents were involved in meeting activities, Jael more so than William. He died in 1750 and she remarried in 1753. Their youngest son, Joshua, married in 1758 at the tender age of seventeen. This would seem to be the kind of situation where emotion and hormones took precedence over proper Quaker procedure, which was just being more tightly enforced under directives from the yearly meeting. But, in fact, Joshua and Sarah Cary were married under the care of the meeting and their first child was born a whole year later. Joshua's brother and sister also married under the care of the meeting and led apparently exemplary lives. Joshua and his older brother William both became very active in Middletown Meeting; William was recorded as a minister.

There were also patterns of negative behavior. The family of Euclydus and Alice (Stackhouse) Longshore is an example (see Appendix 5). Euclydus was about sixty-five years old when the reform reached Middletown in 1757. He lived for another seven years, gradually decreasing his level of activity within the meeting. His wife, who outlived him, was also an active Friend, although neither ever held any offices. There were ten Longshore children, of whom half reached adulthood and married. The eldest son was disowned in 1740, long before the reform took shape, for marrying a non-Friend. The second son was disowned in 1743 for "unchaste action before marriage" (that is, their child was born less than nine months after they were married). However, Thomas acknowledged and condemned his misbehavior, and was reunited with Friends. Eldest surviving daughter Margaret offered a paper acknowledging and condemning her own marriage "out of unity" with a non-Friend, which was accepted. Her younger brother Euclydus[2] did the same thing in 1761. However, this was after the tightening of the discipline, and Margaret had to acknowledge and condemn her attendance at his unauthorized wedding ceremony. She married a second time shortly after, to another non-Friend, and this time she did not try to reverse her disownment.[29] After the first wife of Euclydus[2] died, he married Sarah Gillam under the care of the meeting. Two years later he requested that the six children of his first wife be accepted as members. Two of them died, two were disowned for marriage infractions, and two were disowned for military activities during the Revolution. In the earlier generation, then, four of the five Longshore children who reached adulthood were disciplined, two of them ending up permanently disowned. In the next generation, all five of Thomas's children, and all four of the surviving children of Euclydus's first wife were disowned. The children of his second wife fared somewhat better. Only four of the nine who lived to adulthood were disowned, and one of them was later reinstated.

What was it about the Comfort and Blakey families that caused their children to conform to expectations of Quaker behavior, that was absent in the Longshore family? Since all the Longshore deviations in the earlier generation had to do with marriage or sex, we need to test Barry Levy's thesis that in Chester County in the first half of the eighteenth century, poorer Quakers had difficulty finding Quaker spouses and were disproportionately disowned.[30] Table 4 shows data set men in order of wealth as listed in the 1757 tax record, which is the most complete. The amount of a man's personal estate, inventoried after his death, tended to vary according to his age at death, and whether or not he had previously given grants to his children. All financial amounts are given in constant dollars. The level of activity of the parents is given on a scale of one to six. One is assigned when there were no committee assignments and therefore no visible activity within the meeting for business. A two is given for one to five assignments, a three for six to ten tasks, a four for eleven to fifteen, and a five for sixteen or more assignments. A six is given to someone with sixteen or more tasks who also held an office. Offices included minister, clerk, assistant clerk, treasurer, elder, overseer, or trustee. The number of children who lived to age twenty one and the number

TABLE 4: Relative Income, Meeting Activity of Parents, and Disciplining of Children, Third Quarter 18th Century, Among Data Set Families

Name	1754 Tax in Const. Dollars	1757 Tax in C$	Year of Death	Age at Death	Estate Valuation in C$	Adult Children N	Number Disown	% Disowned	Meeting activity Father	Mother
Joseph Richardson	-	322.67	1772	-	16,568.76	6	0	0	6	5
William Paxson	214.08	214.08	1767	55	1,207.26	11	4	36	6	6
Thomas Jenks, Sr.	171.27	172.10	1797	97	1,746.62	6	1	17	6	6
Stephen Comfort	51.38	158.98	1772	-	1,989.51	9	0	0	6	6
John Woolston	149.86	150.58	1791	83	1,376.17	7	0	0	6	6
Ezra Croasdale	-	-	1794	68	1,851.78	10	5?	50?	6	2
Isaac Stackhouse	149.86	149.86	1791	71	386.10	7	2	28	6	5
John Watson	128.45	129.07	1764	61	1,382.50	2	0	0	6	6
Jeremiah Croasdale	-	-	1749	54	1,387.90	6	1	17	5	6
John Mitchell	119.89	119.89	1789	78	5,153.06	8	2	25	5	5
William Blakey	-	-	1750	-	1,178.59+	3	0	0	3	6
Euclydus Longshore	111.32	111.86	1764	-	386.90	5	4	80	5	5
Robert Croasdale	107.04	107.04	1780	52	-	6	1	17	6	6
Thomas Paxson	107.04	107.04	1790	75	876.96	11	1	9	6	6
James Paxson	1.28	107.04	1769	48	776.83	2	1	50	1	1
Joseph Stackhouse	107.04	107.04	1774	71	1,915.22	7?	4?	57?	1	4?
William Allen	106.60	106.59	1791	76?	843.38	7	4	57	4	3
Samuel Allen	106.60	106.59	1785	83	2,524.21	4	0	0	2?	1
Stephen Wilson	51.38	103.25	1761	67	1,241.55	8	1	12	6	3
Jeremiah Woolston	42.82	103.25	-	-	-	6	2	33	1	1
Samuel Woolston	51.38	64.96	-	-	-	3	0	0	1	1
James Wildman	51.38	64.53	1796	72	-	1	0	0	6	6
Lucas Gillam	51.38	52.27	-	-	-	10	7	70	1	2
Thomas Longshore	42.82	25.80	1777	56	*	5	5	100	1	1
David Wilson	-	25.80	1768	77	4,604.68	9	3	33	5	5
William Croasdale	-	-	1781	91	-	7	2	29	6	1

SOURCE: 1754 and 1757 Middletown Tax duplicates; Bucks County probate records; Middletown Meeting records

* In Penna. currency it was $333.95; because of rampant inflation there is no single number available for converting to constant dollars for 1777.

and percentage of those disciplined are also given. Although an N of twenty six, less those cases which have incomplete data, is too small to run significant statistical correlations, it does make some relationships more visible.

Looking at these figures, it seems that wealth was not the controlling variable in predicting with a high degree of accuracy which children would be disciplined by the meeting. However, the level of involvement of the parents, especially the mother, tends to have some correlation. It should come as no surprise that the factors determining the behavior of adolescent or adult children are much more subtle and difficult to quantify than such crude measures used here.

Inactivity in the meeting tended to appear at the middle and lower end of the income scale because those people had less available time, as well perhaps, as being viewed as less "able" in the colonial sense which assumed a concurrence of economic wellbeing with other kinds of ability. So to an extent these Middletown Friends confirm Levy's thesis, but in a more subtle way. Less wealthy Friends were frequently less able to take time to become involved in the ongoing business of the meeting, and therefore because they were less involved, their children tended to conform less closely to the requirements of the discipline.[31]

John Woolman's deliberate lowering of his financial obligations, realizing that they distracted him from devoting time and attention to God, reminds us that there is not a simple relationship between time, money, and faithfulness. Part of the complexity comes through levels of faith development. As a level four, Woolman was determined to follow the dictates of God in his heart, and would not let money—either too much or too little—deter him.[32] He observed too many wealthy Philadelphia Quakers, with plenty of servants freeing their time to serve in a variety of capacities, but with their hearts still in their counting houses.

In order to understand more fully the dynamics of the reform, let us examine the power structure of Middletown Meeting at the height of the reform period, 1757 to 1785. In the women's meeting there were thirty-eight women who held office or served on a significant number of committees (a value of five or six in Table 4). Some became active part way through the period, some died or removed, so there were not thirty eight actively at work for the entire period.

These women were recognized by the other Friends to have considerable experience and spiritual maturity. Their authority could take one or more of several forms. A Friend could have eloquence and clarity of insight: the ability to express the community's best understanding. A Friend could have competence or expertise: the understanding of how best to get something done. Someone who had borne responsibility for a long time would have authority, as would someone whose official position would give her (or him) access to information. But the greatest authority came from the Holy Spirit, which led one to know, communicate, and act on the Truth. Discernment was a struggle, as well as a gift, requiring humility and openness.[33] In the language of the day, Friends with these kinds of authority were "seasoned" or "weighty". It cannot be assumed that there is complete congruence between such authority and frequent committee assignments, but it is the best that can be done with the data available. These were not the only women who participated in committee assignments or meeting decisions, however. Another thirty three were also involved, but without holding office or being appointed as frequently to specific services (a value of two to four in Table 4).

A closer examination of the thirty-eight weighty Friends reveals that over half held an office and just under half of these held two offices, usually consecutively rather than concurrently. The thirty-eight women had twenty-seven different surnames. Their thirty-three known maiden names represented twenty-two different surname families. So the power within the women's meeting was fairly broad-based and not dominated by a few individuals or families. Jobs were assigned to new or younger women to see how they would perform. A woman with time and ability would be given more responsibilities. Unless she could hire sufficient help, however, a woman with young children usually was given few jobs.

The largest single family constellation surrounded Grace Croasdale. As mentioned above, her daughter Ann (Croasdale) Hampton was a recorded minister, another daughter, Mercy (Croasdale) Comfort was clerk, then an elder, while her daughter-in-law Margery (Hayhurst) Croasdale was an elder. Toward the end of the period, her granddaughter Rachel (Croasdale) Paxson was named an overseer, and three granddaughters-in-law were also very active.[34] But these eight women were only about one fifth of the most active Friends. Overt manipulation or power plays did not seem to have occurred at this time.

When an individual Friend deviated from expected Quaker behavior, it was hoped that whoever became aware of the transgression would take the individual aside and counsel her or him. The procedure was based directly on New Testament teaching.[35] If the deviating Friends accepted the proffered advice and mended their ways, the incident was forgotten. If, however, behavior was not modified, the information would be passed on to the overseers. Usually two overseers would then find an opportunity to speak with the offending Friend. If the situation was rectified, the matter was closed. If the offense persisted, the matter was taken to the monthly meeting.[36] There two or more Friends were appointed to visit and "labor" with the offender. Friends hoped that she would acknowledge that the behavior was inconsistent with Friends' testimonies, condemn it, sincerely repent, and change her ways. Usually a signed statement to that affect was required. When the meeting accepted the paper, often it was read after meeting for worship on First Day, and in some cases posted on the meeting house door. If the offender refused to admit the action was wrong, or was unwilling to go through this public procedure, Friends would spend considerable time laboring with her. Occasionally a case might drag on for over a year. But eventually, if she (or he) refused to give Friends "satisfaction", the meeting disowned her.

The Friends appointed to labor with an offender needed to be clear about Friends' testimonies, to lead exemplary lives themselves, to be firm, but also to lovingly help the offender to repent. It is interesting that four of the thirty-eight weighty women were not asked to serve on a discipline committee (at least in this period), while eight other women were. I assume that there were qualities about the four which led Friends not to give them these sometimes delicate or difficult tasks, while Friends recognized their capacity to do other jobs for the meeting. From 1757 to 1785, forty-one different women labored with other women who deviated in some particular from expected Quakerly behavior. Thus, it was not a small clique forcing its will on the great majority. There was broad consensus about what would be tolerated, and relatively wide participation in enforcement.

In the ten years before the yearly meeting's advice on reform was acted upon by Middletown, eleven women were disciplined, of whom four (36%) were disowned. In the decade after the discipline was tightened, thirty-five women were "labored" with, of whom thirteen (37%) were disowned. The thirty-five women who transgressed Friends' testimonies from 1757 through 1766 had twenty-eight different surnames. But only seven (20%) had married or maiden surnames similar to the thirty-eight weighty women. Although there might be a variety of explanations, it seems likely that within the eighteenth-century Quaker home, those families in which the mother was actively involved in the Friends meeting experienced the Quaker testimonies demonstrated in daily life. The daughters brought up therein tended to absorb and reflect their parents' values.

When the men who were disciplined in that same period are compared with the weighty women, the picture changes somewhat. There were ninety-two discipline cases involving men, some involving the same man more than once. They represented forty-four different surnames, sixteen (36%) of which were the same as the married or maiden names of weighty women. This perhaps implies that daughters were more amenable than sons to their mother's influence.

When the advice came from the yearly meeting to tighten the discipline, Middletown Meeting got into line, albeit reluctantly. The machinery for discipline was fairly broad-based. Among data set families forty-one females from thirty-one nuclear families participated in discipline committees, while thirty-five women in twenty-eight families, and seventy-nine men in forty-three families felt the rod of discipline in the ten year period from First month 1757 through Twelfth month 1766.

The deviations for which individual Friends were disciplined continued to be for irregular marriage procedures, fornication, debt, and others mentioned earlier. But the reform not only advocated a tightening of traditional rules. It also called for a new look at a practice some Friends' families had been involved with since the founding of the colony in 1682, or even earlier in the Caribbean Islands: holding human beings as chattel slaves. We will now turn to look at this issue.

CHAPTER 4: ANTISLAVERY

Slavery and the relations among people of different races—either overtly or by omission—is a continuing issue in United States history and for American religious groups. Its violence, ambiguity, and imperfectly realized potential for putting into concrete reality the highest ideals we profess, runs like a discordant theme through the symphony of American history.

Quakers accepted the dominant culture's use of slave labor when they found it already established in the Caribbean Islands. It was introduced by Dutch settlers in the Delaware valley before 1681, and Friends accepted—and many adopted—the practice in Pennsylvania. But gradually Friends came to see that holding humans as slaves was contrary to the teachings of the Inward Christ.

In this chapter we will look at the outward results of the Society's attempts to redefine slavery to make it one of the testimonies by which Friends separated themselves from the dominant culture. Once they accepted this new understanding they had to bring their practice into conformity with their faith by ending slaveholding among all Friends. There is an extensive literature on Quakers and slavery.[1] Here we will deal only with the story in Middletown Meeting.

Data is not available to chart the inward process by which individual Friends in Middletown Meeting shifted from their unquestioning acceptance of the dominant culture's support for the institution of slavery.[2] Therefore this chapter traces the story of Middletown Meeting's efforts to bring all its members into conformity with the new understanding that relinquishment of slave holding was required for membership in the Religious Society of Friends. Some Friends embraced antislavery willingly and devoted a great deal of time and energy to laboring with others. Some Friends adopted it reluctantly, as the price they had to pay to remain within the group. A few Friends refused to accept the new demands and chose instead to be disowned rather than give up the benefits of slave labor. We will search for patterns among the people who reacted in these various ways. Considering only those who actually owned slaves and therefore were directly affected, it appears that there was a relationship between the amount of time and energy an individual or his immediate family put into the affairs of the meeting and the willingness to accept the new sacrifice demanded by their Religious Society. Those who put more time into the meeting were also those most in touch with the enlarging Quaker understanding that slavery was wrong. But first, a narrative of the reaction of the local meeting to the decision of Philadelphia Yearly Meeting.

Middletown Meeting's Response

When Philadelphia Yearly Meeting decided that Friends should not be involved in buying or selling slaves, the Middletown men's meeting equivocated. Its report from the yearly meeting session did not mention slavery. When the issue could no longer be ignored, there was a disagreement within the men's monthly meeting as to whether the ban applied to all Blacks or only those imported from other countries. The question was sent to Bucks Quarterly Meeting. In Eleventh month 1756 that meeting decided that the yearly meeting intended to restrict the purchase of all slaves.[3] Middletown seems to have quietly ignored the issue for the next two years; at least it minuted nothing on the subject.

But it was impossible to ignore the yearly meeting of 1758, which after "weighty Consideration" minuted that there appeared to be a "unanimous Concern prevailing to put a stop to the Increase of the practice of Importing buying selling or keeping Slaves for term of Life" or even keeping them for so many years that they gave the appearance of "being keepers of slaves."[4] Monthly meetings were asked to discipline members who imported, bought, or sold slaves. The sanction was partial disownment: such a Friend could not sit in business meetings, contribute funds, or serve as a representative of the Society. Slaveholding itself was not banned, although it was denounced, and a five-man committee was appointed to join with others in each quarter "to visit and treat with all such Friends who have any Slaves". One member was John Woolman. He, with Samuel Eastburn of Buckingham, visited Quaker slave owners in Bucks County in December.[5]

Middletown's initial reaction was similar to its initial response to the general reform. They noted with interest and approval the epistle from London Yearly Meeting, and Philadelphia's advice concerning Friends visiting in families, neither of which mentioned slavery. Then they noted the exhortation regarding maintaining Friends' testimonies against war, including furnishing wagons to the belligerents. Almost as an afterthought they reluctantly added that the exhortation was to keep all testimonies, especially those "which relates to Wars and Fighting; and is against Swearing, or keeping of Negroes, or other Slaves."[6] Then the meeting was silent about slavery for another five years.

While the Middletown slave owners might have felt themselves relatively immune from the growing feeling within the yearly meeting, there were other, more tender consciences. In the late spring of 1763 Middletown minuted:

> This Meeting being concerned on Account of so many Friends continuing to purchase Negroes, appoints William Croasdale, Robert Collison, and Thomas Stapler, to visit and treat with all such who have lately purchased any of them, and endeavour to convince them of the Inconsistency of such a Practice with the Discipline of Friends and Principle of Truth, which teaches, "To do to others as we would be done by"; And report their Progress therein to next Meeting.[7]

Who were these three men? William Croasdale was a seventy-three year old widower, the brother-in-law of the recorded minister Grace (Heaton) Croasdale. All seven of his surviving daughters were married. William had been an overseer since 1753, and was active in the life of the meeting. Examples of his activity, recorded in the men's minutes: since 1755 he had been named a representative to quarterly meeting seventeen times, and seventeen times had been asked to visit with someone who transgressed the discipline. He had served on five marriage clearness or oversight committees, and six committees to ascertain if someone was clear of debt and other impediments to removing from the area. In 1756 he was asked to visit families in the meeting, to encourage them in their spiritual growth. What is absent from the list are the requests to do the jobs which had little or no spiritual overtones. Only once was he asked to deliver a certificate and once to help audit the meeting's accounts. He owned no slaves, and at his death in 1781 his personal estate was valued at a prosperous £1,127.8.7.[8]

Robert Collison was one of the most active men in Middletown Meeting. His profile is similar to William Croasdale's, but with a broader range of tasks for which the meeting called on his service. Thirty-nine year old Thomas Stapler had moved to Middletown from Falls in 1757. He was named an overseer in 1760. Like his two colleagues, the meeting tended to appoint him to committees which required tact, firmness, and a certain spiritual maturity.

It took them two months to complete the service. They then reported that

> Henry Harding, Joseph Thornton, Samuel Twining, John Jenks, John Wildman, William Rodman, and John Gregg, have lately been such Purchasers, whom they have endeavoured to convince of the Inconsistency of the Practice with the Doctrine of Christianity and Rules of our Society; but that they have not been able to convince them of the Evil thereof: Wherefore, as they are most of them now present, and hear Friends Sentiments concerning the Matter, it is referred to their solid Consideration until next Meeting.[9]

It could not have been a pleasant afternoon for the seven men, and for the next few months the minutes grumble that "few" of them were present. So the matter dragged on. An additional Friend was appointed, and the committee was asked to speak to the slave purchasers again. In December they reported they

> conferred with them all since last Meeting, and that several of them expressed some Concern and Desire to make Friends easy; and they were requested to attend this Meeting for that Purpose, but some of them not being here, and such of them who were here desiring further Time to consider of it, the Meeting condescends, and leaves the Matter to further Consideration.[10]

Finally the patient labor of the committee began to show results. In First month 1764 John Gregg, "being here, declares he is so sensible of the Evil of the

Practice, that he is for that Reason sorry he ever meddled with them; and that if he were clear of them, he would be careful to keep so for the Future, which this Meeting accepts of as what he can do at present."[11] He was not required to put it in writing, and he was allowed to keep the slaves. The meeting seemed content with an acknowledgment of wrongdoing, and a promise not to do it again.

William Rodman, on the other hand, "constantly persisted in vindicating the Practice of buying and keeping Negroes", in spite of repeated efforts to help him see the Light. In Fifth month 1764 Middletown minuted its "Disunion with him, by refusing to permit him to sit in our Meetings for Business, or to be employed in the Affairs of Truth, neither can we receive from him any Contribution for the Service of the Meeting, untill [sic] he come to be convinced of his Error, and properly condemn the same."[12]

By Second month 1765 the remaining five slave purchasers had followed John Gregg's example. Their acknowledgments of wrongdoing and promises not to repeat it were accepted by the meeting as what they were capable of at the time. It had taken ten years and five months from the time the yearly meeting sent its epistle, and a year and eight months since Middletown appointed a committee to visit recent slave purchasers. The slaves were still held in bondage.

After this burst of activity the meeting once more subsided into silence on the issue. This did not mean that individual Friends in Middletown were not concerned, nor did it mean that the issue was not from time to time raised among Friends and even at the monthly meeting. Its absence from the minutes meant that no decisions were made. Information is not available on the inner work by which individuals in Middletown wrestled with a gradually enlarging understanding of what God was requiring of them, and the slowly stiffening resolve to make a break with the dominant culture's acceptance of slavery.

Philadelphia Yearly Meeting continued to grapple with the concern. That body's recommendations were forwarded to the quarterly meetings, which in turn passed them on to the monthly meetings. For five years from 1769, Middletown Friends noted, with no apparent follow through, that the yearly meeting "again recommended to the Care of Friends in their respective Monthly Meetings, to visit and treat with such who have Slaves in their Possession . . . ."[13] In 1774 the yearly meeting strengthened its position short of completely forbidding slave holding. Middletown noted that the yearly meeting "recommended and enjoined that Monthly Meetings are careful to deal with all such Friends who shall be concerned in importing, buying, selling or giving away Negroes; and unless they condemn such Misconduct to Satisfaction, to be disowned." Nothing was said about continuing to hold slaves. However, the next month the meeting appointed Thomas Wilson and Robert Croasdale "to treat with such as hold Slaves in Bondage." In the Eighth month meeting for business,

> One of the Friends appointed to visit such Friends who hold Slaves in Bondage, reports that he, in company with several Friends appointed by the Quarterly Meeting to that Service, have visited most of such Friends belonging to this Meeting, and are in hopes their Labour hath not been altogether in vain, as several who have such who are of a suitable Age, propose to set them free.[14]

In 1775 the yearly meeting's now familiar advice was received "to continue to labour with such who keep Slaves, in the manner directed last year."[15] Again Bucks Quarterly Meeting appointed a visiting committee, including Thomas Stapler, William Richardson, and William Blakey from Middletown Meeting. Also named was James Moon of Falls Monthly Meeting, whose notes of the committee's work constitute the best extant record of such a committee.[16] The committee began its work in March, visiting Joshua Richardson.

Family Responses

We will look at four families that owned slaves. They are not a statistical sample. Rather, they were chosen because they illustrate the relationship between the ease of manumission of slaves and the degree of involvement in the business of the monthly meeting. Three families freed their slaves and one did not. We will look for factors which might explain the difference, such as the broad outline of activities of the slave owners, in an effort to determine where they were most invested, where their true allegiance lay. It appears that the more time and energy an individual put into the ongoing activities of the meeting, the more likely he was to bring his actions into line with the demands of the Religious Society regarding slavery. The individuals with large involvements of time and energy in activities outside the meeting were less likely to make the sacrifice of manumitting their slaves, just because the meeting demanded it.

Richardson

The Committee began its work with Joshua Richardson, forty-three years old, the eldest son of the immigrant Joseph. Joseph, who had died four years earlier, had been the wealthiest man in Middletown Meeting, at one time owning many slaves. A brief sketch of the Richardson family, which had members on both sides of the slavery issue, also will shed some light on the complexity of the problem for individual families and how divided they were on this issue.

Joseph Richardson had arrived in Bucks County in 1724 with a certificate of removal from Richmond Monthly Meeting in Yorkshire. According to family tradition he had the clothes on his back, a single groat in his pocket, and a flail. The young man hired himself for the winter months to live with William Paxson and thresh his grain. Several years later he married his employer's daughter, Mary. With the help of a small legacy from a relative in England, Joseph bought an acre at the crossroads in the village of Four Lanes' End in Middletown Township. He established a store, the only one between Durham, with its iron forges in the north of the County, and Bristol, with its port and small manufacturing in the south. He traded sugar, rum, molasses, and British goods for deerhides, iron, lime, and farm produce. His healthy profits were invested in land, and slaves to farm it. John Scarborough is reported to have said, "old Joseph Richardson at Four Lanes' End has about 40 [slaves] and is determined to keep them."[17]

One would expect to find such a man quite active in the meeting and in local and provincial politics. Joseph was appointed to the committee which oversaw the use of the meeting's burial yard, and he served as treasurer from First month 1756 to First month 1759. But appointments to other committees only appear before the mid-1750s. Regardless of his wealth, in 1750 he accepted the chore of sweeping the meetinghouse and making the twice-weekly fires in cold weather. Joseph seemed to use the meeting as a collection agency when Friends owed him money rather than as a faith community which could nurture his spiritual growth. For example, in 1744 he brought a complaint against Anthony Wilson for debt, in 1755 against David Wilson, and in 1759 against Eber Croasdale. He brought three such complaints to Falls Meeting between First month 1749/50 and Fifth month 1757.[18] Except for two appointments to grand juries in the 1750s, he does not appear active in public affairs. It seems that Joseph Richardson was much more interested in his own business affairs than politics, and to a certain extent, used the meeting to further his commercial interests. His wife Mary (Paxson) was quite active in the women's meeting, although she never held an office. At his death in 1772 Joseph owned over 1,000 acres. He bequeathed one slave, Joe, to his son Joshua "forever". But otherwise, no slaves appear in his will or estate inventory.[19] By that time Friends were reluctant to set a value on a human being, and therefore simply left slaves out of inventories.

Joseph and Mary had six children, all of whom lived to adulthood. Two daughters never married, one married at the age of twenty, the other at fifty three. The Richardson sons were Joshua and William. Joshua married Sarah Preston and came to own a mulatto slave named Joseph Davenport who was born in her father's household. Joshua inherited 319 acres in Middletown, his father's business, and presumably his father's business skills. He served the meeting as trustee for the meeting house and land, and as treasurer from 1772-1785. But other than that, he was named only to two small committees. Sarah bore six children. She had been given only one meeting appointment before she died in 1777, when her youngest child was not quite four years old.

William Richardson was quite different from his brother. He inherited his father's land in Northampton township, but bought the 319 acres in Middletown from his brother and lived there. He was extremely active in the meeting, appointed overseer in 1773, served as elder from 1781 to 1794, and recommended as a minister in 1794. He married Elizabeth Jenks, appointed as an elder in 1802.

In February 1776 William was one of several Friends named by Middletown Meeting to visit slave owners; Bucks Quarter appointed him to the same service. Thus, on the morning of March 8, 1776, he and six other Friends knocked on the door of his brother Joshua's house for a serious discussion on the issue of holding two enslaved humans. Joseph Primus or Priner, about sixty-six years old, had been purchased some thirty-six years earlier by Joseph Richardson from the estate of Jonathan Woolston, and bequeathed to Joshua "forever". Joseph Davenport, a mulatto, was twenty two and had grown up in Sarah's home. Whatever the ties of sentiment or economics, Joshua was persuaded to free both men, making arrangements that the "antient" Joseph, "being an orderly man", would continue to live in the Richardson household.[20]

Slaveholding was not the only Friends' testimony with which Joshua had difficulty. Two years after his wife Sarah died, Joshua was disciplined for "taking strong drink to excess". After a six-month struggle, Friends accepted his acknowledgment that he would try "to overcome his weakness by refraining very much from the Use of strong Drink." But seven years later the problem resurfaced. This time Friends labored with him, and he with his "weakness", for fourteen months before the meeting was satisfied that it was under control.[21] On the issues of slavery and drinking, where Joshua's outward behavior was not in accord with Friends' principles, he struggled to bring them into conformity.

Paxson

The Paxsons were another Middletown Meeting family that owned slaves. William[2] Paxson, who died in 1733, left two (white) servant girls whose indentured time was worth £15, and a "negro man" valued at £25.[22] William's daughter Mary married Joseph Richardson, described above.

William[3] inherited his father's plantation and the three laborers. When he died without a will in 1767, his estate included "a Negro lad 60£, a wench & child 40£".[23] His wife Anna (Marriott) died in 1773. According to Friends' records she had not manumitted the slaves. But they did not appear in her estate inventory which listed the farm and household gear indicating she died possessed of her late husband's plantation. The inventory was made by John Woolston, Thomas Paxson (Anna's brother-in-law), and Joshua Blakey, all active members of Middletown Meeting. It appears that they refused to include enslaved people in the inventory.[24] James Moon's "Account" noted that Anna Paxson died possessed of a Negro girl named Lucia, aged about twelve. She was probably the "child" in William's estate inventory of 1767. In early 1776 Thomas Stapler and William Blakey visited two of Anna's sons, Joseph and Thomas, who signed away their rights to Lucia. Three days later William Blakey and William Richardson (the Paxsons' first cousin) met with another of Anna's nine sons, Mahlon, who also signed. Then William Blakey had "an opportunity" with son Samuel, who was living in Wilmington, and he, too, signed away his rights to Lucia. But apparently they only gave up their rights to her when she became 18. In 1780 the committee reviewed her situation. She was living with yet another of Anna's sons, Phineas Paxson, and her age was given as "15 or 18". That suggests that she, the committee, and most of Anna's sons recognized that Lucia was now of age, but Phineas was considering her only fifteen, with three more years to serve. On January 20, 1785, five years later, Joseph, Phineas, Mahlon, Joshua, Mary, and Anna, Jr., finally righted the situation by deeding a plot of land to "Luce (a negro)".[25]

James Moon's "Account" also noted that William[3] Paxson had died possessed of an "ancient" Negro woman named Matillah or Matilda, "nearly past her Labour & almost blind", who had belonged to the family for many years. If she was the mother of Lucia, she couldn't be much older than in her early sixties. But she was seen as "advanced so far in age as not to be able to Support herself by her own Labour". William[4], Joseph, and Mahlon set her free and bound themselves to support her for the rest of her life. Joshua Richardson, their first cousin and guardian for their five youngest siblings, agreed to the arrangement.[26] Joshua had freed his two slaves four months earlier when the committee visited him.

Several questions remain. What happened to the "negro lad" valued at £60 in 1767. Had he died? William[3] and Anna had twelve children, the eldest died in infancy, and five youngest were still minors in 1776. The remaining six were all males, but only three had been drawn into the agreement regarding Matilda, although in one way or another all had been party to at least some of the arrangements regarding Lucia. Of those not brought into the arrangements for Matilda, one lived in Wilmington and two had recently been disowned for other reasons.[27] It was agreed that William[4] would be reimbursed £18 for the 18 months he had already supported Matilda. Secondly, the agreement stipulated that William should be "paid in Mony" at the rate of £12 a year "By his Brothers and Sisters". Did that include all of them? Joshua Richardson signed for the five minors. Presumably the two disowned brothers were not required by Friends to be party to the manumission. Did they voluntarily go along? The record is silent.[28]

Other than Phineas who was benefitting from Lucia's labor, none of the Paxson siblings were seriously affected in their purses by the manumission of the girl and promise to support the old woman. It is clear that they did not take any initiative, nor feel any urgency themselves to rectify the situation. Only two of the siblings were active in the meeting: Joshua, whose committee appointments were made later, at the turn of the century, and Joseph whose first task was given in 1778, but who did not become deeply involved for another five or six years, then continued to be active until his death in 1793. It is tempting to conclude from their behavior that with the possible exception of Joseph, none of the Paxson siblings at the time were really engaged in that tough inner work by which one allows the Light to search all areas of one's life, showing where there is a disconnection with God's will. Friends assumed such inward work would find expression in outward lifestyle. It is much easier to be an outward Friend, only modifying behavior under pressure to remain within the Quaker community. This can be one characteristic of second-level faith development, particularly a lukewarm one.

Jenks

The Jenks family was closely connected with the Richardsons. William Richardson, who served on the visitation committee, was married to Elizabeth

Jenks. Her brother, Thomas Jenks, Jr, was married to Rebecca Richardson. Another brother, John Jenks, was the object of the committee's labor.

The father of the family, Thomas Sr., had married Mercy Wildman and moved to Middletown from Buckingham in 1734. He owned 600 acres along Core Creek, where he built a fulling mill and a comfortable stone house. Thomas and Mercy were both active in Middletown Meeting. Thomas served briefly as an overseer; Mercy was clerk of the women's meeting for ten years. Thomas was also active in the public world, serving on five grand juries between 1755 and 1762. He served as executor for at least four estates, including that of Jeremiah Langhorne who manumitted his slaves in his will in 1742.[29] There is no indication that Thomas owned any slaves. Thomas and Mercy had six children, all of whom married. Four were involved in the Meeting, from an occasional appointment to very active. A fifth child, Joseph, was disowned when his third marriage was not under the care of the meeting.

The eldest son John had been a recent purchaser of a slave in 1763. After delaying sixteen months, he finally "appeared and declared he was now more fully convinced of the evil of purchasing Negroes; and that he designed to keep clear of that Practice for the Future, which Acknowledgment the Meeting accepts of for the present."[30] He kept his word and purchased no more; but he did not manumit his one–as he was not required to do at that time.

In March 1776 Friends again began to labor with Jenks, this time to free the slave. The Committee reported that John did not "appear disposed to Set him at Liberty, therefore further Labour is thought necessary." For eighteen months they labored and he wrestled. Finally in September, 1777, the forty-one year old bachelor John was persuaded to manumit his fifty-three year old slave named James. Like Joshua Richardson, slaveholding was not the only testimony with which John had difficulty. In early 1780 there was a rumor that he had fornicated. John declared his innocence but refused to go with Friends to talk with the woman who accused him. After four months of fruitless labor, John was disowned.[31]

We have looked at three families that included slaveholders who were persuaded to free the humans they held as chattels. All the families had some members who were very active in the ongoing business of the meeting. Two of the slave owners had other areas of their lives with which they had trouble being in conformity with Quaker expectations. The implication is that the individuals were somewhat weak in their own internal commitment to God. However, they had enough family members who encouraged them to modify their behavior on the slavery issue so as not to sever their connection with the Religious Society that meant so much to most of the family.

Rodman

The Rodman family divided on whether to give up its slaves, even if refusal to do so meant losing their membership in the meeting. They differed from the other three families in being much more involved in the secular world. Largely accommodated to the dominant culture, they seemed not to identify exclusively with Friends and the Quaker definition of what constituted acceptable behavior. Other interests had higher priority than their religious activities and affiliation.

The first Quaker in the family, John[1] Rodman, had been imprisoned in Ireland, then banished to Barbados in 1655 for refusing to remove his hat in court. He became a slave-owning planter. His son John[2] owned 47 acres and 13 Blacks in 1679 (probably a sugar plantation). John[2] moved to Newport, Rhode Island in 1682, then to Block Island, and finally to Flushing. He was a physician and recorded minister. John[3] was also a physician and slaveholder, a large landowner in New Jersey. Years later the Camden and Amboy Railroad ran through land John had set apart as a burial ground for his slaves. He served first in the Provincial Assembly and then in the Council. Three of his sons were members of Middletown Meeting. John[4] had manumitted or set definite terms of servitude for his slaves by 1782. Thomas[4] moved from Middletown to Burlington, New Jersey, in 1760, where he served in New Jersey's Provincial Assembly, as High Sheriff of Burlington, and as a Justice of the Peace. One of Thomas's sons took the unQuakerly job of barracks master in Burlington. The other son was disowned for marrying out of unity with Friends.[32]

William[4] Rodman was quite active in Middletown Meeting until Friends indicated their uneasiness with his slaveholding. The meeting struggled with him as a recent purchaser of slaves in the 1760s. The result, as noted above, barred him from participation in the meeting's activities, but stopped short of actual disownment. However, he was cut off from the meeting for business. One result may have been a further drifting away from the group and a closer association with non-Friends. In 1776 the meeting required that he liberate the slaves he had purchased. James Moon noted that William "appeared Deaf to the Advice of his Friends".[33] The division between the dominant culture and the Society of Friends became sharper as the Revolution progressed. William was unwilling or unable to bring his life into conformity with Friendly requirements regarding both slave owning and relinquishment of political office. Although Friends did not take action against him while he lay ill for several months, he was finally disowned in February 1778.[34] William seemed freed by the cutting of those ties. He took the affirmation of allegiance in 1778 and was an active supporter of the patriot cause. William's sons Gilbert and William, Jr. followed their father's example and were disowned for military activity and taking the affirmation of allegiance and abjuration. Two daughters were disowned for marrying out of unity with Friends as were two children of John[4]. The interests of the family gravitated outside of the meeting, and when choices had to be made, they parted company with Friends.

By August of 1781 James Moon was able to record that no Negroes were kept by Friends in Bucks County in life bondage except in a few households in which the wife was a Quaker but the husband was not–usually because he had already been disowned for the offense. Bucks Quarter was entirely free of slave holding by 1799.[35]

Pennsylvania and Slavery

As the attitude of Friends toward slavery had shifted, so did that of the dominant culture. After 1772 antislavery activity had increased in the wider colonial American society. Connecticut banned the slave trade in 1774. Both Continental Congresses in 1774 and 1776 adopted resolutions against it. Friends, by and large, supported both this and the growing sentiment against British colonial policies. But by the time fighting broke out Friends and antislavery were diverging from patriotic politics. As historian Patricia Bradley notes, the emphasis of Friends (and others) that slavery was a sin from which the faithful must purify themselves, was at cross-purposes with patriotic rhetoric. Revolutionary rhetoric extolled the innocence of the patriots, an image much more comfortable to slave holders, and one that enabled them to ignore antislavery pleas.[36] However, the revolutionary appeals of the Declaration of Independence had moved opinion in Pennsylvania to the point that on March 1, 1780 the Assembly passed an act for the gradual abolition of slavery. It also appears that the radicals, who controlled the Pennsylvania Assembly in 1779-1780, were influenced by Quaker thought. Anthony Benezet had lobbied each Assemblyman. George Bryan, Presbyterian leader of the fight to pass an abolition bill, found it "irksome" that the heaviest opposition came from his own co-religionists who were "otherwise remarkable for their zeal, and for their exertions in the cause of freedom." The preamble of the bill explained its necessity in terms of demonstrating the sincerity of the American fight for freedom, and offering "substantial proof" of Pennsylvania's gratitude to God for rescue from the British. Bryan remarked that the bill "astonishes and pleases the Quakers. They looked for no such benevolent issue from our new government, exercised by Presbyterians."[37]

The reasons for the passage of the law were slightly different from Friends' reasons for abolishing slavery. There was more emphasis on the Rights of Man rather than on obedience to God owed by a people called apart to be under Christ's governance. Naturally, however, each group used all the arguments it could muster, so there was considerable overlap, as well as borrowing. The final bill prohibited bringing new slaves into the state, and stipulated freedom for the children born of slaves after the passage of the act, after they had served a twenty-eight year indenture. Immediate freedom was granted only to slaves whose masters failed to register them by November 1, 1780. Friends had pushed their members for immediate manumission, although permitting some exceptions provided the terms of indenture were not so long as to give the effect of continuing servitude in all but name. The Pennsylvania Act freed none who were properly registered as slaves; only their children would eventually be free. So, although Quaker testimony and the political agenda seemed to converge for a time, and no doubt influenced each other, there were some important differences having to do with the Quakers' underlying spiritual concern.

Once the manumission battle had been won within the Society of Friends, Quakers shifted their attention to the freed Blacks. Middletown Friends noted that the yearly meeting, "having taken into Consideration the Situation of the poor Negroes who have been set free closely recommends it to the Care of Quarterly and Monthly Meetings, that they help and Advise them on all Occasions when necessary, and that they appoint solid and experienced Friends for that Purpose." Thomas Wilson (of Southampton) and Ezra Comfort were appointed from Middletown to join with the quarterly meeting committee.[38] A decade later Joseph Paxson served on a similar committee. Grace Croasdale had died in 1769, but her daughters Grace (Croasdale) Townsend and Ann (Croasdale) Hampton were remembered fondly for their care of "bound and colored" people.[39] This sympathetic care by women who were also ministers, points to similarities with Soderlund's "exemplary" Friends of Shrewsbury and a fourth level of faith development.

The issue of slavery did not directly touch the large majority of Middletown Meeting families. They did not own slaves, they did not labor with those that did, and they did not serve on the committees appointed to visit the freed Blacks to offer counsel and assistance. However, they had to come to grips with the issue and had to undergo the mental and spiritual process by which they redefined a practice which the dominant culture had long sanctioned but was itself beginning to judge by a new standard. They had to see enslavement in a new Light. They had to change their thinking about what was required of those who identified themselves as Friends. An actual change of outward behavior was only required of those who owned slaves.

Racism

While Friends and the revolutionary culture converged on the issue of antislavery, they also converged on an inability to address the more difficult underlying issue of racism. Here Friends betrayed their deep connection with the dominant culture. Much has been written about racism in western culture.[40] In spite of their enlarged understanding of the work of Christ's Spirit in all people, many Friends accepted antislavery less from a tender regard for the fundamental human equality of people of color because all have "that of God" within and both the potential and the responsibility to obey its instructions, as from their understanding that one of the requirements laid on them as members of the Religious Society of Friends was not to own slaves. In other words, they accepted it from a place of spiritual understanding that we might identify with Peck's level two faith development, or Wilber's blue meme, rather than Peck's level thee or four, or Wilber's green meme or second tier. A second, or blue, level would oppose slavery because it was against the rules of the Society of Friends. A level three or green meme would say slavery is a horrendous wrong to the slave, and we must work to eradicate it everywhere. A level four or second tier Friend would say, yes, slavery is horrendous, and as I come to live as if in God's realm now, I personally behave so that none of my actions give any support to the institution of slavery anywhere, and I reach out to victims of slavery (Black and white) as way opens, because this is how people in God's kingdom live. John Woolman was able to connect seventeenth-century Quaker experience of being marginalized and oppressed with the eighteenth-century condition of oppressed and marginalized enslaved people. By internalizing the suffering linked with marginality he was able to feel the oppression of others. Woolman's own life demonstrated the inner work and pain of "opposing his fellow Friends without breaching harmony."[41] From the outside his fourth-level antislavery work may not look very different from that of second or third level activities, but it came from a different spiritual understanding.

Most Friends seemed unable to break out of the mind set that people of African descent were different in more than skin color. They were at least childlike and inferior, if not innately lazy, debauched, and depraved. Throughout the North most whites maintained a careful distinction between granting Negroes a theoretical right to life, liberty, and property, and granting them actual political, economic, and social equality. Nothing seemed to erase from the public mind the firmly held conviction that the African race was inferior and therefore incapable of being assimilated politically or socially—not to mention physically—with the dominant and "superior" European society. The nineteenth-century reformer Maria Child summed it up in 1852, "even in those [earlier] days, the Society of Friends were by no means all free from prejudice against colour, and in later times, I think they have not proved themselves at all superior to other sects in their feelings and practice on this subject."[42]

Middletown Friends were not immune to these feelings. In 1703 the men's meeting had minuted that:

> There having been formerly some Negroes buryed in ffriends Burying yard which they are not well satisfied with. Therefore Robert Heaton and Thomas Stackhouse are ordered to fence off[f] that corner with as much more as they may see convenient, that ffriends burying place may be of it selfe from all others.[43]

It is hard not to see that as blatant racism, particularly as no other meeting seems to have minuted a similar action. Mitigating the situation somewhat was Friends' reluctance to allow non-Quaker whites to be buried in their ground. Also, it seems that Friends were burying people of color in a recognized place rather than haphazardly on their farms. But a generation later the same mean spirit was alive in Middletown. Perhaps, but not mentioned in the minutes, someone had circumvented the restriction. If so, that would be an interesting insight into someone or some family's attitude. In any event, the men minuted:

> this meeting having had ye Matter under Consideration it is unanimously agreed that hereafter no Deceased Negroes be Buried Within ye Walls of sd graveyard Belonging to this Meeting, & Adam Harker, Jonathan Woolston & Joseph Richardson are appointed to keep ye Keys of ye Said Graveyard & take Care that none be Buried therein but Such as they in ye Meetings Behalf shall allow of.[44]

Jonathan Woolston held at least one slave, and Joseph Richardson had many. It is clear that Middletown Friends, no matter how "kind" they might be as masters, did not welcome Blacks to join the meeting, or in any way encourage them to aspire to other than a theoretical theological equality.[45]

On the other hand, James Moon and William Blakey, who worked most closely with Middletown Blacks, seem to have risen above the prejudices of most other whites of their day. They were involved in the meetings for worship held for Blacks, and in visiting Black families.

Other than the exclusion from the graveyard, and comments in Blakey's Journal, it is difficult to assess the racial attitudes of Middletown Friends. No Blacks applied for membership, although meetings for worship were held, on occasion, just for them. Short of overt acts or references by eye-witnesses, the only way the historian can gauge the degree of racism is to read statements left by Friends—read them with the heightened consciousness of the early twenty-first century. Aware of how much unconscious racism still resides in the caring and thoughtful liberal heart of the 2000s, we are jarred by the us/them language and the unchallenged assumptions of superiority/inferiority which sprinkle eighteenth century Quaker writing. We no longer accept at face value the protestations of, for example, historian Edward Turner who found little or no race prejudice in Pennsylvania before 1800.[46]

The record of Friends in the United States is inconsistent regarding racism. In 1756 a plan to extend Philadelphia's Great Meeting House provided "suitable places" for Black attenders–presumably physically segregated. A quarter century later, in 1783 Philadelphia Yearly Meeting minuted that a white, Indian, or Black woman could be "safely" considered for membership. In 1796, in spite of concern over contravening popular prejudice against admitting any Black members, the yearly meeting determined that membership should be decided "without respect of persons or colour". That minute was decided on the case of a mulatto girl who applied for membership in Rahway Quarter. William Blakey was present at the quarterly meeting and noted the application "brought an exercise over some minds, on beholding the prejudices that exist, because of colour."[47] Robert Purvis, a wealthy and very light-skinned Black, lived in Bensalem. He was probably a member of Byberry Meeting and his second wife was Mary Townsend, a white Friend. An 1804 letter from Quaker minister Oliver Paxson of Buckingham Meeting related the account of a woman of African descent who applied for membership in Oblong (New York) Meeting and was rejected "solely on account of her colour". She took it "very hard" and was greatly distressed. This kind of incident appears to have been rare. Henry J. Cadbury concluded that few Negroes were excluded outright because of race, but people of color were discouraged from applying, consideration of their applications was postponed, or other reasons were cited for rejection.[48]

Racism in the dominant culture increased in virulence, peaking (in the period from 1750 to 1850 covered by this study) in the 1830s. An English Friend reported in 1841 that his American co-religionists "imbibed the prejudice against colour" and many were "caught by the gilded bait of southern commerce".[49] Quakerism found it "difficult to inure itself against the force of public sentiment", which was stronger than "the sting of an occasional English critic", in Leon Litwack's words.[50] He implies that Friends gave in to the dominant culture's racism less because they accepted its ideas, than because they had not the stomach to stand up against the vilification and harassment which would have been the price of taking such an unpopular stand. Whatever was the underlying motive, the outward actions of many Friends in the first half of the nineteenth century demonstrated a lack of the "fruit" of a God-centered, obedient life. The spiritual life of large numbers of American Friends was no longer the radical and empowering experience of their seventeenth-century ancestors.

Although Friends failed to clear themselves of racist attitudes, they did end slaveholding within the Religious Society. They also worked hard to maintain their testimony against war. This position, too, put them at odds with many of their non-Quaker neighbors. We will look at this in the next chapter.

CHAPTER 5: WAR

In the last chapter we saw the seeming convergence between Quakers and the Revolutionary culture in Pennsylvania on the inappropriateness of chattel slavery while maintaining a belief in the "inferiority" of Blacks. They shared arguments and many similar views, although they came from somewhat different starting points. On the question of war as an appropriate instrument for settling the growing disagreements between the colonies and the mother country, however, Friends and the dominant culture were diametrically opposed.

During times of war governments make the heaviest demands on their citizens. The question of ultimate allegiance is thrown into high relief. It is then that the basically theological nature of the conflict becomes apparent.[1]

What was at stake during wartime for Quakers, Mennonites, and the other peace sects, was their concept of discipleship as a distinct way of life. Religious commitment involved a radical rejection of the dominant culture's claim of primacy; instead it provided different models for moral conduct and authority. Ultimate allegiance was to God and not to human government.[2]

When relations began to break down between Britain and her American colonies, passions rose, and pressure increased for Quakers to conform to the political demands of the larger society in which they lived. It was a time of testing. There were several aspects of the test, with varying amounts of data available. The easiest to study and document were the overt demands made upon Friends–and all citizens–through laws passed by the new authorities. These demanded oaths or affirmations of allegiance and military activity, or in lieu of that, payment of fines or assessments. Related demands included the sale, loan, or "gift" of wagons and teams or supplies for the military effort, and the use of rapidly depreciating continental currency. Another dimension of the test which Quakers faced, just as real but much more difficult to document, was the attitude of their neighbors. To what degree were individual Friends subject to ridicule, to loss of status, and to outright hostility? The degree to which such treatment rankled individuals also varied.

This chapter summarizes the political events in Bucks County in 1774-1776 and the role of Quakers in them. Then it briefly describes the consequences Friends faced when they tried to uphold their peace testimony. Finally, it looks at families within Middletown Meeting to see how they reacted to the demands made upon them by the revolutionary events. In particular it examines some families which gave in to the pressure to conform to the political and military demands, and some that resisted. It explores some of the differences between those families and tries to discover which variables were most important in influencing Friends' choices.

Philadelphia and Bucks County Prepare for War

Politically and economically powerful Philadelphia Quakers initially supported protests against British encroachments on their rights as Englishmen. They vigorously protested the Stamp Act and with slightly less enthusiasm, the Townshend Acts.[3] But as England became less willing to compromise and the radical elements in Pennsylvania became increasingly vociferous, the Philadelphia Quaker merchants became more cautious. Their primary goal was to safeguard the Charter of 1701 which guaranteed their religious freedoms. Only secondarily did they protest British infringements on their other liberties.[4]

News of the Boston Port Bill galvanized Philadelphia's Committee of Correspondence into action. It encouraged the formation of county committees to send delegates to a convention which would send "instructions" to the Provincial Assembly, then dominated by conservatives. The hope was to encourage the Assembly to select delegates to a proposed Continental Congress. In Bucks County on July 9 a public meeting held at Newtown, chaired by future Tory Gilbert Hicks, passed a resolution favoring such a move, and appointed seven men to attend it. At least two of the men were Quakers, and a third, Joseph Kirkbride, had been disowned earlier by Falls Meeting.

The resulting First Continental Congress called for non-importation and non-consumption of English goods, and urged county committees to enforce the boycott. Accordingly, the seven Bucks County delegates called for a general meeting to elect the new committee. This was done December 15 at Newtown. The "Committee of Observation for this County" consisted of twenty-nine men, including Thomas Jenks, Joseph Watson, and several other Friends.[5] Snow prevented the committee from meeting until January 16, at which time its first resolve was to "highly approve of the pacific measures" and "render our unfeigned thanks to the worthy gentlemen who compose that august Assembly." It also set up a Committee of Correspondence of five men, including Joseph Watson, a Quaker from Buckingham.

The conservative Philadelphia Quakers, who controlled the Meeting for Sufferings which spoke for Friends between sessions of the Yearly Meeting, were trying their best to apply brakes to the widening rift with Britain. If they failed, they would do all they could to prevent Friends from participating in any way, especially in public meetings and demonstrations. Philadelphia radicals loudly accused Quakers of Toryism. This may have been true for the wealthy international merchants, but rural Friends tended (although not unanimously) to favor the patriot cause while trying to remain neutral in any military sense.[6]

The men of Bucks County who participated in the political process continued to vote for the people they had always chosen. Therefore a number of Quakers found themselves on these quasi-legal committees which were recommending strong anti-British actions. There is no indication that Jenks, Watson, and the others did not support the patriot position. But events rapidly escalated beyond what Friends could conscientiously support. Shots were fired at Lexington and Concord, and on May 2, 1775 the Bucks County Committee resolved that "notwithstanding the disapprobation we have hitherto shown to the prosecution of any violent measures of opposition", it now felt compelled by the British use of force to "earnestly recommend" that people in each township form associations "to improve themselves in the military art". Money was also raised to send to the aid of suffering Bostonians.

Only ten men came to the June Committee of Observation meeting; probably one was a Friend. They decided to publish an advertisement calling on all townships to form associations and choose field officers. At the meeting on July 21, 1775 a "large majority" was present. A man who had said derogatory things about the "general American cause" came and in typical Friends' manner "acknowledged the charge, and made such concessions as were considered as a sufficient attonement [sic] for his former errors." Informers brought additional complaints, so a subcommittee of four men was appointed to examine them. But the main interest of the Committee became encouraging the associations of militiamen. It was becoming increasingly clear that there was less and less business of the Committee in which Friends could be involved. "John Wilkenson, Jonathan Ingham, Thomas Foulke, and John Chapman, being of the people called Quakers and alledging [sic] scruples of Conscience relative to the business necessarily transacted by the Committee, desired to be relieved from any further attendance . . . ." The next month the minutes listed the six people who replaced those four Quakers plus Thomas Jenks of Middletown and Joseph Watson of Buckingham.[7]

Without the moderating presence of Quakers, the Friendly procedures against people accused of slandering the patriot cause began to change. That very month Thomas Smith of Upper Makefield was brought before the Committee and found guilty of saying nasty things about Congress, that the Devil was at the bottom of it, and "taking up Arms was the most scandalous thing a man could be guilty of; & more heinous than an hundred of the grossest offenses against the moral law, etc., etc., etc." He was declared an "Enemy to the Rights of British America" and everyone was to "break off every kind of dealing with him." That was not a Quakerly "disownment". However, after the Committee threatened to send an account of his unpatriotic words to the press, Smith came to it and made a statement very much like a traditional Friends' acknowledgment and condemnation of his act, promising "for the future to coincide with every measure . . . so far as is consistent with the religious principles of the society to which I belong."[8]

With Quakers and other pacifist sect members off the Committees of Observation they grew louder in their calls to the Provincial Assembly to remove the voluntary character of the township associations. In late November 1775 an act was passed conscripting all males between the ages of sixteen and fifty, and providing for a fine or assessment of £2.10.0 for all non-associators. In April 1776 the fine was increased to £3.10.0. But Quakers, Mennonites, Schwenkfelders, Dunkers, and Moravians could no more pay the costs for another to go to war than they could go themselves. The issue was clearly drawn between two views of ultimate authority. The sects viewed themselves as citizens of a heavenly kingdom, subject to the authority of Christ. In times of conflict between the spiritual and the secular, the sects opted to obey God. This vision of religion as legitimately making total demands on the life of the individual, had been protected by Pennsylvania's First Article of the Charter of Privileges of 1701.[9] That was another reason the radicals wanted to change it.

In June 1776 a Provincial Conference was called to propose a new constitution for Pennsylvania, and to encourage the Continental Congress then meeting to declare independence from Great Britain. Pennsylvania's new constitution was signed on September 28 and the old Assembly ceased to exist. In Bucks County a few men met on October 1 for the usual election, but a rowdy group of associators forcibly prevented the attempt.[10]

The Quaker Response

Philadelphia Yearly Meeting in the fall of 1776 had representatives from all the other American yearly meetings except New York, where military activity was centered. The recommendations of a committee representing all of them were approved by Philadelphia Yearly Meeting. They spelled out specific instructions for maintaining the peace testimony: Friends were to withdraw from any activity in the civil government, including elections for public office; they were to pay no substitute fine, tax, or penalty in lieu of military service either openly or by connivance, for themselves, their servants, or children; they were to avoid engaging in any trade or business likely to promote or aid war and were not to partake in the spoils of war, such as prize goods; and they were to give generously to alleviate the sufferings of others caused by war. Monthly meetings were asked to make lists of the sufferings of their members for the sake of conscience. These directions were taken to the other yearly meetings and thus American Friends had a fairly uniform response to war and consistent standard of conduct.[11]

Under the new Pennsylvania constitution there was no legal protection for "tender consciences". Quakers and members of the other peace churches faced fines for refusing to muster with the militia. For refusing to pay the fines their goods were distrained. The distraints usually exceeded the value of the fine. When the British army occupied Philadelphia and Washington was at Valley Forge, both sides felt free to send foraging parties to help themselves to livestock, blankets, and additional supplies owned by Friends and others.

If Friends reacted in any way other than by taking up the cross of suffering with nonresistance, their faith community was standing by to encourage and exhort, and if necessary, resort to disciplinary action and disownment. To see the function of the meeting, as reflected in its minutes, in rather negative terms of enforcing a discipline, is to miss the dynamic of a faith community under siege. Ties among members were strengthened and love deepened as they shared experiences of accepting the suffering which resulted from increased obedience and faithfulness. Each individual had to decide which was primary for him or her: the dominant culture with its enthusiastic cries of patriotism and opportunities for advancement, and its sanctions of economic loss and social derision, or the Society of Friends with its hope of a personal relationship with God and the pressure of expectations from family and Friends to submit to suffering and receive comfort and support. The possibility of closer relationship with God within the Quaker tradition, and the threat of distraint of goods faced each Friend. The degree of social pressure from outside and from within differed from family to family and individual to individual. They cannot be measured, but the decision of each Friend can be seen in whether he, or to a certain extent, she, upheld Quaker testimonies or decided the pain was not worth the gain. Each Friend had to answer the question, where lies ultimate allegiance: to God or to the national cause?

In effect Friends were being offered the opportunity to embrace a "collective dissenting identity"–the stance that early Friends had found to be transformative. By choosing to marginalize themselves as a community in their own land they opened the possibility of revivifying their religious Society.[12]

The Cost of Upholding the Peace Testimony

We need to shift our attention now to the price which was exacted by the larger society as the cost of refusing to accept the patriots' definition of what was required for good citizenship. This price was in addition to the cost of war borne by everyone: soldiers quartered in homes; meeting houses and churches commandeered for hospitals and barracks; fences taken for firewood; blankets, food and other supplies requisitioned; raiders from both sides seizing goods on their way to market. For example, a British foraging party appropriated 2,000 yards of cloth from Thomas Jenks's fulling mill.[13] Friends and other peace sects faced persecution over their refusal to obey the conscription laws, take the affirmation of allegiance and abjuration, pay war taxes, and accept continental currency. We will look in more detail at Friends' sufferings for resisting conscription. Then we will look at one example of persecution over the currency issue.

Conscription

The November 1775 law conscripted all males between the ages of sixteen and fifty, and established a fine for all non-associators. From time to time it was amended. Lists were drawn up for each township, assigning men to militia companies and classes.[14] They included Friends. Exercise days were proclaimed when the men and boys practiced marching. Drums and fifes provided a general festive air. Even though absentees were fined, most Friends stayed home.[15] They also resolutely refused to pay fines. So the local captain would dispatch someone to the Friend's house to seize some goods to cover the fine. It was at this point that gross injustices were perpetrated in the name of patriotism and national security.[16]

For example, in January 1778 local militia officer John Thompson came with two men to Joshua Blakey's house, and charged him with a fine of £2.10.0 for "not going out as a soldier". They took two horses and two bridles, worth £50.12.0. Three months later they came back again and took another horse, saddle, and bridle for the same fine, these being worth £32.10.0. In July they returned, told Blakey he owed a fine "for not taking the test", and took two loads of hay, valued at £5.0.0. In January 1779 John Thompson returned and took a sleigh and various pieces of gear, all valued at £4.2.6, saying it was in payment of the fine for not exercising with the militia. In February two other men came and looked over Blakey's flock of sheep. They selected the eight best and took them, explaining that they had purchased them five weeks earlier from John Thompson, although no one had informed Blakey. In July Thompson visited again because Joshua and his son had not gone out with the militia. This time Thompson took a cow and a bull, worth £6 and £5 respectively. The bull came home again that evening, but in October two men came and collected him, saying they had purchased him from Thompson nine or ten weeks earlier.[17]

In January 1778 John Thompson also visited John Watson of Middletown, and took a mare, saddle, and blind halter in payment for a fine of £3.10.0 for John and another £3.10.0 for his apprentice for non-attendance at the last muster day, even though the apprentice's name was not on the muster roll nor on the official returns. Nine months later the saddle was returned, without explanation. The mare was sold for £32.2.0, and a few days later resold at a handsome profit, for £60. In June Thompson returned with a demand for a substitute fine. He told

Watson that there was £20 or £30 "overplus" in his hands, but nonetheless he drove all of Watson's sheep into a neighbor's barn, selected the best twelve, and took them. The following year a demand was made for £42 for Watson and £42 for his apprentice for substitute fines even though, as Watson pointed out, the apprentice was underage when the draft was first made, and had since been assigned to a class which had not yet been called. Thompson was unimpressed and took a fine mare belonging to Watson's daughter. Unknown to Watson at the time, a neighbor offered to pay £84 to have her returned. Thompson refused, bought the mare himself for £300, although the price could easily have been £1,000 "as the money then went". Watson complained to Joseph Kirkbride, disowned by Falls some years earlier, and very active in the patriot cause. Joseph "seemed to disapprove the conduct yet no redress" was made.[18]

The meeting collected accounts of Friends' sufferings from 1775 on, and forwarded them to the quarterly meeting, which sent them to the yearly meeting. They consist of page after page of distraints, galling in their arbitrariness and injustice. Livestock and gear, wheat, oats, Indian corn, buckwheat, hay, cheese, flour, blankets, feather beds and coverlets, kettles, chairs, and other items were taken. They took what was available–fabric and a clock reel from a weaver, boards from a sawyer. They came with two wagons and drivers to James Moon's farm. They searched all his outbuildings and his whole house, then took an ax to the locked door of the granary. When they couldn't wrench it off its hinges, they climbed up and smashed the glass window to gain access. They cleaned out the Moon supplies, except for five bushels of wheat to last him, his family, and his hired men through from June to the next harvest.[19]

As citizens of God's realm, harassed by people from the "world", Friends needed to respond by following God's rules, not the usual, emotional or "common sense" responses. This meant responding to persecution with love. A party of Continentals headed by a Baptist clergyman came on a plundering party from New Jersey, and stopped at William Blakey's home. The men were ordered to seize horses, wagons, grain, and produce, while their leader insulted William in his own house. But William "remained silent, and perfectly calm and quiet" until the officer himself fell silent. Then he asked William if he ever prayed, and would William pray for him? William said he would. The leader ordered his men to restore all the goods to William. They held more serious conversation, then the party left with professions of friendship.[20] William was a recorded minister. Probably most Friends were unable to attain this level of holy obedience.

Friends knew that following exercise days, they could be subject to harassments. But distraints could come more or less often. Enforcement was arbitrary and uneven. Samuel Mitchell seems to have been hit most frequently. Fourteen fines between 1778 and 1783 are listed in the *Pennsylvania Archives*.[21] Thomas Jenks, Jr., Euclydus Longshore, and Henry Mitchell, among others, were only listed once. But the official list of fines does not always tally with the sufferings recorded by the meeting. Some forage masters had their own agendas. Arbitrariness was widespread, and was complained about from both sides of the political fence. An April 1778 Chester County letter complained, "Part of the County that joyns on my District has not had any Fines demanded of them, which incensces [*sic*] these that is taken from."[22]

There is no way we can explain now why some non-associators were picked on more than others. The answer may lie in geography or the personal animosity or greed of the men charged with foraging. The result must have been serious disruption in the social fabric of the larger community and a tendency for Quakers to turn more closely to members of their own group.

Even though a man had been disowned by Middletown Meeting, that did not mean he necessarily gave up the Friends' peace testimony. This lends weight to the understanding that disownment was not necessarily a severing of ties with the Quaker subculture. It was an official declaration that, due to some action, the disowned person had transgressed a Quaker testimony and the meeting could not be responsible for him, until he acknowledged and condemned the behavior. Eleven disowned data set Friends suffered fines for not co-operating with the military demands made on them. For example, Joseph Allen, disowned in 1761 for fathering a bastard, was fined six times between 1780 and 1783. Thomas Paxson, disowned in 1776 for marrying contrary to discipline, and not reinstated until 1800, was fined four times. Abel Stackhouse, disowned in 1763 for the same reason, also received four fines. Phineas Paxson was disowned in 1776 for exercising with the militia, but in subsequent years was fined seven times for refusing to do it again.[23]

Affirmation of Allegiance

In June 1777, as part of a general militia law, the Pennsylvania legislature enacted an oath or affirmation of allegiance to the Commonwealth and abjuration of allegiance to King George III. Those who did not subscribe to it could not hold public office, serve on juries, sue in the courts, vote, buy, sell, or transfer land, and could be arrested as spies if they ventured beyond their home area. The next year it was extended to strip from non-oath takers most of their civil rights, including serving as an executor or administrator of an estate, as a guardian, or even as a recipient of a legacy, and to bar them from engaging in activities as a teacher, merchant, trader, attorney, clerk, notary, apothecary, surgeon, or doctor. It was not repealed until 1789.[24] The provisions which should have been felt most heavily by Middletown Friends would have been the prohibitions around wills and against transferring land, the closing of the Friends' school, shutting down the Richardson's store, and preventing Friends travelling in the ministry. However, the record is not clear that these things happened, although fines and distraints were levied for not taking the affirmation (as in the case of Joshua Blakey, mentioned above). The loyalty oath provided an additional tool to the local patriot officials; they apparently felt they could use it–or not–at their discretion. It also provided another test for Friends deciding where their ultimate allegiance lay and acting upon that decision.

From the beginnings of the Religious Society of Friends there was a strong testimony against the taking of oaths, and the double standard of truth such oaths implied. Pennsylvania's new law provided for an affirmation in place of an oath. But there was an additional difficulty. A 1762 Philadelphia Yearly Meeting advice stated that Friends cannot consistently join with such as form combinations of a hostile nature against any; especially in opposition to those placed in sovereign or subordinate authority; nor can we unite with those or encourage such as revile or asperse them.[25]

Since the British government was still the lawfully constituted authority, Friends could not abjure allegiance to it, nor shift their allegiance to an irregular government.

The brothers Jonathan, John, and Isaac Stackhouse, and William Paxson, William Rodman, Jr., and John Wildman were all reported to the meeting in Third month 1779 for taking the affirmation of allegiance and abjuration. John Wildman was disowned in Tenth month. He had had trouble with Friends' principles before, over an alleged incident of highway robbery in his youth, and the purchase of a slave in 1764. Of the Stackhouse brothers, Jonathan was married to Grace Comfort, the granddaughter of minister Grace Croasdale. It is not hard to envision her using Friendly persuasion on her husband, and then on her brothers-in-law. All three men told one of the "Powers" to whom they had made the affirmation, of their new-found uneasiness, and their subsequent papers were accepted by the meeting in Twelfth month. William Paxson, oldest son and fourth generation of solid citizens of Middletown, presented an awkward case for Friends. In his twenties he had been made a trustee of the meeting property and had served on a committee, but then his name is absent from the minutes. He married a woman who apparently joined Friends in order to marry him. William seemed to exemplify the kind of birthright Friend who, as an active member of the Quaker subculture was expected to be a weighty Friend, but whose lack of inward spiritual experience meant that when the test came the inner strength and depth were missing. William was disowned in Fourth month 1780.[26]

Continental Currency

The militia and test acts were not the only things for which Quakers had to be willing to suffer rather than compromise their principles. There was also the vexing problem of continental currency. There were several things wrong with it:

it was issued by an irregularly constituted government, it financed war, and its rapid depreciation meant someone was being defrauded. The yearly meeting was unable to reach unity on advice regarding the use of continental currency, only asking that Friends be tender with one another's scruples.[27]

Thomas Watson of Buckingham was one of those who was uneasy about the use of depreciating paper. About 7:00 p.m. on New Year's Day, 1777, three men with swords came to his home without a warrant and without telling him the charge, and dragged him off to Newtown to General Stirling. Although his wife and children were in great distress, he later wrote that he "endeavoured to be still, & was very desirous I might be favoured [with divine wisdom] to Conduct [myself] aright". Stirling questioned if he had ever refused continental money. Watson told him "I had taken it but was not quite easy, & that a neighbor of mine one Bogan had applied to me to buy some Hay, which I agreed to let him have, & let him know I should expect to be paid in hard Money for the same." It was decided he should be hung, to serve as an example. Watson was taken to the guard house, stripped down to his "under jacket", and set with irons on his hands and feet. Towards dawn, at his request, a man loosely hung Watson's coat around his shivering shoulders. Several Friends came to intercede for him. But Thomas Watson was unwilling to be released on the condition that he accept continental currency, "rememb'ring I had been uneasy on taking it, & if that uneasiness should increase, I might be brought into such a bondage, I rather choose to suffer than loose my peace". After remaining there three days and nights his wife came to plead with the General. Susannah (Woolston) asked permission to bring a bed and other things to make her husband comfortable. She told Stirling that she could not persuade her husband "to do any thing contrary to his Judgment". Eventually he was sent home to house arrest, which he scrupulously observed for the prescribed number of days while being nursed back to health. No more was ever heard of the matter.[28]

Some of these larger stories of danger, courage, and suffering have been recorded. But the small indignities have been lost to historians–the slights, the slurs, the ridicule or contempt where before there had been respect and perhaps deference. The historian can imagine the range of responses by non-Friends in a rural area where most people had known each other all their lives. Some people would respect folks who stood by their principles; others would use the opportunity to settle old scores or enhance their own positions. The interactions between individuals say as much about the character of the non-Friend as of the Friend. One wonders how long it took after the war for hurts to heal.

Middletown Meeting Families Face War

We will turn now to look at specific families in Middletown Meeting. As their reactions to the reform movement in general and antislavery in particular had varied, so did their reaction to the pressures brought by war. What we are trying to understand is what led some individuals and families to compromise and what enabled others to stand firm. Under the constraints of available data we will look at political, economic, and meeting activities. The social factors are much harder to study. Finally, we will look for family patterns in the making of choices between the requirements of Quakerism and the demands of the revolution.

In 1775 nine cases involving military activity were brought before Middletown Meeting. Friends wrestled for months with each one, and finally four men were disowned. The next year there were four more cases, and all resulted in disownment. As the war progressed, the average time spent on each case decreased. Perhaps Friends grew tired, perhaps they felt all Friends were now thoroughly familiar with the principles which were at stake. By the end, Middletown Meeting had disowned eighteen men for not upholding the peace testimony. Overall, 420 were disowned from meetings making up Philadelphia Yearly Meeting.[29]

When we look more closely at who compromised the peace testimony we find that compromise was neither random nor across the board. It concentrated in certain families and was entirely absent from others. An immediate question is, did this correlate with families that had sons in their late teens and twenties? We assume that those most susceptible to public pressure for the militia were males no older than thirty in 1775 and no younger than fifteen by 1783. Among the seventeen surname families there were thirty-eight nuclear families that had at least one son born between 1745 and 1768. The number of sons in these families ranged from one to eight. Of the thirty-three families with complete data, nine (27%) suffered a disownment for military activity during the Revolution. Only one family had two disownments. If we look at disownments for other causes during the same period, we find eight more cases, all but two of which were in the same nine families. Thus twenty-two families (67%) which had sons in the at-risk age, had no disownments for any reason during the war years (1775-1783). Inconsistency with Quaker peace testimonies did not stand apart from inconsistency with other Friends' principles. Inconsistency or compromise seems to have been the point, not the specific pressure of military demands.[30]

Disownment was the final step. If a Friend began to bend under the pressure of secular demands, he would be labored with or "eldered" by other Friends. Often that would be enough to strengthen the waverer and bring him back into conformity with the testimonies of the Religious Society of which he was a member. During this period three data set Friends had difficulties regarding the peace testimony and seven in regard to other testimonies. But they acknowledged their inconsistencies and changed their behavior, so they were not disowned. None of the ten families (30% of those with complete data) involved had any members disowned during this period. It is interesting that individuals who lived in families which had no disownments seemed more willing or able to change their behavior to conform to Quaker expectations than those in families which had already experienced a disownment. Once a family had experienced a disownment, it seemed more willing to tolerate additional deviation among its members.

Twelve (36%) of the data set nuclear families with complete data who had some sons in the at-risk age group managed to uphold all Friends' testimonies during the war years. In addition, another ten (30%) faltered but recovered. That is, they were disciplined, but not disowned. One third had one or more family members who were unable or unwilling to completely uphold all Friends' testimonies and were therefore disowned by the meeting.

What were the factors which contributed to these differences among the families? Since the issue was, at root, the theological question of ultimate authority, we need to look at the activities of these families to try to determine where they placed their allegiance. With the hypothesis that one cannot serve two masters, and where one's time and energy are spent indicates where one's heart lies, we will look at the political activity, economic level, and degree of participation in the meeting's business. A fourth alternative to the political, economic, and religious worlds, was the non-Quaker social world. The data for this in rural Middletown is simply unavailable, and probably was less important there than in sophisticated Philadelphia. A rural village had less diversity and less class differentiation. We are forced to ignore this aspect, but can do so with a relatively clear conscience.

Political Factors

Only Job Stackhouse and Thomas Jenks, Jr. among our data set Friends were directly involved in holding elected office in the 1770s, although the Kirkbride and Watson families had close relatives in Falls and Buckingham, respectively, who were involved, and William Rodman, a member of Middletown Meeting, but not part of the data set, was elected to the Assembly. Job Stackhouse accepted the office of tax collector in Bristol in 1777. It would be necessary for him to distrain Friends' goods if any refused to pay what they considered to be a war tax. Job was disowned Tenth month 1778. His office holding was not his only offense. He also took "strong drink to excess". Earlier he had "gone out" with his marriage, but had submitted an acceptable paper acknowledging and condemning the action.[31]

Thomas Jenks, Jr. had a long career in public office. He was thirty six when elected to the Committee of Observation for Bucks County in Twelfth month 1774. The next year he was elected to the Pennsylvania Assembly. He resigned from the former because of religious scruples in Eighth month 1775; the Pennsylvania Assembly was replaced by the new state constitution in the fall of

1776. But while he and William Rodman were sitting in the Assembly, the preparative meeting reported that it considered they had "judged in a military affair". The two Assemblymen allowed as since Friends were unhappy they would not do it again. The next month Thomas's paper was accepted, in which he declared that "he would not do the like were it to do again".[32] As soon as he could after the war was over, Thomas resumed his political career. He became assessor in Eleventh month 1787, served on grand juries in 1788, 1792 (twice), 1794, and 1795, and as foreman for all but the first of these.[33] He was elected to the state constitutional convention in 1789 and became the first Pennsylvania State Senator from Bucks County under the new 1790 constitution. Thomas was clearly involved in the political world, but when the test came during the war, he acknowledged the precedence of Friends' principles and stepped down, not resuming activity until he could do so without compromising Quaker testimonies. He was moderately active in the meeting's business, but both his parents, who lived through the war–his father died at the age of ninety seven–were very active. His mother was clerk of the women's meeting. His father was an overseer. So it appears that, although politics was important to Thomas, his loyalty to the testimonies and principles of the Society of Friends–or his family's participation therein–was more important.

Office holding was not the only indication of political activity and interest. But how can the historian assess it? If one joined the military, and chose the British over the American forces, presumably that was a political decision. There are indications that nine men in three of the surname families may have been Tories.

The clearest example seemed to be Joseph Paxson, the son of James and Hannah (Thornton), whose 125 acre farm in Middletown was attainted and sold in April 1778. Joseph was twenty. His father had died when he was eleven, and Joseph had been apprenticed. The meeting disowned him for running off from his apprenticeship and "joining with a military body of men". The minute had read "taking up arms", but in an effort to be completely accurate, this had been crossed out. The implication is that he joined the British forces in Philadelphia but did not actually become a soldier. He may have been the Joseph "Paxton" who was captured at Stony Point, and eventually released from the "new gaol" in Philadelphia where he had become "dangerously ill".[34] Joseph's parents had been inactive in the ongoing business of the meeting. It seems that at this period the adolescent Joseph was relatively indifferent to the interior life of the spirit and its relation to his outward life.

Joseph's cousin Phineas Paxson, son of William and Anna (Marriott), presented a more ambiguous case. He was disowned in Fourth month 1776 for exercising with the militia. Presumably that meant the local patriot associators. However he reaffirmed his Quaker principles and was fined seven times between 1778 and 1781 for refusing to cooperate with the militia. Phineas owned and operated the Buck Tavern. In Sixth month 1780 he was tried, found guilty, and fined because "he joined the enemy in this city [Philadelphia], and has, in his general conduct and character manifested a disaffection to the American cause, & there is reason to suspect him to be privy to the escape of British Prisoners; Whereupon, Resolved, That he be no longer permitted to keep a Publick house. . . ."[35] Was his aid to British prisoners a simple humanitarian gesture? Had his political views changed? This case demonstrates the difficulties of reading motive into the bare record of events. Both Joseph and Phineas seem somewhat out of step with their siblings and cousins. Joseph had only a single sister; Phineas's many brothers left no evidence of treason to the American cause, all the while maintaining a strict Quaker neutrality.

The Robert Stackhouse family was a different story. Robert himself had been disowned in 1719 for horse racing. Nonetheless his children seem to have been part of the Quaker subculture even if not recorded in the meeting records. In 1750 Robert's twenty-four-year old son James requested and was admitted into membership. Soon thereafter he requested and received a certificate of removal to Philadelphia. James's son Hastings returned to Middletown in 1776. He was disowned in 1779 for leaving in a disorderly manner, putting himself under the protection of a military body, and taking the affirmation of allegiance. The meeting records do not say to whom Hastings affirmed his allegiance, however, he became involved in Loyalist activities. After helping recruit pilots for General Howe's proposed sailing of the British fleet up the Delaware, Hastings fled first to

New York, then after the war to Savannah, Georgia. According to a family historian, three of Hastings's cousins (two sons of his uncle Joseph and one son of his uncle Thomas), were Loyalists who removed to New Brunswick.[36] This branch of the Stackhouse family appeared only peripherally involved in the Friends meeting.

Amos Watson left his father's house, went to Philadelphia while the British army was there, and came out "in a company of armed men". Later he went to New York or Long Island. Friends noted that there was no other reason (than that he was with the British army) for him to leave. He was disowned in Third month 1781. Amos had been in trouble four years earlier for attending a wedding performed by "an hirling minister", but had submitted an acceptable paper of acknowledgment and condemnation.[37]

The Gillam family provides another insight into motivation, mixing economics with politics. Lucas and Ann (Dungan) Gillam were not involved in the committee process of Middletown Meeting. Lucas had been orphaned at a young age, and apprenticed to a cooper. Three years after he married, Lucas purchased a 100 acre farm. He was constable for Middletown in 1757, a relatively low-status public office. In 1760 he was nominated to be Overseer of the Poor, a position often held by more respected men in the community. But there were difficulties in 1760: one Friend complained to the Meeting that Lucas owed him money; he sued another Friend; and he had a "difference" with one of the weightiest members.[38] As an old man, Lucas retained ownership of his farm but it was worked by his son Simon. This son was very active in the Meeting, becoming a recorded minister in 1813. The other seven brothers were disowned, although two were reinstated, one of whom became a "prominent Friend" in Canada. The Gillam brothers' offenses included marriage outside of meeting procedures, leaving an apprenticeship and the area in a disorderly manner, and military activity. The last named occurred after the end of the Revolution. Family tradition labels the three who emigrated to Canada in the 1790s as Loyalists, although the documentary record is unclear. With eight sons and only one farm, economics seems a likely contributing factor to sons leaving the area. This would have been the case with or without the economic pressure of fines and distraints or the pressure caused by unacceptable political views. It also appears that the parents' lack of involvement in the ongoing business of the meeting was emulated by six of their sons.[39]

None of these men who decided to support the British cause or who emigrated to Canada were active in the ongoing business of Middletown Meeting. They were, perhaps, more invested in its cultural and tribal than its spiritual aspects.

Economic Factors

When we look at the economic standing of the heads of the nuclear families, we do not get a clear picture. What would we expect? That wealthy men would be more likely to be Tories? Certainly the wealthiest Quaker in Bucks County, Joseph Galloway, was a Tory. Or should we expect that wealthier people would be more likely to be politically involved in order to protect their investments? Kenneth Alan Radbill found that neither economic and social discontent nor the desire to improve or alter economic or social status were important variables in determining which Philadelphia Yearly Meeting Friends would break with Quaker testimonies and engage in military activities during the Revolution.[40]

Conversely, is there a corollary here to the Levy thesis (mentioned in Chapter 3) that poorer Quakers were disowned because of their inability to find Quaker spouses? Did more poor Quakers also get disowned because they could not absorb the economic losses of fines and distraints?

Thomas Jenks, Jr. and his brother Joseph were among the four wealthiest men in our group, based on the 1785 post-war tax assessment. See Table 5. Of the ten wealthiest men in the group, six had no children who were disowned. The others had one disowned daughter (two cases), one had two sons disowned, and one had four sons disowned. At the other end of the economic scale, there were seven men assessed at fifty cents or less. Only two had children disowned: one with one son and one with two sons. So whereas 60% of wealthy men kept their children within the fold, 71% of the poorer men succeeded. This is contrary to the finding of Levy for Chester County in the early eighteenth century, involving disownments around marriage issues. But since we have found that disownment for military activity did not come from a significantly different group than disownments for any other reason, it seems valid to make the comparison with marriage-only offenses.

TABLE 5: 1785 Tax Valuation and Children Disowned, Among Data Set Men

Name	1785 Tax	Date of Death	C$ Estate Valuation	Sons Age 21	% Disowned	Daughters Age 21	% Disowned	% Children Dis'd
Isaac Stackhouse	$19.58	1791	386.10	4	0.%	3	33.%	14.%
Joseph Jenks	17.12	1820	1,472.93	1	0.%	2	50.%	33.%
William Richardson	15.00	1813	1,167.23	3	0.%	6	0.%	0.%
Thomas Jenks, Jr.	12.78	1799	7,532.26	3	67.%	5	0.%	25.%
John Watson	11.99	1799	-	1	0.%	1	0.%	0.%
John Watson	11.99	1844	7,845.32	4	0.%	3	0.%	0.%
Samuel Mitchell	10.51	1826	1,987.04	5	80.%	2	0.%	57.%
Joshua Richardson	10.00	1800	1,584.33	1	0.%	5	0.%	0.%
Thomas Paxson	9.90	1790	876.96	5	0.%	6	0.%	0.&
Joshua Blakey	8.70	1814	172.31	3	33.%	2	0.%	20.%
Joseph Wildman	7.50	1809	1,681.48	5	0.%	4	0.%	0.%
William Blakey	6.16	1823	-	2	0.%	1	0.%	0.%
Jonathan Woolston	4.21	1828	51,015.99	1	0.%	4	0.%	0.%
Euclydus Longshore	3.70	1804	286.46	6	33.%	7	86.%	62.%
Jonathan Kirkbride	2.82	1804	134.23	1	0.%	9	0.%	0.%
Robert Croasdale	2.33	1821	1,114.81	3	0.%	3	0.%	0.%
James Wildman	2.33	1844	1,734.97	1	0.%	2	0.%	0.%
Solomon Wildman	2.00	1831	456.03	2	0.%	7	0.%	0.%
William Blakey, Jr.	2.00	1831	3,994.49	1	0.%	5	0.%	0.%
Richard Mitchell	1.61	1820	13,797.57	2	100.%	4	0.%	33.%
Jonathan Paxson	1.23	1797	1,300.82	1	0.%	9	0.%	0.%
Joshua Woolston	1.08	1821	3,667.55	2	0.%	5	20.%	14.%
Jonathan Stackhouse	.50	1805	7,621.91	2	100.%	5	0.%	29.%
Isaac Stackhouse	.39	1835	44,530.12	1	0.%	1	0.%	0.%
John Stackhouse	.36	1828	25,305.10	1	0.%	5	0.%	0.%
Joseph Paxson	.31	1793	2,442.65	4	0.%	4	0.%	0.%
John Woolston	.11	1791	1,376.17	3	0.%	4	0.%	0.%
William Allen	.07	1835	1,176.72	1	0.%	3	0.%	0.%
Thomas Jenks	.04	1797	1,746.62	3	33.%	3	0.%	17.%

SOURCES: Bucks County Tax Records, HSP; Will Files, Bucks County Courthouse; Middletown Monthly Meeting records, FHL, Swarthmore College

Neither the political involvement of Friends nor the level of their wealth appears to be an important factor in determining whether the individual or family faithfully maintained Friends' testimonies or compromised with the "world".

Family Patterns

Part of the community in which Friends moved was their own Religious Society, and it encouraged and pressured individuals to conform to its paradigm or view of reality, its standard of behavior. Each Friend had a choice in the face of economic pressure, pressure from the "world", pressure from their Society, and pressure from the Inward Guide. The fourth pressure was the one to which Thomas Watson yielded–that which made him uneasy to the point where he feared he would be in such inner bondage that he preferred outward suffering to the risk of losing his inner peace. Thomas Jenks, Jr. appeared to yield to the third pressure–he would rather give up public office than make Friends unhappy. No one seemed to have left Friends just because of economic pressure, although a few tried to cut their losses. When William Richardson's team was pressed, he prudently sent along a man to look after it and see that it got safely home. He volunteered a paper to the meeting acknowledging the wrong.[41] What we do not know is if this paper was the result of being visited and prompted by overseers or elders, or if his conscience independently stirred him. John Mitchell paid a fine rather than risk distraint. This appears to have been the last straw, added to other offenses involving marriage. He was disowned.[42] Joseph Wildman directed a collector to where he might find money to cover his fine rather than seize goods. Joseph brought a paper of acknowledgment and condemnation which was accepted by the meeting. Four years later he was accused of paying for a substitute soldier, but the meeting believed him when he said he did not realize it was that kind of a tax. Both Joseph and his wife Ann (Paxson) were quite active in the meeting, and were willing to bring their actions into line with Friends' testimonies.[43]

The Rodman family is an example of one which largely gave in to pressure from the dominant culture. To put it another way, other interests had higher priority than their religious affiliation. A brief sketch of this family is in the previous chapter. Thomas Rodman, who moved from Middletown to Burlington, New Jersey, in 1760, followed the pattern of Thomas Jenks, Jr. Although serving in New Jersey's Provincial Assembly, as High Sheriff of Burlington, and as a Justice of the Peace, he resigned as war approached. His half-brother William was quite active in Middletown Meeting until he was disowned in February 1778 for slaveholding and because of Friends' uneasiness with his service as an elected official. Once William was released from Quaker constraints he took the affirmation of allegiance later that year and was an active supporter of the patriot cause. William's older son Gilbert (disowned for military activity) rose to the rank of major in the Continental army. His younger son, William, Jr. (disowned for taking the affirmation of allegiance), pursued a political career that peaked with a term in the U.S. House of Representatives.[44] The interests of the family gravitated outside of meeting, and when choices had to be made, they parted company with Friends.

A different image is provided by the Comfort family. Stephen Comfort had been recorded as a minister in 1747 at the age of twenty six. His wife Mercy (Croasdale) served as clerk of the women's meeting and then as an elder. Eight of their nine children lived to adulthood. They included six sons who were all in the at-risk age during the Revolution. Although Stephen died in 1772 all his children remained steadfast Friends. The eldest married the daughter of John Woolman and moved to New Jersey. Second son Ezra was recorded as a minister in 1777. Stephen, Jr. was an elder. Grace, who married Jonathan Stackhouse, was an overseer. Mercy, wife of Aaron Phillips, was a minister. Jeremiah died at the age of thirty before he could fulfill more than a handful of committee assignments for the meeting. Moses removed to Abington, and thus out of the Middletown records. Robert, the youngest son, was less settled. He seemed to move around a good deal, and probably did not get involved in the business of the various meetings to which his membership was transferred. Moses and Robert, both young when their father died, spent their late teen years in other towns, living with other families, presumably as apprentices. The Comfort family was heavily invested in the Religious Society of Friends. None of them wavered from upholding Quaker testimonies regarding war or any other issue in this period.

The Croasdale family, gathered around the matriarch Grace (Heaton) who was a recorded minister, included Mercy (married to Stephen Comfort), Ezra (whose three wives each died before they were assigned to meeting committees), Robert and his wife Margery (Hayhurst), and Ann, a minister who married John Hampton and moved. These were six very active and involved Friends. The oldest Croasdale daughter, Grace Jr. removed to Abington and out of our view. The youngest son, Eber, did not follow the family mold. After the death of his first wife he left his small son in the care of his mother-in-law and fell into bad habits. The Meeting disowned him for

> keeping loose and idle company and so plunging himself into debt . . . profane swearing and drinking to excess . . . [although] often admonished and cautioned by his religion and [unclear] Mother, and tender and well wishing Friends . . . but after Long forebearance and Patient waiting for his Return he hath like the Prodigal Son turn'd his back of [sic] his friends and Rejected all their tender advices and kind endeavours . . . [and] strayed off without settling his affairs and satisfying his creditors.[45]

The war and all the sufferings resulting from it, tried Friends. But they tended to withstand these pressures similarly to the ways they faced other issues such as endogamy, temperance, and politics. Those whose highest allegiance was to God as perceived corporately by the Society of Friends, or who were trying to orient their lives in that direction, or identified themselves with this way of life, did not give in. If they weakened, they were strengthened by their family and meeting and thus enabled to resist the demands (or opportunities) to compromise by joining with the dominant culture. Those who were deeply involved in the outside world of politics or commerce, or who were "not attending to that which would have preserved [them] from evil" were likely to compromise and then allow themselves to be disowned.[46]

CHAPTER 6: CHANGING ECONOMIC VIEWS

The Revolution presented a clear crisis point for Friends. They had to choose. They could not waffle. After the war was over and emotions had subsided, life eventually returned to calm and order. Friends no longer had the same kinds of sharp crises forcing them to make choices. Instead, they could avoid the hard decisions about the orientation of their lives. They could be Quakers in outward form while going about their own business.

As the eighteenth century closed and the new one opened, the larger society experienced changes associated with at least two different concepts: market capitalism and evangelical religion. This chapter and the next examine the challenges these presented to Friends, and their responses. In some ways the challenges were subtle and almost invisible, but that did not make them any less real.

Particularly in Britain throughout the eighteenth century, increasingly wealthy Quakers had turned from the Spirit to commerce. They became over-involved in making money, and in maintaining the attitudes and status their prosperity conferred upon them. However, in Pennsylvania this process was checked by the self-questioning of the reform movement, catalyzed by the events of 1756. Even after the Revolutionary War was over, Philadelphia Quakers were "never to the same extent or for long" as involved with the pre-1756 worldliness which continued to entice and entrap wealthy British Quakers.[1] However, although they did not go to the extremes of British Quakers, American Friends were continually tempted by the economic opportunities around them.

In the new United States the growing "go-getter" entrepreneurial mentality diverged increasingly from Quaker principles, while the ideals of good business practice remained among approved Quaker behaviors. But because the dominant culture and Friends' practices had some outward similarities it became easy for Friends to forget the very different bases of the two, and to slip over from the one to the other.

Between about 1790 and 1820 there was a shift in popular thinking away from the republican traditions of the Revolution towards modern liberal capitalism.[2] Friends had always had many characteristics in common with the newly emerging mentality. Yet there is a "yes, but" quality about Friends' adherence to these traits. Their initial underlying motive had been spiritual, not capitalistic. Therefore the characteristics they had in common with the new "go-getter" were coincidental. But because of the similarity, Friends found themselves open to the possibility of thoughtlessly slipping over the line separating their concentration on God's realm, and the world's preoccupation with getting ahead.

Before we examine individual Friends and their behavior, we need to look at the guidelines Friends set for themselves regarding business practices. The official Quaker position is perhaps best summed up in this 1797 epistle from London Yearly Meeting:

> We do not condemn industry; which we believe to be not only praise-worthy, but indispensable. It is the desire of great things, and the engrossment of time and attention, from which we desire that all our dear friends may be redeemed. We doubtless owe duties to ourselves and to our families; but we owe them also to society; and do we not owe even our own selves to our all-wise, all-protecting, and provident Creator?[3]

Friends were deeply involved in business and industry, especially in England and in American cities. Because of their honesty, hard work, willingness to try new methods, and constraints on conspicuous consumption that enabled profits to be reinvested, Quakers tended to prosper. But underlying and suffusing their lives as business people, Friends were supposed to carry the understanding that they were primarily God's people, with a set of rules different from those of other, "worldly" entrepreneurs. They were to participate in the world of commerce but not be part of its ungodly practices or values. Friends were not to go into business beyond their ability and capital; they were to call on more experienced Friends for advice; they were not to engage in hazardous enterprises at the risk of their family's or investors' well-being. There were specific advices against circulating bills of credit (in lieu of scarce currency or specie). But even more important, they were not to allow business concerns to so fill their lives that they were unwilling to serve God whenever and however God should require.[4]

There were a few examples of Quaker entrepreneurs who deliberately limited their income and wealth. Josiah White (1781-1850) was an engineer who played a major role in the development of canals, especially for the transportation of anthracite coal.[5] John Woolman (1720-1772) is the best known Friend who integrated his inward spiritual life with his outward life. He deliberately chose an occupation (tailor) that provided sufficient income for his family while not consuming too much time, energy, or thought, so that there were adequate amounts left for spiritual life and work. He clearly understood and wrote about the relation among inward spiritual orientation, goals in life, the use of time and resources, and the presence or absence of societal injustice and war. His gentle invitation to a counter-cultural life was as difficult for Friends in the third quarter of the eighteenth century as it was for those in the nineteenth–or the twenty-first.[6]

If Friends' businesses failed, they were to repay all of their debts, even if bankruptcy laws allowed them legally to settle for less.[7] The rationale was not to punish the debtor nor to extract every last penny into the coffers of the lender. It was to protect the reputation of the Society of Friends as a group of totally honest people living under the governance of God. Living under this leader meant a different set of priorities. Joseph White, a minister in Falls Meeting who died in 1777, expressed the ideal Quaker priorities in this advice to his son Samuel:

> I have not been anxious to gather a portion of this world, nor make to myself mammon of unrighteousness, for I think I have seen that a snare has attended many young people on these accounts. I have from my youth had a desire to be more in substance than in show: let me appear as I might in the sight of men, their praise I sought not for; but I have sought the honor of God, ...[8]

The idea was to be a participant in the economic world while not buying into its values and definitions. Friends were to be in the world but not of it.

Business Failure

Many bankrupt Friends were disowned. At first glance it appears that Friends were punishing business failure. But not all bankruptcies resulted in disownment. The meeting wanted to know why the Friend's business failed, and how he (or she) handled the situation. Was failure due to overextension, speculation, disregard of meeting advices, and generally putting too high a priority on getting ahead, as the world defined it? Or was failure due to forces beyond the Friend's control, and had he dealt in a thoroughly upright and open way with those who were affected by his default? We shall look at several cases of business failure among Middletown Meeting members in order to see how the meeting handled it, as well as to try to get a sense of the underlying choices the individual Friends had made.

There were several failures in the economic depression of the early 1820s. Simon Gillam, who with his socially proper wife Anna (Paxson) had prospered after the Revolution, turned from the eager cultivation of his outward plantation to his inward one. He was recorded as a minister in 1813, at the age of fifty four. Simon was described as a "much esteemed man" who "was careful to adorn the doctrine he preached with a meek and quiet spirit". In February 1821, the meeting noted that he had assigned all his property to an assignee for the benefit of his creditors. In other words, he was bankrupt. Friends investigated, and reported that his difficulty was due to his becoming surety for others plus the fall in property which "disables him from fulfilling his engagements". He had, however, acted completely "agreeable to discipline". There was no need for Friends to disassociate from him. His fine house and imported carpets were sold, and Simon and his family removed the next month to Upper Springfield Meeting, to make a fresh start.[9]

Simon's brother Isaac Gillam was caught in the same economic downturn. But when he sought a certificate of removal to start afresh elsewhere, the meeting noted that he was unable to discharge his just debts because of "launching into trade and business beyond his ability to manage". His stone house, barn, and fruit trees on a half acre in Attleborough, were sold at a sheriff's sale. When it was clear that his debts would be covered, Friends gave him a certificate of removal.[10]

Joseph Hulme, president of the fledgling Farmers' National Bank of Bucks County, and member of a family of mill owners and entrepreneurs, also failed in the early 1820s. Friends determined that Joseph had launched into business and trade beyond his ability and at the risk of others. Furthermore, as he was going bankrupt he assigned his real and personal property to the directors of the Farmers' National Bank, giving them preference over his other creditors. It was clear to Friends that Joseph was not being completely honest with all of his creditors. The implication was that Hulme was more concerned with gaining wealth, than with laying up spiritual riches. The meeting disowned him in 1822.[11]

Phineas Paxson, nephew of the Phineas who had operated the Buck Tavern during the Revolution, was reported in reduced circumstances and unable to pay his debts in early 1823. The meeting found that he, like Isaac Gillam and Joseph Hulme, had launched into trade and business beyond his means. Furthermore, he had converted part of his assets into building a house on his father's land and thereby put it beyond the grasp of creditors. However, as Friends labored with him, he came to see his actions in the Light, and offered a paper of acknowledgment and condemnation, which the meeting accepted. Phineas continued intermittently to have financial difficulties. His home in Attleborough was sold at sheriff's sale in March 1829 and the family moved to Falls, then ten years later, to Maryland. His widow, Rachel (Woolston), returned to Middletown in 1851.[12]

Phineas's father, Thomas Paxson, also had financial problems. His 218 acre farm with its two "nearly new" stone homes was offered for sale in November, 1822, and finally sold for the benefit of his creditors in January, 1824. He was disowned in Fifth Month, 1824 for assigning his property contrary to discipline.[13]

Thomas's financial dealings were not his only actions which failed to meet the highest standards of Friends. At the age of nineteen Thomas had been apprenticed to his cousin Benjamin Paxson of Buckingham. When his term was completed, he returned to Middletown with a certificate testifying that he had settled his (financial) affairs, was clear of marriage entanglements, and "some-times" attended religious meetings. Although "by birth and education [Thomas] had right of membership and was deemed a member [he] so far deviated from truth" as to marry a non-Quaker. Their first child was born a scant seven months after marriage. Thomas was disowned. Twenty-four years later his wife Elizabeth (Randall) requested and was granted membership, and Thomas also rejoined. Two years later, their eldest son, Phineas, followed suit. While neither Thomas nor his wife ever became active in the ongoing business of the meeting, Phineas was moderately active and Phineas's wife Rachel (Woolston) was very active, serving as clerk and recorded as a minister.[14]

We can speculate about the roles of these two wives in their husband's decisions regarding financial dealings and Friends' testimonies. As we have seen in previous chapters, during this period there was a correlation between activity in the meeting and steadfastness in upholding Friends' testimonies. It seems likely that Rachel actively encouraged her husband to pay closer attention to living in conformity with Friends' testimonies, while perhaps Elizabeth did not feel so strongly. However, Elizabeth did care enough about being part of the Quaker subculture that she applied for membership, as did her husband.

As we have seen in these five cases of business failure in the early 1820s, Friends did not punish failure *per se*. Simon Gillam had no action taken against him when it was found he behaved entirely according to discipline. Isaac Gillam was given a certificate of removal once his financial obligations were fulfilled. Phineas Paxson's acknowledgment and condemnation of his wrong actions was accepted. Friends were concerned that no Friend would engage in fraud or dishonesty. The two men whose conduct raised questions were disowned.

The ideal was exemplified by Cyrus Hillborn. His father Thomas lived on a farm in Newtown that had been in the family for 120 years. He went bankrupt in 1821, assigned everything to creditors, and moved to Philadelphia. His two young sons worked hard. After Thomas had died, and eighteen years after the bankruptcy, his son Cyrus sent $5,000 to John Paxson asking him to repay his father's debts in full, plus eighteen years of interest.[15]

There is no evidence whether or not Middletown Meeting was seriously concerned to keep a close watch on all members to see that they had their priorities straight. The meeting tended to get involved in a situation only after a business failure signalled that something had gone wrong. Whereas on occasion the meeting minutes note that Friends had frequently warned a young woman not to become involved with a certain non-Quaker young man and she had ignored their advice, the minutes do not indicate that Friends had been working with, and warning any of the above five Friends that they were getting into economic difficulties. There is no evidence whether economic ends and means were a subject of conversation during visits of ministers to each family in the meeting. Without journals or other personal records we have no information on what was discussed between Friends. While the minutes, advices, and epistles regularly exhorted Friends to be careful with plain speech and dress, for example, warnings against being sucked into the whirlpool of greed and over-concentration on making money were relatively rare.[16] Because the virtues of Quaker businessmen so nearly approximated the emerging "go-getter" mentality, it was more difficult for Friends to see the danger of forgetting the fundamental differences from which the two grew.

We will now look at one final case of bankruptcy, that in some ways is the most interesting because it appears to contradict the findings from the 1820s cases. Upon closer examination, it points to the necessity of individual Friends to discern the different orientation of traditional Quaker life and that of the emerging capitalist culture, and then to make the daily choices aligning themselves with the former rather than with the latter.

Mardon Wilson, living in mid-century, was lauded in a local history as "a man of ability, integrity and energy, and an advocate of all the reforms of the day". He was remembered more candidly, perhaps, by the son of a neighbor. Samuel Eastburn wrote that Mardon Wilson was ambitious, and wanted to have the "most water power of any mill on the creek". So he built a large pond and mill race. But when a "freshet" came, the water backed up to Jenks's mill upstream and spoiled $10,000 worth of flour. Jenks sued Wilson and won his case.[17]

Middletown Meeting reported in Third month, 1848 that Wilson "has failed and does not appear to be able to pay his debts; which failure we believe has arisen in a great measure from a want of due attention to the advice contained in the discipline". Furthermore, Wilson told a few creditors early so that they could place themselves to get paid, to the disadvantage of others. Several committees labored with Wilson. He produced two papers acknowledging his wrongdoing, but Friends were not satisfied. Opinion within the meeting was evidently divided, and it took several drafts to produce a minute which was acceptable to all. But finally in Fourth month, 1849 Mardon Wilson was disowned. He appealed to the quarterly meeting, which, as usual, upheld local Friends. Wilson appealed to yearly meeting, which in an unusual move reversed the lower bodies.[18]

What makes Mardon Wilson's case different is that before 1848 he was active in the ongoing activities of the meeting. He had thirty-two assignments over three decades. His wife, Ann (Dewees) had only one. How do we reconcile Mardon's activity in the meeting with his lack of observance of the meeting's economic advices? A careful examination of the kinds of things he was asked to do indicate that they were mostly attendance at quarterly meeting and service on nominating committees and committees to clear and oversee marriages. At that time these were not perceived as requiring great spiritual weight. Mardon Wilson was secretary of the Bustleton and Somerton Turnpike Company, and involved in "all the reforms of the day". Perhaps his activity in the meeting was of similar quality–the thing a public-spirited man was expected to do, not the outgrowth of a deeply religious exercise. Despite his reinstatement by the yearly meeting, Middletown Friends never again asked him to serve them in any capacity.

We have looked briefly at some Friends' testimonies regarding economic affairs. Six men in Middletown Meeting failed by the standards of the larger society. In each case the meeting tried to apply moral or religious rules to economic behavior, disowning those who failed to adhere to strict principles of honesty.

However, it is less clear how carefully the meeting encouraged Friends to keep their priorities straight between religion and economics. Next we will look at the formation, mainly by Quakers, of a bank. To some extent, these Friends brought their religious ideas into this secular institution.

The Farmers' National Bank of Bucks County

Historian Richard D. Brown described banking as an institution that encouraged thrift and capital formation while expanding credit and financing speculation.[19] Friends approved the first two and opposed the last. The Farmers' National Bank of Bucks County is a good case study of the selectivity with which some Friends picked their way through the new economic environment. This first bank in the county was established through the efforts of men who were mostly members of Middletown Meeting. They attempted to shape it to their needs and vision rather than to accept unquestioningly the new enthusiasm for money making. However, it was still a bank, and its purpose was to make money as well as to provide a service.

Bray Hammond claimed that before the Civil War most farmers did not want to borrow, and most lenders considered agriculture a poor risk. Therefore, the main users of credit were businessmen.[20] But in lower Bucks County, even though many of them were farmers, a group of men were sufficiently involved in the market economy to need credit and a reliable currency. On December 5, 1814, they met, elected thirteen directors, and chose Hulmeville as the site for the new bank. Of those thirteen directors, eight were currently Friends and all the others came from Quaker backgrounds.[21]

John Hulme, a member of Middletown Meeting, played a key role in the establishment of the bank. He was born in 1747 and had started out in poverty. In 1796 he had exchanged his Manor Farm for Joshua Woolston's Milford Mills on the Neshaminy. Eventually he was able to buy several hundred more acres and with his five surviving sons laid out and developed Hulmeville, which quickly became a thriving center of industry. He was described as one of the most prominant businessmen in Bucks County, "one of the most useful and respectable men", who served several times in the Legislature. John Hulme was named the first president of the Bank; space for it was rented in his son George's house.[22]

When John died in December, 1817 his son Joseph was immediately named president of the Bank. He, too, was a Friend. But where his father's bold business ventures had been crowned with success, Joseph and the Bank got caught in the hard times following the panic of 1817. He resigned as Bank president on July 3, 1821, and as described above, Friends disowned him. The Bank's tangled financial affairs were straightened; it received an infusion of fresh capital and was moved to Bristol. Some of the directors were replaced, and from then on the Bank was on firm financial footing.[23] It remained in Quaker hands.

During the early unregulated days of state-chartered banks, business practices and ethics varied widely. The predominantly Quaker directors of the Farmers' National Bank of Bucks County were fiscally conservative and scrupulously ethical. They provided a sort of safe deposit system whereby customers could deposit specie which would be held, untouched, in the bank's safe. During the panic of 1837, when Philadelphia banks suspended specie payment, the Bucks County bank continued to redeem in gold its own notes, and to pay "small sums" on other notes so that its depositors would not be hurt.[24] The bank even dealt with would-be robbers in a Quakerly way. One night in 1845, Benjamin Swain who lived in an apartment above the bank

> heard hammering on the stone wall of the building outside the vault, and as he always kept a heavy log of wood on the window sill above, he cautiously raised the sash and called, "I don't want to harm thee, friend, but I am about to drop this log on thee if thee don't go away." The log fell, but the would-be burglars had decamped.[25]

If banking is taken as a quintessential capitalist enterprise, Middletown Friends embraced the institution but shaped it to their own ends, insisting that it follow their standards. The Farmers' National Bank did not overextend its credit. It did not print notes beyond its ability to redeem them. It acted for the prudent interests of its shareholders and depositors rather than financing speculation.

However, even here there was some ambiguity. Its first president, John Hulme, confided to the Quaker minister Edward Hicks that if he had been obedient to the Heavenly vision he would not have been where he was now, meaning, "nearly lost among the rocks and shoals of skepticism and intemperance."[26] Hicks clearly saw the connection between too vigorous a cultivation of the outward estate, being drawn into the secular currents and other temptations which accompany it, and neglect of the interior estate. John Hulme's skepticism may have indicated Peck's third-level faith development.

William Blakey, a minister of Middletown Meeting, in early 1776 was made aware of the "states and stupid condition which my fellow members and countrymen were fallen into, through lukewarmness of spirit, and an anxious pursuit after the honours and profits of the world."[27] For his own life, he chose obedience to the Spirit rather than the latter course. His Journal offers many glimpses of fourth-level spiritual development. The point is that John Hulme seemed to orient his life towards economic advancement while William Blakey seemed more interested in spiritual life. The two men, facing the same new economic opportunities, made different choices.

Inventions and Improvements

Nineteenth century capitalists, entrepreneurs, and assorted go-getters were fascinated by new technologies and eager to invest in a wide variety of schemes for improvements. There is evidence that many Middletown Friends were similarly engaged. We will mention first some indications of Quaker support for new technologies, and then we will list some of their participation in the promotion of canals, rail-roads, and other enterprises.

New Products

Newspaper advertisements for new products often listed the names of local people who endorsed them. The entrepreneur thought these individuals had sufficient importance in the community to lend cachet to the product; these individuals were willing to have their names publicly linked with a new technology. In 1827 Samuel Comfort endorsed a patented spinning machine for family use, by which a family could spin up to four times the amount of yarn it had previously done on a normal wheel. In 1832 John Paxson endorsed a patented threshing machine. In 1845 his brother Isaac Paxson's name was listed in an advertisement for the Bucks Patent Wood Cooking Stove. Michael H. Jenks, his non-Quaker cousin Daniel T. Jenks, and three Friends recommended another new improved threshing machine in 1835. Joshua Woolston and Robert Longshore endorsed a "portable horse power and thrashing machine" the following year.[28]

In addition to their interest in new machines, as the century progressed they became increasingly involved in organizations dedicated to the general improvement of agriculture. Most Bucks County Friends continued farming even while some were dabbling in more lucrative opportunities in business and industry. William Richardson, Jr. seems to have been the only Middletown Meeting Friend involved in the first Bucks County Agriculture Society. It met in Doylestown and promoted new farming methods by offering premiums for the best stock and produce at its annual fair. William died relatively young and no other Middletown Friend took his place. Dr. Phineas Jenks of Newtown, disowned by Middletown when he married a non-Friend, was deeply involved in all three successive agriculture societies. His cousin Michael H. Jenks served as secretary of the second agricultural society in 1829. When a third agricultural society was organized in the 1840s, more Middletown Friends got involved.[29] With this incomplete evidence it appears that Middletown Friends constituted a spectrum of picking and choosing with which new inventions and technologies to be involved. They may have matched fairly closely their non-Quaker neighbors.

New Investments

In order for market capitalism to bloom fully in the young republic several things were needed. The transportation infrastructure that was necessary to get goods to markets had to be built. Capital had to be raised with which to finance its construction. Friends were involved with both these endeavors.

In the early nineteenth century stocks and bonds for banks and a variety of improvement companies could be found in Quaker estate inventories. Out of ninety-nine data set inventories made between 1790 and 1850, sixty five (65.6%) included assets in some sort of paper: notes, bonds or stock. Some notes were money lent to relatives and neighbors, as had been the practice since the earliest days of Bucks County. But others were what we generally associate with the term nowadays. For example, Thomas Jenks (died 1828) owned stock in the Bucks County Bank, New Hope Bridge Company, and the Long Beach Great Swamp Company. William Gillam (died 1848) owned stock in the Bustleton Turnpike Company, Farmer's National Bank, a Bridge Company, and Yardley Villa. He also owned shares in the Attleborough High School and the hay scale.[30]

In addition to investing in banks and a variety of improvement companies, many Friends were directly involved in their organization and direction. As noted above, a number of Middletown Friends served as directors of the Farmers' National Bank. Friends were also involved when banks were established in Newtown, Langhorne, and Doylestown. Jonathan W. Gillam, a farmer, (grandson of Simon and Anna) was a director of the first two of these three banks. Joshua Richardson was secretary of the Neshaminy Lock Navigation Company, while Thomas L. Allen, a physician, and Joseph Jenks served as two of its commissioners (1832). Perhaps enthusiastic to be in on the ground floor of an even newer technology, Allen chaired a public meeting in 1836 for the promotion of a railroad. In 1832 Joseph Allen, Joshua C. Canby, Joseph Gillingham, John Paxson, and Giles Knight, all Friends, were elected directors of the Philadelphia and Trenton Railroad Company. Joshua Woolston, John Paxson, Mardon Wilson, Samuel Comfort, John W. Stackhouse, and five Jenkses were commissioners of the Newtown and Bristol Railroad Company. John Kirkbride chaired a public meeting against the Morrisville and New Hope Railroad because, he argued, it would benefit only the railroad contractors and stock speculators, and perhaps more important, would compete with the Delaware Canal—a company in which he had an interest. Mardon Wilson was secretary of the Bustleton and Somerton Turnpike Company.[31] When the Doylestown Insurance Company solicited subscriptions in 1835, included in its long list of Associators were Phineas Jenks, Michael H. Jenks, William Watson, and John Paxson, among other Friends.[32]

Although these brief notices of Quaker involvement in new technologies and new financial instruments indicate how comfortable at least some Friends were with the economic *zeitgeist* of "improvement" and "progress", not all Friends were so cozy with these active planners and creators. Edward Hicks became a member of Middletown Meeting in 1803, and moved to Newtown in 1811 where he painted many "Peaceable Kingdoms". Hicks clearly saw the theological choice confronting his generation. He understood that the qualities needed for "this world"—the "enterprising, aspiring, restless, warlike America"—were not those called for by God's kingdom. He railed against

> lawyers, doctors, office-hunters, and office-holders; speculators in bank, bridge, steamboat, railroad, and canal stocks, money mongers, land jobbers, and teachers of the higher branches of fashionable learning such as the dead languages, and even painting, a link in the chain of anti-Christian foibles next to music and dancing.[33]

It is hard to tell how many Friends shared Hicks's views, and how many supported the economic activists. In his *Journal* Hicks implies he was a small minority.

If Hicks was at one end of a spectrum of Quaker positions, Joseph Eastburn probably typified the broad middle. He was the first to use a mowing machine in Middletown, attracting an audience of 500 locals. His basic philosophy was not to get rich, but to earn "a good, generous healthy living for a large family and the help, and with a pride in accomplishment in honest toil." The surplus produce was sold in Philadelphia for cash which was "handled with care".[34]

It seems that a majority of Middletown Friends in varying degrees according to their financial situation and willingness to take risks, accepted the emerging culture of liberal capitalism, but fit it into their own perception of distinctive Quaker requirements. Their goal diverged from the world's desire to get rich; they were content with making "a good, generous healthy living". They appreciated the labor-saving advantages of new technology. There were probably many of them who were unaware of the seductive attraction with which new machines and new consumer goods could draw them, bit by bit, from a concentration on God to a fascination with the world. It was not a matter of a rule against this or that, it was a question of where ultimate allegiance lay.

It was a relatively short step from an interest in new enterprises to the spirit of speculation in bank, bridge, steamboat, canal, and railroad stocks. Speculation goes a step farther away from Friends' principles of "prudent investment" while it remains one of the "world's" acceptable methods of getting rich. Since it is impossible to sort out the motives behind Quaker purchases of such stock, we will look briefly at two speculative manias (merino sheep and mulberry trees and silkworms), and try to determine Friends' attitudes towards them.

Speculation

The first of these speculative fevers involved merino sheep, which produce long, silky wool much prized for making fine soft yarn. From 1810 to 1815 the excitement raged over merino sheep. Full-blooded merinos sold for as high as $300 to $500 each, and in a few instances even brought $1000. One man sold his whole wheat crop (200 bushels at $3 each) for one sheep. When the bubble burst merino sheep sold for $5 to $10.[35]

A quarter century later, the next generation seemed just as eager to be gulled, this time over mulberry trees and the silk worm industry. The *Bucks County Intelligencer* began boosting them early in 1828. By June 1835 it was printing instructions for raising silkworms. Gradually public interest was roused. In the wake of the 1837 panic and collapse, a business convention of delegates from several states meeting in Philadelphia passed a resolution urging that the economy could be stimulated and the foreign debt relieved by promoting the growth of a domestic silk industry. Acres of *morus multicaulus* (Chinese mulberry) trees were planted to supply leaves for feeding the silkworms. Dr. Phineas Jenks was a principle backer in the establishment of a cocoonery in Newtown;

David Comfort built one in Byberry. Others were built in Doylestown. A Bucks County Silk Society was established, offering advice and premiums to stimulate the infant industry. The *Bucks County Intelligencer* carried an increasing flood of articles and letters urging citizens to buy into this sure ticket to wealth.

Not everyone was caught up in the mania. A letter to the newspaper from "Caution" warned against speculation in silk culture and the greed he saw driving it. He noted that silk had been tried and failed before the Revolution. He compared the present mania to that of merino sheep and western land speculation. He decried the state tax subsidy on silk. But he was ridiculed, drowned out by a chorus of enthusiasm for *morus multicaulus*.[36] Edward Hicks wrote of two Friends from Newtown Meeting who succumbed to the temptation. One was a "worthy, exemplary elder", the other was a poor but honest hatter with a "lovely wife" and a family of young children. When the bubble burst the elder was out by $700 to another "very clever Friend", the hatter by $300 to a Presbyterian.[37]

"The pernicious excitement which the expectation of sudden wealth, produced among all classes, has passed away like a golden dream," the *Bucks County Intelligencer* announced without a trace of shame for its prominent role in that same pernicious excitement. It urged "the sober and reflecting owner of Mulberry trees" to continue to cultivate them and to expect "reasonable profits" to result.[38]

No member of a data set family went bankrupt because of speculation in either sheep or mulberry trees. Some were, however, involved. Joseph S. Longshore was advertising mulberry trees for sale in 1839.[39] But Middletown Friends do not seem to have been as deeply involved as those who lived in towns in which avid promoters were at work. It does not seem likely that the quality of the religious commitment of Middletown Friends, as a group, was different from those in, for example, Newtown, but perhaps the temptation was not as strenuously advanced. Phineas Jenks, partner in a cocoonery and avid promoter, lived in Newtown. No one seems to have played his role in Middletown.

The evidence from contemporary newspapers, local histories, estate inventories, biographies, and collections of family papers is that in the first half of the nineteenth century most Friends in Middletown did not differ markedly from their non-Quaker neighbors in terms of their participation in the economic activities of their time. Friends and non-Friends experimented with new technologies and with new forms of economic institutions for financing new modes of transportation. They joined in groups to promote agricultural improvements, to provide public hay scales, or to organize banks and build bridges.

How then did Middletown Quakers differ in the economic sphere from their neighbors? Edward Hicks grumped and railed against the newly emerging culture, like an Old Testament prophet, a lonely voice crying in the wilderness. Gentle William Blakey quietly chose to follow God, never allowing his outward concerns to push aside his concentration on his spiritual life. As early as 1780 he had observed, "When the world calls, how we scuffle! but when religion calls, how we hang back. My desire is to be delivered from the over-anxious thoughts and cares about these perishing things; that there may be more leisure for better thoughts."[40]

More typical was Michael H. Jenks, who probably thought he had the best of both worlds. He noted in his unpublished memoir that among the resolves that he tried to live by was "To carry out the Queries of the Discipline of my Religious Society—Viz. To live within the bounds of my [means?], keep to moderation in my business, punctual to my promises and just in the payment of my debts—To be industrious, and economical[.] To avoid bad company and dissipation and try to make myself a useful citizen."[41] Jenks gave up farming and moved to Newtown in 1837, at the age of forty two. He was a surveyor, conveyancer, Justice of the Peace, real estate and insurance agent, County Commissioner, and U. S. Congressman. His name often appeared on lists of citizens promoting "improving" activities. He was secretary of the second agricultural society, and won a premium in 1827 for his peach brandy. Although he was deeply involved in most of the economic, political, and public affairs activities of his time, Jenks appears never to have stepped over the line of what was considered acceptable by Friends. But there is little indication in the meeting records, his own memoir, or in the evidence of his outward life that he seriously engaged in the hard lonely spiritual work of developing a lively relationship with the Inward Christ. This rather superficial adherence to the rules of the religious institution is one mark of a second level of faith development.

We have seen that Friends required a higher degree of prudence and honesty than did the law, including repaying debts that had been forgiven by the courts. It was still a question of ultimate allegiance, but the question was less insistent. Unless there was a business failure, it does not appear that the meeting inquired about a Friend's priorities. It was easier to avoid asking to whom one belonged in the economic sphere than it had been under the conflicting demands surrounding the peace testimony at the time of the Revolution.

The point is, there seems to be some truth in the warning that one cannot serve two masters. There was a basic incompatibility between pursuing the economic and social goals of newly emerging liberal capitalism while at the same time hoping to attain the traditional spiritual goal of Quakerism: the cultivation of a living relationship with, and obedience to, the Inward Christ. Because there were no sharply visible crisis points, most Friends seemed not to have realized that as a group they were losing the internal reality of an intimate, radicalizing relationship with God, while steadfastly maintaining the outward patterns of behavior which earlier Quakers had learned were the fruits of that relationship.

These early decades of the new republic offered a temptation to Friends to take the Quaker virtues of thrift and industriousness, innovation and anti-authoritarian independence and join the swelling river of new entrepreneurs flowing, rushing, to prosperity.

There was another temptation for some Friends to look outside their narrow Society and join in the flood of evangelical Christianity united in emotional enthusiasm against the threat of infidelity. The next chapter will examine how Friends reacted to the shift in the dominant religious culture from Enlightenment rationality and deism to the fervor of evangelical revivalism.

CHAPTER 7: EVANGELICALISM

The economic sphere was not the only area in which Friends absorbed ideas from outside their Religious Society. New theological ideas also crept in. Of these, evangelicalism was the most important. Since these ideas played such a large part in the Separation within Philadelphia Yearly Meeting in 1827, we need to examine them a little more closely.

Evangelicalism is not easy to define precisely.[1] Two elements of it with which we are most concerned were its emphasis on the conversion experience and on the authority of the Bible. Evangelicals stressed the crucial importance of each believer's specific, emotional "new birth" into an acceptable personal relationship with God, usually with the assistance of a "spirit anointed" preacher. The ultimate authority for evangelicals was the inspired Bible which was to be believed as literally true and accurate. They also stressed the necessity of moral regeneration combined with self-reliance. There is a compatibility between evangelicalism and the second level of faith development. This does not mean that every evangelical was a level two, nor that every level two was an evangelical. It just points to the certainty of the conversion experience and belief in the inerrancy of the Bible as two positions which fill the second level's need for answers. The level two comes to religion to escape ambiguity and mystery. Evangelicalism tends to supply unequivocal answers.

Historian Boyd Hilton describes evangelicalism as the formative ideology in nineteenth century Britain, and it had a somewhat similar influence, although perhaps not as monolithic, in the United States.² In addition to being a pervasive ideology in the American dominant religious culture, it played an important role in the 1827 Separation within Philadelphia Yearly Meeting. This chapter will sketch some of the main differences and similarities between the evangelical movement and the Religious Society of Friends in general.³ Then, searching the thin documentary evidence, it will try to assess its impact on Middletown Meeting in particular.

When Quakerism arose in the seventeenth century it had no difficulty defending its unique theological understandings against all other varieties of Christianity. A large part of its strength came from the experiential quality of its proclamation. But "status quo" is not a term that accurately pertains to spiritual life (as opposed to religious institutions).

We have seen that in the middle of the eighteenth century Friends, individually and corporately, were having to reassess their faith and practice, and make choices regarding accommodation to or rejection of various aspects of the dominant culture. The reform movement of the third quarter of the century strengthened the Society of Friends, enabling it to survive the Revolution in unity, albeit smaller, and to uphold its peace testimony. The changing economic climate proved to be a tougher challenge because it was subtly seductive and insidious, and provided few sharp points at which choices had to be made in terms of declaring allegiance to God or to the "world".

The compromises made by many Friends regarding the new economic climate were similar to compromises made with the new intellectual and emotional climate of evangelical religious thought. They were subtle and almost unnoticed, but had a profound impact. The history of Friends in this period suggests there is a connection between not needing to make difficult choices in taking a stand on declaring one's highest loyalty, and on neglecting hard inner spiritual work. In other words, it seems that during the seventeenth-century persecutions or the harsh demands of the Revolutionary War, those who chose to be Friends did so out of strong conviction. In times of peace and prosperity many Friends got spiritually lazy, and one result was that the vitality of meetings for worship declined.

Historian Larry Ingle suggests that the reform of the third quarter of the eighteenth century continued after the Revolution.[4] But if it did, it seemed sapped by the War, and its emphasis seemed to be on decrying declension in terms of outward behavior and clothing. The essential integrity of a life demonstrating the reality of its inward experience of the divine seemed too often to be replaced with an emphasis on obedience to a set of rules for the sake of preserving the Society. An English Friend observed that in the decades after the Revolution, "error, formality, and worldly ease were silently altering . . . Quakerism into a merely fossilized imitation of that of earlier days."[5] An 1804 letter from Jonathan Evans to Elias Hicks noted, "It seems a very low time among us as to the life of religion . . . a round of Duties may be performed and a regular deportment adhered to, yet from my feelings, I should conclude without breach of charity, we need to be shaken from our inferior dependencies and more certainly know our feet established upon the sure foundation."[6]

When individual Friends lacked personal experience of the presence of God, and the spiritual vitality of meetings for worship ebbed, Friends sought alternate sources of spiritual nourishment. First there was a vacuum, then it was filled. The vacuum was the lack of a radicalizing personal relationship with God, and the uninspired and uninspiring "dead" meeting for worship. It was the result of an interplay of factors: an over-emphasis on quietism, a decrease in vocal ministry, an increase in the power of elders, and most important, individual Friends spending more time on their outward affairs than on their inner, spiritual lives. That "God has no grandchildren" is particularly true for Quakerism, because it is based on a personal experiential relationship with the divine that cannot be inherited. Each individual must choose to listen to the Spirit and bring his or her life into conformity with it. Historian John Sykes concludes, "as soon as Quaker practice falters, [along with] the tending of the inward fires, with all that that implies, then the soul of the Society is amongst those most easy to capture."[7]

The dominant culture offered a variety of theological alternatives to Quakerism with which to fill the vacuum. The rational deism of the Revolutionary generation appealed to only a few Friends, perhaps because it was at its height at the time war was forcing Friends to reexamine their beliefs and take an outward and public stand on Friends' principles. Those who remained Friends were not overly influenced by Enlightenment theology, although rationalism in other areas of life was very appealing and not incompatible with Quakerism. The rationalist "New Lights" in New England, who became Unitarians, influenced some Friends, or found parallel ideas among them. These ideas produced a fierce backlash among Presbyterians and other mainstream denominations and also among some Quakers. The French Revolution symbolized the excesses resulting, it was feared, from the worship of reason, and in both Britain and the united States rationalism gave way before the rising tide of evangelicalism. As J. William Frost and Hugh Barbour observed, evangelicalism flourishes when there is an enemy to identify, and that enemy was identified in the 1820s as free thinkers, rationalists, and Unitarians. Evangelicals seemed to know no words other than "deist" or "infidel" to describe people with whom they disagreed.[8]

There was a small minority of Friends, centered around the periodical *The Berean*, who could accurately be called liberals in that they attempted to use reason as they tried to understand the Bible. However, both they and the evangelicals were at odds with the traditional Quaker quietists.[9] In time the Longshore family in Middletown Meeting came to be associated with this liberal position.

Among these theological alternatives, the one with the greatest influence on Friends was the evangelical revival, whose repeated waves were originally stirred up by the Great Awakening and Methodism. Friends had been largely immune from contagion from that first Awakening. Frederick Tolles suggests that class differences provided a large factor. In the seventeenth century, lower class folks were drawn to the enthusiasm of the first Quakers, but by the 1730s and 1740s Pennsylvania Quakers had become respectable and prosperous and found religious enthusiasms unappealing. They emphasized the quietist fear of creaturely activity, and thus avoided the emotionalism and organized revival meetings of the evangelicals.[10] Another hypothesis is that many Friends in the first half of the eighteenth century were satisfied with their spiritual experience within Quakerism and felt no need to search elsewhere.

By the end of the eighteenth century, however, some Quakers were looking beyond the Religious Society of Friends to their evangelical neighbors. There were some points on which evangelicals and Friends agreed. However, there were some distinct differences from the original Quaker understandings, although at first it is probable that Friends did not notice that a new tone had crept into the messages of some ministers.

Friends and evangelicals both emphasized experiencing the Holy Spirit, the depravity of unregenerate "natural" humans, freedom of will, the universality of Christ's atonement, the possibility of perfection, a prophetic note, an austere moral code, a strong humanitarian impulse, the disparagement of reason and theological education as the means for understanding spiritual truths, and a certain democratic tendency.[11] However, how they arrived at their positions, and how they interpreted them, often differed.

Three of the most obvious differences between original Quakerism and early nineteenth century evangelicalism lay in their understanding of the authority of the Bible, the necessity of a second birth, and the importance of the historical acts of Jesus' death, resurrection, and atonement.[12] We will discuss the Bible issue first, then return to the others.

The very first Quaker imprisonment, in 1649, was over the authority of the Bible. A preacher in Nottingham "told the people that the Scriptures were the touchstone and judge by which they were to try all doctrines, religions, and opinions, and to end controversy." But George Fox cried out, "Oh, no, it is not the Scriptures", it was "the Holy Spirit, by which the holy men of God gave forth the Scriptures". It was the Spirit that led into all Truth, and by which all opinions, religions, and judgments were to be tested.[13] Early Friends understood that the Bible was not the final authority, but pointed the way to the ultimate authority, namely the Spirit of Christ. They also understood that parts of the Bible, especially the Old Testament, while still historical fact, were best understood as "types and figures" of inward struggles, or perhaps as metaphor. The events of the Bible could help explain an individual's inner struggles, and inner events could aid in understanding the Bible—both happening under the tutelage of the Holy Spirit.[14]

Evangelicals, on the other hand, maintained the Protestant idea (in protest against the authority of the institutionalized Roman church) that the written Bible was the ultimate authority. In the face of a gradually enlarging sphere of science, they also increasingly insisted that the Bible was literally true.

The cases of Hannah (Jenkins) Barnard, of Hudson, New York, and Abraham Shackleton of Ballitore, Ireland, in the first decade of the nineteenth century illustrate the extent to which some "establishment" Friends had drifted from the original Quaker understanding. Friends in positions of influence and power in Irish meetings pilloried Barnard and Shackleton for suggesting that there was a discrepancy between the God whom they experienced, who instructed them against outward war, and the God of the Old Testament who directed the Jews to annihilate whole cities. Although these two were firmly in the tradition of the original Friends, they were disowned because their positions seemed too close to those of the despised and feared deists. Their disownments illustrate the growing schism between traditional Spirit-centered Quakers and the newer Bible-centered evangelical Friends. The schism was exacerbated by evangelically-inclined travelling ministers spreading all over the Quaker world this new interpretation of the authority of the Bible.[15]

The early Quakers had spoken of the outer work of the historical Jesus, meaning his death, resurrection, and atonement. But they insisted that this alone was inadequate. It must be matched with what Friends called the inner work of Christ. This meant the universal Light of the Logos, or Spirit of Christ, revealing areas of darkness and sin in the individual, and then that person cooperating with the Light as it seeks to transform, guide, gift, and empower. It is the inward work of Christ that leads, not to a mouthing of salvation formulas, but to a transformation of human personality.[16] Quakers saw the process as a long-term growth into wholeness or holiness, rather than the all-at-once new birth emphasized by evangelicals.

Some scholars who have studied the growing influence of evangelicalism within Quakerism have connected it to city-dwelling, the growing influence of new modes of commerce and industry, and reform enthusiasms. Wealthy urban

Quaker elites who also accepted evangelical ideas appeared to have had a high involvement with these interests. Rural, threatened, fearful, conservative Friends were more likely to cling to traditional visions of Quakerism, and of life in general.[17] While this theory was largely true for Great Britain and Philadelphia, it does not hold up well when used with a closer examination of Middletown Meeting. As we shall see, many Middletown Friends adopted a good many of the views often associated with evangelicalism, without seeming to accept the theology.

Both Edward Hicks of Middletown and then Newtown, and his more famous cousin Elias Hicks of Long Island, were opposed to newfangled inventions as well as evangelical (newfangled?) theology. Their journals are often quoted to demonstrate the firm connection between Hicksites and reaction. But Edward felt himself to be in a small minority, a lonely voice crying in the wilderness.

Unfortunately, there are no known journals of other Middletown Friends. William Blakey, who lived to 1822, had stopped writing by 1816. There are indications that Blakey did not adopt evangelical ideas. For example, he stated his belief, "Divine contemplation, and a strict attention to the revelation of Jesus Christ, in our own hearts, only and alone can make us true Christians." Later, he approvingly mentioned the visit of Abel Thomas, "an old fashioned Quaker; which made me think of what William Penn's father said to him—'Son William, if you and your friends keep to your plain way of preaching, and plain way of living, you will make an end of the priests to the end of the world.'"[18]

Evidence for Evangelicalism in Middletown

Because of the lack of personal records, the historian is forced to look for outward events and work back from them to try to ascertain what might have influenced members of the meeting. Several scholars have noted trends in the dominant culture that had an impact on some Quakers in the nineteenth century. They posit a correlation between evangelicalism and revivals and reform movements and new opportunities in commerce. We looked at the latter in Chapter 6, but now will review it in the light of possible evangelical leanings. Then we will investigate the degree to which Middletown Monthly Meeting Friends engaged with the former. Typical evangelical activities of the early nineteenth century included forming groups to encourage evangelical revivals, Sunday schools and Bible societies, a variety of reforms (such as temperance), and philanthropy.

In 1771 a Methodist preacher came to Bristol, and after the war, in 1788 a Bristol circuit was formed. That year William Blakey accompanied James Moon to the Friends Meeting in Trenton and observed it was "Small, but rather upon the revival. It is hard work for us, Quakers, to get quiet enough."[19] By the turn of the century there were both Presbyterian and Methodist churches in Bensalem. Several disowned Friends became active in the Methodist Church. This did not mean that Quakers in good standing joined in ecumenical evangelical endeavors. However, the evangelical British Quaker Joseph John Gurney did preach in the Methodist Church in Bristol.

There is some additional evidence of evangelical activity in lower Bucks County. A revival was held in 1827. An 1831 newspaper article recounted how Augustine Willit (who had Quaker relatives) in his later years invited revivalist preachers to use a place in his woods where the rocks made a natural pulpit. Camp meetings continued there after his death. The names of Middletown Friends do not appear in various accounts of these activities.[20]

About 1811 the first Sunday School was organized in Bristol. In 1816 a Bible Society began in Bucks County, the purpose of which was to give a Bible to every destitute family. No Friends seemed to be involved in either of these organizations until 1827 when a newspaper account listed Dr. Allen, a member of Middletown Meeting.[21] With this small evidence, it appears that except for Thomas L. Allen, Middletown Friends were not participating in typically evangelical activities.

Allen was a physician, involved in a number of civic endeavors. He was a commissioner for the Neshaminy Lock Navigation Company, chaired a public meeting promoting a railroad, and served as president of the Attleborough High School.[22] He also served as administrator for several estates, as well as guardian for some orphaned children. He was not, however, particularly active in the ongoing work of Middletown Meeting. His first wife, Susanna Marmaduke Watson, died in 1823, two months after the death of their third infant, leaving two- and four-year old children. Allen raised them to adulthood before he married for a second time, in 1844. It is not an unexpected reaction to grief and loneliness to throw oneself into useful activities. For whatever reason, Thomas L. Allen appeared to be the only Middletown Friend who worked with people of other denominations on typically evangelical projects.

There are other ways of ascertaining what was influencing individuals. For example, historian Thomas Hamm found that evangelically-inclined Friends in the Midwest were becoming increasingly involved with members of other Christian denominations in a variety of reform activities: temperance, prison reform, education, sabbatarianism, tract distribution, and relief for the worthy poor.[23] The joint effort encouraged Friends to think of themselves as members of a broad stream of generic evangelical Christians rather than as a small band of peculiar people. Some of these activities also were taking place in Bucks County, but few Friends were involved. Since the Bible Society and various reform organizations accelerated their activities in the second quarter of the century, after the Separation, they will be taken up later, after we have examined the split.

Temperance was vigorously promoted, and from the late 1820s the activities of a number of fledgling temperance societies were reported in the *Bucks County Intelligencer* and the *Doylestown Democrat*. Frequently listed were Quakers Mahlon B. Linton, Penquite Linton, Joseph S. Longshore, and Marmaduke Watson, as well as former Friend Phineas Jenks.[24] Marmaduke Watson was the father-in-law of Thomas L. Allen, both leaning to the evangelical persuasion.

Joseph S. Longshore, on the other hand, was a theological liberal. The poverty of Longshore's grandfather and great grandfather was described in Chapter 3. We will see in Chapter 9 how one branch of the family was ahead of its time in progressive thinking. Suffice it to say here, that Joseph was an active abolitionist, an ardent advocate of total abstinence, and helped establish the Female Medical College of Pennsylvania.[25] The point is, in Middletown Meeting temperance drew its few supporters and activists from both ends of the spectrum of theological positions. The great majority of Friends were not involved. This is further evidence that most Middletown Friends were not being drawn into the constellation of reform activities which often characterized evangelicals.

New Modes of Commerce

In order to examine the theory that Friends who were involved in new modes of commerce and industry as well as a variety of reform movements were the ones who were more open to evangelical ideas, we can look at who was involved with these things in Bucks County. Chapter 6 described a number of Quaker men whose names came up repeatedly for their involvement with the bank and various schemes for canals, turnpikes, railroads, and new agricultural technologies. Although there were several women listed as shareholders in the bank, and many had stocks in their estate inventories, they do not seem to have been active economic players.

Members of the data set families involved in the Farmers' National Bank of Bucks County included John Paxson, director from 1814 and president from 1838 until his death in 1850, and directors Joseph Jenks, Thomas Jenks, John Kirkbride, Joseph Kirkbride, William Richardson, and Isaac Stackhouse. Jonathan W. Gillam was a director of two other Bucks County banks. Joseph Allen, Thomas L. Allen, Joseph Jenks, Michael H. Jenks, John Kirkbride, Mahlon B. Linton, Joseph S. Longshore, Isaac Paxson, Joshua Richardson, William Richardson, Jr., and Mardon Wilson were actively involved in a number of progressive, improving schemes. Of all these men, Thomas L. Allen was the only evangelical.

Non-agricultural occupations and advanced market agriculture have also been seen as correlating with evangelicalism. A few Friends in Middletown Meeting took opportunities for non-farming occupations. One was Joshua Mitchell, who went from being a farmer to a shopkeeper, and then moved to the city and became a Philadelphia alderman "noted for his administration of justice". Sarah Stackhouse had a shop in Bristol in 1824, but apparently went out of business when she married Isaac Paxson the next year. Stephen Wilson was a tailor who advertised that he would do "fashionable, plain, and common work", would take produce as partial payment, and also carried a line of ready-made clothing and uncut yard goods. A number of Friends moved into medicine or some form thereof: James Linton (dental surgeon who also sold dentifrice), Maurice P. Linton (physician and dental surgeon, who also manufactured and inserted false teeth), Anna Mary Longshore, Joseph S. Longshore, and their sister-in-law Hannah E. (Myers) Longshore, John S. Mitchell, and John Wilson. Wilson's obituary in 1835 described him as "active in business, a kind neighbor, a good example for economy, industry and moderation."[26] Presumably these Friends were not alienated from the emerging culture of economic change, but as near as can be determined, none of them could be considered evangelicals.

The data set families missing from these lists are Blakey, Comfort, Watson, Wildman, and Woolston. They, along with a good many members of the other families, were farmers. According to the generally accepted theory, subsistence farmers should not have been connected with evangelicalism, particularly if they were not profiting from the new economy, while farmers deeply involved in market agriculture, should have been drawn to evangelicalism. These families do seem to have been financially successful. But, among them, only the Comforts took the evangelical side in the 1827 Separation. The rest did not.

Therefore, to make the jump, as many scholars do, that involvement in what Doherty calls the new "acquisitive society" was directly related to evangelical leanings, does not seem to follow with members of Middletown Meeting. Since we have no access to the inner thoughts of these Friends, we are forced to rely on the somewhat thin and scattered evidence of their outward behavior. There was very little involvement in and commitment to the activities of ecumenical evangelists on the part of Middletown Friends that Anthony Wallace, for example, found so prevalent in Chester County's "Rockdale".[27] The interesting thing is that Middletown Friends seem to have ignored the reforming activities of evangelicals, while, for the most part, participating actively in the economic activities often associated with evangelicals.

To create a hypothesis which might explain such an apparent anomaly, we need to return to the second dimension of spiritual life. Rather than look at these Friends in terms of second- or third-level faith development, we should, perhaps, look at them on the spectrum of indifferent to passionate. Many evangelicals were passionate about their spiritual life and about helping others become saved. Many of these Middletown Friends seem rather perfunctory. They were not so indifferent that they opted out of the business affairs of the meeting. But they did not seem actively engaged in the inner work which is the mark of spiritual growth. They seem to have been Friends by habit, by birth, by tribal affiliation. Many of them were probably level twos, but unreflective, instinctive conformists. Because economic affairs were such an important part of many of their lives, and rationalism was well-honed as a tool in that sphere, it is likely that without realizing it, some were slipping into level three skepticism. But it was, at this point, an unexamined and almost unconscious skepticism.

We will see evidence for the presence or absence of evangelical leanings in the decision each individual made when the Philadelphia Yearly Meeting split. We need to turn now to the Separation of 1827 and see which Friends in Middletown chose the Orthodox faction and which chose the so-called Hicksite faction.

SEPARATION

The differences in theological emphasis discussed in the last chapter merged with other issues and resulted in a separation within Philadelphia Yearly Meeting in 1827. This chapter will not recount that story, which has been done at great length elsewhere.[1] Instead it will review some relatively recent approaches to and interpretations of the schism, and see how the concept of faith development might increase our understanding of it. Then we will look at Middletown Monthly Meeting to see how these various interpretations hold up when applied to one rural meeting. Finally we will examine the data set families and see who went which way. All this is designed to help us explain why individuals in the data set families identified with the group they chose.

But first a few words about labels. Both factions called themselves Friends, and assumed they were the true heirs of the Religious Society. The Orthodox were so named because they favored bringing Quaker theology into line with orthodox Protestant theology as expressed most vividly in the revivals connected with the Second Great Awakening. They called the other group Hicksites, after the most egregious of their opponents. It is really a misnomer, intended to be pejorative. That group was united only in its opposition to the Orthodox. After about 1818 Elias Hicks's theology became increasingly idiosyncratic, but it was understood or accepted by very few of those who opposed the Orthodox.[2] As a minister, however, Hicks was a powerful preacher, a much loved (or reviled) elderly Long Island farmer who staunchly witnessed to his antislavery beliefs. He was a tireless traveller in the ministry, and remained extremely popular among rural Friends. I wish there was another name by which to call this diverse group, since "Hicksite" obscures its diversity. Larry Ingle calls them "reformers". Sometimes, in frustration, I have labelled them "so-called Hicksites".

The Scholarly Trail

If we look at how some scholars have viewed the hundred years of Quaker history leading up to 1827, we can get a sense of movement towards schism. Frederick Tolles, in *Meeting House and Counting House* and *Quakers and the Atlantic Culture*, discussed the problems for genuinely life-changing Quakerism when, in the colonial period, some of its members began to acquire great wealth. The time and attention necessary to build and maintain a fortune, and the lifestyle assumed to accompany wealth took time and attention away from concentration on the inner life. In practical terms, individual Friends demonstrated that there was truth in the Biblical warning that one cannot serve two masters.

Jack Marietta, in *The Reformation of American Quakerism*, described the growing division between those nominal Friends whose hearts and minds were in the marketplace or the statehouse, and the reform-minded Friends who exhorted all who would listen to turn inward and obey the Spirit. Because of the trauma of the French and Indian War, the reformers, with their politically attuned British allies, prevailed on Pennsylvania Friends to relinquish positions of provincial political power. The reformers also succeeded in tightening the discipline to ensure outward uniformity of behavior among Friends.

J. William Frost posited the existence of two strands within the impulse for reform: those who focussed on eliminating the evil of slavery and those who worried most about the corruption stemming from a laxly enforced discipline, most obvious in the marriage regulations.[3] Jean Soderlund, in *Quakers & Slavery,* took the analysis a step further, seeing the concern for discipline as adhering to what Max Weber called the "emissary" form of prophecy, that is, the need to purify the Society and separate it from the larger world. The concern over slavery had characteristics of Weber's "exemplary prophecy" which emphasized the need to live according to God's will, inwardly possessed.[4]

It is helpful to take this another step by using the concept of faith development. The "emissary" form has similarities with people in Peck's second level of development or Wilber's blue meme who are attracted to the authority of the institution and loyally support its rules and mores. The "exemplary" form has similarities with Peck's fourth level and perhaps Wilber's second tier which embrace the mysteries of spirituality, are able to live with paradox, and experience at a deeper level the reality of a personal relationship with the divine.

In his dissertation, "A Saving Remnant," David Robert Kobrin employed the term "evangelical" to mean the effort of reform-minded Friends to proselytize nominal Quakers. This definition masked the growing differences among the reformers, differences which Soderlund had emphasized.[5] Kobrin theorized that because their basic ideology depended on the direct guidance of the Spirit of Christ, Friends were unable or unwilling to change to meet the emerging new climate of opinion in independent America. The change he saw in the American dominant culture was an increase in rationalism and faith in human progress and in the efficacy of individual effort. He appeared to confuse genuine, radical dependence on the Spirit, which allows for and even demands bold new directions, with the fearful, conservative clinging to the *tradition* of dependence on the Spirit.

Kobrin also ignored the strand in the dominant culture involved with evangelical revivalism. It was this strand that Thomas Hamm studied in *The Transformation of American Quakerism*. Hamm saw the great bulk of midwestern Friends over the course of the nineteenth century slough off distinctively Quaker bits of faith and practice. As a result, by the late twentieth century, one large group (Evangelical Friends International) was virtually indistinguishable from other fundamentalist Protestant sects. Another large group (Friends United Meeting) had lost a good many Quaker "distinctives" and had more in common with Methodists than with seventeenth-century Friends. In other words, the story of eighteenth- and nineteenth-century Quakerism can be seen as demonstrating the difficulty of escaping the pull of the dominant culture. As individuals and groups accepted, in differing amounts, various thought patterns and behaviors from the "world", tensions led to a series of schisms.[6]

Scholars have interpreted the story of these schisms in different ways. Larry Ingle's study of the 1827-28 Separation pitted the "reformers" against the "Orthodox". The reformers were those who wanted to continue the work of the third quarter of the eighteenth century in the traditional understanding of the Inward Christ and the primacy of the authority of the Spirit. The Orthodox wanted to bring Quaker doctrine into line with evangelical Protestantism. Robert W. Doherty, in *The Hicksite Separation*, concluded that the split was the result "of an argument about sect and church", a disagreement over proper organization and belief. The Orthodox wanted a church, while the so-called Hicksites wanted a sect.[7]

If we tie together the work of these scholars, we can trace a line connecting Jean Soderlund's "inner", "exemplary" Friends with Ingle's "reformers". The Orthodox, who were interested in proving the doctrinal soundness of Friends and wanted to tighten the outward discipline, were in the footsteps of the "outer" or "emissary" Friends of the eighteenth century.

As Larry Ingle points out, during the Separation Friends in opposing factions spoke past each other. The Orthodox, in an effort to reform and revitalize the Society, turned to doctrinal orthodoxy. Their attacks on Elias Hicks and others whom they found "unsound" were an attempt to purify the faith. They were opposed by a broad coalition of Friends who sought to reform and revitalize the Society by reconfirming the value of the unique Quaker understanding of the relationship between God, the Inward Light, and each individual. Many of them saw the conflict in terms of a power struggle: *who* would make the doctrinal decisions by which Philadelphia Yearly Meeting defined itself?

Scott Peck notes that people at different levels of faith development have great difficulty communicating with each other.[8] That can account for some, but not all, of the deepening misunderstanding within Philadelphia Yearly Meeting.

There is a certain incongruity in the more authoritarian, wealthy, urban establishment Friends identifying with evangelicalism that attacked not only Calvinist predestinarianism and preoccupation with damnation, but also hierarchical ecclesiastical structures and upper class privilege. Joyce Appleby sees evangelicalism embracing Jeffersonian democracy and self-reliance as compatible with the personal salvation they preached. Self-made economic men needed a personal religion, but rejected rationalism and free-thinking. In a sense evangelicalism became for them more a cultural orthodoxy than a doctrinal one. They extolled piety expressed in virtuous habits and good works. Not coincidently disciplined lives and self-mastery provided the invisible framework for market capitalism.[9]

The Separation in Philadelphia Yearly Meeting

Matters came to a head in 1827. The Meeting for Sufferings, acting as an executive committee of Philadelphia Yearly Meeting, attempted to over-rule the removal by a local meeting (Green Street) of ministers and elders with whom it was not in unity. The Meeting for Sufferings tried to impose others more to their liking on Green Street Meeting. The issue came to Philadelphia Yearly Meeting, but before that body could take it up, it had to agree on a clerk. When, in a noisy and disorderly session, it was unable to come to agreement, the previous year's clerk, Orthodox Samuel Bettle, remained at the table and recognized only Friends who shared his Orthodox views. In despair and frustration, a large segment of Friends withdrew to the Green Street meeting house and organized their own parallel yearly meeting.

Since both of these yearly meetings sent reports, epistles, and visiting committees to the quarterly and monthly meetings, each subordinate body had to choose which to receive. It did not seem conceivable to Friends that both be received, since each claimed sole legitimacy. Consequently, the split rippled out to the farthest corners of Philadelphia Yearly Meeting, and then to other yearly meetings in North America. But this is not the place to retell the story of the Separation in Philadelphia Yearly Meeting. Instead we will look at our one rural monthly meeting and the families we have been following.

The Separation in Middletown Meeting

As early as Second month 1827, local Friends had learned about the proposal to change the way elders and members of the Meeting for Suffering were appointed.[10] Middletown, along with other rural meetings, was afraid the evangelically-inclined wealthy Philadelphia "establishment", which was threatening through the Meeting for Sufferings to impose ministers and elders on Green Street Monthly Meeting, would make these appointments without listening to traditional, rural Friends. Therefore Middletown and many other meetings named twice their usual number of representatives to the upcoming yearly meeting. They hoped this would ensure them a fair hearing. The Orthodox sympathizers in Middletown objected. But in a move which would be repeated frequently at all levels of Quaker organization, Friends' process was ignored and the objections were passed over. The meeting did not wait for divine guidance. It did not wait for a solid sense of unity to emerge before taking action.[11]

After Friends returned home from the yearly meeting sessions, the minute prepared by the Green Street group was read in Middletown Meeting. The two factions gave varying interpretations of the minute's reception. It was "generally united with" state the Hicksite minutes; it was approved "over objections" note the Orthodox minutes.

At the Bucks Quarterly Meeting a few weeks later (31 Fifth month) the twenty representatives who had attended the yearly meeting, reported

> that from the unprecedented manner in which the business of the said Yearly Meeting was conducted we feel it to be our duty to inform the Quarterly Meeting that amidst great disorder a Clerk was imposed on the Meeting contrary to the prevailing sense of the Representatives and the Meeting at large, and at the close a Committee was appointed to visit the subordinate Meetings by the will of a party over the heads of a large proportion of the Meeting and contrary to the solid sense of many exercised brethren then expressed . . . proceedings calculated to abridge our Christian privileges and to lay waste all order and condescension in Society.
>   It is therefore our united judgment that it will be unsafe by receiving such Committee, reading the Extract or in any other manner to acknowledge the authority of the late Yearly Meeting.[12]

Among the eight signatures were those of Middletown Friends John Watson, Benjamin Mather, and Mardon Wilson.

When this was reported to the next Middletown Monthly Meeting, the minute was accepted and the visitors from the Orthodox Yearly Meeting were turned away. At the following monthly meeting (Seventh month) an epistle "from a general meeting of Friends held the 4th and 5th last month at Green Street" was read and accepted. It suggested setting up a new quarterly and yearly meeting, and recommended several queries, for which three men were asked to prepare answers. The Eighth month Bucks Quarterly Meeting appointed representatives to the proposed new yearly meeting, thereby separating themselves (in the eyes of the Orthodox) from the "ancient Yearly Meeting". Those loyal to that "ancient" body continued to hold their own quarterly meeting, and to appoint their own visiting committees.

When Orthodox visitors came to Middletown, their minutes were not accepted and endorsed by the Clerk; when visitors from the "separated" yearly meeting came, they were welcomed and their travelling minutes were endorsed as being in unity with Middletown Friends. The Orthodox sympathizers in Middletown could not accept this insubordination. They withdrew to one of the sheds in the meeting house yard and appointed their own clerk, Samuel Hulme. After adjourning to Grace Stackhouse's nearby home, they appointed a committee to get the minute books and other papers "belonging to this meeting" and a nominating committee to replace the overseers who had "separated". They read the minutes from the yearly meeting of which they felt a part, and graciously received all Orthodox visitors.

In the next few months it became clear that the "other" meeting had no intention of relinquishing the minute books to the Orthodox faction. The Orthodox felt that there were too few Orthodox Friends in Bristol to keep up the preparative meeting there, so it was laid down, retaining only the meeting for worship. Then in First month 1828, the Orthodox began to disown Friends who had "deviated from discipline and good order by having unity with the opposition yearly meeting".

Meanwhile, the remaining Friends (a majority) went about their tasks. In response to the queries asked by Green Street, Middletown responded that

> from the best information obtained there appears to be within the compass of Middletown Preparative Meeting about 153 adult members who are favourable to a representation in the Yearly Meeting to be held in the 10th month next, and about 20 who are those called Orthodox and consequently opposed thereto[;] besides these there appears to be about 14 neutrals.
>
> Within the compass of Bristol about 67 Adults who are favourable as afores'd and about 21 orthodox making within the compass of this Monthly Meeting 220 Friends, 41 Orthodox, and 14 neutral.[13]

There was no list of "neutrals" in the minutes of either faction, but there is a fragment of an Orthodox Quarterly Meeting list of members at the time of the separation. The only neutral listed was Mary Stackhouse. However, six members of the data set families were not disowned by either group, and therefore it is possible that they were among those who refused to take sides. They included Samuel Allen (d. 1833), Hannah (Comly) Mitchell (a recorded minister whose children were disowned by the Orthodox for being Hicksite), Elizabeth (Townsend) Stackhouse (d. 1836, whose husband Isaac was disowned by the Orthodox for being a Hicksite), her daughter Mary Stackhouse (d. 1838) listed above, Rachel (Walton) Myers Wildman (d. 1834, her husband was an active Hicksite, and children were disowned by the Orthodox), and Jonathan Woolston (d. 10/1828).

As for the traditional query asking if "love and unity [are] maintained among you", both groups answered, apparently with a straight face, that "Love and unity we believe are generally maintained amongst us . . . when differences appear endeavours [sic] are used to end them." Since they seemed not to recognize those who had separated as "us", there was unity. On Second Month 8, 1828 the Hicksite women minuted an explanation: "a separation having taken place in the Society of Friends the answers [to the queries] are adapted to the state on [sic] members comprising about four fifths of this meeting."[14]

The larger group (so-called Hicksites) also had to appoint new overseers and elders to replace those who had separated. Each group appointed its own visiting committees. But after the Orthodox began to disown Hicksites, the latter group felt it necessary (in Fifth month 1828) to minute their own explanation of the upsetting events.

> In the 9th month last several Individuals of both sexes withdrew from our Monthly Meeting and set up and held in private houses Meetings of Business which they call Middletown monthly and preparative meetings. And since they have set up and in like manner held Meetings for Worship in which tho' not inattentive to their Deviations, Friends have given them no Interruption. For as they separated from us under a religious Pretext we were willing they should exercise the Inestimable Privilege of liberty of conscience concluding that as they had gone from us and assumed the form of a separate organiz'd Body without the consent of this Monthly Meeting (of which they had been members) They had themselves sever'd the Tie and Virtually dissolved the Connection between us and while they persisted in such Deviations we could have no Unity with them nor consider ourselves accountable for their Conduct and therefore but little Notice was taken of them on our Minutes. But they having lately Issued Testimonies of Disownment against some of our members in the name of Middletown Monthly Meeting of which (having separated therefrom) they themselves are not members. It now seems necessary in order to prevent future confusion that their Names be placed on our Minutes. With the Explicit Declaration that we do not acknowledge them members of our Religious Society whilst they continue in the disorder above mentioned.[15]

There followed thirty-seven names, including these from the data set families: Pierson Mitchell, Sarah Comfort, Samuel Comfort, Elizabeth Comfort, Thomas L. Allen, Mercy Stackhouse, Ann Richardson, Rebecca Richardson, Elizabeth Richardson, Susanna Richardson, Hannah Richardson, Ann Mitchell, Sidney Wilson, William Allen, William Allen, Jr., Sarah Allen, Martha Allen, Jane Allen, Rachel Allen, Ann Paxson, and Mary Ann Jenks. In addition, the women's meeting also included Mary Jenks, Jr.

The difference in tone between the two sets of minutes is striking. True, the Hicksites with the large majority of members and possession of the property, could afford to be forbearing. But they really did put a high value on freedom from doctrinal controls, since that was what they thought the Separation was about: a small group of powerful, urban Friends who wanted to change the traditional Quaker faith by usurping power over local meetings. The Orthodox minutes, on the other hand, seemed obsessed with upholding the letter of the law. For years they would keep track of children in the pre-1827 meeting. As they came of age, a committee was delegated to visit them, and they were then formally disowned—a procedure which kept open the wounds and fed animosity. Edward Hicks noted "the cold, supercilious and insulting manner in which they entered our houses, assuming a jurisdiction over our families. I confess I got angry . . . ." A later (Orthodox) Friend, looking back, observed "evident rancour and bitterness."[16]

The other interesting comparison is between the men's and women's minutes. The above account was taken through the men's eyes. The women seemed more swept along by events than precipitating them. They seemed somewhat reluctant to have the affair culminate in separation. As representatives to the Fifth month Bucks Quarterly Meeting, the women sent two who would identify themselves with the Orthodox and one Hicksite. This does not seem to be the move of a group positioning itself for optimum political advantage. The representatives reported back rather blandly that "they attended and it was then recommended from the Yearly Meeting that the scriptures of truth be read frequently in our familys [sic] and that we be more explicit in answering our queries." Ignoring a possible break, they also read "an acceptable epistle from the Women's Yearly Meeting held in London." In Seventh month, the very last item of business was to read "an Epistle from a general meeting held at Green Street Philadelphia (of Friends)". There was no comment as to local approval or disapproval. In Eighth month, again two Orthodox sympathizers were among the three official representatives to quarterly meeting. There was a separation in Bucks Quarterly Meeting in Eighth month, and only two women from the majority Middletown Meeting attended the Hicksite session. In Ninth month, the Middletown minutes did not mention the report of the quarterly meeting, nor did they mention that the Orthodox women walked out. Here is the minute of the Orthodox women:

> On account of various things that we as members of the religious society of friends could not unite with, being out of our regular order of preceedure [sic], and the separatists refusing to recognize the minute from the [Orthodox] quarterly meeting of Bucks, and not being willing to acknowledge our [visiting] committee from that meeting, their [sic] being

considerable expression purporting that their [*sic*] could not be any other quarterly meeting than that they represented, believing contention would continue if we attempted further to urge our rights, they were informed that we viewed their proceedings as designed to reject us, and not allow our transacting the regular business of the meeting and feeling under the necessity of leaving the house, retired to the shed near the meeting house, where we were favoured to feel the flowings of that love which is better than life—we then appointed Ann Richardson to act as clerk, and adjourned to meet in half an hour at the dwelling of Grace Stackhouse.[17]

And so the die was cast. But why did these Friends choose to walk out? What was it about them as individuals or as members of the Allen, Comfort, Mitchell, Richardson, or other families that inclined them to Orthodoxy?

Who Went Which Way, and Why

Doherty studied the two sides in the 1827 separation and concluded that the positions taken by the participants were conditioned by socio-economic factors, the single most important variable being their relative degree of alienation. He found the Orthodox were committed to the values of an acquisitive dominant culture, were benefiting from the processes of change, had not suffered in the 1816-1819 agricultural depression, and dominated in non-agricultural or commercial-agricultural occupations. In contrast, he found that so-called Hicksites tended to be non-commercial farmers who were either not gaining in wealth or were actually hurting economically, and were alienated from the dominant culture.[18] Doherty's hypothesis can be tested on Middletown Friends by using the 1820 and 1830 tax returns to try to determine which Friends were hurt in the agricultural downturn following the War of 1812.

Doherty used the poor tax records for Chester and Delaware Counties and discovered that the Orthodox had slightly larger and more valuable farms than the Hicksites, although the difference was not great. He concluded that it was not a question of rich versus poor.[19] The mean tax valuation on Middletown Hicksite data set families in 1830 in constant dollars was C$6,649 (N=25) while the mean for Orthodox data set families was C$6,219.25 (N=4). See Table 6. The wealthi-

TABLE 6: Taxable Wealth, Middletown Hicksite and Orthodox Data Set Families, with Constant Dollar Values, 1820, and 1830

Name	1820 Tax	1820 C$ Valuation	1830 Tax	1830 C$ Valuation	1820-1830 % change	Inc. or Dec.
HICKSITE:						
Isaac Gillam	-	-	.25	170.		
Jonathan Kirkbride	-	-	.27	171.		
Jonathan Woolston, Jr.	-	-	.28	189.		
James Wildman, Jr.	-	-	.30	186.		
Joshua Linton	-	-	.30	186.		
Euclydus Longshore	.14	95.	.30	186.	+95	<
William R. Richardson	-	-	.36	224.		
Joseph Watson	-	-	1.76	994.		
William Blakey, Jr.	5.25	3,543.	5.08	3,159.	-384	>
Thomas Paxson	.30	204.	5.32	3,304.	+1,520	<
Thomas Paxson, Jr.	-	-	5.08	3,433.		
Thomas Linton	-	-	7.46	5,036.		
Jeremiah W. Croasdale	12.05	8,136.	7.85	4,875.	-40	>
Abraham Longshore	6.90	4,658.	8.18	5,081.	+9	<
Joseph Wilson	9.49	6,408.	8.85	5,500.	-14	>
Robert Croasdale, Jr.	.38	257.	8.94	5,555.	+2,061	<
Mardon Wilson	6.92	4,673.	11.01	6,850.	+47	<
William Richardson	12.44	8,397.	11.31	7,029.	-16	>
John Allen Mitchell	11.21	7,567.	11.60	7,209.	-4	>
William Mitchell	12.27	8,284.	12.63	7,843.	-5	>
Joseph Jenks	20.33	13,722.	12.89	8,010.	-42	>
Amos B. Stackhouse	-	-	13.31	8,266.		
James Wildman	20.68	13,962.	13.31	8,267.	-41	>
Isaac Paxson	-	-	14.10	8,760.		
William Gillam	11.34	7,653.	14.33	8,899.	+16	<
Michael H. Jenks	-	-	16.23	10,078.		
Jonathan K. Stackhouse	.28	189.	17.17	10,663.	+5,542	<
John Blakey	21.54	14,543.	20.30	12,609.	-13	>
John Watson	22.42	15,138.	21.64	13,441.	-11	>
Jonathan Woolston	38.11	25,728.	30.70	19,072.	-26	>
ORTHODOX:						
Pierson Mitchell	.10	68.				
William Allen	.28	189.	.60	373.	+97	<
Thomas L. Allen	2.34	1,580.	6.96	4,323.	+174	<
Clayton N. Richardson	-	-	10.03	6,231.		
Samuel Comfort	22.49	14,851.	22.46	13,950.	-6	>

SOURCE: Middletown and Bensalem Township Tax Records, HSP

est individual was Hicksite Jonathan Woolston, followed by Orthodox Samuel-Comfort. But Comfort was the only Orthodox above C$6,500, while 56% of the Hicksites were in that prosperous category. Middletown data set Hicksites were somewhat more wealthy, but as Doherty notes, that does not seem to be an important variable.

Instead, Doherty observed that the crucial variable was the degree of alienation, measured especially by relative economic loss or gain over time. Table 6 shows some data set tax returns for 1820 and 1830. This gives us a picture of the direction an individual family's fortunes were headed as the Separation occurred.

Table 7 summarizes the findings of Table 6, and shows that among Hicksites, 29% experienced large gains, 24% experienced large losses, and 47% had only a small gain or loss, staying essentially the same. The very small N of 3 for the Orthodox shows 67% with large gains, 33% with a small loss. These differences appear very significant numerically, but in fact there were only 2 large Orthodox gains compared to 5 large Hicksite gains. The Hicksites seem to be relatively evenly distributed over the economic spectrum, although only 41% of them found their economic situation had improved in the decade. By contrast 68% (2) of the Orthodox increased their wealth. The N is so small, though, the results cannot be given much weight.

TABLE 7: Percentage Change in Tax Valuation 1820 and 1830, Hicksite and Orthodox Data Set Families

	Large gains		Small Gains		Small Losses		Large Losses		Total
	N	%	N	%	N	%	N	%	
Hicksite	5	29.%	2	12.%	6	35.%	4	24.%	17
Orthodox	2	68.%	0	0	1	33.%	0	0	3

SOURCE: Bucks County Tax Records, Middletown Township, HSP. Constant Dollars (C$) were calculated on the basis of $105.80 for 1820, and $80.50 for 1830. See Chapter 2 for method of computation.

Doherty looked at the number of cattle families had, in order to judge how deeply involved they were in the market economy. But he did not compare the number of cattle with the number of residents. If we calculate that one cow can provide the milk products for four persons for a year, then a family of two with two cows, would have the excess production of 1.5 cows, while a family of nine with two cows, would have to purchase the output of one quarter of a cow.

TABLE 8: Household Size, Cattle Owned, Cattle Producing Potential Marketable Surplus Dairy Products, for Hicksite Data Set Men Resident in Middletown Twp.

Name	Died	1800 P	1800 C	1800 Srpls	1810 P	1810 C	1810 Srpls	1820 P	1820 C	1820 Srpls	1830 P	1830 C	1830 Srpls
William Blakey, Jr.	1831	9	3	0.75	8	2	0	8	2	0	7	4	2.25
Wm1822/John Blakey	1836	8	4	2	9	4	1.75	12	6	3	7	8	6.25
Jeremiah Croasdale	1829	11	3	-.75	9	4	1.75	10	0	-0.25			
Robert Croasdale	1847										15	10	6.25
Robert Croasdale	1821	3	1	0.25	11	4	1.25	9	2	-0.25			
Jerem. W. Croasdale	1873							5	3	1.25	10	7	4.50
William Gillam	1843							10	7	4.5	12	8	5.00
Joseph Jenks	1869							-	3		6	5	3.50
Michael H. Jenks	1867							8	-		12	4	1.00
Jonathan Kirkbride	1870										5	4	2.75
James Linton	1854				9	2	-0.25				10	6	3.50
Abraham Longshore	1858				8	1	-1.	9	3	0.75	11	3	.25
William Mitchell	1868							9	4	1.75	10	8	5.50
John Allen Mitchell	1863							6	6	3.5	13	7	3.75
Isaac Paxson	1858										8	3	1.00
William Richardson	1813	19	5	0.25	16	8	4						
Wm. Richardson, Jr.	1832	7	-	-	7	6	4.25	12	4	0	8	4	2.00
Joseph Richardson	1826	6	0	-1.5	-	4		10	4	0.5			
Joshua Richardson	1874										8	0	-2.00
Isaac Stackhouse	1835	7	7	5.25	11	6	3.25	10	6	3.5	12	4	1.00
Jonat. K. Stackhouse	1841										9	8	5.75
Amos B. Stackhouse											8	7	5.00
John Watson	1844	10	9	6.5	10	3	1.2	16	6	2	12	5	2.00
James Wildman	1844	11	8	5.25	7	5	3.25	7	7	5.25	7	5	3.25
Solomon Wildman	1831	7	2	0.25	8	3	1.						
John Wildman	1842	6	0	-1.5	10	2	-.5						
Hampton Wilson	1831				11	8	5.25	10	9	6.5			
Joseph Wilson	1840				8	3	1.	8	5	3	10	5	2.50
Mardon Wilson	1874				8	14	12.	11	14	11.25	18	14	9.50
Jonathan Woolston	1828	11	3	0.25	11	8	5.75	6	5	3.5			
Jonathan Woolston Jr	1842										6	4	2.50

Surplus product of 1 cow or more, 27 families, 87%; surplus product of 5 or more cows, 11 families, 35%. (N=31 families).

SOURCE: Middletown Township Tax Records, HSP; US Census schedules, WRHS.

P = number of persons in household; C = number of cattle; Srpls = number of "surplus" cattle potentially produced for market

TABLE 9: Household Size, Cattle Owned, Cattle Producing Potential Marketable Surplus Dairy Products, Among Orthodox Data Set Husbands and Widows Resident in Middletown and Bensalem Townships

Name	Died	1800 P	1800 C	1800 Srpls	1810 P	1810 C	1810 Srpls	1820 P	1820 C	1820 Srpls	1830 P	1830 C	1830 Srpls
William Allen, Jr.	1837	7	3	1.25									
Thomas L. Allen	1856							7	2	.25	9	2	-0.25
Stephen Comfort	1826	9	6	3.75	10	6	3.5	4	1	0			
Sarah (Stevenson)											5	1	-0.25
Samuel Comfort	1860							10	12	9.5	11	15	11.25
Mary (Newbold) Jenks											8	0	-2
Pierson Mitchell	1834	12	5	1	11	8	5.25	4	2	1			
Joseph Richardson	1826	6	2	0.5	-	3							
Rebecca (Newbold)								8	3	1	11	2	-0.75
Clayton N. Richardson											6	3	1.5
Jonathan Stackhouse	1805	13	7	3.75									
Grace (Comfort)	1827				6	2	0.5	3	-				

Surplus product of 1 cow or more, 7 families, 78%; surplus product of 5 or more cows, 2 families, 22%. (N=9 family units).

SOURCE: Middletown and Bensalem Township Tax Records, HSP; US Census schedules, WRHS

P = number of persons in household; C = number of cattle; Srpls = number of cattle potentially producing surplus for market

Tables 8 and 9 show the number of people in the household (P), the number of cattle (C), and the estimated number of surplus or deficit cows (Srpls) for dairy production calculated for data set families at decade intervals over a thirty-one year span. In order to allow for the natural ebb and flow of economic activity due to the life cycle, we will credit each family at its point of highest production within this time span, and those figures have been made in bold type. Eighty-seven percent of Hicksite families enjoyed the surplus production of at least one cow over and above the needs of their households. See Table 8. Only 78% of Orthodox families had that much excess to dispose of on the market. See Table 9. But as the tax records do not differentiate among dairy cows, heifers, steers being fattened, or bulls, let us be more conservative, and only look at families who had, in addition to one cow for every four household members, more than three "extra" cattle. Sixty-one percent of the Hicksite families had at least three extra cattle, while only 44% of the Orthodox did. In addition, 35% of the Hicksites (11 families) had the surplus of five or more cows, while only 22% of the Orthodox (two families) had that much.

Ignoring the number of people within the household, Doherty calculated that in Chester and Delaware Counties, 59% of farmers owning more than four cattle became Orthodox, while 63% of the farmers who owned three or less, became Hicksites. It must be remembered that in the Middletown data there are only eleven Orthodox and thirty-one Hicksite cases, so the statistical comparison can not be given excessive weight. There is enough, however, to cast doubt on the universal applicability of Doherty's model.

Doherty concluded that the Orthodox were more likely to be involved in commercial agriculture, and not highly alienated from the world; in short, that they were committed to the acquisitive values of the wider society. Hicksites, he hypothesized, were not caught up in the world to the same extent. Their values were more likely to be non-commercial, they were more likely to be hurt by economic change, and therefore they should have been highly alienated from the world. But then we look again at John Paxson, president of the Farmers' National Bank; Michael H. Jenks, real estate and insurance agent and politician; and Mardon Wilson trying for the biggest mill on the creek and (in 1810) having the largest surplus of cattle among the data set families. All these men, who would seem to fit Doherty's profile of typical Orthodox Friends, became Hicksites.

A helpful consideration is Joyce Appleby's observation that an integral part of the broad evangelical movement aligned itself with the democratization of Thomas Jefferson. It extolled self reliance, disciplined work habits, and self mastery, thus eagerly embracing the new economic and civic opportunities.[20] With challenge and opportunity in the air, one was not obligated to accept a complete package predetermined by any authority. One could absorb the nascent market opportunities and the vigorous anti-authoritarian and anti-hierarchical attitudes while rejecting specific doctrinal ideas. This seems to be what many Middletown Friends did. It could be seen as a potential move toward Peck's level three skepticism.

Family Connection

The most important variable within Middletown Meeting was family connection. After the schism at the Philadelphia Yearly Meeting sessions the representatives went home and tried to line up support. It was then that the family and social linkages became critical. It should come as no surprise that Friends tended to choose the side where most of their friends and relations clustered.[21] Of the seventeen surname families under study, nine, or 53%, were completely monolithic: every individual in each of those surname families who was a member of Middletown Meeting between 1827 and 1850 was a Hicksite (in eight families) or an Orthodox (in one family). Three families (18%) were nearly monolithic, with only one or two exceptions, usually due to a spouse of the other branch. That leaves only five surname families that were anomalous.

Why were some families monolithic and others not, and why did they choose the faction they joined? We will look first at the issue of family solidarity.

The Comfort, Croasdale, Gillam, Kirkbride, Linton, Longshore, Watson, Wildman, and Wilson families were completely monolithic in terms of meeting affiliation of those who were Friends in Middletown between 1827 and 1850. See Appendix 5. The Blakey, Paxson, and Woolston families had only a few exceptions, and as we shall see, they tend to prove rather than overturn the rule of family solidarity. It seems, then, that the evidence is clearly weighted in the direction of family solidarity. Therefore we must examine the exceptions to this general pattern in order to try to understand them.

There appear to be three general explanations for individuals who broke with the pattern of their family's affiliation. Some married into another family with a different affiliation. In those cases the couple generally chose to adopt one family's pattern. Other individuals exhibited a general disaffection for the Society of Friends and its behavior surrounding the Separation. This might be called the "plague on both your houses" syndrome. This could also be an opportunity for someone near the "indifferent" end of the passion scale to drop out, while not actually resigning. However, the disaffection or indifference was not severe enough to lead them to make a formal relinquishment of membership. Finally, for some Friends there appeared to be occasional instances of low family cohesion, or family tension that did not encourage the value of solidarity.

We will look first at cases of individuals marrying into a family with a different affiliation, what might be called "mixed marriages". The only two Blakeys who joined the Orthodox were Rachel and Tacy, who both married Orthodox men. The only Middletown Orthodox Paxsons were William and his wife Ann (Canby) and their daughter Frances. The Canbys were a strongly Orthodox family. William J. Jenks, of a Hicksite nuclear family, became an Orthodox when he married (in 1851) Lydia Ann Martin, a member of that branch.

The Hicksite Stackhouse family intermarried with the Orthodox Comforts, and displayed an interesting pattern. See Appendix 5, pages 256-257, 278-281. When a Comfort woman married a Stackhouse man, she and her children were Orthodox: Grace (widow of Jonathan), to whose house the Orthodox retreated on Ninth month 7, 1827, and her two Middletown daughters Mercy (unmarried) and Macre (with her husband John Buckman, Jr.). Another branch of the family were the children of William Stackhouse (died 1826). Their grandfather Samuel Allen was named guardian. The eldest, Sarah Stackhouse, amicably resigned her membership in the Hicksite meeting in 1837 when she married Samuel Comfort, an Orthodox. After her death, Samuel married her younger sister, Mercy Ann. The Hicksites disciplined her, but do not seem to have disowned her; the Orthodox never accepted her as an official member. Their sister, Elizabeth Y. Stackhouse, married William Gillam, of a monolithic Hicksite family, and she remained an active Hicksite. Their youngest brother, Samuel Allen Stackhouse, married his third cousin, Sarah Allen and joined her in the Orthodox Meeting.

Another example was John Wildman, who removed to Falls in 1811 and therefore dropped out of the data pool. But it is of interest to note that he married Ann C. Comfort and joined her in the Orthodox meeting, leaving the rest of his family who were Hicksites.

The only Orthodox in the Woolston family in Middletown were Lydia (Jordan), the third wife of Joshua (1755-1821), her daughter Lydia, and her step-daughter Ann who married Aaron Comfort in 1816. They all removed to Falls in 1817, before the Separation. The other step-children were Hicksites, along with their Middletown Woolston cousins.

Perhaps the most striking case of "mixed marriages" was the Richardson family. See Appendix 5, page 277. The first generation of the family in Pennsylvania was Joseph, the shopkeeper merchant who became quite wealthy, but whose many activities in the meeting (including serving as treasurer) could be interpreted as subordinate to his business interests. His wife Mary (Paxson) was more active in the meeting. All of their children, with the exception of Rachel who died at the age of twenty-three, were active to some degree in Middletown Meeting. Joshua, who overcame drinking and slave-owning problems, and Ruth, served as treasurers of the men's and women's meetings, respectively. William was a minister, and he and his wife Elizabeth (Jenks) were very active. Nearly half of the third generation lived through the Separation. They divided roughly evenly between the two branches. Two of Joshua's daughters became Hicksites while the one who married William Allen became an Orthodox. The widow of an active son, Joseph (d. 1826), was very involved in the Hicksite meeting. Not unexpectedly, the children of the Allens remained Orthodox, while the children of the others were Hicksites. The children of Joshua's brother William, the minister, and his wife Elizabeth (Jenks) included two very active Orthodox daughters and an Orthodox widowed daughter-in-law. Their son William, who married Anna Paxson, was, with his wife, an active Hicksite. The pattern here is that the nuclear family of Joshua was Hicksite except for those who married into strongly Orthodox families; the nuclear family of William was Orthodox except for the son who married into a strongly Hicksite family.

Thus we can conclude that while most families remained monolithic, a few individuals changed their affiliation to match that of their spouse. This happened most often when the spouse was a Comfort. The Canbys and Allens were also strongly Orthodox and influenced most of their spouses to join them.

There were some exceptions, that is, spouses who refused to change their affiliation. As the decades went by, the Hicksites were untroubled by this, but the

Orthodox continued to require an acknowledgment and condemnation of such a marriage "out of unity" with the meeting. Examples were Sarah Taylor, the second wife (married in 1844) of strongly Orthodox Thomas L. Allen, and Sarah Rodman Paxson, the wife of his son Marmaduke W. Allen (married in 1856). Both women remained active Hicksites. Another exception was Joseph Jenks, an inactive Hicksite who voluntarily relinquished his membership in 1844. In 1827 he had married his second cousin Elizabeth Jenks, an Orthodox. By the time of her death in 1884, Elizabeth was associated with the "Primitive" splinter of the Orthodox branch. Elizabeth Pierson Jenks was an Orthodox who married the Hicksite George Yardley, while her brother William Pierson Jenks was a Hicksite who married the Orthodox Elizabeth Story. All four seem to have maintained their pre-marital affiliations.

The second explanation of a break in the solidity of a family's affiliation is perhaps a disillusion with the Society of Friends, and its disunity and lack of love. It could also be an indifference to the spiritual dimension of life. It appears that two cases fell into this "plague on both your houses" category.

Samuel Allen (1757-1833) was one of the few Friends who was not disowned by either faction. He was also not given any committee assignments by either meeting after the Separation. In his earlier years Samuel had been quite active in the meeting, serving as assistant clerk and overseer. But in 1803 the family removed to Falls. When Samuel returned in 1821 he was in his 60s, and was given fewer and fewer jobs, his last assignment being before 1827. In 1826 he was named guardian for his widowed daughter's children. Ann (Allen) Stackhouse returned to her father's house in Bristol from New Garden Meeting, but did not turn in her certificate of removal until 1828, after the dust of the Separation had had time to settle. She handed it to the Hicksite meeting.

Her father is not mentioned in the minutes of either Orthodox or Hicksite meeting. But except for him, his children, some of his grandchildren, and the two mid-century Hicksite wives mentioned above, all the Allens were staunchly Orthodox. Why wasn't Samuel disowned by one or the other? It may be that he attended meetings for worship of both groups from time to time. He may have been one of the fourteen "neutrals" identified but never named, in Eighth month, 1827.

It may be that he lost faith in Friends because of their unloving behavior towards each other and towards him and his grandchildren. A descendant claims that Samuel's grandson David Stackhouse, the only grandchild who did not appear in either Orthodox or Hicksite lists, was barely literate. David was on the Bristol township records in 1827 as a poor child, to be educated at public expense.[22] If young David Stackhouse was acknowledged as a member of either meeting, Friends should have provided for his education. It is peculiar that although his siblings were members as adults, David never appeared in the records after his certificate of removal was recorded. Although the documentary evidence is slight, one hypothesis is that Samuel Allen became disaffected with Friends around the Separation, and while never actually relinquishing his membership, distanced himself from both meetings for business, tending to the real needs of his daughter's destitute children. It appears that perhaps his grandson David, whose descendants were not Quakers, shared those feelings. Samuel's eldest son, Samuel (1782-1868), however, became an active Hicksite. Another son, David, who removed to Philadelphia, was also a Hicksite. But youngest son Benjamin's widow, Sarah (Gaskill) with her four children, returned to Middletown in 1846 and the Orthodox meeting.

Another possible example of apparent disaffection was Richard S. Paxson. One of his brothers was John Paxson, active Hicksite, farmer, and president of the Farmers' Bank. Another brother was William who, with his wife Ann (Canby), lived in Philadelphia where both were Orthodox. His oldest sister, Anna, was an elder and clerk of the Hicksite women's meeting.

Richard and his wife Elizabeth (Shoemaker) lived in Philadelphia at the time of the Separation. He had been apprenticed to his uncle Isaac Paxson to learn the hardware business, and had become a successful hardware merchant. In 1843, at the age of fifty-five, he "retired" to become a gentleman farmer at "Farley", an estate in Bensalem. Ordinarily, the family would have sought and obtained a certificate of removal from their Philadelphia monthly meeting to the Middletown meeting of their choice. This was not done. Nor had it been done when the family had moved from the Western District Monthly Meeting (Orthodox) to the central area of Philadelphia. In 1832 a certificate of removal for their minor children had been forwarded from Western District Monthly Meeting to Philadelphia Monthly Meeting (both Orthodox), and in 1843 a certificate was sent from Philadelphia to the Orthodox meeting in Middletown. This was Orthodox practice for any children listed on their books, including those from before the Separation, regardless of the affiliation of the parents. As an indication of where the sympathies of the family might have lain, the parents were not included in the certificate, and their two eldest daughters, after they turned twenty one, were disowned for being Hicksite by Philadelphia Monthly Meeting. Because the parents were neither disowned, nor appear in the minutes, the assumption is that by the time they moved to Bucks County Richard and Elizabeth must have been fairly nominal Quakers. Their children likewise appeared uninterested. Although their certificate of removal was duly recorded by the Middletown Meeting (Orthodox), there was no other mention of them, not even when they married. The point here is that Richard and Elizabeth and their children did not care enough about the two factions within Quakerism to make their affiliation clear.

A third explanation of the breakdown of family solidarity, at least in the Jenks and Mitchell families, seemed to be the presence of coolness, if not animosity within the family. In other words, there was a lack of a sense of family solidarity in general, which would be expected to be reflected in a lack of solidarity of choice of affiliation. The evidence is quite strong in the Jenks family but purely circumstantial in the Mitchells.

At the time of the Separation Pierson Mitchell and his sister-in-law the widowed Ann (Willett), joined the Orthodox branch. Pierson had been very active before the split, and continued to be active, in a decreasing role as he aged, after the schism. He was named to the committee to visit, assist, and advise preparative meetings as they struggled to find their footing after the Separation. The family solidarity pattern would predict that the children of both these Friends would be Orthodox. By 1827 all of Ann's children were removed from Middletown, disowned, or dead. A number of her grandchildren, however, namely the children of Hannah (Comly), were Hicksites. As the Comlys were a strongly Hicksite family, this could be explained by the "marrying into another family" rule. However, two of Pierson's sons were married, living in Middletown, and also very active in the Hicksite Meeting. All their children and grandchildren remained Hicksites. Pierson's wife (she had died in 1815) had been an Allen; in his will Pierson bequeathed $30 to his brother-in-law William Allen, "as a mark of my esteem for him"; his estate included a note for $36.30 of Thomas L. Allen's. Pierson's son John Allen Mitchell had married Tacy Stackhouse, a family that was noted for switching from Hicksite to Orthodox to match their spouse's affiliation. But in spite of all those close ties with the strongly Orthodox Allen family, John Allen Mitchell became a Hicksite, as did his brother. It is tempting to speculate that there was something in the relations between the father and sons that encouraged a break. But without better evidence, we must not carry it beyond speculation.

Evidence is stronger that the Jenks family displayed a lack of family solidarity. See Figure 5. There seemed to be a combination of disaffection within the family, and a lack of deep commitment to spiritual growth.

The progenitors of the family, Thomas and Mercy (Wildman) Jenks were both very active in Middletown Meeting and extremely long-lived. Thomas died in 1797 at the age of 97; Mercy had died ten years earlier. Their six children were a mix. Son John was disowned for fornication; his young widow was later disowned for the same offense. Son Joseph was never assigned any meeting jobs, two daughters and son Thomas, Jr. were given minimal tasks. But daughter Elizabeth and her husband William Richardson were very active in the meeting. In the third generation, none of the family were actively involved in the ongoing business of the meeting, and two sons of Thomas, Jr. were disowned for fornication. Perhaps clinging to the memory of their grandparents' piety, the three members of that generation who were still alive in 1827 and could be traced, became Orthodox. The fourth generation, however, shows a scattered pattern. Three of the sons of William (d. 1818) and his wife Mary (Hutchinson) followed their mother's example and were Hicksites, even though two married Orthodox women.

The fourth son, who died in 1823, left a young widow who followed her natal family's pattern and became Orthodox. The four daughters, however, were Orthodox, although one married a Hicksite.

This record, by itself, would not tell us that the family was undergoing tension. But in his unpublished memoir, Michael H. Jenks tells his story of hard feelings between himself and his brother Joseph over the affections of a young woman. Joseph deceived their father over the matter, with the result that Michael was "cut short of at least $1,000" in his father's will. Joseph, who did not have much business sense, finally married his Orthodox second cousin Elizabeth Jenks, and (Michael snidely recorded) lived off her money. Although Michael and his bride moved in with his step-grandmother, who was "a pretty tart individual and liked to have her own way in most things", the younger woman was able to get along well with her and help care for her. But when the old woman died, she left "all" to her blood relations, even though she had come into the marriage a "poor girl". Later Michael recorded that he visited New York to scout future sites in case he and his brother William could not agree on a price for him to buy out William's share of their father's homestead.[23] So running throughout Michael's account were tensions and distrust among family members.

The references to religion in Michael's unpublished autobiographical notes took the form of surface pieties rather than the deep spiritual exercises with which these tensions could have been met and overcome. Therefore, since neither family solidarity nor spiritual growth were operative priorities for Michael and the others he wrote about, individuals drifted into whichever branch of the Religious Society of Friends best suited. But which branch suited best, and why?

Although it seems clear that family solidarity was the most important variable for determining why an individual chose to join the Hicksite or Orthodox branch, that begs the question of why the various families made the choices they did. Some Friends who were closer to the indifferent than to the passionate end of the scale of commitment would probably continue attending meeting for worship in the same building to which they were accustomed to go whichever faction was in control of it. Since in Middetown that was the Hicksites, such Friends would

THIRD GENERATION

⎡Joseph R. m(1) 1792 Sarah Watson
⎢ 1767-1858; 1767-ca. 1800
⎢ removed 1797 to Philadelphia
⎢ m(2) Ann West (d.1842)
⎢ m(3) 1844 *Ann Ely* (d. 1854)
⎢*Rebecca* m 1801 *Jonathan Fell*
⎢ 1775-1832; 1771-1829
⎢ removed 1801 to Philadelphia
⎣*Mary,* unmarried
  1777-1854

⎡Margaret m 12/11m/1783 Samuel
⎢ Gillingham
⎢ 1764-1841; 1762-1846
⎢ removed 1781 to Buckingham
⎣William m 1790 **Mary Hutchinson**
  1766-1818;

Italic = Orthodox
Bold = Hicksite

FOURTH GENERATION

⎡*Elizabeth* m 1827 **Joseph Jenks**
⎢ 1793-1884; 1792-1869
⎣*Watson* m *Julianna Justice*
  1794-1855; -1852
  removed to Western District MM
─**Hannah W.** m 1843 *Stacy B. Collins*
  removed to New York MM
  -1885; 1791-1873

⎡**Joseph** m 1827 *Elizabeth Jenks*
⎢ 1792-1869; 1793-1884
⎢**Michael Hutchinson** m(1) 1821
⎢   **Mary Earle Ridgeway**
⎢ 1795-1867; -1846
⎢ removed 1837 to Makefield
⎢ m(2) 1848 Mary Canby (d. 1849)
⎢ m(3) 1851 Ann Higgins (d. 1854)
⎢ m(4) 1856 **Sarah Leedom** (d.
⎢   1880)
⎢*Elizabeth Pierson* m 1725 **George**
⎢   **Yardley**
⎢ 1797-1884;
⎢*Charles* m 1823 *Mary Ann Newbold*
⎢ 1798-1823;
⎢*Mary Palmer* m 1827 Edmund
⎢   Morris
⎢ 1804-1875;
⎢**William Pearson** m 1837 *Elizabeth*
⎢   *Story*
⎢ 1807-1886;
⎢*Ann* m 1831 *Charles M. Morris*
⎢ 1810-1870;
⎢ removed to SDMM
⎣*Susan W.* m 1838 **Franklin Fell**
  1812-1837
  removed 1837 to SDMM

Fig. 5: Simplified Jenks Family Chart Showing Hicksite and Orthodox Affiliation
For more detail see Appendix 5, pages 262-263.

become, by default, Hicksites. This inertia might explain the affiliation of the seven unmarried Kirkbride sisters, who did not appear to be active in the women's meeting. Their youngest brother, Jonathan, was absent from Middletown during the split, but after his return in 1830 he became very active in the Hicksite men's meeting. It could also explain the affiliation of the widow Sarah (Hirst) Linton who was never given a task by the women's meeting. She had no close relatives in Middletown Meeting until April, 1827 when her son returned from eight years in Stroudsburg. James was nominally active in the meeting. He and his wife Ann (Croasdale) and the younger children who lived with them, joined the Hicksite branch. But inertia might only account for a few Friends.

An investigation to uncover other factors starts with the Comfort family because it exhibits a remarkably simple pattern plus a connection with a well-known Friend. There were nine Comfort siblings who grew up during the reform movement of the third quarter of the eighteenth century. The oldest, John, married Mary, the daughter of saintly John Woolman. Although John Comfort and Mary removed from Middletown in 1771, and both had died before 1827, all of their children who can be traced, were Hicksites. However, every single one of John Comfort's siblings and their spouses, children, children-in-law, and grandchildren and their spouses who were traced were Orthodox.

If we assume that the Comfort family should have been uniformly Orthodox, and this was a simple case of "mixed marriage", nevertheless we want to know what it was about the influence of John Woolman that made his grandchildren Hicksites.[24] Woolman epitomized a genuine experiential radical Christian Quakerism. The fundamental thrust of his life was to bring ever more parts of himself into obedience to the Inward Christ. Although he was concerned about maintaining the discipline, he came to this position not because he wanted to enforce rules, but because he knew that outward behavior reflected the inward spiritual condition. It was this inward relationship with God that he worked to encourage and nurture in himself and other Friends. A large strand of Hicksites held to the traditional Quaker position emphasizing the necessity of the inner work of Christ. Orthodox, on the other hand, were very verbal about the outward work of the historical Jesus, through his death, resurrection, and atonement. A strand of Orthodox were the ideological descendants of those who wanted to tighten enforcement of the rules for the sake of conformity.

This is a very intriguing theory. But is it too simplistic to explain the Comforts? Were they level twos compared to the advanced fourth level of John Woolman? The Comforts were the grandchildren of Mercy (Croasdale) Comfort, who was the daughter of the minister Grace (Heaton) Croasdale, one of the spiritual rocks of her generation. See Appendix 5, pages 256-257. Among Mercy's children, Ezra and Mercy (Comfort) Phillips were ministers, Grace (Comfort) Stackhouse and Stephen and his wife Sarah (Stevenson) were elders. Her grandson Samuel (the son of Stephen and Sarah) was very active. Why were Mercy, Grace, Sarah, and Samuel all ardent Orthodox? Could it be that as they sought to gain for themselves the strong faith their mother and grandmother had had, they had trouble finding it within the growing indifference of Middetown Meeting? In frustration did they seek for spiritual guidance outside of their meeting, among Philadelphia Friends? We have not found their names among non-Quaker Bucks County evangelical associations. But with their wealth and ties to Philadelphia Friends, they would have been well aware of the messages brought by evangelically-inclined British Friends and their American sympathizers.

The Comforts fit the economic profile of wealth which Doherty advanced, but they were not the recently upwardly mobile (and hence socially insecure) model he hypothesized. They had ties with wealthy urban Philadelphia Orthodox Friends. For example, William Evans, an important Orthodox player in the 1827 Separation, stayed with the recently widowed Sarah (Stevenson) when he visited Middletown Meeting Eleventh Month 30, 1826.[25] Without diaries or other primary materials, the historian cannot "prove" why the Middletown Comforts identified with the Orthodox branch of Friends. We can note that they, more than any other Middletown Orthodox family, fit the economic profile other scholars have found correlated with the Orthodox position. But so in many respects did Hicksites like John Paxson, Michael H. Jenks, and Mardon Wilson. It appears that the Comforts, with their wealth and compatibility with Orthodox Friends in Philadelphia, were drawn into the network of city Friends deeply influenced by travelling British ministers and other evangelically-inclined Friends. With their tendency to be actively involved in the meeting and a family pattern of being deeply concerned with spiritual life, it is quite possible that the Comforts were not satisfied or nourished by the growing indifference or level two contentment in Middletown Meeting. As a family they seem more concerned with their faith than most in the meeting at this time, and probably sought out others who could share with them on a deeper level. Their connections led them to Friends in the city who happened to be evangelical and who were eager to share their new insights and enthusiasm.

In some respects the Blakey family paralleled the Comforts in its attention to spiritual matters. Minister William Blakey was a quiet but strong influence on his children, as was his brother Joshua on his family. But these Friends seemed to find the nurture they sought within the traditional Quaker framework of the "inner work of Christ".

The Allen family is more difficult. They were not especially wealthy. There was only Thomas L. Allen's ecumenical activity to enable us to predict that the family would be identified with the Orthodox, and he was not involved in the business meeting committee assignments of the Orthodox meeting to the same degree as, for example, his uncle William, and cousin Martha. Thomas was only asked to help purchase the land and materials for the construction of a new meeting house. The close ties between Pierson Mitchell and the Allen family probably had a strong influence on reinforcing their mutually-held ideas and ideals.

Let us turn the question around and ask why the other families became Hicksites. First, we should note that this label is a misnomer. It was used as a pejorative attempt to smear all non-Orthodox with the characteristics and beliefs of their most aggravating and extreme spokesman, Elias Hicks. The only thing Hicksites had in common was their opposition to the Orthodox. Although much of the language of the dispute concerned doctrine, and indeed that is the way the Orthodox saw the struggle, at bottom the fight was over who would exercise moral and spiritual power within the Society. Who would decide the answers to the doctrinal questions?

The evangelical theology led to a rigid morality that sought to impose strict rules of outward behavior concerning such things as temperance, education by rote, Bible reading, and sexual restraint. Traditional Quaker morality had stressed that right living would grow out of a right relationship with God.[26] Orthodox saw tendencies to dilute the Christian content of Quaker faith, and to admit undesirable ideas from Unitarians which undermined what they had experienced as necessary for salvation. Hicksites saw the wealthy urban elders and Meeting for Sufferings attempting to force the rest of the Society to subscribe to their views. The Orthodox treatment of Green Street Meeting, when it tried to appoint its own ministers and elders, was seen as a naked power grab, and a warning of what could happen to other non-Orthodox meetings. An unknown number of Hicksites saw it in political terms, or as a reflection in the religious arena of the struggle over enlarging democracy which was taking place in American politics.[27]

Although there is an element of truth to the description of Orthodox as enforcers of outward rules and Hicksites as seekers of an inward relationship with the divine, this distinction is too partial and incomplete. Not all Orthodox were at level two; not all Hicksites were at level four. While it might be justified to suggest that a majority of Orthodox were level two, it certainly cannot be said that a majority of Hicksites were level four. A good number of them were also level twos, and some were level threes.

Historians have identified a variety of factors which characterized Hicksites. However, because they were such a disparate group, joined only by their opposition to the Orthodox, we should not expect to find all the factors present in any given Hicksite. One factor was a distrust of the city, of powerful wealthy urban Friends, and of newfangled changes that were threatening the known, seemingly ageless, rural life. Edward Hicks epitomized this aspect most stridently. William Blakey, in his quiet, consistent, and gentle way, simply turned his back on aspects of the emerging culture that were at variance with his life with God. But many Middletown Hicksite Friends, like John Paxson, Mardon Wilson, Isaac Stackhouse, and Michael H. Jenks, energetically and enthusiastically embraced the new changes. They seemed not to spend a lot of time working on their spiritual lives. From time to time they exhibited actions which seemed like level two and at other times like level three.

A quite different factor of opposition to the Orthodox that became Hicksite by default, were the small minority of Friends who accepted Enlightenment rationality. The Longshore family, increasingly as the century progressed, less so before 1827, epitomized this position.

There was little in the earlier generations to hint of the nineteenth-century developments in that family. The first generation, Euclydus and Alice (Stackhouse) were active in the meeting, but never held office; they were not wealthy. None of their children were active in the meetings for business; none became wealthy. The second Euclydus had two wives and sixteen children; the family was so poor that the children were sent out as they grew large enough to go elsewhere for work. His son Abraham had a "natural taste for reading", and a desire to get ahead, with the willingness to work hard. Abraham's wife, Rhoda (Skelton) was characterized as having "quiet, solid hard sense" and "earnest, practical goodness"—traits much needed by reformers. Their son, Thomas Ellwood Longshore, was fifteen at the time of the Separation. He "read Elias Hicks' sermons carefully, and much of the controversial Friends' literature of that period with interest and eagerness". He became "the first in the family to embrace antislavery, total abstinence, non-resistance, woman's rights, hygiene in diet, and to work for the enlightenment of others." All of the family eventually came over to those views. In his later life Thomas (or T. Ellwood as he sometimes appeared) read widely in higher criticism of the Bible, and wrote extensively, introducing these ideas to many Friends. His wife, Hannah E. (Myers) graduated from the Female Medical College, and Thomas supported her practice with clerical and "practical" help. His brother, Joseph S. Longshore, was a physician, helped to establish the Female Medical College, and was very active in the temperance movement. Their youngest sister, Anna Mary, was also a physician.[28]

A significant group of Middletown Friends who did not subscribe to the liberal social ideas of the Longshores, were caught up in the rationalism and economic liberalism seen in the emerging capitalist culture. It is interesting that in the city this trend correlated with Orthodoxy. In rural Middletown it cut across both factions. Both Orthodox and Hicksites were involved in improvements and "progress". In fact, because there were more Hicksites, more of them were involved. So it is not very helpful to posit economics as a determining factor.

Referring back to the discussion in Chapter 6, it is possible to suggest that those who were deeply involved in the "acquisitive society", who spent the majority of their time and energy on improving their financial position, were probably not level fours. A level four has a higher priority than the single-minded determination to get rich, although it is the rare one who follows John Woolman's example of conscientious attention to the *full* implications of his or her livelihood and possessions. But here we can begin to trace the split between level twos, with their interest in the institution of the church (meeting) and the enforcement of the discipline, and level threes with their skepticism of dogma and of religious establishments and authorities, and of a deeper interest in social action. As the century progressed the faint outlines emerge that the Orthodox were settling into level two, and the Hicksites into level three.

A great deal of anti-Orthodox rhetoric concerned the defense of religious liberties against the domineering Philadelphia elders who sought to impose doctrinal orthodoxy on Friends who traditionally treasured the relationship each individual had with the Inward Spirit of Christ. Earlier Friends had assumed that the Light would lead into unity. It was a relatively short step from the importance of the individual relationship with God to assigning increased importance to individual belief and individual responsibility for salvation. With this new emphasis, doctrinal unity was felt to be less important than individual liberty of conscience.[29] It is hard to find evidence of this new interpretation in the records of Middletown in the 1820s, although as the century wore on, a broad toleration began to emerge as more clearly defining the Hicksite branch.

To sum up, in Middletown Meeting, most of the conflicting pushes and pulls experienced by others in the Religious Society of Friends and in the wider society were present. In the details of a single meeting we can see the complexity of these forces. Within the family, Friends learned, set, and reinforced their priorities. There they discussed and shared their ideas, fears, and dreams. Within the close-knit family culture, it is not surprising that families tended to orient, as a unit, to one faction or the other. So whole families tended to be involved in the wider culture of economic improvements and "progress", or tended to value the family farm and the old ways, or got caught up in progressive social activities, or felt deeply that only through doctrinal orthodoxy could the Society of Friends be renewed, or clung to their understanding of the old traditions and values.

In the final analysis, we can't say with total certainty why any given family joined the branch it did. All we can say is there are distinct patterns and few surprises.

The Separation indelibly shaped the Religious Society of Friends. Without the creative tension between the two factions, each was freed to emphasize its own peculiar and partial vision of Quakerism, unhampered by a corrective from the other side. The lure of the dominant culture increased its pull. Members of the two Quaker groups, who had so much in common before 1827, began to diverge on some issues.

CHAPTER 9: POLITICS, REFORM, AND FURTHER ACCOMMODATION

The last chapter described the 1827 split in Philadelphia Yearly Meeting. The Orthodox faction hoped to revitalize the Society by stressing the evangelical doctrines about which their non-Quaker neighbors and associates were so enthusiastic. The so-called Hicksite branch resented the authoritarian manner in which the urban wealthy Philadelphia Quaker elite was seeking to impose its will and doctrines. The dynamic at work in Middletown was more complex than the economic or social alienation Doherty hypothesized as the controlling variable for predicting who would become Orthodox or who would be Hicksite. In Middletown Meeting there were plenty of economically forward-looking men who were involved in a number of civic and improving projects, who rejected the Orthodox faction and its reforms.

It has been alleged that many Orthodox adopted a religion which enabled them to slough off the inconveniences of Quaker peculiarities for a set of formalized beliefs which would enable them to conduct their worldly affairs unencumbered by potential demands to subordinate ever-increasing areas of their lives to God's will. Among wealthy Philadelphia Quakers, or in the mid-west centered around Richmond, Indiana, this may have been the case.[1] However, in Middletown the strain which emphasized an outward conformity to the discipline, specifically the marriage and dress rules, was carried on in the Orthodox branch. In the years after the Separation, it was the Philadelphia Yearly Meeting Orthodox who kept rigidly to the letter of the law regarding marriage procedures and plainness of speech, dress, and house furnishings. The Hicksites, on the other hand, are usually stereotyped as conservative, clutching their traditional Quaker distinctives. They began to loosen enforcement of the marriage rules and the dress code long before the Orthodox did. In their growing acceptance of the importance of religious freedom, it must have seemed inconsistent to disown someone for marrying a non-Friend, or for marrying without proper meeting procedures, if the individual expressed an interest in remaining within the meeting. In a way this could be a faint continuation of that strand of the eighteenth century reform's emphasis on the need for the inner work of Christ. An individual's relationship with God was what was of crucial importance. Right actions would presumably flow from that relationship. However, it is only a very faint continuation of it because the serious intent to put one's spiritual life first seemed to be fading from individual Middletown Quaker's priorities. There were no Friends of the spiritual maturity and stature of William Blakey or Grace Croasdale in the second quarter of the nineteenth century in Middletown Meeting. Instead, there were dedicated workers enforcing the Orthodox discipline and upholding all the proper Quaker peculiarities. Across town in the older meeting house (rebuilt in 1793), Hicksites were equally involved in maintaining their meeting. As we have become familiar with the concept of faith development, it appears that Middletown Friends were mostly settled comfortably into the second level of formal, institutional faith.

This chapter will look at the political activities of members of the two branches, and their involvement in a variety of reform and civic activities. As in the case of economic opportunity and the new evangelical ideas, Friends were not faced with clear-cut decisions that forced them to confront difficult issues. Instead there was a lack of sharply defined crisis points in the political and social worlds. So Friends were able to drift and avoid tough choices. As the dominant culture grew more complex, reaching more pervasively and seductively into individual Quaker lives, the focus of life imperceptibly but decisively changed. More and more individual Quakers, in more and more areas of their lives, were drawn away from the inward spiritual focus to an outward accommodation with, even enthusiastic embrace of, elements of the dominant culture. This chapter will examine three areas of the dominant culture and Middletown Friends' relations with them: politics, reform movements, and other secular organizations.

Jacksonian Democracy and Middletown Friends

The relationships among government, the political process, and the Religious Society of Friends changed considerably in the seventy-five years after 1750. In 1750 Quakers were active in local and provincial politics and effectively controlled the levers of power at the provincial level and in many counties and localities. Because of the upheavals and traumas of the Great War for Empire and the American Revolution, members of the Religious Society of Friends had withdrawn from public office and refrained from voting. Gradually they became reinvolved in the political process. But the advices, culled from their marginalized dissenter experience in Great Britain as well as from their experiences in Pennsylvania, remained in the *Books of Discipline*.

These advices seemed curiously out of date for the hustling world of Jacksonian politics. They reflected a worry about taking of oaths, and advised Friends not to accept office nor promote other Friends for offices in which they might have to give or tender oaths. Mixed in with advice against becoming involved in war or military preparations, was the phrase from 1798 warning against "in any wise encouraging the unstable deceitful spirit of party, by joining with political devices or associations, however speciously disguised under the ensnaring subtleties commonly attendant thereon".[2]

Although the *Book of Discipline* did not give unequivocal guidance for coping with the enthusiastic and boisterous political activities of the second quarter of the century, not all Friends were at a loss concerning what course to follow. The experience of John Comly of Byberry (1773-1850), just over the county line from Bensalem, stands at one pole of the spectrum of Quaker options. As a young man John went with his father to exercise "his civil right of voting". There was high partisan rhetoric over the governor's race. Comly voted for the man the Philadelphia Quakers recommended even though Comly did not know anything about him. The opponent won and the country did not fall to ruin as prophesied in the heat of the election campaign. The same thing happened in the Senate race. When the governor was up for reelection, the Quakers urged Comly to vote for the incumbent—that same man they had so strongly opposed the time before. Comly, in disgust, refused to vote, and never voted again.[3] At the other end of the spectrum stood Michael H. Jenks (1795-1867) who plunged wholeheartedly into partisan politics and was rewarded with election as a Bucks County Commissioner, a term as county treasurer, a seat in the state legislature, and one term in the U. S. House of Representatives. Both of these men were Hicksites.

One of the underlying themes in the literature on the 1827 Separation is that American culture was moving in the direction of greater democratic participation. The Orthodox in some respects seemed like Federalists: knowing what was right for the masses and determined to keep power firmly in their own capable hands. The Hicksites, this theory says, were struggling for greater participation in decision making, for more local autonomy, and for the rights of individuals to their own private beliefs. There is no doubt that the latter saw the 1827 Separation in these terms. In the wider world of politics, therefore, we might expect to find the Allens and Comforts (Middletown Orthodox families) in the Federalist camp, and the rest of the Middletown Meeting data set families in the Jacksonian camp. This was not the case.

Historian Lawrence Kohl studied the political rhetoric of the Jackson era and concluded that at base it was a fierce argument over the shape of human relationships in the face of rapid transition from a "tradition-directed" society to one of individuals who were increasingly "inner-directed". The major issues of banking, currency, corporations, tariffs, and internal improvements were discussed in language that pointed to underlying fears about how each of them affected human relationships. Kohl found the Democratic party appealed to those who tended to cling to a web of traditional social relationships, and who felt that the modern institutions coming to birth were constricting and degrading. Although they liked the economic benefits of the new order they criticized its moral foundations, while struggling to break free of artificial social bonds. Whigs were more comfortable with the self-assurance of impersonal relations, with contracts, corporations, and voluntary associations. They were trying to reweave the social fabric— to preserve law and order—but on the basis of their own self-interest rather than on traditional communal interests.[4] There was no clear-cut Quaker stand in this argument. Elements within Quakerism embraced ideals of community and the integrity of personal relationships. Other elements within Quakerism espoused individual responsibility and equality. Friends were left to find their own way: whether to engage in politics or not, and if so, which party to support. By the 1820s the Religious Society did not see politics *per se* as a religious issue on which Friends were called to witness. However, there were issues within the realm of political discourse that could be interpreted as having religious ramifications.

In order to explore where individual Friends drew the line between the requirements of their faith and the opportunities which the dominant culture offered in the field of politics, we need to find two things. One is to discover which Friends were involved in political activities in the period from roughly 1824 to 1850, and the other is to discover which partisan causes they espoused.[5]

Most Bucks County Quakers who were active politically affiliated with the candidates and parties who supported internal improvements, the Bank, and encouragement of commerce and manufacturing. We must remember that within the confused squabbling of Pennsylvania politics there were Jacksonian Democrats who supported the bank and internal improvements as well as those who hewed more closely to the national party line espoused by Jackson himself.[6] The names of the anti-Jackson parties changed, from Federalist to Federalist-Republican, to Federal and Independent Republican, to Republican, to Democratic-Republican, to Democratic, to Whig. The names got so confusing that in 1824 many had given up on party labels altogether and just called it the party of the administration.[7] For a list of data set Friends involved to one degree or another in political activities, see Table 10. Out of 106 data set men who were living in the area as adults for at least part of the period from 1822 to 1850, 42% were involved in some political activity in addition to voting. Political activity of the period involved a number of activities. One called, attended and chaired public meetings or local conventions (formerly called caucuses) to advance or protest issues and nominate candidates. One could be on a local vigilance committee to watch that the election was conducted fairly. One could run for office.

Of the data set men listed in Table 10, nearly all were involved with the Federalist-Adams-National Republican-Whig configuration. Joseph S. Longshore,

TABLE 10: Data Set Men whose Names Appeared in Bucks County Newspapers as Involved in Political Activities, 1822-1850.

In Bensalem: William Allen Jr. (d. 1837), William Allen, Charles H. Paxson, Elihu Paxson, Isaac Paxson, John Paxson*, John R. Paxson, Jonathan Paxson, Joseph Paxson, Richard Paxson, William Paxson (dis), William H. Paxson, Thomas Stackhouse (N), Elwood Wildman (N), John Wildman, Jr. (dis, d. 1842), Joshua Wildman (N).

In Bristol Borough: Joseph W. Allen (dis), Samuel Allen, esq. (d. 1833), Samuel Allen, Jr., esq.*, William B. Wilson.

In Middletown: Marmaduke W. Allen, Dr. Thomas L. Allen, William Blakey*, William W. Blakey, Samuel Comfort*, Jeremiah W. Croasdale, Jonathan Gillam, William Gillam, Harvey Gillam*, Joseph Jenks, Michael H. Jenks* (before 1835), Thomas Jenks (dis, d. 1828), Jonathan Kirkbride*, Carey Longshore, John S. Mitchell, Joshua Mitchell, Samuel H. Paxson (after 1835), Clayton N. Richardson (dis), Joshua Richardson*, William R. Richardson, Jonathan [P.] Stackhouse, John Watson, Jr., William H. Watson, John Wildman (after 1840), William Wilson.

In Newtown: Michael H. Jenks* (after 1835), Phineas Jenks (dis), John Linton, Jr. (N), Mahlon B. Linton (N), Penquite Linton (N), Joseph S. Longshore.

In Northampton: Benjamin Croasdale (d. 1846).

In Southampton: Benjamin Croasdale (d. 1841), Ezra Croasdale (d. 1849), Robert Croasdale (d. 1847), Israel Paxson.

SOURCE: *Bucks County Intelligencer* and *Doylestown Democrat*
dis = disowned sometime before 1850
N = member of another monthly meeting: Byberry, or Newtown/Makefield
* = candidate or office holder

however, worked for Jackson in 1828. With his participation in temperance and abolition groups, he seemed to fit the level-three, social-activist, liberal mold. There were non-Quaker Stackhouse cousins who were active Democrats, as was Daniel T. Jenks, son of the disowned Thomas Jenks. At different times the names of Clayton Richardson and Penquite Linton appeared with both parties. But by and large Middletown Friends of both branches were Whigs.

A literal interpretation of the official yearly meeting advices regarding political activity left plenty of room for Quaker men to be drawn into the enthusiastic, highly-partisan political world. Friends who were already involved with non-Quakers in forming banks, buying stock in canal and other improvement companies, and worrying about the need for various reforms, easily and naturally joined political activities aimed at advancing their interests. The spirit of the age called for forming local associations to fix whatever needed to be remedied, to change what needed to be modified, and to invent what new institutions and methods needed to be created. The political style of the day was highly partisan, with very little regard for truth, sensitivity to others' motives, or compromise and conciliation.[8] There was no room for the old-fashioned Quaker values of moderation, strict honesty in all speech, and looking for the witness of God in everyone including opponents, in the no-holds-barred arena of Jacksonian politics. These virtues also played an unfortunately insignificant role in intra-Quaker disputes. No matter what Quakerly rhetoric these Middletown Friends might use, their mind set was in sync with the humanistic, improving doers of the antebellum northeast.

A small incident will illustrate how far the majority of Middletown Meeting men had moved from the understandings which had underlain the adoption of the advices noted above. Early Friends took seriously the biblical injunction to "swear not at all", and they had suffered greatly for refusing to take oaths. Colonial Pennsylvania provided for an affirmation in place of an oath, and after the first flush of republican zealotry, so did the new Commonwealth.[9] When a tender conscience noted that the affirmation had become a formula replacing the words of the oath but seeming to have taken on its spirit, the Quaker establishment was not prepared to weigh seriously the concern.

Thomas Elwood Longshore was an interesting character who came from a rather poor family and embraced most of the radical reform ideas of the nineteenth century. He left home at the age of twenty-three, walked out to Ohio where he became a Garrison abolitionist in 1835, and returned to Middletown shortly thereafter. In 1850 he moved into Philadelphia so his wife could attend the Female Medical College. After she graduated he helped with the "clerical and practical part" of her practice. In 1844 he was concerned about the affirmation and how it had become a mere substitute for the forbidden oath. Earlier he had signed a will as a witness. After the woman died he was called to the probate court to affirm that he had witnessed it and that it was his signature on the document. He refused to say the words, but stated that he had watched her sign it. The judge threatened and cajoled. Joseph refused to alter his language. Finally in frustration the judge declared him deranged, and ordered alternate methods of probating the will.[10]

The absence of this affair from the minutes of Middletown Meeting is significant. Thomas should have brought his concern to the overseers, who should have helped him clarify and test his "leading". If they supported his act of civil disobedience, the meeting should have been informed. If they counseled him to stifle the leading and accept the approved formula of affirmation, then they would have reported his insubordination to the meeting. It appears that Thomas did not ask for help and support. This probably indicates both his own lack of humility and his not-unfounded sense of the probable lack of sympathetic understanding on the part of men in positions of authority in the meeting. In any event, it appears the spiritual state of the meeting was far different from what it had been, for example, during the Revolutionary War, when the probability of suffering for refusing to take the oath or affirmation of allegiance and abjuration forced Friends to think deeply about Quaker testimonies around these issues.

If we take the incident of Friendly silence around Thomas E. Longshore's refusal to affirm as an example of Middletown Meeting's general lack of interest in the internal questions of conflict between a politically-sanctioned demand and the leading of conscience, were there external issues to which we might expect

Friends to react differently from their neighbors? We will look at three issues: the Bank, Cherokee removal, and restriction of Black suffrage.

The Bank

The Bank of the United States was a major issue in Jacksonian politics. But it was not an issue which impinged directly on any well-known Quaker testimonies. It was not a cause for great excitement in Pennsylvania in 1828 because by and large Pennsylvanians were content with the system, centered as it was in Philadelphia. However, after Jackson's removal of federal deposits from the United States Bank, it became an issue of political controversy.[11] Because of the deep involvement of Middletown Friends in the formation and management of the Farmer's National Bank of Bucks County we would expect them to have firm opinions on bank issues. At the time of the fledgling Farmers' Bank's difficulties following the depression of 1817, assistance had been requested and received from Nicholas Biddle himself.[12]

Throughout the first half of 1834 the *Bucks County Intelligencer* reported a series of public meetings, the establishment of committees of correspondence, delegates sent to a convention in Harrisburg, and so on, protesting Jackson's "usurpations". The foremost usurpation complained of was his treatment of the United States Bank. It appears that the Friends involved with the Farmers' National Bank of Bucks County identified with Biddle and the U. S. Bank.[13] John Paxson, long-time Director of the Farmers' Bank, Michael H. Jenks, Jeremiah W. Croasdale, Thomas L. Allen, Joshua Mitchell, and Joshua Woolston were among those who spoke out. The bank became a major campaign issue in the fall of 1834. More data set Quakers joined the local "committees of vigilance": Jonathan Kirkbride, Joshua Richardson, James Linton, Jr., William W. Blakey, and Isaac Paxson in Middletown; Israel Paxson, and Ezra and Robert Croasdale in Southampton; Joseph W. Allen and William B. Wilson in Bristol Borough. Additional non-Quaker members of these families were also involved. The *Doylestown Democrat* shrilly insisted that the anti-Jackson faction was really pro-Bank.

The editor declared that "Jos. S. Pickering is a blockhead". He was a Friend and long-time Clerk of the Farmers' National Bank.[14] The "national whigs", as the local anti-Jackson party sometimes called itself, won the Congressional and two of the four Pennsylvania Assembly seats in the County.

Banking was not a religious or spiritual issue *per se*. A Friend at Peck's level two would see that the meeting's advice did not prohibit it. Someone at level three would not care what the advices said if right or justice demanded action. Friends largely indifferent to all but formal membership could be drawn into secular activities supporting their economic, or other interests. Many individual Friends from both branches of the Religious Society of Friends were involved with the Farmers' Bank and the larger banking issue. Nearly all of them supported the Bank against Jackson. They worked hard to influence public policy concerning it. Clearly Friends were quite ready to become involved in political activity if they felt moved. The next two issues were ones in which Friends might have felt moved to become involved, not because of their economic interests, but because of their religious principles.

Cherokee Removal

President Andrew Jackson refused to enforce the U. S. Supreme Court's order setting aside Georgia's conviction for murder of a Cherokee Indian. He also refused to enforce the Supreme Court's 1832 *Worcester v Georgia* decision forbidding Georgia's removal of the Indians. The Jackson-dominated House of Representatives tabled an order which would have allowed federal forces to restrain Georgia's eviction of the Cherokees. Friends responded to the blatant injustice fueled by greed and racism with which whites grabbed Cherokee farms, houses, factories, and land, forcing them on the death march which became known as the Trail of Tears. Quakers had a long tradition of friendship and support for Native Americans. Middletown Meeting had experienced a personal tie when young Henry Simmons, Jr., the son of Mary (Paxson), went to western New York from 1796 to 1800 to work with the Oneida Indians, teaching them farming.[15]

Even before the *Worcester* decision there had been a flurry of editorials and letters in the *Bucks County Intelligencer* protesting Jackson's policies towards the Indians. It was listed as the next important reason, after support for internal improvements and domestic manufacturing, for voting against Jackson in 1830.[16]

Although presumably Middletown Quakers were outraged by this uncivilized treatment of Indians who had largely adopted "white" social, economic, and political institutions, there is no evidence of public meetings, petitions to Congress, or the sorts of activities engaged in when the Bank was threatened. There were large numbers of Middletown Friends involved in the pre-election activities of the early 1830s but there is no direct evidence that it was Jackson's treatment of the Indians rather than his treatment of the Bank which galvanized Friends into action. Friends were involved in meetings called to protest the deposit withdrawals. There were no meetings called to protest the Cherokee removal. The outcry regarding the Bank was louder than that regarding the Cherokees, at least as recorded in the *Bucks County Intelligencer*.

Carroll Smith-Rosenberg found the Davy Crockett myth used to justify jingoism, racism, and sexism as "natural" for young American males. If the sexual language and diatribes of Jacksonian America were metaphors for the political, economic, and sexual power relations within the dominant culture of the time, it is interesting that the Quakers rejected it. Friends seem to have stuck to their older ideas of peace and fair treatment of Native Americans. As a result of the tenacity with which they resisted the new mythology, Quakers were harshly depicted. When an elderly Philadelphia Friend was jailed for not paying a fine in lieu of military duty, the *Doylestown Democrat* thought it right and just. The *Bucks County Intelligencer* was outraged by the sentence.[17]

There is no direct evidence that Middletown Meeting Friends were exposed to excoriation or that they took substantive action or spoke out publicly against the injustice being done to the Cherokees. So on an issue where one might expect God-centered people to cry out, the reaction of complacent Middletown Friends seems to have been mostly silence. This can be interpreted as the reaction of level twos. The rules did not require involvement, and thus activities which could have had potentially unpleasant social costs could be avoided. The level two need not be seen as so calculating, however. There is a fair amount of genuine unawareness at this level.

Restricting Black Suffrage

Pennsylvania's revolutionary 1776 state constitution had been replaced with a more conservative one in 1790. By the mid-1830s discontent was voiced over excessive gubernatorial patronage, life terms for judges, and restrictions on the power of the legislature to charter corporations and authorize banks to issue notes, among other things. An uncontested referendum to hold a constitutional convention was passed quietly in 1835. The convention sat from May 1837 to February 1838, with a long recess for the October elections. The end result, with one exception, was a more democratic document.[18] The exception was a new restriction of the suffrage to white males.

The issue might not have been raised at all if it were not for an incident in Bucks County. In the October 1837 election, the Bucks County Democrats attributed their defeat to Black votes, and went to court. Judge John Fox ruled that Blacks were not and never had been eligible to vote.[19]

With their early struggle to gain clarity regarding opposition to slavery among Friends, and their concern for Black people as evidenced by meeting committees to oversee the welfare of freed Blacks, one might expect Friends to be outraged at this assault on Black civil rights. The *Bucks County Intelligencer* printed a letter to the editor deploring the exclusion of Blacks from the suffrage. In response, "OPQ" launched a diatribe against abolitionists on the grounds that Negroes "are created inferior in all respects". "A Republican" in Newtown then protested disqualification on the basis of skin color. But the writers of the rest of the articles in the period fell all over themselves trying to prove that the anti-Jackson candidate for governor, Joseph Ritner, and his party were or were not abolitionists–the hated epithet of the time.[20] There was no outcry by numbers of Friends against this injustice, although there is no reason to suppose the two letters opposing such racism were not written by Friends. There were a few individual Quakers, including Oliver Schofield in Newtown, who were well known for their stands in favor of abolition and increased rights for Blacks. What is clear is that Friends as a group did not see this as a moral issue upon which they felt compelled to act. Again, as in the case of the Cherokee removal, the lack of Middletown Friends' reaction implies a second level of faith development.

Summary

This brief look at a few political issues of the Jackson period indicates that in places where a wholehearted commitment to the radical implications of Quakerism might have led Friends to political positions very different from those of their non-Quaker neighbors, Friends did not move in those directions. A large group of Middletown Meeting men were deeply involved in partisan politics in ways that supported their social and economic interests. In this respect they did not differ from their neighbors who similarly worked the political system to favor their interests. Black suffrage and injustice to Native Americans, which we in the early twenty-first century might regard as moral issues, had identifiable roots in earlier Quaker testimonies. But they were not energetically addressed by the group of politically active Middletown Friends. When there was a choice to espouse causes that had no direct economic interest to them and carried potential social costs, Friends were mostly silent. The silence was greater regarding the issue closer to home. It was much easier—then, as now—to champion the cause of the distant oppressed than to become involved to fight local oppression which is embedded in our own psychological, social, economic, and political matrix. One hallmark of a radical living faith is its willingness to do just that. Judged by this criterion most Middletown Quakers in the antebellum period had traded the radical imperative of their faith for comfortable and convenient conformity.

Although there was no official Quaker stance regarding political activity, there is more to Quakerism than official pronouncement. From its rise in seventeenth-century England, and never completely forgotten, the Religious Society of

Friends has understood that it calls for living amid the political and economic world of humans while giving ultimate allegiance to God. Friends are to be in the world but not of it. This implies more than obeying the do's and don'ts of the *Book of Discipline*. It implies orienting one's life to the divine. It means to be involved in the ongoing life of the wider community without accepting the standards or moral blinders of that society.

John Comly, who eschewed even the minimal act of voting, steadfastly set as his goal the inward life. His outward life of farmer and school teacher was organized so that he could be free to follow the urging of the Inward Guide to travel in the ministry. His *Journal* is more detailed than many, in its insights into his spiritual growth and the process of Quaker ministry and its relationship with the faith community. With his priority on the kingdom within rather than the rewards of the world, Comly found politics a distraction.

Michael H. Jenks, on the other hand, while giving lip service to Quaker values in his unpublished memoir, put his priority on his own agenda: getting on in the world, evening scores regarding old hurts and slights, and taking pleasure in the rewards which the world can offer. I think we can assume that members of Middletown Meeting ranged along a spectrum bounded by the inward and the outward orientations symbolized respectively by Comly and Jenks, with the great majority finding Jenks decidedly more compatible.

Reform Movements

Historiography

Sydney James noted the trauma which Friends suffered as they lost political and social influence at the Revolution, and he hypothesized that Friends then turned to humanitarianism in order to retain or regain some degree of influence and social approval. He ignored the experience of British Friends, also deeply involved in philanthropy and reform without having suffered the trauma of Philadelphia Friends. He also ignored the roots of humanitarianism dating back to the very beginnings of Quakerism.[21] Historian Joyce Appleby notes that the geographical, economic, social, and political mobility of the post-Revolutionary War generation unravelled the older authorities and constraints on behavior. In response many people enthusiastically embraced a new role as reformers, hoping to demonstrate that "uncoerced cooperation and voluntary efforts could do the work of central government and established churches."[22] In other words, active engagement to improve society was wide-spread. There is no doubt that at the close of the eighteenth century, and increasingly as the nineteenth century progressed, numbers of Friends were deeply involved in philanthropy and efforts to reform society at large—as were non-Friends. Some of these efforts involved only Quaker allies, others were undertaken with members of a variety of denominations.

There was another dynamic at work, possibly unnoticed at the time. The traditional Protestant dogma held that right doctrine would inform social consciences, which in turn would galvanize action to build a just social and political order. In the individualism of the new republic, however, benevolence was privatized and separated from the public sphere. The result was a permanent divorce of religious bases from political policies addressing poverty and charity.[23] Whether as cause or result, there was a flowering of voluntary associations to promote a variety of worthy charities and tackle a plethora of perceived social problems.

Historian Thomas Hamm points out that coalitions with evangelicals encouraged Friends (consciously or unconsciously) to change their thinking to be more in tune with their ecumenical partners.[24] If, as James suggested, the initial impulse of Friends to humanitarianism came from an urge to gain respectability and influence, evangelicalism provided another push into reform movements. English Quaker Joseph John Gurney, for example, urged Friends to become involved with non-Quaker evangelical reformers because it was the Christian thing to do to promote Sunday Schools, Bible study, temperance, and so on. Gurney was identified with the most evangelical wing of the Orthodox faction, his name eventually providing their label: Gurneyites.

On the other hand, probably the most famous nineteenth-century Quaker reformer was Lucretia (Coffin) Mott, a Hicksite at the opposite end of the spectrum from the Gurneyites. There is, then, confusion over which branch of Friends was involved in reform movements. Not all Orthodox followed Gurney's example. There was also a strain which followed John Wilbur who exhorted Friends to uphold the old advice against mixing with other denominations, and to beware of "creaturely activity" (that is, any kind of outward activity which was not directly prompted by God).[25] The anti-Orthodox were also divided into outward-looking ecumenists who joined reform movements and inward-looking conservatives who banded only with other Friends. And, of course, within all strains of Quakerism the majority went about their daily business and did not become involved in any reform activities. Although some of these variations can be understood in relation to levels of faith development, the passion/indifference scale is also helpful. There were apparently some Friends whose commitment to searching for the implications of their faith was such that they did not see the connections between Quaker beliefs and the need to work for peace and justice.[26]

What these analyses lack is the larger context of the major shift in the dominant culture from what historian Lawrence Frederick Kohl calls the old "tradition-directed" world of personal relationships and communal controls and the new individualism of the "inner-directed" Whig world of rational self-interested human relationships and the need for self-control. The latter, largely congruent with evangelical Protestantism, saw church, school, and voluntary associations as the major tools for inculcating morality and self control. Their goal was to enable every man [sic] to be able to seize the opportunities being offered for material success.[27] Friends were found in both tradition- and inner-directed camps.

Quaker Response

What was the "correct" stance for Friends? The different answers to that question fueled further separations. The spectrum of Quaker responses to reform was more complicated than the spectrum of responses to political activity. Parallel to political action, Friends could keep entirely free of reform work, or throw themselves into it, with all steps in between. But there is another dimension.

Quakers have had a series of testimonies which require them to behave in certain ways: the peace testimony, for example, and the testimony against owning slaves. In other words, built into Quakerism is the requirement that one's outward life reflect one's inward obedience to God. It also holds out the possibility that this obedience might call an individual Friend to a more strict application of principle than the lowest common denominator of Friends. For example, the refusal to use products made by slave labor never became an official testimony, but some Friends felt compelled to abstain from such articles, while others felt free to buy, sell, and use them. Building on their understanding of the necessity for one's outward life to witness to living under divine instruction, Friends could expect to see a variety of responses to calls for action to promote God-favored causes.

Another way to draw a spectrum of responses to reform movements is to return to the concept of levels of spiritual growth. A level-two person would be more likely to engage in reform movements in order to control disorderly elements of society. The level-three person often throws himself or herself into social action out of a passionate desire to work for peace, justice, or whatever is seen as necessary to improve the lot of the downtrodden. Sometimes this is done to avoid doing the personal inner work necessary for spiritual growth. The level four, however, will personally live in such a way as to witness to his or her understanding of what is required to live in God's realm. From the outside, many of the activities may look very similar, but they spring from different motivations. The ways individuals at different levels interact with reformers from different denominations might also vary. We can assume, I think, that all these levels were present to some degree among members of Middletown Meeting, with level twos probably being the most prevalent. Two reform issues, temperance and abolition, will serve as case studies.

The Temperance Movement

Rather than labelling the temperance movement as a conservative response to social change, historian Ian R. Tyrrell wrote that it was supported by people concerned with economic and moral improvement who saw it as a means of perpetuating social progress. Temperance flourished in a society in transition, strongly supported by people trying to bring about the changes which were convulsing the United States. There was a correlation between commercial farmers and manufacturers, those who were optimistic promoters and beneficiaries of social and economic change, and those who supported temperance. These people wanted to shape society in their own image, to manipulate the environment to remove the obstacles to moral and material progress. Those with deep faith in human potential for improvement fueled both the evangelical and the temperance movements. One did not cause the other; they both arose from the same social and economic ferment.[28] These people most typically represent elements from both second and third levels of faith development.

The per capita alcohol consumption was higher between 1790 and 1830 than at any time before or since in the USA. By 1830 an average of 4.3 gallons of hard liquor and 2.8 gallons of beer, cider, or wine—over seven gallons per year— were consumed by each person in the United States including children, slaves and those who did not drink. With the rise of the temperance movement the tide abruptly turned; by 1840 the annual per capita consumption fell to a little over 3 gallons total. By 1850 it was well below three gallons.[29] The *organized* temperance movement began in 1811 among Presbyterians in Philadelphia, followed by Methodists in 1816. In 1826 the American Temperance Society was formed.[30]

Quakers had begun advising moderation much earlier. See Table 11. One of the earliest voices for temperance was that of Elizabeth Lewis (or Levis), whose 1761 writing was "suppressed" at the time, but reprinted seventy years later.[31] Anthony Benezet spoke and wrote against distilled spirits in the early 1770s. Bucks Quarter took the initiative against the use of distilled spirits at vendues in 1724. In 1794 it suggested that Philadelphia Yearly Meeting make distilling or participating in such activities in any way a disownable offense.[32] In 1845 the Orthodox yearly meeting reported that only fifty members out of several thousand used alcohol, down from the previous year; the Hicksite yearly meeting reported its use was "nearly banished".[33]

The influence of well-known early temperance advocate Benjamin Rush (died 1813), who had a knack for public relations, did much to publicize the ideas in social circles which were, perhaps, less receptive to Quaker or Methodist moralizing.[34] Temperance activity began picking up steam in the second decade of the nineteenth century as the social and psychological conditions were changing. In the 1820s the movement shifted its goal from moderation (temperance) to total abstinence. In the 1840s reformers entered the political arena, pressuring local governments not to renew or grant new tavern licenses. Next came the move for legal prohibition, exemplified by the Dow laws of Maine. Political election campaigns stopped the practice of treating potential voters with free booze, and the long newspaper columns reporting toasts at July Fourth celebrations faded away. The type of hard cider campaign run for William Henry Harrison quickly became anachronistic. Through the end of the 1830s the reform campaign had been led by an elitist coalition of evangelicals, industrial promoters, and general reformers. In 1840 the Washingtonian movement exploded onto the scene, led by reformed alcoholics who were reaching out to their blue collar brothers. They were concerned with saving individual alcoholics, not with general social reform. But by 1844 this movement was in decline, some elements co-opted and some frozen out by the reform establishment. Nevertheless, between 1830 and 1845 consumption of alcohol had halved and the public mores had shifted from acceptance of heavy drinking as manly, hardy, and brave, to being seen as a form of deviance.[35] With this very brief overview of the temperance movement to provide the context, let us turn to the data set families.

In 1804 Oliver Paxson, a minister in Buckingham Meeting and cousin of the Middletown Paxsons, wrote complaining about excess drinking at weddings with one or two hundred guests and feasting for two days. He wrote of harvests with twenty or thirty men of dissolute character and much rum: a quart per man. He worried about "the revelling,—the noise,—the obscene conversation,—the striving, and the waste of grain,—the gifts of heaven!"[36] By the late 1820s Mahlon B. Linton's name was in the newspaper connected with temperance activities. In 1831 he was recording secretary of the Bucks County Society for the Promo-

TABLE 11: Philadelphia Yearly Meeting Actions Against Alcohol Use and Abuse

---

1704 Discipline listed "drinking to excess" a disorderliness to be labored with

1706 Advised Friends to avoid vain and idle company, sipping and tippling drams and strong drink

1726 Friends forbidden to give or take distilled spirits at vendues

1738 Friends urged to discourage the granting of licenses for sale of any intoxicating liquors

1746 Friends advised to avoid unnecessary attendance at taverns

1762 Query: "Are Friends careful to avoid excessive use of spirituous liquors, the unnecessary frequenting of taverns, and places of diversion, and to keep in true moderation, and temperance, on the account of Births, Marriages, Burials, and all other occasions?"

1777 Friends ordered not to distill grain or sell it to be distilled (a time of bread shortage)

1784 Friends to be cautioned and dissuaded from importing or retailing distilled spirits

1788 Friends advised not to use distilled spirits as medicine without due caution

1789 Friends not to use distilled spirits at births, marriages, or burials

1796 Friends to be labored with who trade in or use distilled spirits

1806 Query addition: "Are Friends careful to discourage the unnecessary distillation or use of spirituous liquor?"

1831 (Hicksite) disownment for distilling, importing or selling liquor

1834 (Orthodox) disownment for manufacture, trade in, or sale of any intoxicating liquor except for medicinal, chemical, or mechanical purposes

1841 (Hicksite) Friends advised not to rent property or furnish any materials to "any such as our testimony against spirituous liquors may be violated"

1877 (Hicksite) Friends advised to avoid all intoxicating beverages

1883 (Orthodox) encourage Friends to abstain from all that can intoxicate

---

SOURCES: W. J. Rorabaugh, *The Alcoholic Republic*, 37-38; various Philadelphia YM *Books of Discipline*; Ezra Michener, *Retrospect of Early Quakerism*, 323.

tion of Temperance, and later served on its executive committee. His brother Penquite Linton was also involved. There were non-Middletown Paxson and

Watson cousins of data set families who took part. But the most active Middletown Meeting members in the temperance movement were Thomas Ellwood Longshore and his brother Joseph S. Longshore.[37] In view of how comfortable so many Middletown Friends felt with the political activities of the secular world it is somewhat surprising that so few were involved in temperance activities. We will return to this puzzle later.

During the 1830s local temperance groups were established in various townships and villages. In mid-1835 the Bucks County Temperance Society unanimously adopted total abstinence. An observer noted of Buckingham, that the "people are chiefly of the denomination called Hicksite Friends; very numerous in all this region, and, according to the rules of their sect, very exemplary, a great proportion of them, in respect to the use and traffic in strong drink."[38]

Joseph S. Longshore was a controversial Friend, as was his brother Thomas Ellwood Longshore who had refused to affirm in 1844. Thomas helped Joseph admit that he drank too much, and after his reform, Joseph threw himself wholeheartedly into the total abstinence movement.[39] He held temperance meetings in a local schoolhouse until the spring of 1845. Then, frustrated that the local tavern in Attleborough (formerly Four Lane s End), Middletown Township, continued to operate, Joseph set up sandwich boards warning of the evils of drink, rang a bell to draw further attention, and held weekly street meetings near the tavern. On September 2, 1846 a disturbance broke out, with tavern patrons and local Negroes hurling rotten eggs and epithets. Joseph was arrested, charged with "violent, abusive, intemperate, and inflammatory language", and tried. The trial lasted three days, with several Friends being called as witnesses. The judge left the bench three times during the proceedings to avail himself of liquid refreshment. Statements from both sides were rather provocative and intemperate. The jury found him guilty on three of four counts, and Joseph was fined $50. The fine was eventually remitted by the Governor. In spite of Joseph's strenuous efforts, in February 1847 the license was renewed for the tavern in Attleborough.

The interesting thing about the incident, however, was the heavy involvement of Friends supporting the tavern owner, and the response of Middletown

Meeting. The lawsuit was instituted by Joshua Richardson and three other men. Joshua also complained to the overseers of Middletown Meeting that Joseph had used "violent, inflammatory, and slanderous language in the public street, calculated to produce a riot and disturb the peace of the neighborhood, and for speaking evil of the dead." A few days earlier in a private conversation with Simon Gillam (grandson of Simon mentioned in Chapter 6), Joseph had questioned how ministers all could be considered preaching with divine authority when some damned the temperance and other reform movements, and some praised them. From this conversation Simon forwarded to the overseers a complaint that Joseph "says that Quaker inspiration is all a humbug, and will carry the society to the devil".

Two overseers, John Allen Mitchell and Jeremiah W. Croasdale, called on Joseph. A second visit was scheduled to bring Joshua Richardson and Simon Gillam face to face with him. Charges and denials were made, reconciliation was eluded. The complaint was reworded to charge Joseph with "tale-bearing and detraction, slandering his neighbors and the Society of Friends" and taken to the preparative meeting, and then to monthly meeting. A committee consisting of John Paxson, Jeremiah Bunting, and young Jonathan Paxson was appointed to look into the charges against Joseph. Things were getting a little irregular, but Joseph agreed to proceed with the charges as rewritten, even though they were different from what the overseers originally had discussed with him.

At a second meeting at which all parties might bring witnesses, all the charges were dropped except one, that growing from Simon Gillam's original complaint. This was carried over because Simon had not been present. As there were no witnesses to the original conversation between Joseph and Simon, it was one man's word against the other's. The committee apparently believed Simon. Joseph refused to make an acknowledgment of his wrongdoing because he insisted Simon had misquoted him and misconstrued his intent. The two older members of the committee reported to monthly meeting that Joseph's conduct required an acknowledgment, which was not forthcoming. Jonathan Paxson, in opposition to his father, suggested that the matter be dismissed from the minutes.

Instead a committee was appointed to draw up a minute of disownment. Joseph was disowned Second month 5, 1847, even though there was clear disunity: nine Friends spoke in favor of the disownment and ten spoke against it. Friends do not vote in their business meetings, so it was not a question of majority rule. The clerk minuted that the weight of the meeting approved proceeding with the disownment. However, with such obvious disunity, it does not seem like right order to have minuted such a decision.

Joseph appealed to the quarterly meeting, held Fifth month 27 in Buckingham. A large committee was named to hear the case, and as permitted by Friends' custom, Joseph asked for the replacement of a number of men he felt would be biased. The committee brought its recommendation to the following quarterly meeting: Joseph was reinstated as a member in good standing. He thereupon immediately brought charges to the Middletown overseers complaining that Joshua Richardson and Isaac Livezey had defamed and slandered *him* and prosecuted him at law, a clear violation of the Discipline. Neither overseers or meeting ever took any action on Joseph's charges.[40]

The incident illustrates how far the men in authority in Middletown Meeting had strayed from putting spiritual concerns foremost in their lives. John Allen Mitchell received 6% interest on his investment in the tavern—in spite of the advice of 1841 not "to rent property or furnish any materials to any such as our testimony against spiritous liquor may be violated". See Table 11. The spirit of this advice would have prohibited furnishing the use of capital. But the literal words did not mention it, so as in the case of political activity, someone looking for a way around an inconvenient advice could ignore it. Joshua Richardson was an important shop owner in town. John Paxson was President of the Farmers' National Bank of Bucks County. Jeremiah W. Croasdale was a fairly wealthy farmer. By Tyrrell's account, one would think that these men, presumably profiting from the changes in the economic and social scene, would be attracted to the reform position. But perhaps because the irreverent, iconoclastic and outspoken Joseph Longshore, from a poor, non-socially respectable family, pre-empted the abstinence position, these establishment men felt the need to distance themselves from him and his stand. Richardson, Mitchell, Croasdale, and Paxson all held positions of authority in the meeting and were frequently named to the small committees involved in doing the meeting's work. There is no evidence that they concentrated on the inner qualification that is necessary for a life of spiritual depth.[41] Longshore's faction characterized Paxson as "well known for his judgment . . . but he esteemed that the majority should govern the church as well as the state, and that their decision should be law". Jeremiah Bunting, another elder, was described as one who "loved the reputation of the brotherhood much more than he valued truth and fair upright dealing."[42] The person who maintains the outward institution, who is concerned about upholding rules and appearances and maintaining proper respect, represents second-level faith development. A level-two Quaker might not understand that Quakerism is an invitation to a growing relationship with the divine, and instead would work hard to uphold its rules and institutions, thus missing the main point.

Joseph S. Longshore, in this period of his life, appeared as a man of third-level faith development. He was skeptical of received wisdom, questioned authority, and was passionately concerned with pursuing the particular social changes he felt were crucial. He lacked tact, forbearance, and love. His relationship with the divine seemed to have been theoretical and intellectual.

The meeting seemed to lack seasoned and wise elders and ministers who could sense where each individual was coming from, and encourage that which was good, while admonishing the pride, arrogance, and self-righteousness which marred the work of all involved in the affair.

Except for Longshore, the men participating in this incident seem to have had their attitudes formed by the secular culture. Without realizing the spiritual depth and richness which Quakerism could offer to reorient their lives, they unthinkingly acted as men "of the world". They did not seem to realize there was a difference between what they were doing and what Quakerism ought to have stood for—in terms of Quaker process, "sense of the meeting" decision making, the way to proceed with a "concern", and most of all, the inner work that is necessary to separate and clarify God's will from the world's way.[43]

It seems likely that other men in Middletown Meeting were so interested in distancing themselves from Longshore that they refused to become involved in the temperance movement. Phineas Jenks, a disowned Friend, and Mahlon and Penquite Linton of Makefield Meeting, all lived in Newtown. They were the only other members of data set families to appear in newspaper accounts of temperance activities.[44]

Abolition

Temperance and abolition were the two most important reforms of the antebellum period. Although members of the Religious Society of Friends understood that Quakers were not to own slaves, they were not united on how—or even if—that testimony was to be extended to others. As the idealism of the Revolution's rhetoric faded and was replaced with language and ideals of the market place, racism became increasingly overt. Many Quakers absorbed the dominant culture's attitudes.[45] However, there seems to have been a residue of either some sort of affection or a sense that Friends were not as hostile as other whites, because at least in Middletown people of color preferred (or were invited) to live in as employees of Friends more often than with non-Friends. See Table 12. In 1850 in Middletown Township slightly less than 4% of non-Quaker households included non-white residents, while about 33% of the Quaker households did.

TABLE 12: Residence of Blacks and Mulattoes in Quaker and Non-Quaker Households, Middletown Township, 1850

	Households headed by:				
	Non-Quaker white	*Quaker*	*Black*	*Mulatto*	*Total non-white*
Non-white persons living in household	23	36	99	51	150
Households in which non-whites live	11	26	29	10	39
Total households	294	79	29	10	39

SOURCE: U. S. census schedules, Middletown Township, 1850, WRHS.

Although most Friends in Middletown seem not to have done anything overt to oppose slavery in the 1830s or 1840s, there were a few Friends who felt that they must not only speak against slavery but work actively to change the situation. Such work took a variety of forms, from petition campaigns, to public meetings against slavery, refusal to use slave produce, work to aid free people of color kidnapped into slavery, aid to support and better the lot of free African Americans, and aid to escaping slaves—the underground railroad.

An examination of antebellum Middletown Quaker activities regarding what might broadly be termed race relations reveals an interesting spectrum. We can assume that underlying these actions was an even broader array of motivations, at which we can only hint. The great majority of Middletown Friends was silent and did nothing on this issue, as least as far as traces of words and actions can be found by the historian. It is not unlikely that some had business or commercial connections with the South and sympathized with, or tolerated, the white Southern position. Some eschewed controversy; they did not want to get in "trouble" with their neighbors. To some degree, most accepted the racism of the people around them, labelling Blacks as morally and intellectually inferior, hating racial "amalgamation" and social mixing, sharing racist jokes and stories.

A few Friends, troubled by slavery but also troubled by the thought of living with free Blacks, joined the Bucks County Colonization Society: Thomas L. Allen, a physician; Stephen and Joshua Woolston, half brothers who had moved with their father, Joshua, from Middletown to Falls; and Phineas Jenks, disowned for marrying a non-Quaker. The first was Orthodox, the second two were Hicksites. Joshua Woolston was one of the twenty-four managers of the Colonization Society, the other three were among the eighteen vice presidents.[46] Some members of the Colonization Society castigated the Buckingham Female Anti Slavery Society on the tired old biblical grounds that women should stay home and keep silent. A lively debate ensued in the pages of the local press.[47] The Buckingham women seemed to be on the cutting edge of the movement. They resolved not to purchase any goods made with slave labor, which the (men's) Bucks County Anti Slavery Society then adopted.[48] Phineas Jenks's non-Quaker wife Amelia (Snyder) was a member of the Newtown Female Temperance Society; Stephen Woolston's wife Elizabeth (Kelly) signed an antislavery petition. So it is hoped that these men did not subscribe to their colleagues' narrow view of the "proper" role of women. In any event, the more radical antislavery societies broadly castigated the Colonization Society, and the latter faded from the Bucks County scene.

During the petition campaigns of 1831, 1837, and 1841 a number of Quaker and other women in Bucks County—and all over the North—memorialized Congress to abolish slavery in the District of Columbia and the territories, to prohibit interstate slave trade, and/or not to admit any new slave states.[49] The following signatures of Friends with some Middletown connection were identified on what was probably a petition from Falls: Phineas Paxson and his wife Rachel W[oolston] and daughters Mary W. and Elizabeth; Carey Longshore, brother of T. Ellwood and Joseph S.; Susanna S. Albertson married to Charles Wildman (who as a boy had moved from Middetown to Byberry, which was the meeting of John Comly and Robert Purvis); Elizabeth (Stockton) Woolston, second wife of Stephen, an elder in Falls Meeting and half-brother of Rachel (Woolston) Paxson; Moses Comfort, Jr. and Mary and Rebecca Comfort. The last two women were either wives of brothers Stephen and Samuel, or daughters of Samuel; they were granddaughters-in-law or great granddaughters of John Woolman. All of these Friends were Hicksites except for Moses Comfort, Jr. A search through the National Archives' petitions was not exhaustive but it seems probable that only a minority of Middletown Friends either agreed with the request of the petitions or risked putting their signatures on them.

Moving towards more radical positions regarding abolition, next would be membership in the Bucks County Anti Slavery Society. Marmaduke Watson held meetings in his schoolhouse in Lower Makefield. Penquite Linton served as vice president of the organization. Mahlon B. Linton and the peripatetic Joseph S. Longshore were on the executive committee.[50] Marmaduke Watson, who married Mary Richardson and whose daughter married Thomas L. Allen, was Orthodox; the others were Hicksites. Being publicly identified with the Anti Slavery Society meant taking a public position greatly at odds with the popular sentiment of the

1830s. Longshore and the Linton brothers were also involved in abstinence activities. Joseph S. Longshore, in particular, seemed to have delighted in being a nonconformist. At this stage in his life he seemed to exhibit characteristics of the third level of faith development: a certain disregard for authority and a passionate concern to work for social justice.

A few Friends in Bucks County were involved in the underground railroad. The record, of course, is difficult to find as their acts were often illegal and therefore not publicized. Later hagiography can be suspect. However, it appears that among data set families, Mahlon B. Linton and his wife, Jolly Longshore and others in his family, and "the Paxson family" (probably of Solebury rather than Middletown) were involved. There were known to be stations in Bristol, Yardleyville, Buckingham, and Newtown. The story of one escaped slave secreted in the attic has come down in the William Richardson family. However, the majority of Friends did not approve of such activities. Oliver Schofield of Newtown was disowned by Makefield Meeting on charges obliquely arising from his underground railroad activities; it was overruled by Philadelphia Yearly Meeting and he was reinstated, but his health was broken.[51]

Although the dominant culture gave lip service to denouncing the evil of slavery, it was essentially a racist society and in the 1830s abolitionism was a dirty word.[52] After the October 1837 election Bucks County newspapers were filled with charges and countercharges surrounding a defeated candidate claiming his opponent's seat on the grounds that Blacks had voted for the opponent and their voting was contrary to law. Public meetings were called by the Democrats. Both parties competed to prove that they were not abolitionist.[53] But after the passage of the federal Fugitive Slave Law, public opinion in Pennsylvania began to shift rather rapidly. Although most Pennsylvanians detested Blacks, they discovered they hated slave catchers even more.[54]

Friends who chose to be involved in antislavery activities before the 1850s were definitely swimming against the current of public opinion, and against many of those wielding power within their own meetings. As with temperance, there must have been a variety of motives that can be analyzed with reference to levels of faith development. Some Friends would ask what Quakerism required as an institution. The answer could be narrowly interpreted in terms of what appeared in the *Discipline*: Friends could not own slaves themselves, they were to obey the constituted government unless expressly forbidden by a higher law, they were to be careful about joining with non-Friends for promoting social actions.[55] These were level-two formalists. It is most likely that the great majority of Middletown Friends, Hicksite and Orthodox, fell in this category. Some Friends would accept the liberal *zeitgeist* of a small group which strongly felt the need for reform on many fronts. Joseph S. Longshore fit this category at this stage in his life; he was not active in the ongoing committee work of the meeting. This is the social activist and skeptic of level three. Finally there may have been those Friends who asked not the question of the first group, but rather what God required. These Friends would have spent a great deal of time pondering, praying, and meditating. Their highest priority would have been to obey God's will, not the institution's, not public opinion's. It seems that John Comly and Oliver Schofield fit this category of level-four, mature faith. But it is hard to locate Friends of this level in Middletown Meeting; they were rare anywhere by mid-century. With the lack of these solid, centered Friends to form its core, Middletown Meeting was in danger of losing its foundation.

Looking through the names of data set Friends who were connected in some way with abolition activities reveals a connecting web. Few were involved who were not related in some way. But not all those who had family connections joined in the action. Joshua Woolston married Mary Richardson, whose first cousin, William Richardson, harbored an escaped slave. William's wife was Anna Paxson, sister of Phineas who married Joshua Woolston's sister Rachel. William's sister Mary Richardson married (her first husband) Marmaduke Watson and their daughter married Thomas L. Allen, the only Allen who seems to have been involved. Marmaduke was an out-of-town distant cousin; no other Middletown Watsons seem to have been involved. Several members of the Longshore and Linton families were engaged in the underground railroad.

Summary

This look at the temperance and abolition movements reveals the great majority of Friends observing from the sidelines. There is little evidence of congruence between those who accepted more evangelical theologies being drawn into these reform movements. More Hicksites than Orthodox were involved, given the proportions of the two branches of the Society in Middletown. Perhaps the lack of support from the majority of Middletown Friends indicates that they saw these activities in terms of evangelicalism, and therefore were not disposed to be sympathetic. But more likely it was their dislike of the radical Longshores and their desire to distance themselves from the causes the Longshores espoused.

There was a great deal of overlap between involvement in temperance and abolition. One hypothesis is that if one is going to risk social stigma by being a reformer, one might as well go all the way and embrace all the reform causes. Another is that once involved in one radical group, one meets people supporting a variety of other causes, and gets drawn into them.

Reform activity tended to run in families: one member would try to involve other family members. Thomas Ellwood Longshore made this explicit, claiming that he was the first to adopt each of the many reform enthusiasms, but eventually "all" his family came over at least "in part" to support these views.[56] It seems likely that the Longshores and Lintons got their primary support and sense of community not from Friends but from fellow reformers. But their identity as Quakers was important enough that they fought against disownment. In spite of lack of support or even hostility from other Friends, these reform-minded Quakers did not want to sever their ties with the Religious Society of Friends.

Non-Reform Secular Organizations

The Bucks County Intelligencer and other antebellum newspapers revealed a close-knit, face-to-face community which formed associations and societies to chase horse thieves, monitor elections, improve agriculture, study natural science, and engage in a host of other projects. The men exuded a spirit of self confidence, that they controlled their local destiny even if the nation was in the hands of a "tyrant" (i.e. of the "wrong" political persuasion). They considered themselves to be the ones who made things happen: canals, reforms, schools, the booming economy. The community seemed to accept and include white middle class males from a variety of protestant denominations. But they were incredibly, unself-consciously, unashamedly chauvinistic, sexist, racist, and prejudiced, bantering around their comfortable, accepted stereotypes of Jews, Irish, Blacks, and women. Some Quaker men undoubtedly found themselves quite comfortably part of this dominant WASP male culture.

How did Quakers react to the proliferation of societies and associations springing up around them? How should they have reacted? The answers to those two questions will help us to see how individual Friends drew the line between the requirements of their faith and the blandishments of the dominant culture. If a seventeenth-century Friend were magically transported to antebellum Bucks County how would he have reacted to the beckoning variety of voluntary groups? I suspect that he would first ask what God wanted him to do. The question would not be, whether to join or not join this group or that one. The question would be, where is the Light leading? That most nineteenth-century Friends did not see it that way is an indication that they had left the fringe of society where radically God-centered people congregate and had entered the social mainstream. They absorbed the assumption of their time that of course one formed societies—there were lots of things that needed to be done, and the way to do them was to form societies, hold public meetings, pass petitions, and so on. Their question then became whether to join only other Friends, or join whoever was working toward the same goals. Only those who devoted considerable time to the inward struggle to find God's will seemed to conclude that joining any extra-curricular group was superfluous. John Comly and Edward Hicks, for example, do not seem to have joined any associations. I am not trying to imply that joining a voluntary, secular organization was an un-Quakerly thing to do. Rather I am suggesting that most Friends at this time did not seem to address the option in terms of seeking God's will. Instead, they unconsciously absorbed their attitudes of acceptance from the dominant culture. They asked the wrong question.

Virtually every adult male in Middletown Meeting joined one or more groups in the 1830s and 1840s. Probably the data set family name most frequently seen in local newspapers was Dr. Phineas Jenks. He had been disowned for marrying a non-Friend, and attended the Presbyterian church in Newtown. Perhaps because he no longer felt constraints from the meeting he was able to throw himself into so many activities with such enthusiasm. He symbolized the energetic urge to join which characterized the age. He was president of the fledgling Bucks County Medical Society and of the Bucks County Lyceum; he was listed as part of the Bible Society. He and Joshua Mitchell were involved in a public meeting in Newtown of "friends of education" advocating public schools. Other Friends from Bucks Quarter named from time to time in this effort were Mahlon B. Linton (of Newtown), Stephen Woolston, George Comfort, Thomas L. Woolston (these three from Falls), J. Allen Mitchell, William Gillam, William Mitchell, Jeremiah W. Croasdale, Joshua Richardson, and Robert Croasdale (all from Middletown). The indefatigable Phineas Jenks chaired a public meeting of a Committee to Collect Relief for Ireland; Edward M. Paxson (Buckingham Meeting) was secretary, and Jolly Longshore, Jonathan Paxson, Mahlon B. Linton, Marmaduke Allen, Jonathan W. Gillam, Jonathan Kirkbride, Paxson Blakey, and Benjamin Croasdale of Bucks Quarter were also involved. Phineas was president of the Bucks County Agriculture Society, the third attempt to get such an organization going. Serving on committees, judging exhibits, or winning prizes between 1844 and 1850 were Bucks Quarterly Meeting Friends Jonathan Watson, Edward M. Paxson, John K. Paxson, Robert Longshore, William Watson, Abraham Paxson, James Longshore, Jolly Longshore, Ellen Longshore, Margaret Longshore, Reuben Watson, Thomas Jenks, James Wildman, James Stackhouse, John Linton, Benjamin Croasdale, Joshua Woolston, Abdon B. Longshore, Joseph Watson, Jonathan L. Watson, Marmaduke W. Allen, and Samuel Johnson Paxson.[57] It is obvious that being a Quaker, or from a Quaker background, did not prevent these people from participating in the group life of their secular community.

The Attleborough Protective Company

We will look in more detail at one voluntary organization to which most Middletown Meeting men who resided in that township belonged. (The meeting drew its membership from all or part of five townships.) This was the Attleborough Protective Company for the Detection of Horse Thieves and Other Villains and the Recovery of Stolen Property. Table 13 shows data set members as published in the *Bucks County Intelligencer* each year.

Horse thief pursuing companies proliferated in Bucks County from the establishment of the first one in 1809. In the 1830s, through the use of advertising, they shifted somewhat from their original role of reacting to thefts to preventing them. By the 1850s deterrence was seen as their primary function. By then there were over forty companies, averaging about fifty members in each. The prevailing view is that these horse companies grew out of the spirit of self-help endemic to the period. The annual meetings provided a welcome social event which helped cement the bonds of their white, male, Protestant members.[58]

The perceived problem needing to be addressed was rising crime spawned by proximity to Philadelphia with its riots and unrest. The city was close enough for thieves to sneak out, raid the peaceful and prosperous country side, then escape back to anonymity in the city's slums. However, although the population of Bucks County rose 66% from 1820 to 1850, property crimes (cases appearing in the criminal court docket) actually only rose 30%.

Historian Craig B. Little has shown that more was at work than a perceived rise in crime. This was a period of rapid and far-ranging change, inevitably accompanied by stress and insecurity. In particular, strains were felt around three issues: immigration of non-white Anglo Saxon Protestants (WASPs), increased urbanization, and industrialization. Increased immigration of Irish and people of color fostered a reaction of nativism. Although Friends had been involved in raising funds for Irish famine relief and in a variety of efforts to help freed slaves, this did not necessarily mean Friends wanted these people to live next door. However, in Middletown there was no overwhelming influx of Irish or of African Americans. See Table 14. The fear was not based on reality.

TABLE 13: Data Set Family Members of the Attleborough Protective Company with Hicksite/Orthodox Affiliation, 1839-1851

O Allen, Marmaduke W.- 1/1844, 1/1845, 1/1846, D1/1848, D1/1849, 1/1850, 1/1851
H Blakey, Paxson - 2/1839, 2/1841, 1/1844, D1/1845, 1/1846, 1/48, 1/49, 1/50, 1/51
H Blakey, William – 1/1846, 1/1848, D1/1849, 1/1850; Esq.: 1/1851
H Blakey, William W. - 2/1839, 2/1841, 1/42, 1/44, 1/45, 1/46, 1/48, 1/49, 1/50, 1/51
O Comfort, Jesse - 2/1839, D2/1841, D1/1842, D1/1844, Sec 1/45, S1/46, S47, 1/48
O Comfort, Samuel, Jr. – 1/1849, 1/1850, 1/1851
H Croasdale, J. Wilson – 1/1851
H Gillam, Harvey – 1/1846, Pres 1/1848, D1/1849, D1/1850, D1/1851
H Gillam, Jonathan W - 2/1839, D2/1841, D1/1842, D1/1844, 1/1845, D1/1846, D1/1848, 1/1849, 1/1850, 1/1851
H Gillam, Simon – 1/1846, 1/1848, D1/1849, 1/1850, 1/1851
n Jenks, Howard - 2/1841, 1/1842, 1/1844, 1/1845, 1/1846, 1/1848
H Jenks, Joseph - Pres 1/1842, 1/1844, Pres 1/1845, 1/1846
n Jenks, Thomas - 2/1841, D1/1842, D1/1844, D1/45, 1/46, 1/48, 1/49, 1/50, 1/51
H Kirkbride, Jonathan - D2/1839, 2/1841, 1/1842, T1/1844, T1/1845, T1/1846, T1/1848, T1/1849, T1/1850, T1/1851
H Linton, Joseph W. – 1/1850, 1/1851
H Longshore, Abraham – D1/1846, 1/1848, 1/1849, 1/1850, 1/1851
H Mitchell, Gove – 1/1851
H Mitchell, John S. – 1/1851
H Mitchell, Joseph Paul – 1/1845, 1/1846, 1/1848, 1/1849, D1/1850, 1/1851
H Mitchell, Pierson – S1/1848, S1/1849, S1/1850, S1/1851
H Paxson, Isaac - D2/1839, P2/41, D1/42, D1/44, 1/45, D1/46, 1/48, 1/49, 1/50, 1/51
H Paxson, Samuel H. – 1/1850, 1/1851
O Richardson, Clayton N. - 2/1841, D1/1842, D1/1844, 1/1845
H Richardson, Joshua - P2/1839, S2/1841, S1/1842, S1/1844, D1/1845, P1/1846, 1/1848, 1/1849, 1/1850, D1/1851
n Stackhouse, Joseph – 1/1846, 1/1848, D1/1849, 1/1850, D1/1851
H Watson, John, Jr. - D2/1839, D2/1841, 1/1842, 1/1844; without Jr: D1/1845, 1/1846, D1/1848, 1/1849, 1/1850, 1/1851
H Watson, Joseph - 2/1839, D2/1841, 1/1842, 1/44, 1/45, 1/46, 1/48, 1/49, 1/50, 1/51
n Watson, Stacy – 1/1851
H Wildman, Edward – 1/1851
H Wildman, James – 1/1846, D1/1848, 1/1849, 1/1850, 1/1851
H Wildman, John – D1/1848, Pres 1/1849, P1/1850, P1/1851
H Wilson, Mardon, Jr. – 1/1850, 1/1851
H Wilson, William – 1/1846, 1/1848, 1/1849

SOURCE: *B. C. Intelligencer*, in months and years published in the newspaper.

H = Hicksite; O = Orthodox; n = non-Quaker (i.e. disowned or the child of disowned parents); D = Director; P = President; T = Treasurer; S = Secretary

TABLE 14: Place of Birth of Inhabitants of Middletown Township and With Whom They Lived in 1850

People Born in:	People Living in Households Headed by:					Total
	Quaker	Non-Quaker				
		Irish	Other White	Black / Mulatto	Total non-Quaker	
Ireland	18	40	39	0	79	97
England	0	0	26	0	26	26
Germany	1	0	10	0	10	11
Scotland	1	0	0	0	0	1
Canada	0	0	1	0	1	1
Africa	0	0	0	1	1	1
Unknown	0	0	0	1	1	1
Pennsylvania	352	12	1389	106	1507	1859
New Jersey	3	0	80	12	92	95
Maryland	4	0	2	3	5	9
Delaware	0	0	4	3	7	7
New York	2	0	2	1	3	5
Ohio	1	0	4	0	4	5
Virginia	0	0	1	1	2	2
Connecticut	0	0	1	0	1	1
Georgia	0	0	1	0	1	1
Total Inhabitants	382	52	1560	128	1740	2122

SOURCE: U. S. Census schedules, Middletown Township, 1850, WRHS.

The urbanization of Philadelphia fostered an urban-rural stress that was reflected, for example, in the 1827 Quaker Separation. But how much of an actual threat was this to Middletown Meeting men who were deeply involved in improvement schemes and new financial opportunities? Having shaken off the constraints of Orthodox Philadelphia Yearly Meeting elders, were Middleotwn Hicksites at some level still fearful of urban interference and control?

The third cause of stress, industrialization, which was occurring in nearby areas, accentuated the division between factory workers and the small agricultural entrepreneurs of Bucks County who owned their own land, tools, and animals, and felt fiercely the need to protect them. Middletown Quaker farmers would have felt this. They probably had an "us/them" attitude toward immigrant canal laborers or textile mill workers. This attitude, of course, was quite contrary to the traditional Quaker call to respond to the Seed or Light of God in everyone.[59]

It is interesting to see who was absent from the membership list. Joseph S. Longshore, who seemingly joined every reformist cause, but was obviously not appreciated by the Middletown Meeting establishment, was not a member. As a reforming zealot, would he have wanted to join such a status quo club? Most horse companies acquired members by invitation; it seems the Middletown establishment did not want Joseph, whether or not he had wanted to join them. His father Abraham, however, was a member.

The Woolstons were the only data set family not represented in the Attleborough Protective Company. At this time there were no Woolston males living in Middletown township. Although several horse companies did list an occasional female member, the Attleborough Company did not. It is unclear if female members were expected to help ride a route (chasing a thief), or to take part in the social conviviality of the annual meeting, or if they just paid their dues.[60]

Should we have expected Quakers to join horse companies? Can we expect them to have been infected with their neighbors' uneasiness over immigration, urbanization, and industrialism? Would Quakers, too, fear crime—the loss of private property? In spite of advice from the Bible about not laying up treasures on earth where they are prey to thieves (as well as moths), or from William Penn about not becoming too attached to the things of this world, it is clear from the earlier discussions in this chapter that Middletown Quakers were heavily invested in the dominant culture and considerably less so in the deep spiritual orientation which Quakerism could offer.

Summary

It seems that as the middle of the nineteenth century approached, individually and corporately Middletown Friends had become less and less conscious of the distinctive imperatives to which their ancestors had been called. While this became increasingly true for the Hicksite branch in terms of plain dress, speech, and house furnishings, that is not really the point. It can be argued that these represented only outward rules and signs, and as such were a distortion of the original Quaker message anyway. More importantly, it seems that Middletown Friends wore their religion by habit rather than by conviction. While these men and women lived upright and respectable lives, the spiritual fires seem to have burned quite low. They seem to have unconsciously absorbed so much of the dominant culture that they did not even realize something was missing from their own well-ordered practice of Quakerism. What was missing, of course, was evidence of the palpable presence of the living God, the Inward Spirit of Christ who transforms and empowers. Early Friends expected this inward experience to transform their outward lives. They saw many of the hypocrisies of their time and refused to participate in them. Such fruits seemed quite scarce among Middletown Friends in the nineteenth century.

An application of faith development analysis helps us understand the great majority of Middletown Meeting in this period. As Wilber's blue memes, or Peck's level twos they were concerned for the literal interpretation of the discipline while unaware of the deeper spiritual implications of the advices. In addition to being stuck at the formalism of level two, many also were somewhat indifferent to faith issues, as measured by their involvement in the ongoing business of the meeting. We will examine this more closely in the next Chapter. Without sharp crisis points, they were not forced to examine their beliefs. Unexamined beliefs easily are pushed aside by more vigorously accepted ideas. Thus the dominant culture reached increasingly deeply into more and more areas of their lives.

We cannot prove this is what happened. All we can see are the recorded actions. Many of the men in Middletown Meeting absorbed the assumptions of the dominant culture that one should form and join organizations to address a variety of perceived problems. The Friends who chose political organizations tended to choose to become involved in issues that directly affected their economic well-being, while remaining silent on issues with a strong moral imperative which might have exacted a social cost. Most Middletown Friends identified with the

Federalist-National Republican-Whig parties and supported candidates against Jackson and in support of the Bank. They mostly avoided issues of injustice to Native Americans or people of color.

While they identified with forward-looking economic and financial activities, most Middletown Friends were not involved in the two most important reforms of the antebellum period, temperance and abolition. The most likely reason for a level two to avoid the temperance issue would be its local linkage with the unpopular, scandalous Longshore brothers. Before 1850 a level two was unlikely to be involved in abolition activities because the class of people who would be "improved" by the work were living at a distance, because the success of the movement might mean an influx of undesirable people, and because the most significant part of the work was against the law. A level-three person, however, questions authority and can be fired with zeal to help the downtrodden. It appears that in this period there were relatively few level-three Friends in Middletown Meeting. There is no historical evidence of active level-four Friends in Middletown at this time. Such people's lives would have spoken eloquently, even if they used few words.

As we have seen in other contexts, it was family connection rather than Hicksite or Orthodox orientation, which seemed to count most strongly in determining the degree and direction of an individual's social action. Those who were involved in temperance or abolition formed two webs of relatives: the Longshores, and the Woolston-Paxson-Anna (Paxson) Richardson-Mary Richardson-Marmaduke Watson web. The Lintons, sons of John in Newtown, formed a third web, just beyond our data set area.

As we approach the mid-nineteenth century mark, we need to put these families back into the context of their meeting and larger community.

CHAPTER 10: DATA SET, MEETINGS, AND TOWNSHIP IN 1850

Early on we compared the data set individuals and families with Middletown Meeting as a whole, and Friends as a group with Middletown Township, using a variety of economic and political yardsticks available for the mid-eighteenth century. During the hundred years covered by this study, many Friends absorbed a great deal of the dominant culture. In order to see if the data set people remained relatively representative of the rest of the meeting, or if Friends as a group had grown increasingly like their non-Quaker neighbors, we will make similar comparisons for the mid-nineteenth century. Because more data is available from 1850 than from the colonial period, we will be able to consider additional factors. However, the available data only allows us to examine external aspects of people's lives.

The Data Set Families and Middletown Meetings

The most obvious difference between Middletown Meeting of 1750 and of 1850 was that by the latter year there were two groups of Friends using that name. The lack of formal membership lists, noted in 1750, remained.[1]

The Orthodox assumed that every pre-1827 Friend was a member until disowned. They carefully and deliberately carried out the disownment procedure as each child, born before 1827, came of age, even if that person clearly identified with his or her parents' Hicksite affiliation. Therefore, reference to a disownment in the Orthodox minutes does not necessarily mean the individual had been, or intended to be, a member of that branch of the Religious Society of Friends.[2]

The situation with the Hicksite meeting was easier. On Ninth month 10, 1858 an official list of members was inserted in the men's minutes.[3]

In 1750 there had been 378 members of Middletown Monthly Meeting, some living in nearby townships. In 1850 there were eighty-six members of Middletown Monthly Meeting (Orthodox) and 292 members of Middletown Preparative Meeting (Hicksite), for a total of 378 Friends.[4]

Although the numbers stayed the same, there were other differences between 1750 and 1850. In the nineteenth century there were non-resident members; Friends had been disowned in the eighteenth century for leaving the area without a certificate of removal. In 1850 there were many "mixed" marriages in which only one spouse was a Friend, or a member of the same branch of Friends. Although the reform movement in the third quarter of the eighteenth century had tried to tighten up on marriage irregularities and strengthen the hedges separating Friends from the "world", by the mid-nineteenth century most Friends had come to see some people on the other side of the hedge as fellow Christians rather than as apostates. The Orthodox tended to feel more comfortable with Methodists and evangelical Christians. As the century drew to a close, increasing numbers of Hicksites became more comfortable with Unitarians and "social gospel" Christians who employed higher criticism in Bible study. These non-Friends did not seem as different, or as dangerous, as they had appeared earlier.

Participation

In 1750 approximately 35% of Middletown Meeting data set members never received an assignment to an office or one of the many committees which carried out the business of the meeting. We can assess this for four different groups in 1850, each of which had its own meetings and minutes: Orthodox and

Hicksite, men and women. But rather than do all the calculations for each meeting, we will use slightly different tests with each, resulting in a more varied picture of Friends.

Over the twenty-four years from Ninth month 1827 through Twelfth month 1850, nineteen Orthodox men were given tasks. See Table 15. These tasks represent all the official activities of the meeting, from clearing and overseeing marriages, to procuring a meeting house, to disowning "separatists" or others who did not adequately maintain the various testimonies. Through death or removal, not all men were there the entire time. The most jobs in any single year were thirty nine given to Samuel Comfort in 1828, when the Orthodox were obsessed with disowning the majority of the meeting which had separated from the (Orthodox) yearly meeting. Calculating on an annual basis, eleven men averaged two or more assignments a year, and four averaged eight or more, while one man, Samuel Hulme, averaged fourteen a year for the four years until his death in 1830. But this is misleading because of the huge bulge of activity in 1828 and 1829. By 1830 the situation was stabilized, and for the next twenty-one years the Orthodox men's meeting averaged 27.8 tasks per year, assigned to an average of 6.2 men.

Only slightly over six men, on average, were involved in any given year. There was an oligarchy consisting of William Allen, William Allen, Jr., John Buckman, Jr., Samuel Comfort, Aaron Eastburn, and both Samuel Hulmes. John Newbold and Evan Roberts were slightly less active. This lack of participation, or to put it another way, this concentration of power in the hands of a relative few, had been one of the major complaints by Hicksites against the way Philadelphia Yearly Meeting was being run, although it does not seem to have been a complaint within Middletown Meeting. Perhaps it became a characteristic of the Orthodox branch to feel that ability was concentrated in a few able hands and there was no need to broaden the power base.

A similar oligarchy ran the Orthodox women's meeting: Macre (Comfort) Buckman, Elizabeth (James) Comfort, Sarah (Stevenson) Comfort, Ann (Maris) Gregg, Mary (Richardson) Watson Hulme, Mercy (Comfort) Phillips, Ann Richardson, Rebecca (Newbold) Richardson, and Mercy (Comfort) Stackhouse. There

TABLE 15: Number of Tasks Assigned to each Man per Year, Middletown Orthodox Men's Meeting, Ninth month 1827 through Twelfth month 1850

Name	1827	28	29	30	31	32	33	34	35	36	37	38	39	40	41	42	43	44	45	46	47	48	49	50	died
Thomas L. Allen	1	28				1																			1856
William Allen	2	15	1	3	6	1	2																		1837
Wm. Allen, Jr.	4	21	9	4	9	5	10	7	4	4	5	3	5	5	4	3	2	1	1		1				1856
Thos. Branson																					3				1845
John Buckman, Jr.	36	20	14	9	6	14	8	6	6	7	8	3	2	4	6	7									1880
Jesse Comfort																1									1852
Josiah Comfort	21	4																							1880
Samuel Comfort	6	39	14	15	16	5	13	9	9	7	4	8	4	2	5	8	4	2	10	7	4	9		10	1860
Aaron Eastburn	1		1	2	4	5	3	2	1	2	6	2	4	3	2	7	4	6	5		22	1889
Jonathan Eastburn			2		1	2		7	2	3	4	3	6	1											1840
Joseph Eastburn																								3	
William Hicks														1		2	2	1		5	2	5		14	
Samuel Hulme	3	30	24	2													2	4							1830
Samuel Hulme																				5	5	4	6	3	
John Milnor		1																							
Pierson Mitchell	2	10	1	2	1																				1834
John Newbold	3	30	1	3	2	3	2	2	1																1842
William Paxson	2	5					3			3															1858
Evan Roberts									2	4	4	3	2	3	3	1	4	4	3	4	3	
M. Satterthwaite																			1						
Men involved	9	10	11	7	7	8	5	6	6	6	6	6	6	5	7	7	7	6	7	6	5	5		6
Total Tasks	23	178	83	43	45	24	41	37	27	26	19	24	31	19	18	27	23	11	33	23	20	29		45

SOURCE: Middletown Monthly Meeting (Orthodox) Men's Minutes, Quaker Collection, Haverford College.

NOTE: Josiah Comfort and William Paxson removed in 1829; Evan Roberts arrived in 1837; Thomas Branson arrived in 1839, removed 1846; William Hicks requested membership 1839; young Samuel Hulme turned 21 in 1837; Joseph Eastburn arrived 1847.

was an interlocking directorate of family connections. Macre was married to John Buckman, Jr., Elizabeth was married to Samuel Comfort, and Mary was married to Samuel Hulme. Mercy Stackhouse and Macre Buckman were daughters of Grace (Comfort) Stackhouse, and nieces of Mercy (Comfort) Phillips, as well as sisters-in-law of Elizabeth (James) Comfort. Sarah was Elizabeth Comfort's mother-in-law.

Rather than constructing a table for the women similar to the one for Orthodox men, we will use the women to calculate the percentage of involved Friends. During the period from Ninth month 1827 through Twelfth month 1837 there were fifty-six women who were members for all or part of that time. Of them, the nine above named, who constituted 13.8% of the women's meeting, were assigned 80.4% of the jobs. Each of the nine women handled from twenty-six to fifty-one tasks. Fourteen women, or 21.5%, had fewer jobs, while forty two, or 64.6% were not asked to do anything. From 1830 through 1837 the work was spread among twelve women, of whom two averaged 3.25 jobs a year, six averaged two assignments a year, and four women were only given an average of 0.4 tasks each year.

If oligarchy was a characteristic of the Orthodox branch, it is somewhat surprising that the Hicksite women's meeting shared a similar situation. As near as can be calculated, there seem to have been 300 women who were members at one time or another between Ninth month 1827 and Twelfth month 1850. However, this number is deceptive because of the high mobility of Friends. At least 106 arrived after Ninth month 1827, and ten attenders requested membership, meaning that 38.6% were not in the meeting at the time of the split. At least nine died (and probably a good many more), ninety three removed, nine relinquished their membership, and five were disowned in the period. So 120 women, or 40%, were not there by Twelfth month 1850. Of the 300 women who passed through the meeting in these twenty-three and one-third years, 116 or 38.6% were given at least one assignment by the meeting. Twenty-eight women, or 9.3% did the bulk of the work with sixteen or more jobs each. There were 184 women, or 61.4% who were given no tasks at all.[5]

Considering that women with young families were rarely given jobs, and if a newcomer was not already known by Friends it would take a while before she was entrusted with a task, and considering the high mobility, it is difficult to judge if general participation in the ongoing business of the meeting was greater or less than it had been under more stable conditions a century earlier. The figure for data set members in 1750 had been 35% non-participation. In the second quarter of the nineteenth century it appeared to be about 62% for all Friends—slightly lower among Hicksites, slightly higher among Orthodox. Two factors make the comparability of these figures suspect. One is the higher mobility in the nineteenth century. The other is the likelihood that the data set families, by virtue of their characteristic of remaining in the meeting over generations, were more likely to be involved actively in the business of the meeting. Still, it seems safe to conclude that there was less wide-spread participation in the ongoing business of the meeting by 1850. The most likely explanations involve an increase of numbers of Friends at the indifferent end of the passion/indifference scale, and the increase in seductive alternatives offered by the world outside the meeting.

Discipline

The situation regarding discipline was quite different in the mid-nineteenth century from what it had been a century earlier. In the earlier period 50% of discipline cases involved breach of marriage procedures or sexual mores. One sixth were alcohol related. The remaining third were a variety of miscellaneous offenses. One third of all cases ended in disownment.

Discounting Friends who were disowned for joining the Hicksite branch, and carefully selecting among those disciplined by both branches to assign them to the meeting to which they seem to have belonged, we arrive at the figure of twenty-one cases brought before the Orthodox meeting between 1828 and 1850. They involved nine women and twelve men. There were thirteen cases (62%) involving marriage procedures, one (4%) involving strong drink, and the remaining third (seven cases) for all other offenses. Several Friends were disciplined more than once. Five of those whose marriages were irregular offered acceptable expressions of regret. All of the other cases (71.4%) ended in disownment. Of the nineteen individuals being disciplined, fourteen, or two thirds, were disowned. This was twice the rate of disownments from a century earlier.

Five of the Orthodox Friends being disciplined had the same surname as a member of the oligarchy. Of them, two gave acceptable expressions of regret, although one of those was later disowned for another offense. The remaining three were disowned also. So the oligarchy did not treat its own relations more easily. However, the situation is a little less clear when viewed more closely. Samuel Comfort's son Jesse's acknowledgment for "outgoing" in marriage was accepted, as was that of Rebecca Richardson's son Clayton. Rebecca removed to Philadelphia in 1829, and two years later Clayton was disowned for swearing, suing a Friend, and striking a man in anger. Thomas Canby Hulme who joined the military, was the nephew, not son, of Samuel. The relationship between Emily Newbold, who joined the Episcopalian church, and Elizabeth Newbold who married without following proper procedures, and active Orthodox John Newbold, has not been traced. We can hypothesize that immediate family of deeply involved meeting members were persuaded to do what was necessary to remain within the fold. It seems clear that those joining the military or another church had no interest in conforming to what was required by being a Quaker.

The Friends most deeply involved in the discipline process were the group of most active members. Here I am discussing the discipline committees appointed by the monthly meeting, which visited each offender and counselled him or her to acknowledge the error, condemn it, and change behavior. Any quiet, one-on-one counselling did not appear in the minutes. Among the Orthodox, in 1828 fourteen women (87.5% of those who did any task) did discipline committee work, while only two who were assigned tasks, were not given these jobs. In the peak year of 1828, the six Orthodox men (66.6%) with heavy assignments did all the discipline committee work. The three men with three or fewer assignments served on no discipline committees. In the following years discipline committee work was spread among eight men, with two others being asked to do one, once.

That represents 50% of the men who did any meeting task. After that hectic year, from 1829-1837 eight women did all the discipline committee work while ten women did other committee tasks. Of the eight, four women did only one each, while the other four women did all the rest. It appears then, that once the extraordinary post-Separation discipline backlog was cleared up, the Orthodox women had a more closed system than did the men, but both had changed from the mid-seventeenth century when a larger percentage of Friends was engaged in the discipline process.

There was a considerable difference between the way Orthodox and Hicksites dealt with offenders. The former tried to adhere strictly to the rules, the latter tended to make allowances for individual circumstances. The most obvious example is the way each branch dealt with its "separated" former members. The Middletown Meeting Orthodox minority set about with great energy disowning the majority. They carefully followed the prescribed procedures: visiting each separated Friend, reporting his or her unwillingness to acknowledge and condemn the error, approving and signing a testimony of disunity, delivering a copy to the individual, then recording it in the meeting records. Children of Hicksite parents were visited when they became of age or married. That this was an unpleasant process is indicated by the numbers of Hicksites who refused to receive the Orthodox visits. Hard feelings were kept alive by this continued meddling, long after the Separation had occurred.

Once the Orthodox had begun to publish the names of Friends "disowned by Middletown Meeting", the Hicksite majority who also claimed that name felt compelled to compile their own list of those who had separated and for whom the group no longer "owned" responsibility. But rather than visiting each Orthodox twice, and writing up papers of disownment, the Hicksites merely minuted that these Friends were released from membership—it was obvious that they no longer considered themselves part of the majority meeting. As the years passed the Hicksite minutes mellowed, merely referring to a soon-to-be-former member as one who was "in unity with those friends called Orthodox".[6]

Economic Profile

In the mid-eighteenth century Quakers in Middletown had been wealthier than non-Friends. The four most wealthy men in the township were Friends. But in spite of that, Friends could be found across almost the entire economic spectrum. While most Friends, like most residents of Middletown, were farmers, they were also represented among the various secondary industries which serviced the predominantly agricultural economy.

The data on occupations and real estate valuations in the 1850 census show the relative positions of Friends a century later. See Table 16. Not surprisingly, the largest single occupational category continued to be farming, which accounted for 134 (37%) male heads of household in Middletown. The next largest category contained eighty-one men (26.6%) listed as "laborer". It is assumed that these were farm hands. In Middletown no Friends were listed as a laborers. In Bensalem Township the two categories were apparently merged; there were no "laborers" in Bensalem but 68% of the male heads of household were "farmers".

In 1850 Quakers did not mirror the general population as closely with regard to occupation as they had in 1750. One category in which Friends differed from their non-Quaker neighbors was the comparatively large number of men listing "none" for their occupation. Over 16% of male Quaker heads of household were retired, gentleman farmers, or otherwise unemployed, while only 7% of the non-Friends were unemployed, and that included disowned Friends. One unemployed non-Friend was twenty-eight years old, married with a child, and probably looking for work. If he was omitted from the non-Friends with no occupations, they averaged 64.5 years old, ranging from fifty to eighty years. Quakers, on the other hand, included three men in their thirties, and averaged 55.9 years of age. They ranged in age from thirty-one to seventy-four years. There was no clear pattern pointing to an explanation of the high percentage of unemployed Friends. They varied in age, value of real estate, activity in the meeting's business, and length of time their family had resided in Middletown Township.[7]

TABLE 16: Occupations of Quaker and Non-Quaker Male Heads of Household in Middletown and Bensalem Townships, as Listed in the 1850 Census

Occupations	Middletown Township					Bensalem Twp.	
	Township Totals		Non-Quakers		Quakers		Township Totals
Farmer	134	37.3%	97	32.0%	37	67.2%	229	68.5%
Laborer	81	22.5%	81	26.6%	1	0	-	-
Shoemaker	21	5.8%	21	6.9%	0	0	15	4.4%
Carpenter	17	4.7%	14	4.6%	3	5.5%	11	3.3%
"None"	16	4.4%	7	2.3%	9	16.4%	13	3.9%
Blacksmith	11	3.0%	11	3.6%	0	0	11	3.3%
Mason	7	1.9%	7	2.3%	0	0	5	1.5%
Miller	6	1.7%	5	1.6%	1	1.8%	0	0
Merchant	5	1.4%	4	1.3%	1	1.8%	9	2.7%
Physician	4	1.1%	2	.6%	2	3.6%	3	.9%
Teacher	2	.5%	0	0	2	3.6%	1	.3%
Other	54	15.0%	54	17.7%	0	0	37	11.0%
Left blank	2	.5%	2	.6%	0	0	0	0
Total	360		305		55		334	

SOURCE: U. S. Dept. of Commerce, Bureau of the Census, August 1850 census returns, WRHS.

There were other occupational differences between Friends and non-Friends. There were no Quaker shoemakers, blacksmiths or masons—although in earlier years there had been. There were no non-Friends who taught school, although one styled himself a "college principal". Half of the four physicians were Quakers, considerably above their proportion in the population. The other occupations in which there were no Friends, included such low-paying and low-status jobs as weaver, huckster, wool spinner, boatman, drover, and tinman. There was an assortment of artisans usual in an antebellum rural town, such as wheelwright, tailor, butcher, cooper, and so on, which also included no Quakers. By 1850 Friends were concentrated in farming, or living on farms without actually doing the work themselves, with a few white collar merchants, physicians, and teachers. The only artisans left among meeting members were Samuel Comfort, Jr., a miller, and carpenters William Blakey, and brothers Carey and Isaac Longshore. Friends, then, were diverging from the rest of the Middletown population in occupational terms as well as wealth. The later nineteenth century novels of Bayard Taylor (1825-1878), set among Chester County Quakers, point to the almost Jeffersonian value Quakers were coming to place on rural, agricultural life.[8] This is, perhaps, confirmed by the retirement of Philadelphia Quakers like Richard S. Paxson out to farms in nearby counties, including Bucks.

TABLE 17: Most and Least Valuable Real Estate Holdings in Middletown Township in 1850, with Age of Owner and Quaker Affiliation (QA)

Holders of the 10 Most Valuable Plots					*Holders of the 10 Least Valuable Plots*				
Name	QA	Age	Real Estate Value	C$ Value	Name	QA	Age	Real Estate Value	C$ Value
Thomas L. Allen	O	61	$33,900.	41,852.	Gilbert Randall		40	$ 80	99
Samuel Comfort	O	71	33,000.	40,741.	Margaret Slack		66	175	216
Ann Woolston	H	55	27,000.	33,580.	George Burr		50	250	309
John Paul		81	27,000.	33,580.	William Williams		45	260	321
James Moon		68	27,000.	33,580.	Mary Rice		50	300	370
Alexander H. Smith		36	26,000.	32,099.	John Race		51	300	370
Franklin Vansant		48	25,000.	30,864.	Samuel Comfort	O	32	300	370
Kasey Boos		73	20,000.	24,691.	Carey Longshore	H	36	300	370
John L. Janney		51	16,000.	19,753.	Abraham Brooks		49	300	370
Isaac Paxson	H	61	15,850.	19,568.	Isaac LaRue		50	350	432

SOURCE: US census, 1850, WRHS.
O = Orthodox   H = Hicksite   C$ = Constant dollars

From the information supplied to the census takers in 1850 we see that as in 1750, the owners of the most valuable real estate, and probably the wealthiest people, were Quakers. See Table 17. However, by 1850 fewer than half the top ten most wealthy landowners were Quakers. Their shrinking proportion of the top ten reflects their shrinking proportion among the entire population. See Table 18. The average value of land owned by Friends ($7,145) was more than half again as much as that of land owned by non-Quakers ($4,459). Moreover, the poorest Quaker landowner owned land worth more than three times that of the poorest non-Quaker landowner. Slightly more Friends had their own dwellings, but the statistical difference is too small to be significant (93% to 91%). Many more Friends owned their own land (78.6%) as non-Friends (45.6%). Adjacent Bensalem Township, with fewer Quakers spread among Middletown, Bristol, and Byberry Meetings, had percentages of land ownership and dwellings, and average values of real estate quite comparable to those in Middletown Township.

TABLE 18: Value of Real Estate Owned by Quakers and Non-Quakers in Middletown Township, 1850, Compared with Bensalem Township

	Middletown Township			Bensalem Twp.
	Totals	Households Headed by:		Total Households
		Non-Quaker	Quaker	
Total Family Units	412	342	70	366
Number of Dwellings	375	310 91.0%	65 93.0%	342
Families Owning Land	211 (51.2%)	156 45.6%	55 78.6%	227 (62.%)
Value of Land Owned	$1,037,780	$637,680 61.5%	$400,100 38.5%	$1,125,775
Average Value of Land	$4,942	$4,459	$7,145	$4,959
Highest Value of Land	$33,000	$27,000	$33,000	$30,000
Lowest Value of Land	$80	$80	$300	$100

SOURCE: U. S. Census schedules, 1850, WRHS.
NOTE: The 1850 census indicates whether each family unit occupies a separate dwelling. Landowners are assumed to be those for whom a figure is given in the column "value of real estate". Only one landowner is counted for each family unit even if, for example, the widowed mother also owned property.

As in 1750, Friends in 1850 also owned some of the smaller and less valuable parcels of real estate. In other words, Quaker-owned properties could be found along nearly the entire spectrum of real estate values. However, many of the Quaker owners of the smallest, least valuable lands in 1850 were comparatively young. It could be expected that they would inherit or purchase additional land by the time they reached middle age. For example, Samuel Comfort, owner of real estate worth only $300 was a miller, and thus his net worth was masked by small real estate holdings. He was not likely to be left in that situation by his father, Samuel Comfort, aged 71 and owner of $33,000 worth of land.

In the century after 1750, Friends in Middletown as a group outstripped their non-Quaker neighbors in terms of the average value of real estate owned. Differences regarding land ownership between Hicksite and Orthodox Friends in

Middletown are statistically unreliable because of the small number of cases. An examination of real estate values in both census and tax listings, show clearly that all five of the data set Orthodox in Middletown were well-situated financially.

The Hicksite data set members, with nine times more individuals, displayed a greater spectrum of individual differences. At the lower end were John W. Croasdale, twenty-one years old and still living at home, and most of the sons of Abraham Longshore. At the upper end were men whose wealth was reflected in paper as well as real estate. Isaac Paxson, for example, had the most valuable Hicksite farm at $15,850, but it was less than half the value of the wealthiest Orthodox Friend's farms valued at $33,900. Isaac also had $300 in bank shares. J. Allen Mitchell had $3,350 in bank shares, $13,000 put out at interest, and a $1,262 promissory note, not to mention a $500 judgment to which he was entitled. His state tax of $38.15, along with that of his brother William Mitchell for $32.06, was higher than that of any Orthodox Friend. At least in Middletown, the few Orthodox Friends were comfortably wealthy while Hicksites covered a much wider range. There do not appear to be significant differences in the forms of wealth between Orthodox and Hicksites. Few were mortgaged. Men in both groups had money lent out at interest and held shares of bank stock.

Finally, we need to compare the data set families with the other members of their respective meetings. See Table 19. Using the 1850 state tax returns it appears that the average state tax bill of data set Hicksites was only 88% of that paid by the Orthodox: $12.27 for the former, $13.91 for the Orthodox. The average for all Orthodox was $9.79, and $11.72 for all Hicksites. By adding the non-data set Friends, Hicksites appeared wealthier in comparison to Orthodox. Thus, once again, Middletown Meeting data does not support the theory of Robert Doherty, who wrote that the Orthodox were the wealthy and successful men, while the Hicksites were frustrated and in danger of being marginalized.[9]

The data set families averaged higher state taxes than the rest of the meeting members: $12.48 compared to only $9.53. Among Orthodox there was an even more striking inequality in wealth between the data set and non-data set families: $13.91 (N=9) to $7.60 (N=17). So by the middle of the nineteenth century,

TABLE 19: Comparison of Taxable Wealth Among Data Set and non-Data Set, Hicksite and Orthodox, Members of the two Middletown Monthly Meetings, 1850

Residence	Data Set Hicksite N	Data Set Hicksite Average Tax	Data Set Orthodox N	Data Set Orthodox Average Tax	Total N	Total Average Tax
Bensalem Twp.	10	$12.37	4	$4.28		
Bristol Borough	2	3.94	0	-		
Bristol Twp.	2	12.80	0	-		
Middletown Twp.	46	12.59	5	21.61		
Total	60	12.27	9	13.91	69	$12.48

Residence	Non-Data Set Hicksites N	Non-Data Set Hicksites Average Tax	Non-Data Set Orthodox N	Non-Data Set Orthodox Average Tax	Total N	Total Average Tax
Bensalem Twp.	2	$11.46	1	$9.47		
Bristol Borough	1	8.60	1	.90		
Bristol Twp.	3	8.13	8	6.70		
Middletown Twp.	24	10.95	7	9.35		
Total	30	10.62	17	7.60	47	$9.53
Grand Total	90	$11.72	26	$9.79	116	$11.29

SOURCE: Bucks County Tax Returns, 1850, on microfilm at HSP.

there was clearly an economic advantage to being an "old" family, with land or wealth to inherit.

What can we conclude from this welter of statistics? In the outward aspects of their lives such as occupations, ownership and value of real estate, and size of family, there were some aggregate differences between Friends and their non-Quaker neighbors. The most significant differences, statistically, were the higher percentage of land ownership and the greater wealth among Friends as a group. Their wealth can be explained partly by the fact that these families were descended from original settlers. However, there were also non-Friends descended from original settlers. Friends continued to eschew conspicuous consumption, preferring things which were of plain style, while of good quality materials. Profits tended to be invested rather than consumed, with the result that wealth accumulated.

The growing economic difference between data set and other meeting members seemed a direct result of the way they were selected. In 1850 they lived on land they had largely inherited, or purchased with assets they had inherited. Thus, by definition, they were more established.

There seemed to be a certain inertia of economic position. Families that had been wealthy remained wealthy. Families that had been poor found it difficult to break out of that pattern. The period of rapid growth and "rags-to-riches" changes mostly had come for these families before 1750. The relative poverty of the Longshores, who had been poor back in 1750, can be compared with the Paxsons or Richardsons or Mitchells who had been wealthy in 1750. However, these positions were not completely static. Some of the Longshore descendents were improving their financial picture, some of the other families were moving downward, in a relative sense. Lucas Gillam was relatively poor in 1750. His son Simon had become quite comfortable, financially, by 1800. Then he went bankrupt and left town. Simon's son Isaac was quite modestly situated, but Simon's grandsons Jonathan and William were again comfortably set by 1850. Although William[3] Paxson had been quite wealthy in 1750, his nine sons were not equally well to do. One son, Joseph, lived on his wife's family estate in Bensalem. Joseph had the use of the land, but did not own it. Three of Joseph's four surviving sons moved to Philadelphia. The remaining son, John, acquired land from his mother's family, and became quite prosperous. Of his six sons, two left the area, two never married, and one, Samuel H., was invited by a widowed aunt to manage her Middetown farm. To complete the picture of economic shifts, Samuel H. Paxson's son went bankrupt in the agricultural depression of 1893, and his widow ended up working as a housekeeper for two Richardson bachelors. Quaker families were subject to the same economic variables as other people, such as number of sons, wealth of wives, ability, and economic forces beyond their control. Quaker testimonies against speculation, conspicuous consumption, and the advice to tend the inner plantation offered Friends some means and ends that varied from those advocated by the "acquisitive society". Not all Friends followed them.

This brief economic profile of Middletown Friends at mid-century underscores certain aspects that the Quaker subculture was assumed to encompass. Correlation, however, is not proof. The fact that, on average, Middletown Friends were twice as likely to own land, and that the land thus owned would average nearly twice the value of that owned by non-Friends, indicates to me that there was something about these Friends that made them different. As we have seen in Chapter 7, even when not completely followed, or followed to the letter rather than in the Spirit, Quakerism offered a number of advices and testimonies in the economic field which encouraged Friends to chart a somewhat different course from that offered by the "world".

Political Profile

Chapter 9 discussed several political issues and the responses of Middletown Quakers. There was a large group of Middletown Friends who were deeply involved in partisan politics in ways that supported their social and economic interests, rather than advancing specifically Quaker moral issues. Here we are interested in paralleling the 1750 political profile drawn in Chapter 2.

The character of local Pennsylvania politics changed considerably between 1750 and 1850. But one thing remained the same: out-going men with ambition or concern for their community became involved in local governance. In Bucks County it was still largely a face-to-face society, although it had never been self-contained or autonomous. Toward the end of the antebellum period national politics increasingly affected the local scene, as had the repercussions of the Great War for Empire a century earlier.

The percentage of Quakers in Bucks County steadily decreased as the population of non-Friends rose. In 1850 the population of Bucks County was 56,091. There was no official tally of Quakers.[10] One way to calculate numbers of Friends is to look at the yearly meeting assessments. The Hicksite monthly meetings were assessed the following percentages of the amount expected from Bucks Quarter:

Buckingham, 21%; Falls, 13%; Makefield, 19%; Middletown, 16%; Solebury, 11%; and Wrightstown, 20%.[11] On the assumption that these were per capita assessments, it is easy to calculate the Hicksite population of the County since Middletown Meeting minuted in Eighth month 1849 that there were 411 members of the two preparative meetings making up Middletown Monthly Meeting. On the basis of this formula, there were about 2,569 Hicksite Quakers in Bucks County. If the Orthodox equaled about 20% of Bucks County Friends at the time of the Separation, and county-wide their numbers remained parallel with Hicksite numbers (which is a big assumption, and perhaps not entirely warranted), then in 1850 they would have numbered about 514 (20% of the Hicksites). Therefore, the total number of Friends in the County could have been about 3,083, or 5.5% of the total population.

We can estimate that there was another approximately 5% or 6% who had Quaker ancestors and relatives but for one reason or another were no longer Friends themselves. How much they identified with Quaker positions would have varied considerably. Some would have been an integral part of the Quaker subculture in all but official designation.[12] Others would have left completely. The presence of this unquantifiable segment of the population cannot be discounted.

To what degree—if any—the Quaker subculture influenced the surrounding dominant culture is an important question, but beyond the scope of this study. A letter from a New York man who spoke to a temperance group in Newtown in 1833 observed with pleasure

> the plain attire, the perfect neatness, and the refined intelligence that distinguished the assemblage, for, you must know that our "Friends" who are appropriately designated by that appellation, are numerous in this county . . . and have given a chaste [sic] to the manners of the people.[13]

Whether or not Friends actually had political clout, they were the subject of occasional appeals, or comments, in the *Bucks County Intelligencer*. There did not seem to have been similar appeals singling out members of any other denomination. A letter "To the Quakers of Bucks County" in 1828 mentioned rumors of war in Europe and hence the need for a "man of peace" as president; the writer urged Friends to vote against Andrew Jackson. Eight years later a similarly addressed letter urged Friends to vote against Martin VanBuren because of Jackson's unfair policies toward Native Americans and Blacks, because he had signed the gag bill against antislavery petitions to Congress, and because of impending war against Mexico. The assumption was that Friends cared enough about these issues for them to affect Quaker votes. In 1848 a piece from the (Philadelphia) *Pennsylvanian* was reprinted which noted that Friends "almost to a man" had voted for Zachery Taylor, thereby exposing their hypocrisy in proclaiming pacifism while voting for a general. The editor leaped to their defense against such slander, insisting that General Taylor was a man of peace.[14] Whether or not Friends were still a subculture, they seem to have been considered an identifiable voting bloc.

In 1750 there had been several routes to public office, including appointment by various officials and bodies, election, and a combination of the two. Regardless of the method of attaining office, Quakers dominated all the political offices in Bucks County except for the geographically-named justices of the peace. This was no longer true in 1850.[15] Comparatively few Quakers held office above the county level. Michael H. Jenks, with his long resumé, comes to mind. Joshua Mitchell moved to the City of Philadelphia and served as an alderman for many years. Joseph Watson (whose mother was Ann Jenks) was mayor of Philadelphia from 1824 to 1828. Lucretia M. Longshore, daughter of Thomas E., married Rudolph Blankenburg who was a well-known reform mayor of Philadelphia in the early twentieth century.[16]

As we have seen in Chapter 9, about two-fifths of the adult male members of Middletown Meeting were involved in local politics in some way beyond the act of voting between 1822 and 1850. The difficulty of ascertaining this on the county level is that many owners of recognizable Quaker surnames were no longer members. Other people had joined, bearing unfamiliar names. A quick tabulation of known Middletown Meeting members who held local offices between 1823 and 1850 revealed seventeen men. There were four Orthodox and the rest, about three-quarters, were Hicksites. This list makes no pretense of being exhaustive. They ranged from Samuel Allen who held a number of posts in Bristol Borough such as tax collector (1823 and 1837), justice of the peace (1845), and election judge (1848), to Samuel Comfort who served as overseer of the poor for Middletown in 1847 and 1848. William Blakey was tax assessor for Middletown in 1846 and justice of the peace in 1850. William Hicks was Middletown Township supervisor in 1847.[17]

On the other hand, in spite of the obvious political involvement of a number of Friends, the opposite image also continued. This was the image of John Comly or Edward Hicks. "A Friend" wrote to the *Intelligencer* hoping to rouse Quakers out of their apathy or disinterest, in support of the writer's political agenda. He explained how many Friends had

> been backward in expressing their sentiments on public men or public issues. In passing through life they have been satisfied with performing their duty towards God and man, with obeying the laws and constituted authorities of the land, without aspiring after the honours and emoluments of office. They have on this account, rarely taken an active part in any of the great political questions that have arisen in the United States, nevertheless, they have not been backward in remonstrating against what they believed unjust or contrary to the principles of Christianity.[18]

He ended with a campaign appeal for John Quincy Adams against Jackson. Even though Middletown Friends had mostly been silent in the face of injustice against the Cherokees or Pennsylvania's Blacks, they continued to enjoy a reputation for championing just causes.

More intriguing than numbers of officeholders who were members of the Religious Society of Friends, is what influence, if any, Quakers had on Bucks County politics. In the election of 1828 the townships that went for John Quincy Adams were the same as those in which Friends lived and had meetings. The exception was the meeting in Richland Township, never a part of Bucks Quarterly Meeting, and some Adams supporters in townships bordering Montgomery County, within the verge of Horsham and Gwynedd Meetings. See Figure 6. This political map closely resembles the description in Chapter 2 of various ethnic settlement patterns. Did the eastern quarter of the county vote for Adams because of Quaker influence, or because they were mostly of English descent, or

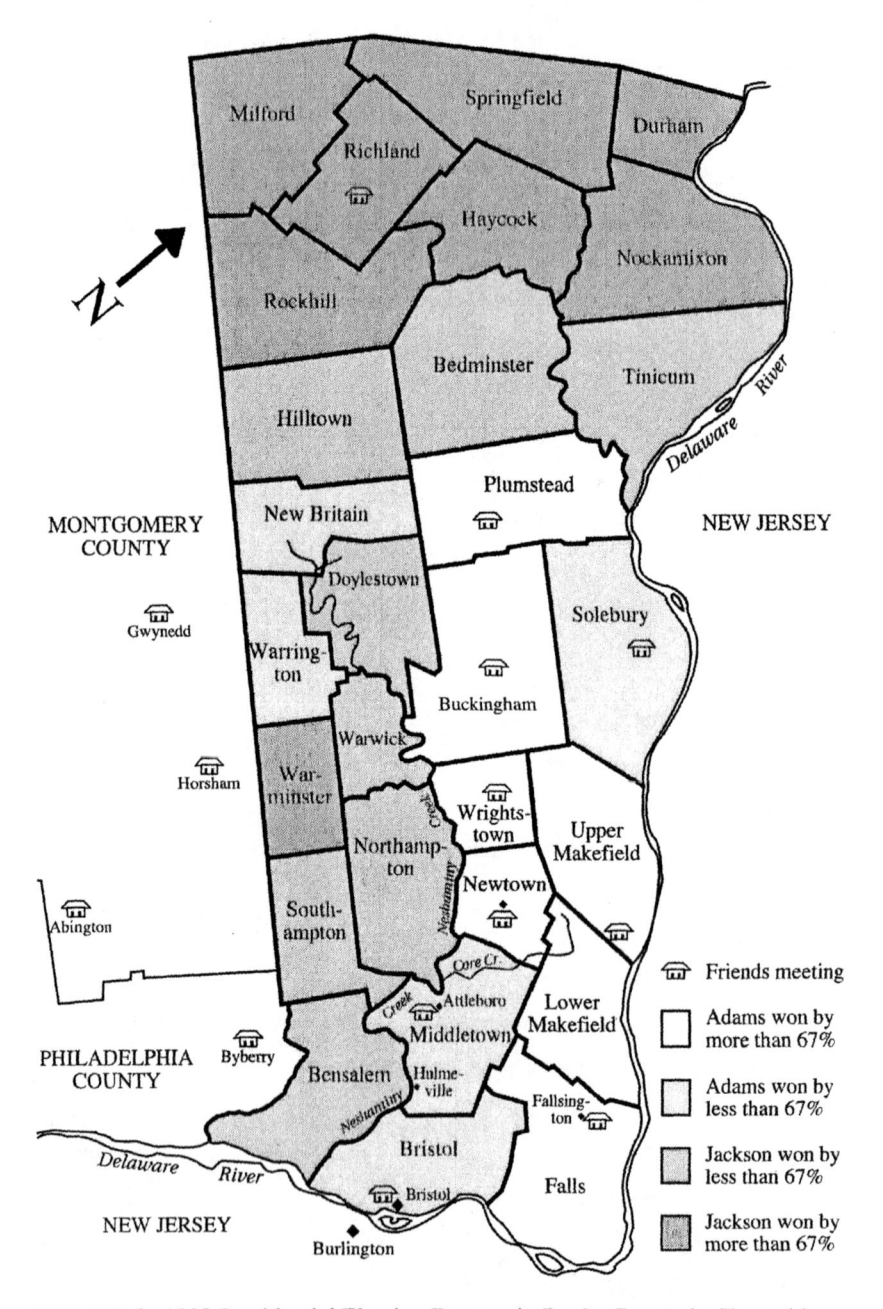

FIGURE 6: 1828 Presidential Election Returns in Bucks County by Township

some combination of the two? Were Friends influencing their neighbors, or being influenced by them? The sources used for this study do not provide answers. We have found clues that a good many Friends were more influenced by the surrounding dominant culture than, perhaps, they themselves were aware. But there have also been indications that Quakers did help set the general tone in the areas of the county in which they lived.

The comparison between the data set Friends and other members of their meetings showed that in the century under study they increasingly diverged. This was to be expected, considering that they were chosen for their longevity in the area. The main way in which they differed was that they tended to be more wealthy. Over the generations some sons moved out of the area, so that the ones remaining had viable-sized farms or other means of livelihood.

We have compared Middletown Meeting members with non-Friends living in the area using various demographic, economic, and political factors. This provides an aggregate statistical picture of certain external features of Friends' lives. It shows that in some respects Quakers were different. They had twice the rate of land ownership, and their land was worth nearly twice as much, on average. A significant number felt no need for a steady occupation. Their families tended to be slightly smaller, and single women were more likely to have their own households. See Appendix 1. Significant numbers were involved in local politics, although there still remained a cultural norm permitting disinterest in political activity. None of these factors tell us why Quakers chose to behave somewhat differently from the non-Friends among whom they lived. As we have indicated in previous chapters, Quaker advices and testimonies pointed to reasons Friends ought to have differed from non-Quakers in many of these respects, but they do not prove that these were the causes of individual situations.

These statistical differences cannot tell us how individual Friends chose between a God-centered life or a secular life, or between Quakerism or some other denomination. They cannot tell us if the Friends, whose aggregate behavior produced these statistics, did so out of habit or because they were intent on following the instruction of the Inward Guide. They only show us that there were some differences between the outward behavior of Middletown Friends and other people in their community.

CHAPTER 11: CONCLUSIONS

The ideal of early Friends was to be "in the world but not of it". That meant that they were not to withdraw from the world, but to participate in the economic and political life of the larger community. However, they were not to absorb the standards and values of that culture. They were to be citizens of God's realm, living as ambassadors of that kingdom. Over the years some individuals, families, and meetings have come closer to approximating this ideal than others.

It seems that Middletown Friends lived farther from the ideal in 1850 than they had at a high point of consistency required by witnessing to testimonies against war and slavery. But to see their story as merely one of declension is to oversimplify. Each generation meets a new situation and must "work out its own salvation". Each makes its own choices, charts its own path. This could be seen, then, not as one four-generation story of decline, but as four stories, each of a distinct historical period, confronting distinct problems. To assert that a community is in decline implies that each successive generation is less able to follow its ideals than its predecessor, that faced with the conditions of 1776, for example, the 1850 people would not have done as well as their ancestors. Conversely, if the 1770s people were transported to 1850, they would have presumably done a better job than their descendants. This seems to be based on a static sense of history, or a lack of application of Toynbee's thesis to individuals: that people tend to rise to the challenges facing them, as long as they are not crushed. It is important to examine each age cohort in its own historical context.

When an obvious challenge was presented by the outside world's demands which ran counter to Friends' testimonies, Friends had to choose between conforming to the world or upholding Friends' witness. During times of crisis Friends tended to do the internal work and make the internal choices that resulted in bringing their outward behavior more closely in line with Quaker testimonies. So, when forced by outward events such as the American Revolution to examine their own beliefs in respect to Quaker testimonies on such things as war or oaths, most Friends rose to the challenge and refused to join the militia or pay fines for substitutes. They suffered distraints of their goods and lost political and social standing among non-Friends. Friends who were unwilling or unable to take this road lost their membership in the Religious Society. Friends who chose to uphold the testimonies rather than conform to the world's demands, might act from several motives. They could do what Friends required just because it was required, or because they identified as part of a group under siege, or they could submit to the tough work of the Inner Christ. The latter choice was an important path of spiritual growth. The former two also could lead through suffering to growth.

In the antebellum period most Friends were prosperous and respected in their communities. With outward things going so well, most Quakers had more trouble choosing to do the lonely, painful self-searching necessary for embarking on a God-centered life. When faced with new opportunities and ideas from the economic or political world beyond the Religious Society of Friends, and without sharp, clear points requiring choices, it was relatively easy to slide off, make compromises, do what "everyone else" was doing. In many ways the story of Middletown Meeting families, like the history of Quakerism in the nineteenth century in general, can be seen as "a remarkable example of the subtle means by which the dominant culture draws outgroups under its influence and closer to the mainstream".[1] As they accommodated to the dominant culture Friends were no longer marginal, dissenting outsiders—the experience that helped transform and empower the first generation of Friends back in the seventeenth century.

Family Patterns

The family was the core unit of the Religious Society of Friends in this period. Friends developed a subculture based in the family that flowered in the eighteenth and nineteenth centuries. Therefore it is not surprising that family is a critical variable in understanding how people behaved.

Both positive and negative patterns of behavior were found among the families studied. Positive patterns included an active spiritual life: individuals who were deeply involved in the meeting tended to have children who followed that example. Families of these people tended to uphold Friends' testimonies more faithfully, as measured by fewer disciplinary actions taken against them.

Negative patterns such as "taking strong drink to excess", or fornication (usually with one's fiancé) tended to concentrate in some families and be absent in others. Some families were not very involved in the regular business of the meeting. From other evidence in their lives, it seems they were not as interested in working on their spiritual lives, either. But families were not complete monoliths. Individuals made their own choices, with or against family patterns.

Comparisons between the data set families and the rest of Middletown Meeting made in 1750 and 1850 show increasing divergence. In 1750 the data set families were slightly more wealthy, and had slightly more children. In 1850, reflecting their longevity in the area, the data set families were considerably more wealthy, on average, than other members of the meetings, and had fewer children.

Patterns illustrated by the data presented in this study confirm the importance of family as a prime motivator in matters of social behavior and in spiritual issues insofar as they are reflected in outward behavior.

Another Look at the 1827 Separation

Robert Doherty hypothesized that Orthodox Friends were in tune with their evangelical neighbors, more involved with the new economic opportunities of the early nineteenth century, and generally forward-looking entrepreneurs. He posits the Hicksites as being conservative, in danger of being marginalized, and generally alienated from the emerging "acquisitive society". It is clear from this study of Middletown Meeting that Robert Doherty's conclusions about the economic profile of Orthodox and Hicksite are inappropriate for at least this rural meeting. In Middletown Meeting a substantial number of Friends were deeply involved in the local bank, in promoting improvements such as the Delaware Division of the Pennsylvania Canal and local railroads or turnpikes, and in using new agricultural implements. Yet 80% of the meeting became Hicksite. By 1850 the taxes paid by the Hicksites averaged considerably higher than those paid by the Orthodox, an indication that they were financially successful.

Another assumption has been that the Orthodox were deeply involved in ecumenical evangelical activities and reforms. In Middletown, only one Orthodox Friend was involved in a Bible Society. The other Friends who joined the Orthodox branch were not. Other scholars have found a close correlation between evangelicals and the temperance movement. Again, Middletown Orthodox were not involved. Instead, a few Hicksites were active.

These observations about Middletown Friends who joined the Orthodox branch undermine the generally accepted psycho-social and economic profile. It forces us to suggest an alternate hypothesis, which is that the spiritual nourishment available within Middetown Meeting was inadequate for the needs of some Friends. Therefore they looked elsewhere for nurture and encouragement. The Comfort family had been deeply involved in the ministry and life of the meeting for over three generations. It can be presumed that for many of them the spiritual life was of great importance. For help they turned not to non-Quaker neighbors, but to Philadelphia Friends who happened to be enthused with new evangelical ideas. The research done for this book does not address the accuracy of the commonly accepted explanation for the reasons wealthy urban Philadelphia Quakers accepted evangelical ideas.

The so-called Hicksites initially were united only by their opposition to Orthodox efforts to impose a more evangelical doctrine on Philadelphia Yearly

Meeting. There was little danger of local Friends forcing this on Middletown. But the events in Philadelphia precipitated action in each quarterly and monthly meeting as Friends had to choose which epistle to read or which visitors to accept from the two competing yearly meetings. Without the inflamed passions, the theological differences, and the power plays at the yearly meeting level, it is very doubtful that Middletown Friends would have separated. But once the die was cast in the city, the tragedy was played out at the local level.

The Friends in Middletown who opposed the Orthodox gave a more accurate forecast of the later characteristics of the Hicksite branch than does Doherty. Later Hicksites, particularly in the last decade of the nineteenth century, accommodated to the economic world in which they found themselves, and eventually clustered around the "social gospel" that is most closely identified with the politically liberal, social activist, rational, skeptical level three of Peck's faith development model, or the green meme of Ken Wilber.[2]

This study corroborates the importance of family connection in how individuals chose which faction to join at the time of the Separation. Nine families (53%) of the data set were completely monolithic in that every family member who was part of Middletown Meeting joined a single branch. In three families (18%) only one or two members, and in two (12%) a larger part of the family, joined the "other" faction. The reason in the former cases was to unite with a spouse of the other persuasion. Two possible explanations emerged for the more mixed character of the latter families. First, one individual seemed to be generally disillusioned with Friends and perhaps refused to choose between them; he was not active in either meeting. Second, one family exhibited signs of dysfunction or lack of the loving unity commonly attributed to Friends. Members of this family scattered over the two branches.

Within the Middletown Meetings we can see the seeds of future directions of the Hicksite and Orthodox branches of Friends. The general indifference to deep spiritual searching, and the enthusiastic involvement in social action to bring about a better world, combined with rationalism and intellectual enquiry into the Bible were characteristics of a good many Hicksites by the beginning of the twentieth century. In this respect, the Longshores were forerunners of the future shape of the Friends General Conference branch of Quakerism. In order to avoid further separations, the Orthodox Philadelphia Yearly Meeting cut off relations with all other yearly meetings. It still had its Gurneyite and Wilburite factions, but they did not separate. Except for Elizabeth Jenks joining a "Primitive" group of extreme quietist Wilburites, it is harder to get a sense of where the other Orthodox were in Middletown. They seemed to turn inward and continued vigorously to enforce the discipline, thereby systematically reducing their numbers. Their pattern was different from midwest Orthodox who, especially after the Civil War, enthusiastically absorbed a great deal from the revival and holiness movements.

Another way of looking at the Separation has been to bring forward the thread used by historians Frost, Marietta, and Soderlund when dealing with the reform of Philadelphia Yearly Meeting in the third quarter of the eighteenth century. They found that there were two kinds of reformers in Philadelphia Yearly Meeting in the 1750s, those who wanted to purify the Society by stricter enforcement of endogamous marriage and other "tribalistic" rules, and those who advocated humanitarian concerns, particularly antislavery. Soderlund suggested a parallel between Max Weber's "emissary" type and those Friends concerned with outward conformity and enforcement of a moral code. Weber's "exemplary" type she found similar to those Friends who were more concerned with the inner demands made in the course of trying to live according to God's will. I have noted the similarity between the "emissary" moral code enforcers and Peck's second level of faith development. Likewise, the "exemplary" is similar to his fourth level of faith development. We will now look at how this concept has helped to understand events in Middletown Meeting.

Faith Development as an Analytical Tool

The concept of faith development is explained in the first chapter as the process or stages through which an individual passes in the development of spiritual commitment and belief. A simple, four-stage model developed by psychiatrist M. Scott Peck was chosen because it seemed to explain the phenomena most satisfactorily. Briefly, these levels are, first, chaos, in which the individual is self-centered and lacking in discipline. One moves by way of a conversion experience and/or family nurture into the second level, the formal, institutional stage. This stage craves certainty. One is loyal to the institutional church's rules and mores. If one becomes skeptical of received answers one can move to the next or third level which combines theological skepticism, questioning of authority, and social action to help the downtrodden. Gradually some people realize that skepticism and rationalism do not provide all the answers. Almost imperceptibly they move into a fourth level which accepts ambiguity and mystery, welcomes the mystical, and returns to the language and symbolism of the second stage, but at a far deeper level.

The use of this simplified schema of four levels of faith development helps us understand behavior in specific incidents, and provides some insights into the dynamics of broad movements. For example, Joseph S. Longshore's passionate attacks on the local tavern, and his disrespect towards the meeting's authorities can be understood if we view him in terms of third-level faith development. The desire of many Orthodox to appeal to the authority of the Bible and stress the importance of following the rules as laid out in the *Book of Discipline* point to the second level's need for certainty.

Another scale that helps in understanding the dynamics of people within the religious arena is a spectrum running from passionate to indifferent. It cuts across the faith levels and separates individuals along another dimension. The Rodman family, most of whom were disowned during the Revolution for military or political activity, taking the affirmation of allegiance, or deviations involving marriage procedures, seemed to exhibit a general indifference to spiritual matters. It is more helpful to use this scale for them, than to describe them as unaware level twos. On the other hand, Joseph S. and Thomas E. Longshore's abstinence and abolition activities mark them as not only level threes, but as passionate level threes, at least for this period in their lives.

These tools ought to be useful for application in other studies of groups that define themselves in terms of religion. They have enabled us to understand better the variety of responses and to glimpse some ambiguities and subtleties of individual behavior. As we know at a gut level when examining our own behavior, the broad generalities offered by those who study the "big picture" often fail to explain satisfactorily the range of complicated individual responses.

The ideals of the Religious Society of Friends have always diverged in some respects from the dominant culture. We have dealt with ways in which the Middletown Meeting community sought to encourage and enforce conformity to its view of right behavior. We have seen interactions between members of that community and the larger society. Some members of the meeting failed to conform to the dictates of the larger society in order to follow the teachings of their faith community. Others adjusted their behavior in the hopes that they could somehow balance their lives between the two communities. Still others, no longer demonstrating by their behavior a commitment to the beliefs of the meeting, abandoned or were abandoned by it. This is the story of human interactions and personal values, as individuals struggled to live out the implications of being "in the world but not of it".

APPENDIX 1: DEMOGRAPHICS OF THE DATA SET AND MEETING

The data set consists of individuals in seventeen surname families who were members of Middletown Monthly Meeting and were alive in 1750, plus all those born between then and Twelfth month 31, 1828, who lived to the age of twenty one.[1] It includes all adults, even those who remained single, left the area, or were disowned. It does not include the children of those who left the area or the meeting. Nor does it include the wives from non-data set families. There are a total of 624 men and women in the data set.

There were 378 members of Middletown Meeting in 1750, of whom 167, or 44%, were members of the seventeen surname families. Adults represented 53.7% of the entire membership. There were proportionately more children among the seventeen families—101 (57.7%)—probably because they had put down roots in the area and they were, perhaps, more accurately recorded. Eliminating all the children under the age of twenty one, there were sixty-six adults in the data set (32.5%) out of the total 203 adults in the entire meeting in 1750. So the sample of seventeen families is not quite demographically representative of the entire meeting. It was not chosen for that purpose.

One hundred years later, in Eighth month, 1850, there were also 378 members of the Middletown Meetings. Of these total members there were 266 Friends (232 Hicksite and thirty-four Orthodox) living in Middletown Township. Together they constituted 12.5% of the township's population of 2,122.[2] See Table 20.

The 166 Quaker adults were 13.9% of the adult population of the township. Quaker children were a smaller proportion, only 10.7%, of the total population of children.

The two meetings included 292 members of the (Hicksite) Middletown Preparative Meeting and eighty-six members of the (Orthodox) Middletown Monthly Meeting. There were 173 members of the data set families, constituting 45.7% of the 378 members. In the Hicksite branch the data set were half of the 292 members, and were 49% of the 176 adult members. Among the Orthodox, the twenty-six members of the data set families were 30.2% of the eighty-six members, or 32.7% of the fifty-eight adults. So in the Hicksite branch the data set families' proportion of the adult membership increased and their percentage of children decreased from a century earlier.

TABLE 20: Comparative Numbers of Data Set, Hicksite, and Orthodox Friends Who Were Residents of Middletown Township in 1850

	Middletown Mtg. (Hicksite)				Middletown Mtg. (Orthodox)				Middletown Twp. Population
	Data Set		Total Members		Data Set		Total Members		
	Mid. Twp.	Total	Mid. Twp.	Total	Mid. Twp.	Total	Mid. Twp.	Total	
Adult Males	35	37	58	72	6	9	10	23	
Adult Females	48	51	86	104	7	10	12	35	
Total Adults	83	88	144	176	13	19	22	58	1188
Males Under 21	25	30	39	51	1	2	4	13	
Females Under 21	24	29	49	65	4	5	8	15	
Total Children	49	59	88	116	5	7	12	28	934
Total People	132	147	232	292	18	26	34	86	2122

SOURCE: 1850 U. S. census schedules for Middletown Township, Bucks County, HSP; Middletown Meeting records, Hicksite and Orthodox.

In 1750, 57.7% of the meeting was twenty-one years old or younger. In 1850 only 46.3% were that young. The Orthodox were a somewhat more aged group than the Hicksites, 67% of them were over twenty-one compared to 60% of the Hicksites. This difference may have been due to the Orthodox propensity for disownment, usually of younger members. The data set families had fewer children than the rest of the meeting. Only 38% of the data set members were twenty-one or under.

These smaller than average Quaker families are in line with Robert Wells's thesis that Friends began restricting the size of their families earlier than other groups.[3] More recent demographers have suggested that the availability and quality of land, that is, whether an area had been settled recently or several generations previously, or if it was suffering from what was termed "agricultural stress", were more important variables in determining family size and fertility.[4] By that criterion, there should have been a relatively low birth rate for all of Middletown Township. However, Middletown Friends had fewer children than their non-Quaker neighbors. Quaker women married later and had their final baby somewhat later than non-Quaker women in Middletown.[5] See Table 21.

TABLE 21: Comparison of Fertility between Middletown Township Quakers and Non-Quakers in 1850 with 102 Rural Northern Townships from New Hampshire to Kansas in 1860

	Bateman-Foust Sample			Middletown	
	Total	Older Areas	Newer Settlements	Total	Quaker
Number of Households	2,870	757	312	412	70
Children 0-9 per Woman Aged 20-49	2.11	1.77	2.22	1.42	.93
Age of Mother at First Birth	22.7	23.3	23.7	22.9	24.6
Age of Mother at Latest Birth	29.6	28.9	29.9	27.6	28.6

SOURCE: Easterlin, Alter, and Condran, "Farms and Farm Families in Old and New Areas" as quoted in Richard A. Easterlin, "Factors in the Decline of Farm Family Fertility in the United States: Some Preliminary Research Results" in Michael Gordon, ed., *The American Family in Social-Historical Perspective*, 2nd ed. (New York: St. Martin's Press, 1978), p. 535. Middletown data from the 1850 US census, WRHS.

Because of the traditional Quaker understanding of the spiritual equality of women and men, and because Quaker women had generations of experience running their own meetings for business, it might be expected that Quaker women would be more independent than their non-Quaker sisters. In 1850 Middletown Quaker women were twice as likely as non-Quaker women to head their own households. See Table 22. While 11% of the non-Quaker households were headed by women, 23% of the Quaker households were so headed. It is not surprising to find widows in such a situation. But unmarried daughters, sisters, and aunts were expected to live under the roof of a male relative. In Middletown five never-married Quaker women headed their own households: Sarah Blakey (whose unmarried sister Phebe lived with her), Helena Kirkbride, Jane Richardson, Mercy Stackhouse, and Eliza Woolston. Four were Hicksite; Mercy Stackhouse was Orthodox. That ratio is comparable to the total proportion of Hicksite and Orthodox Friends in Middletown.

TABLE 22: Heads of Household by Gender and Quaker Membership, Middletown Township, 1850

	Quaker		Non-Quaker		Total
Households Headed by Males	54	77.%	305	89.%	359
Households Headed by Females	16	23.%	37	11.%	53
Total Households in Middletown	70	100.%	342	100.%	412

SOURCE: U.S. census for Middletown, 1850, and Middletown Meeting records.

There were some statistical differences between Quakers and non-Friends in Middletown regarding such demographic variables as number of children and percentage of independent women heading their own households. These factors by themselves do not prove the existence of a Quaker subculture. But they point to a somewhat different understanding, on the part of Friends, regarding the place of women. This understanding is articulated in various Quaker writings.[6]

APPENDIX 2: MIDDLETOWN MEETING ADULT MEMBERS, 1750

There was no official list of members in the eighteenth century. The following list has been reconstructed by gleaning all the names in the Middletown Meeting records for the period and subtracting those who had been disowned or removed from the area by 1750. Names are found in the minutes of the men's and women's meetings and in lists of births. There is no guarantee that this reconstructed list is totally accurate.

Allen, John & Rebecca + 1 child:
  Sarah
Allen, Mary
Allen, William & Mary + 4 children:
  Joseph
  Jane
  Samuel
  Mary
Alsop, Mary
Arbuckle, James & wife (Mary?)
Ashburn, William
Atkinson, Margaret
Bartholomew, Thomas
Baynes, Thomas & Janet
Baynes, Elizabeth
Biles, Charles & wife
Blakey, Jael, widow of William + 3 children:
  Lydia
  Joshua
  William
Blakey, William
Briggs, John & Mary (Watson) + 4 children:
  Mary
  Hannah
  Margret
  John
Briggs, Mary (Croasdale), widow of William, Jr.
Carlile, John
Carlile, Samuel
Carter, Sarah
Carter, Sarah [Jr.]
Carter, Rachel
Cary, Samuel & Sarah (Stackhouse) + 7 children:
  Sampson

Sarah
Ann
Samuel
Hannahmeel
Bethula
Thomas (b 7/7/1750)
Collison, Robert
Comfort, Stephen & Mercy
   (Croasdale) + 3 children:
John
Ezra
Jeremiah (b. 26/8/1750)
Cooper, Hannah
Croasdale, Ezra
Croasdale, Grace (Heaton), widow
   of Jeremiah + 4 children:
Eber
Abijah
Macre
Achsah
Croasdale, Robert & Margery
   (Hayhurst)
Croasdale, William & Grace
   (Harding) + 3 children:
Rachel
Hannah
Phebe
Cutler, Benjamin & Mercy (Bills) +
   7 children
Cutler, Elizabeth
Doan, John
Doan, Mary, wife of Daniel
Doan, Mary & sister Sarah
Doan, Thomas
Dungan, Jeremiah, widower
Dunn, Anna (Heaton)
Edwards, Mary
Field, Ann married 7/1750
Field, Benjamin, Jr.
Field, Sarah, widow of Benjamin + 4
   children
Field, Stephen & Susanna
Gillam, Lucas & Ann (Dungan) + 1
   child:
Susannah
Griffith, Abraham & Elizabeth

Harding, Henry & Mary (Shaw, Jr.)
Harding, John Thomas & Jane
   (Scott, Jr.)
Harker, Adam & Grace
Harris, George & Mary arrived
   10/1749
Hayhurst, Cuthbert & Deliverance
   (Bills) + 8 children:
John
Margery
Cuthbert
William
Thomas
Rachel
Elizabeth
Joseph
Hayhurst, Elizabeth
Hayhurst, John
Hayhurst, Ruth
Hayhurst, William & Rebecca + 1
   child:
Cuthbert
Heaton, Robert, Jr. & Ann (Carver)
   + 1 child:
Susanna (b. 11/5m/1750)
Heston, Alice
Hibbs, William & Ann + 7 children
Hillbourn, Thomas & Mary
Hyatt, Mary
Ingledice [?], __
Janes, Abigail (Sands) married
   8/1749
Jenks, Thomas, Sr. & Mercy (Wild-
   man)+ 6 children:
Mary
John
Thomas
Joseph
Elizabeth
Ann
Jenny, Elizabeth
Jolly, Letitia, disowned
Lamb, Thomas & Alice (Longshore)
   + children
Latham, Ann
Linton, Isaac of age 10/1750

Linton, Joseph & Mary (Blackshaw)
+ 5 children:
  Elizabeth
  Joseph
  Mary
  Phebe
  Jonathan
Lloyd, John & new wife Susanna (Field)
Longshore, Euclydus & Alice (Stackhouse) + 2 children:
  Euclydus
  Benjamin
Longshore, Thomas & Johanna (Vances) + 4 children:
  Euclydus
  Elizabeth
  Cyrus
  Thomas
Mays, John
McVaugh [?], Sarah
Mitchell, John & Margaret (Stackhouse) + 6 children:
  Richard
  John
  Henry
  Sarah
  Samuel
  Margaret (b. 25/12/1749/50)
Mode, Andrew
Moon, James & Hannah (Price)
Naylor, Jane
Naylor, John
Naylor, Mary
Paxson, James
Paxson, Mary, widow of William[2]
Paxson, Thomas & Ann (Paxson) + 6 children:
  Mary
  Ann
  Henry
  John
  Elizabeth
  James
Paxson, William[3] & Anna (Marriot) + 4 children:
  William
  Joseph
  Phineas
  Thomas
Plumley, Charles & Ann (Stackhouse)
Plumley, John
Poole, Joseph & Rebecca + 4 children
Poole, William
Preston, Jonas & second wife Sarah (Carter)
Randle, Elizabeth
Randle, George & Mary (Hardin) + 3 children
Randle, John
Randle, Joseph & Rebecca
Randle, Rebecca, Jr.
Richardson, Joseph & Mary (Paxson) + 6 children:
  Joshua
  Mary
  William
  Rachel
  Rebecca
  Ruth
Roberts, Elizabeth
Rodman, John, Jr. & Mary + 1 child
Rodman, William & Mary
Sands, John
Sands, Richard & Mary + 1 child
Sands, Richard, Jr.
Sands, Stephen
Sands, William & Mary + 5 children
Satterthwaite, William & Pleasant (Mead)
Scott, Benjamin & Jane (Twining) + 2 children
Scott, Benjamin, Jr.
Scott, Thomas
Shaw, George
Shaw, Joseph & Mary + 5 children
Smith, Joseph & Rachel (Wildman)
Stackhouse, Caleb of age 1749
Stackhouse, Elizabeth (Janney) widow of John, Jr. + 2 children:

Lucilla
Abel
Stackhouse, Hannah (Watson)
    widow of Jacob + 5 children:
Moses
Job
Deborah
Mary
Hannah
Stackhouse, Isaac & Mary (Harding)
    + 4 children:
Thomas
Mary
Ann
Jonathan (b. 31/8/1750)
Stackhouse, John
Stackhouse, Joseph & Sarah
    (Copeland) + 5 children:
Joshua
Sarah
Mary
Joseph, Jr.
Benjamin
Stockdale, William & Sarah (Field, Jr.)
Stokes, Susannah
Thackray, James & Rachel + 2 children
Thornton, Joseph & Margaret + 12 children
Tomlinson, Thomas & Elizabeth (Stackhouse)
Twining, Samuel
Walker, Benjamin & wife
Walker, George
Walker, Joseph & Sarah (Heaton)
Watson, John & Ruth (Blakey) + 2 children:
John
Ruth, Jr.
Watson, Joseph
Watson, Martha (Neeld) widow of
    Thomas, + 2 children:
Amos
John
Wildman, James
Wildman, Martin
Wildman, Rachel m 1750 James Spicer
Wildman, Sarah (Wilson) widow of
    Joseph, + 2 children:
Joseph
John
Wilson, Anthony + 4 children
Wilson, David & Elizabeth (Stackhouse)
Wilson, David & Grace (Stackhouse) + 6 children:
Grace
Jonathan
Dinah
Rachel
Asaph
Jesse
Wilson, Jonathan
Wilson, Samuel
Wilson, Stephen & Rebecca (Hoge) + 4 children
Wilson, Stephen
Wilson, Thomas of Southampton
Woolston, Benjamin
Woolston, John & Elizabeth (Wildman) + 6 children:
Sarah
Mary
Elizabeth, Jr.
John
Mercy
Jonathan (b. 22/11/1750/1)
Woolston, Samuel & Hannah (Palmer) + 2 children:
Sarah
Jonathan
Worstal, Edward
Worstal, James
Worstal, John
Wright, Joseph & Rebecca

APPENDIX 3: MIDDLETOWN TOWNSHIP 1757 TAX LIST

Name	Quaker Affiliation	Penna. Currency	Constant $
Ashborn, John	?	6.1.0	25.80
Ashton, Thomas		6.1.0	25.80
Belfford, Benjamin	Q	6.1.0	25.80
Belfford, Daniel	?	6.1.0	25.80
Belfford, Jacob	?	10.1.8	43.02
Belfford, John	?	20.3.9	86.13
Belfford, Nathan	?	10.1.8	43.02
Besonet, John		25.4.2	107.55
Bratt, Daniel		10.1.8	43.02
Bratt, Daniel, Jr.		60.1.0	25.80
Broadnecks, Robert		10.2.4 est 4.0.0	60.22
Carpenter, Ashman		10.1.8 est 10.1.8	86.05
Cawlly, John	?	25.9.2 (or 25.4.2?)	107.55
Cawlly, John, Jr.	?	15.2.6	64.53
Collison, Robert	Q	25.9.2 (or 25.4.2?)	107.55
Comfort, Stephen	Q	12.5.2 est 25.0.0	158.98
Cowgill, Edmund	Q	8.1.9	34.51
Croasdale, Robert	Q	25.4.2	107.55
Cutlar, Benjamin	Q	12.2.0	52.27
Dungan, Jeremiah	Q	25.9.2 (or 25.4.2?)	107.55
Dunn, George		15.2.6	64.53
Dye, Jonathan		6.1.0	25.80
Field, Joseph		12.7.0 est 30.0.0	138.03
Gillam, Lucas	Q	12.2.0	52.27
Gosiin, William		12.2.0	52.27
Gregg, Patrick		12.4.0 est 12.0.0	103.25

Table Continued

Name	Quaker Affiliation	Penna. Currency	Constant $
Hatcher, Nicholas		6.1.0	25.80
Headley, Joseph		15.2.6	64.53
Hudleston, William		12.2.0	52.27
Jackson, Thomas		6.1.0	25.80
Jenks, Thomas	Q	40.6.8	172.10
Longshore, Euclydus	Q	26.4.4 (or 26.9.4 ?)	111.86
Longshore, Robert	disowned	8.1.9	34.51
Longshore, Thomas	Q	6.1.0	25.80
Mackray, Matthew		6.1.0	25.80
Mannasa, widow		10.3.0 est 8.0.0	77.44
Mitchel, John	Q	28.9.8	121.54
Mode, Andrew	Q	12.2.0	52.27
Moon, James	Q	25.4.2	107.55
Morgan, Thomas	?	15.2.6	64.53
Morgan, William	?	6.1.0	25.80
Paxson, James	Q	25.4.2	107.55
Paxson, Thomas	Q	25.9.2 (or 25.4.2?)	107.55
Paxson, William	Q	50.8.4	215.10
Praul, John	?	50.8.4	215.10
Praul, John, Jr.	?	10.1.8	43.02
Pugh, Joseph		8.1.4 (or 8.1.9?)	34.42
Richardson, Joseph	Q	75.12.6	322.67
Row, Matthew		40.6.8 (or 90.6.8?)	172.10
Rue, Matthew, Jr.		6.1.0	25.80
Rue, Richard		10.1.8	43.02
Shaford, Leonard		6.1.0	25.80
Slack, Henry		19.2.8	81.63
Stackhouse, Isaac	Q	35.5.10	150.58
Stackhouse, James	Q	8.1.4 (8.1.9?)	34.42
Stackhouse, Joseph	Q	25.4.2	107.55
Stringer, Vinfrey		6.0.0	25.80
Suber, John Peter		20.3.4	86.05
Tate, Anthony		35.5.10	105.58
Teytos, Francis		15.5.10 est 20.0.0	107.90
Thackery, James	Q	12.2.0	52.27
Thackery, James, Jr.	Q	10.1.8	43.02
Vanhorn, Barnit		10.3.4 est 10.0.0	86.05
Vanhorn, Gabriel		35.5.10	105.58
Vanhorn, Garret		15.2.6	64.53
Vansant, Garret		20 .3.4	86.05
Vansant, Isaiah		8.4.0 est 16.0 .0	103.25
Walker, George	Q	12.2. 0	52.27

Table Continued

Name	Quaker Affiliation	Penna. Currency	Constant $
Walker, Joseph	Q	40.6.8	172.10
Watson, John	Q	30.5.0	129.07
White, Peter		18.3.0	83.89
Wildman, James	Q	15.2.6	64.53
Williams, Stephen		45.7.6	193.60
Wilson, David	Q	6.1.0	25.80
Wilson, Stephen	Q	12.4.0 est 12.0.0	103.25
Wilson, Thomas	Q	1 0.1.8	43.02
Winnar, Isaac		6.1.0	25.80
Winnar, John		6.1.0	25.8.0
Woolston, Jeremiah	Q	12.4.0 est 12.0.0	103.25
Woolston, John	Q	35.5.10	150.58
Woolston, Samuel	Q	12.2.0	52.27
Woolston, Samuel	Q	15.2.6	64.53
Wright, Charles		12.2.0 est 18.0.0	128.43
Wright, Joseph	Q	15.2.6	64.53
Wright, Joseph	Q	25.12.6 est 50.0.0	322.67
Wright, Thomas	?	6.1.0	25.80
Young, Martin		6.1.0	25.80

* Constant $ (C$) is based on the wholesale price in Philadelphia, calculated on the geometric average of the monthly price of 20 commodities from 1821 to 1825; for 1757 this is 62.5.

est = land rented from someone else, taxes paid by the resident

mean C$ tax for entire township of 87 taxpayers:	C$82.43
mean C$ tax for 36 known Quaker taxpayers:	103.50
mean C$ tax for 38 known non-Quaker taxpayers:	69.50

Single Men

Each was taxed on 6sh Penna. currency = $.80 = C$1.28

Name	Quaker Affiliation
Price, James at his place	
Richardson, Joshua at his father's	Q
Smith, Joseph at Charles Wright's	?
Subers, George at his father's	

Table continued

MIDDLETOWN TOWNSHIP TAX LIST, 1757

Name	Quaker Affiliation
Subers, John at his father's	
Taylor, Thomas at James Moon's	
Teytos, Francis at his father's	
Thackery, Isaac at his father's	?
Vanhart, Adam	
Walker, Robert at his father's	?
Watson, Benjamin	Q
Wildman, John at Jeremiah Dungan's	disowned
Wildman, Joseph at Jeremiah Dungan's	Q
Wildman, Martin	disowned
Wostor, James at John Watson's	

mean tax of township of 117 including 30 single men:	C$61.62
mean tax of 40 known Quakers including 4 single men:	93.29
mean tax of 56 known non-Quakers including 18 single men:	47.57
mean tax of 38 known non-Quakers (excluding 18 single men):	69.50

APPENDIX 4: MEMBERS OF MIDDLETOWN MONTHLY MEETINGS, 1850

Bristol Preparative Meeting (Hicksite)

Reconstituted list of members as of August 1850, in household groups as they were listed in the 1850 census.

Sarah Adam

Samuel Allen
Sarah Allen
Dorcas Wharton

James W. Allen

Simeon Brooks

Edwin D. Buckman
Rebecca E. Buckman

Joshua V. Buckman
Mary (Knight) Buckman
Elizabeth Taylor
Rebecca T. Buckman
James Buckman
Grace Knight

Elizabeth Cabeen
 (wife of Samuel)

Elizabeth Cary

Miriam Comfort

Joseph M. Downing
Mary Ann Downing
Margaret Ann Downing
Joseph K. Downing
Hannah C. Downing
Maria F. Downing
Cornelia Downing
Hannah Coleman

William Milnor
 Downing
Allen Downing

Beulah Gilbert

Joseph B. Huchinson
Elizabeth Huchinson
Catharine Huchinson
John Huchinson

Ann Huchinson
Sarah Huchinson
Elizabeth H. Huchinson

Rebecca Hulme

Charles T. Iredell
Rebecca N. Iredell
Hannah Ann Iredell
Louisa Iredell
Samuel N. Iredell
Abigail N. Iredell
Mary Iredell
Charles Iredell, Jr.
Susan Iredell
Elizabeth Iredell
Hannah Iredell

James Ivins
Frances Ivins
Joshua G. Ivins

MIDDLETOWN MONTHY MEETING (HICKSITE) MEMBERS 1850

Rebecca (Warner) Johnson

David Jones
Barclay Jones

Esther Knight

Jesse W. Knight

Mary Knight
Phebe Knight

Charles Laing

Edward Laing
Frances Laing
Florence Laing

Walter Laing
Anna L. Laing
Elizabeth Laing
Catherine R. Laing
Mary Laing

John Longstreth
Ann W. Longstreth
Eleline Longstreth
Alfred Longstreth
Mary W. Longstreth
Edgar T. Longstreth
Anna Longstreth
Sallie Ann Longstreth

Lydia Lukens
Sarah Ann Lukens
Mary Jane Lukens
Peter Lukens
Garrett Lukens

Elizabeth Parry
Charles Trump Parry
Edward Trump Parry
Tacy Ann Parry
Caroline Parry

Anna Parry
William Henry Paxson

Jonathan Paxson
Elizabeth Paxson

Joshua Paxson
Anna W. Paxson
Edward Paxson

Sarah Paxson
Mary Paxson
Anna Paxson
Margery Paxson

Willett Paxson
Sarah C. Paxson

Charles W. Pierce
Mary S. Pierce
William C. Pierce

Joseph Kirkbride Rickey

Amos Rockhill

Benjamin Smith
Elizabeth Smith
Robert Henry Smith
Mary G. Smith

Rebecca Stackhouse

Anthony Swain
Abigail Swain
Edward Swain
Joseph W. Swain

Samuel Swain
Letitia B. Swain
Eliza Swain
Asenath Swain
Martha Swain

Mary Taylor
Edward Taylor
Michael Taylor
Caleb N. Taylor
Thomas N. Taylor
Emma Taylor
Franklin Taylor

Joames W. Thorn

Mary B. Tonkin

Edward Trump

Elizabeth Warner
Joseph F. Warner
Abigail Warner
Anne Warner
Sarah Warner
Mary Warner
Gulielma Warner
Ellen Warner

Lewis M. Wharton
Mary W. Wharton
Euphemia C. Wharton
Samuel A. Wharton
Jacob Clark Wharton
Sarah W. Wharton

Susanna S. Wildman
John K. Wildman
Benjamin A. Wildman
Charles Wildman
Ellwood Wildman

Middletown Preparative Meeting (Hicksite)

Members as of August 1850, in household groups according to the 1850 census.

George W. Adams	Samuel S. Briggs	Joseph Comly
	Mary R. Briggs	Elizabeth T. Comly
Sarah T. Allen	Mary Ann Briggs	Sarah T. Comly
	Ruth Anna Briggs	Ellwood T. Comly
Sarah Atherton	Sarah S. Briggs	Anna G. Comly
	Elizabeth Jane Briggs	Susan B. Comly
Amos Bailey	William Taylor Briggs	Isaac Tyson
Esther A. Bailey	Edward Briggs	
		Jeremiah W. Croasdale
Paxson Blakey	William Bunting	Sarah Croasdale
Letitia Blakey	Margery Bunting	John Croasdale
Anna S. Blakey	Abigail Bunting	Hannah Croasdale
Edward H. Blakey	Blakey Bunting	Robert Morris Croasdale
Elizabeth S. Blakey	Elizabeth P Bunting	
	Hannah Headley	Macre Croasdale
Sarah Blakey		Ruth Croasdale
Phebe Blakey	William Burgess	Anna Croasdale
Sarah Blakey, Jr.	Anna Mary Burgess	Mary R. Croasdale
	Elizabeth Burgess	Benjamin R. Croasdale
Thomas Blakey	Franklin P. Burgess	
Lydia W. Blakey		Ann Drake
Elizabeth W. Blakey	Benjamin Cadwallader	Rachel Gilbert
John Blakey	Elizabeth Cadwallader	Joanna [Ann?] Gilbert
James W. Blakey	Sarah Cadwallader	
Achsahanna Blakey		Isaac Eyre
Thomas Blakey	Mary Canby	Elizabeth K. Eyre
George Blakey	Joseph Canby	William Eyre
Caroline Blakey	Margaret P. Canby	Mary Eyre
	Mary H. Canby	
William Blakey	John P. Canby	Harvey Gillam
Elizabeth Blakey	Sarah Canby	Hannah Gillam
Mary Ann Blakey		Mary W. Gillam
Sarah L. Blakey	Hannah Carlile	William Henry Gillam
William T. Blakey		Harvey H. Gillam
Henry C. Blakey	Martha Carter	
		Jonathan W. Gillam
William W. Blakey	Mary C. Cary	Hannah C. Gillam
Anna Blakey		
Susan G. Blakey		Susanna Gillam
Elizabeth Blakey		Simon Gillam

245

MIDDLETOWN MONTHY MEETING (HICKSITE) MEMBERS 1850

William Gillam
Elizabeth Y. Gillam
Laura Gillam

Joshua S. Hulme

Richard Hulme
Anna M. Hulme
Elizabeth P. Hulme
Anna Rebecca Hulme

Robert Ivins

Helena Kirkbride
Elizabeth Kirkbride

Jonathan Kirkbride
Hannah Kirkbride
Charles W. Kirkbride
John Blakey Kirkbride
Jonathan Kirkbride, Jr.
Thomas Kirkbride
Mary Kirkbride

Abi Knight
Barclay Knight
Mary P. Knight
Anna T. Knight
Joshua Knight
Jane Knight
Martha Knight
Jane Knight

James Linton
Ann Linton
Ann C. Linton

Joseph W. Linton

Elias Livezey

Isaac Livezey
Deborah Livezey
William T. Livezey
Mary Jane Livezey
Edwin Livezey

Abraham Longshore
Mary W. Longshore
Cary Longshore

Joseph S. Longshore

Samuel C. Longshore

Thomas E. Longshore
Hannah E. Longshore
William H. Longshore
Wm. E. Channing
  Longshore
Lucretia Mott Longshore

Richard Mather
Esther Y. Mather
Lewis M. Mather
Benjamin Franklin
  Mather
Charles E. Mather

Benjamin Mather
Catherine Mather
Mary Mather
Elizabeth Mather
Benjamin Mather, Jr.
Patience Mather
Clara Mather

Rowland Mather
Sarah S. Mather
Tacy M. Mather
Anna C. Mather
Mary S. Mather
Jonathan K. Mather
Rebecca Mather
Joseph Mather

Gove Mitchell
Catherine M. Mitchell
Isaac S. Mitchell

John Allen Mitchell
Tacy Mitchell

John S. Mitchell
Phebe G. Mitchell
Emma Mitchell
Tacy Ann Mitchell

Pierson Mitchell
Caroline Mitchell

William Mitchell
Sarah P. Mitchell
Elizabeth Mitchell
Joseph Paul Mitchell
Hannah H. Mitchell
William P. Mitchell
Anna Mitchell

Mary Newbold
Elizabeth I. Newbold
William Penn Newbold
Rachel Wildman

James W. Newbold
Rebecca Newbold

Thomas F. Parry
Mary E. Parry
Rachel E. Parry
Elizabeth R. Parry
Henry C. Parry
John E. Parry

Mary Paul

John Paxson
Susan K. Paxson

Isaac Paxson
Sarah S. Paxson

Samuel H. Paxson
Sarah R. Paxson
Mary R. Paxson
John Paxson
Anna R. Paxson
William R. Paxson
Anna Richardson

Rachel Price
Granville W. Lukens
Letitia Lukens

Joseph Rich
Mary Rich
Mark Palmer Rich
John C. Rich
Tamar Ann Rich
Elizabeth Rich
Mary Rich, Jr.
Hannah Rich
Susanna Rich

Deborah C. Ridge

Jane Richardson
Benjamin Borden
Mary D. Borden

Joshua Richardson
Mary Richardson
Joseph Richardson
Edward Richardson
Mary J. Richardson

John Scarborough
Hannah Scarborough
Charles Reeder
   Scarborough
Amy Ann Scarborough
John W. Scarborough
Synthia Scarborough

Gilbert H. Shaw

Mary T. Smith

Elizabeth L. Stackhouse
Elizabeth Stackhouse
Mary L. Stackhouse
David L. Stackhouse
Sarah Stackhouse

Jonathan Thomas
Sarah Thomas
Jane Thomas

Ruthanna Tyson
Nathan Comly Tyson
Lukens C. Tyson

Ann B. Walton
Phebe Ann Walton
Sarah B. Walton
Blakey Walton
Lydia Walton
Rachel Walton
Martha Walton

John Warner
Lydia Warner
Lydia Ann Warner
Abner Buckman

Joseph Watson
Elizabeth Watson
William G. Watson
Mary Elizabeth Watson
Susan G. Watson
Joseph John Watson
Franklin Watson

Lydia Watson
John Watson
Isaiah Watson

Edward Wildman
Abi Wildman
Hector Wildman
Anna Wildman
Mary H. Wildman
Abigail Wildman

James Wildman
Rachel W. Wildman

John Wildman
Abigail T. Wildman
Jane T. Wildman

Ann Wilson
Sarah P. Wilson
Mardon Wilson, Jr.

Margaret Wilson
Mary Stackhouse

Mary S. Winder

Ann Woolston

Eliza Woolston

Rebecca Worthington
Rebecca Worthington, Jr.
Chalkley Worthington
Asa Curtis Worthington

Middletown Monthly Meeting (Orthodox)

Members as of August 1850, in household groups as listed in the 1850 census.

MIDDLETOWN MONTHY MEETING (ORTHODOX) MEMBERS 1850

William Allen
Martha Allen
Samuel Allen Stack-
 house

Thomas L. Allen
Marmaduke Allen

Sarah E. Allen

Emma A. Allen
Elizabeth C. Allen
Robert J. Allen

John Buckman
Martha Buckman
Mercy Buckman
John B. Buckman
Macre Buckman
Susanna Buckman
Mercy Buckman

Mary Burgess
Ann Burgess

Samuel Comfort
Elizabeth Comfort
Mary Ann Comfort

Jesse Comfort
Elizabeth Comfort
Elizabeth Comfort [Jr.]

Samuel Comfort
Anna E. Comfort
Samuel F. Comfort
Clara Comfort
Mercy Stackhouse

Elizabeth Cooper

Aaron Eastburn
Sarah C. Eastburn
Mary C. Eastburn

Cyrus Eastburn
Mercy Eastburn
Franklin Eastburn

Joseph Eastburn
Elizabeth Eastburn
Samuel C. Eastburn
Anna C. Eastburn

Sidney Eastburn

Grace Eastburn
Mary Ann Eastburn

Hannah Harvey

William Hicks

William S. Hilles
Sarah L. Hilles

Samuel Hulme
Rachel S. Hulme
John Hulme
Mary Hulme
Elizabeth Hulme
Albert Hulme

Lydia Jenkins

Elizabeth Jenks
 (wife of Joseph)

Elizabeth Jenks
 (wife of William P.)

Mary Jenks

Ann Elizabeth Kirkbride

Richard Maris Kirkbride

Samuel McIlwain

Edward Newbold

Evan Roberts
Rhoda Roberts
Caleb P. Roberts
Deborah Roberts
John Roberts
Charles Roberts
Nathan D. Roberts
Sarah C. Roberts

Joshua W. Roberts

Mercy Stackhouse

Michael Satterthwaite
Tacy Satterthwaite
Deborah Satterthwaite
Sarah Satterthwaite
Michael Satterthwaite

Robert W. Satterthwaite
Elizabeth R.
 Satterthwaite

Elizabeth Story

Lydia Tayler

Jenett Vanhorn

Mary Ann Vanuxum

Myers Fisher Warner

John Watson (Jr.)

John Wetheral

Hannah Willis

APPENDIX 5: GENEALOLGY CHARTS OF THE DATA SET FAMILIES

The data on the following family charts have been assembled from many places. The main source has been the records of Middletown Monthly Meeting, followed by other Friends' records, including Hinshaw's *Encyclopedia of Quaker Genealogy*. The federal census, wills, and Bucks County newspapers have provided bits of information. There are published genealogies for a few families, and W. W. Davis's three-volume history of Bucks County has some biographical sketches. Information has been gleaned from articles in various genealogical journals. Occasional dates or names have been supplied by descendants of the families. Some genealogical material has been collected from the web, but this can be problematical because sources are rarely cited. There is widespread confusion between Old Style and New Style dates in information copied from secondary sources.[1] I have tried to check all dates, but suspect that some inaccuracies have inevitably crept in.

The entries take the following form:

    Jane-2 m 13/4/1727 Jonathan Knight
    24/2/1696-7/5m/1745; -1/1782
    rem 1727 to Abington

The first name is a person of the surname family whose page it is; the number after the hyphen stands for his or her level of committee activity in the monthly meeting (see page 251 for an explanation of the code); m stands for married, followed by the date of the wedding (if known). A number in parentheses after m indicates a first or second (etc.) marriage. This is followed by the name of the spouse.

The first set of dates under a name is the family member's birth and death; the second set of dates is his or her spouse's birth and death (when known). They are given day/month/year, with m (for month) added to avoid confusion if the day is 12 or less. All dates before January 1, 1752 are Old Style, with the year beginning on March 25. Then, December was Tenth month, February was Twelfth month, so years between January 1 and March 24 are given with a slash, as in 5/12m/1723/4 (which is equivalent to February 5, 1724 New Style).

Names of Middletown Meeting **Hicksites** are printed in bold face. Names of *Orthodox* Middletown Friends are italicized. The affiliation of Friends who removed to other meetings before 1827 usually has not been noted.

Below the dates is additional information as to whether individuals were disowned, and when they arrived in or left Middletown Meeting. Removals are from meeting certificates, granted by one monthly meeting to another, and do not necessarily reflect residence in a given township. The date given is when the certificate was signed or received, not when the person may actually have moved.

The following abbreviations have been used:

dis	disowned for an offense other than the four specified below; occasionally other offenses are spelled out, such as "debt" for a business failure without complete transparency or honesty
dis (D)	disowned for taking strong drink to excess
dis (F)	disowned for fornication, usually with fiancé(e)
dis (M)	disowned for marrying out of unity with Friends or in some way contravening Friends' marriage procedures
dis (W)	disowned for military activity
dis +	disowned for one of the above named offenses plus additional breaches of discipline
(F)	charged with fornication but acknowledgment accepted, and the individual was not disowned

m	married
M	minister, see chart, below
MM	monthly meeting
NDMM	Northern District Monthly Meeting (in Philadelphia)
NS	New Style date, i.e. with the year beginning January 1
[non-Q]	a spouse who was not a Friend
OS	Old Style date, with the year beginning March 25, and January being Eleventh month; see page 294, n. 19.
rem	removed
res	residence in
ret	returned [to Middletown Monthly Meeting]
SDMM	Southern District Monthly Meeting (in Philadelphia)
unm	unmarried
WDMM	Western District Monthly Meeting (in Philadelphia)

A numeral from 1 to 6 after a name (Jane-2 in the example) indicates the level of activity in the meeting for business, in terms of committee assignments and offices. No effort has been made to correlate the number of assignments with the length of time a Friend was a member of Middletown Meeting.

1	no committee assignments	5	16 or more assignments
2	1-5 assignments	6	16 or more plus holding an office
3	6-10 assignments	6M	16 or more plus being a recorded minister
4	11-15 assignments		

The names in the following family charts are not included in the index. It has been impossible to fit into these charts all individuals who were not members of Middletown Meeting at one time or another from some of the larger extended families. Tracing movements from meeting to meeting gives a sense of the mobility of people, especially after the end of the Revolutionary War.

Allen Family

- Mary m 1716 David Palmer
  26/1/1692-1735;
  15/4/1692-10/9m/1731
  rem 1731 to Falls

- Ann- m 3m/1721 John Palmer
  12/7m/1694-   ;   -1/1782

- Jane m 13/4/1727 Jonathan Knight
  24/2/1696-7/5m/1745;   -1/5m/1745
  rem 1727 to Abington

- Priscilla m Thomas Smith
  22/2/1699-

- Samuel-2 m 1752 Elizabeth Clawson-1
  1/3m/1701-3/2m/1785;   -2/8m/1780
  rem 10/1744 to Falls MM (Bensalem)

- Richard 8/1m/1702/3 unm. "defective"

- William-4 m (1) 1740 Mary Welsh
  1715-13/2/1791;   -1747
  m (2) 1748 Mary Clothier-3
  1722-5/3m/1801

- Nicholas m 1743 Margaret Johnson
  -1750;
  he dis (M) 5/1743; she joined 2/1757

- Martha m 1738 James Welsh
  res: Bristol

- John-1 m (1) 1737 Elizabeth Walsh
  -1763;
  m(2) 15/10/1741 Elizabeth Large
  m(3) 1746/7 Rebecca Gibbs
  she rem 1765 from Falls to Burlington
  she rem 1780 Burlington to Falls

- Sarah m 1744 William Large
  rem 1744 to Falls; ret 1785
  rem 1787 to Buckingham

- Ann m 20/7/1774 Joseph Paul
  18/11/1755-
  res: Warminster

- Samuel-6 m 23/5/1781 Sarah Brown
  16/7/1757-12/12/1833;
  27/11/1758-20/5/1795
  rem 1803 to Falls; ret 11/1821

- Jane m 16/11/1784 Benjamin Shoemaker
  27/1/1761-
  res: Cheltenham

- Sarah unmarried, 23/1/1767-

- Joseph m 13/3/1764 Sarah Plumley
  28/8/1741-1803;   -1809
  he dis (F) 11/1761; she dis (F) 7/1760
  res: Bensalem

- Jane m 15/11/1768 Samuel Wright
  12/3m/1744-
  rem 1769 to Chesterfield
  ret 1789 from Upper Springfield

- Samuel m Sm/1773 Sarah Allen
  4/12m/1746-
  dis (M)1773; res: Bensalem

- Mary m 1780 Daniel Severns
  18/9/1749- she dis (M) 1780

- Sarah 27/10/1751- 1759

- Abigail m(1) 19/5/1774 Henry Lippincott
  18/10/1754-
  rem 1774 to Chesterfield; ret 1784
  m(2) 1787 Robert Ennis or Innis;
  she dis (M) 1787

- Margaret m 14/10/1779 Thomas Stapler
  10/2m/1757-   ;
  rem 1780 to Wilmington

- *William*-6M m 1m/1785 *Sarah Richardson*-2
  2/8m/1759-8/3m/1837;
  4/2m/1762-16/9/1828

- John 19/17/1763- died before 1802

- Sarah m 5m/1773 Samuel Allen
  ; 4/12m/1746-   ; he dis (M)1773

- Mary m 3/5m/1763 Joseph Rodman
  he dis (M)1763;

- Sarah m William Dickinson (he was b. 1738)

- Achsah died young

- *Rebecca*-6 m 15/6/1773 *Pierson Mitchell*-6
  26/9/1754-27/7/1815;
  7/9m/1751-4/4/1834 (see pp 270-271)

- William-2 m 31/10/1786 Sarah Lancaster
  11/4m/1757- 1818; 1765-12/10m/1792
  res : Bristol Township

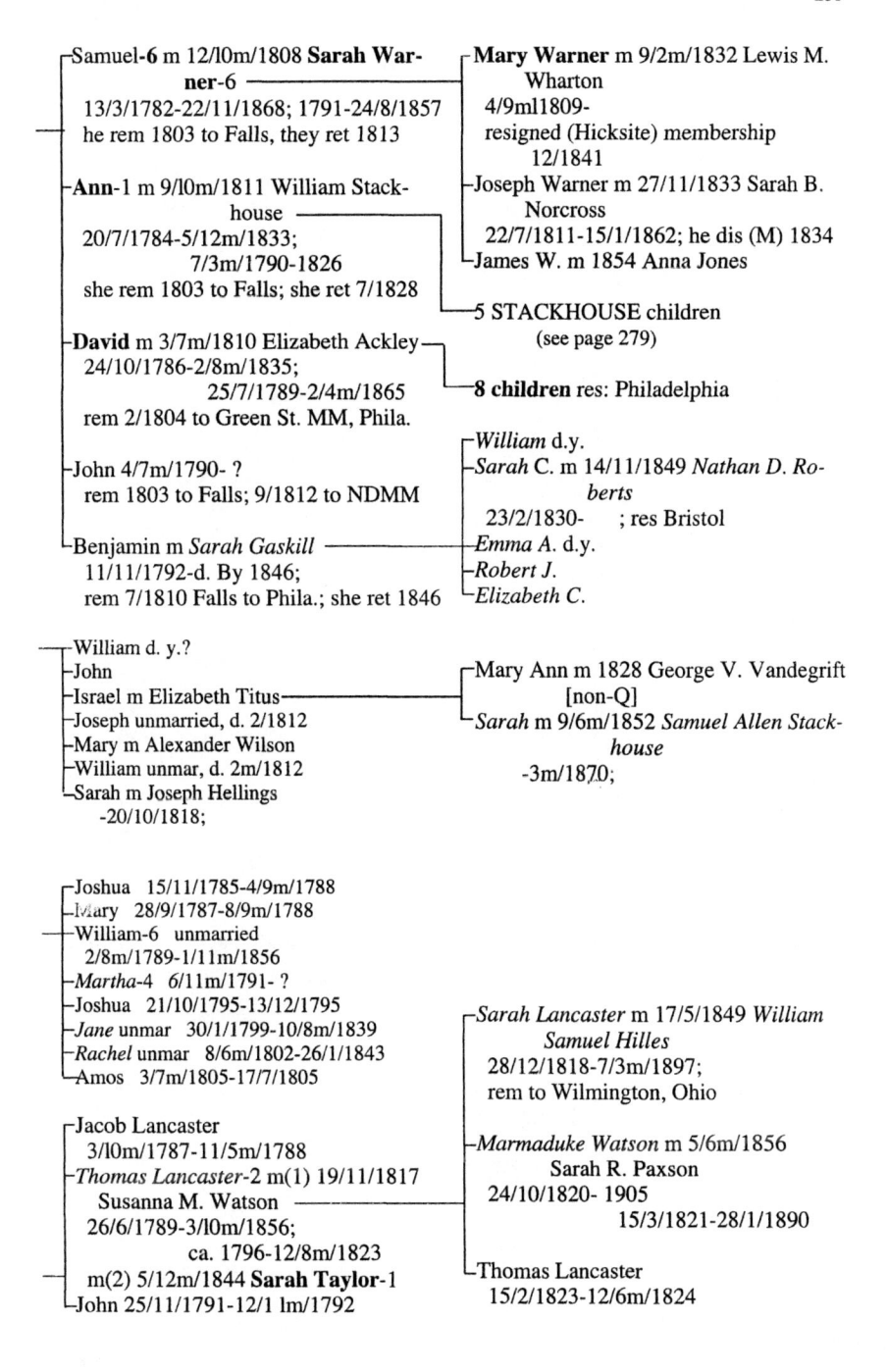

┌Samuel-6 m 12/10m/1808 **Sarah Warner**-6 ─────────
│   13/3/1782-22/11/1868; 1791-24/8/1857
│   he rem 1803 to Falls, they ret 1813
│
├**Ann**-1 m 9/10m/1811 William Stackhouse ─────
│   20/7/1784-5/12m/1833;
│   7/3m/1790-1826
│   she rem 1803 to Falls; she ret 7/1828
│
├**David** m 3/7m/1810 Elizabeth Ackley ──
│   24/10/1786-2/8m/1835;
│   25/7/1789-2/4m/1865
│   rem 2/1804 to Green St. MM, Phila.
│
├John 4/7m/1790- ?
│   rem 1803 to Falls; 9/1812 to NDMM
│
└Benjamin m *Sarah Gaskill* ─────────
     11/11/1792-d. By 1846;
     rem 7/1810 Falls to Phila.; she ret 1846

┌**Mary Warner** m 9/2m/1832 Lewis M.
│   Wharton
│   4/9m1809-
│   resigned (Hicksite) membership
│   12/1841
├Joseph Warner m 27/11/1833 Sarah B.
│   Norcross
│   22/7/1811-15/1/1862; he dis (M) 1834
└James W. m 1854 Anna Jones

─5 STACKHOUSE children
    (see page 279)

─8 children res: Philadelphia

┌*William* d.y.
├*Sarah C.* m 14/11/1849 *Nathan D. Roberts*
│   23/2/1830-   ; res Bristol
├*Emma A.* d.y.
├*Robert J.*
└*Elizabeth C.*

┌William d. y.?
├John
├Israel m Elizabeth Titus─────
├Joseph unmarried, d. 2/1812
├Mary m Alexander Wilson
├William unmar, d. 2m/1812
└Sarah m Joseph Hellings
   -20/10/1818;

┌Mary Ann m 1828 George V. Vandegrift
│   [non-Q]
└*Sarah* m 9/6m/1852 *Samuel Allen Stackhouse*
   -3m/1870;

┌Joshua 15/11/1785-4/9m/1788
├Mary 28/9/1787-8/9m/1788
├William-6 unmarried
│   2/8m/1789-1/11m/1856
├*Martha*-4 6/11m/1791- ?
├Joshua 21/10/1795-13/12/1795
├*Jane* unmar 30/1/1799-10/8m/1839
├*Rachel* unmar 8/6m/1802-26/1/1843
└Amos 3/7m/1805-17/7/1805

┌Jacob Lancaster
│   3/10m/1787-11/5m/1788
├*Thomas Lancaster*-2 m(1) 19/11/1817
│   Susanna M. Watson ─────
│   26/6/1789-3/10m/1856;
│   ca. 1796-12/8m/1823
│   m(2) 5/12m/1844 **Sarah Taylor**-1
└John 25/11/1791-12/1 1m/1792

┌*Sarah Lancaster* m 17/5/1849 *William*
│   *Samuel Hilles*
│   28/12/1818-7/3m/1897;
│   rem to Wilmington, Ohio
├*Marmaduke Watson* m 5/6m/1856
│   Sarah R. Paxson
│   24/10/1820- 1905
│   15/3/1821-28/1/1890
└Thomas Lancaster
    15/2/1823-12/6m/1824

Blakey Family

```
                                    ┌─Lydia m 1769 Jacob Paxson
                                    │  ca. 1734-3/8m/1772;
                                    │         6/11m/1745/6-13/7/1832
                                    │  rem 1769 to Buckingham
                                    │  he m(2) 1777 Sarah Shaw
                                    │
William Blakey, Jr.-3 m 25/7/1733   │
    Jael Bickerdike-6M ─────────────┼─William-6M m 30/6/1763 Sarah
3/2m/1697-1750; 1703-28/10/1782     │    Kirkbride-6 ─────────────
  she m(2) 3/10m/1753 Jonathan      │  19/2/1739-20/6/1822;
    Palmer (his third)              │         31/10/1739-1/10m/1821
  she rem 12/1753 to Falls; ret 2/1766
                                    │
                                    │
                                    │
                                    └─Joshua-6 m 28/11/1758 Sarah Cary —
                                       1741-29/12/1814;   -21/11/1823
```

The first set of dates under a name is the Blakey family member's birth and death; the second set of dates is his or her spouse's birth and death. The letter m in a date indicates month. Bold names are **Hicksite**; italicized are *Orthodox*. Other abbreviations include:

dis = disowned; dis (M) = disowned for a marriage offense
m = married
rem = removed [to another location]
ret = returned [to Middletown Meeting]

The numeral from 1 to 6 after a name indicates the level of activity in the meeting for business, in terms of committee assignments and offices.

1	no committee assignments	5	16 or more assignments
2	1-5 assignments	6	16 or more plus an office
3	6-10 assignments	6M	16 or more plus being a recorded minister
4	11-15 assignments		

- Mary-2 m 1792 **Joseph Wilson-6** — 4 WILSON children (see page 287)
  1/8m/1764-21/3/1821;
  17/3/1762-1/12m/1840
  he m(2) 15/12/1825 **Margaret Stackhouse-6**
  10/7m/1784-3/11m/1859
  - **Ann-3** m 29/4m/1830 **Yarnall Walton**
    18/4/1806- ; -d. by 1845
    rem 1830 to Byberry MM; ret 8/1845
  - **Sarah** 17/11/1807-
  - **Thomas-1** m 16/5/1833 **Lydia Walton-1**
    23/4/1810-16/4/1868; -5/2m/1859
    rem 1851 to Little Falls MM, Md.
  - **William-2** m 25/12/1839 **Elizabeth Gilbert-3**
    23/12/1811-16/8/1862; ca. 1819-
    she joined 10/1840
  - **Paxson-5** m 10/10/1838 **Letitia Smith-6**
    15/2/1815-10/7m/1882; ca.1814-d. by 1867
    rem 1867 to Richland MM

- **Thomas-6** m 12/6m/1805 **Laetitia Paxson, Jr.-2**
  14/8/1766-25/8/1823;
  ca. 1779 -2/3m/1815

- John-6 unmar. 18/9/1768-3/10m/1836

- Grace unmar. 3/8m/1771-1/8m/1775

- **Lydia-6** m 19/12/1799 **John Watson-6** — 7 WATSON children (see pages 283)
  19/9/1774-22/2/1859;
  1/8m/1768-7/1m/1844
  - **Mary-4** unmarried 25/7/1793-8/4m/1837
  - **Ann-3** m 1821 **Jonathan Woolston-6**
    24/4/1795-27/4/1865;
    9/2m/1791-15/4/1842
  - Elizabeth 31/12/1796-3/10m/1823
  - **Sarah** 21/5/1799-
  - **Phebe-1** 1/8m/1801-
  - **William Watson-5** m 12/4m/1832 **Anna Gillam-5**
    22/5/1805-19/11/1879;
    12/8m/1812-19/3/1876

- Sarah -twin, 22/3/1777-19/7/1777

- William twin, 22/3/1777-26/5/1813
  rem 1796 to Philadelphia

- **William-6** m 17/10/1792 **Elizabeth Watson-6** — 6 PAXSON children (see pages 274-275)
  29/11/1759-9/10m/1831;
  5/10m/1766-1/6m/1845
  - Beulah 24/1/1799-29/10/1801
  - **Mary W.** m 14/5/1823 **William Bunting**
    7/8m/1800-6/4m/1858; 1795-22/2/1863
    rem 1816 to Falls; ret 1823; rem 1824
  - **Joshua-1** m 20/1/1825 Elizabeth Flowers
    26/6/1802-
    rem 1824; dis (M) 10/1825
  - **Mark W.-1** m _____ Greene?
    29/10/1804-
    rem 1836; resigned membership 1837
  - **Sarah-1** m 18/2/1830 **Yardley Briggs**
    2/5m/1807-22/8/1892; 1805-4/1873
    rem 1830 to Makefield; ret 1833
    rem 1836 to Burlington
  - *Rachel M.* m James L. Peirce MD
    11/6m/1809-
    rem 1824 to Falls; rem 1833 to NDMM
  - *Tacy* m John Robbins
    2/4m/1812- ; 1818-27/4/1880
    rem 1836 to NDMM (Orthodox)
  - John unmarried 8/6m/1815-

- Esther m 23/5/1782 Hezekiah Linton
  2/7m/1761- ; 23/9/1748-
  rem 1783 to Buckingham

- **Sarah-6** m(1) 22/5/1783 Thomas Paxson, Jr.-5
  26/3/1763- ; 4/5m/1753-25/9/1809
  m(2) 14/5/1812 **George Walker**
  she rem 1812 to Falls

- Samuel m 1796 Elizabeth __ [non-Q]
  20/4/1765-ca. 1818;
  dis (D, M) 2/1797

- Joshua-3 m 1798 Rebecca Watson-1
  13/12/1767-11/2m/1815;
  ca.1771-17/9/1823
  he dis (D) 9/1809, reinstated 3/1813

- Beulah 6/10m/1769-6/9m/1775

- Hephzibah 3/11m/1771-2/7m/1772

- Mary 6/6/1777-21/6/1777

Comfort Family

Stephen-6M m 25/6m/1744 Mercy Croasdale-6
26/12m/1720/1-27/9/1772;
28/12/1723/4-12/1m/1800
rem 5m/1754 to Wrightstown; ret 6m/1755

- John m(1) 3/4m/1771 Mary Woolman —
  5/8m/1745-1/7m/1803;
  18/10/1750-6/4m/1797
  rem 1771 to Burlington; 1790 to Falls
  m(2) 14/11/1798 Ann English ———
  she d. 3/3/1803

- Ezra-6M m 1/9m/1772 *Alice Fell*-5 ———
  11/8m/1747-15/1/1820;
  3/9m/1754-6/11m/1840
  rem 1785 to Gwynedd MM

- Jeremiah unmarried
  26/8/1750-6m/1780

- Stephen-6 m 9/5m/1776 *Sarah Stevenson*-6 ———
  26/2/1753-1/10m/1826;
  13/2/1754-16/4/1837

- *Grace*-6 m 14/4/1774 Jonathan Stackhouse-4
  5/8m/1755- 11m/1827;
  31/8/1750-15/4/1805

- *Mercy*-6M m 14/10/1790 Aaron Phillips
  18/9/1757-
  rem 1/1791 to Buckingham; ret 1/1821

- *Moses*-1 m 10m/1782 *Elizabeth Mitchell*-2 ———
  4/4/1760-17/4/1838;
  17/3/1758-11/2m/1837
  rem 1784 to Abington,
  rem 1786 to Falls

- Robert-1 m 11m/1786 Mary Parry
  24/12/1763-2/6m/1851;
  10/5m/1769-6/2m/1861
  rem 1781 to Mt. Holly; ret 1784
  rem 1787 to Horsham; ret 12/1789
  rem 5/1791 to Falls; 1795 to Horsham

- Hannah 10/7m/1765- d.y.

```
┌─9 children +
├─Samuel m(1) Rebecca Moon
│   1776-   ;   -1836
│   rem 1790 to Falls
│   m(2) Elizabeth Cox

 ┌─Ezra-1 2/12m/1799-
─┤  to Middletown 4/1819
 │  disciplined (F) 1820 but not disowned
 │  rem 5/1821 to Centre MM, Del.
 │
┬┴─5 children +
 └─John-6 m 17/10/1798 Ann Eastburn ──
       17/9/1775-20/10/1840;
              27/12/1774-19/9/1867

 ┌─David m 1799 Beulah Walton
 │   27/4/1777-21/8/1856;
 │          16/9/1772-29/7/1848
 │   rem 1799 to Falls; 1800 to Horsham
 ├─Samuel-6 m 21/2/1809 Elizabeth
 │       James-6
─┤   6/12m/1778-21/2/1860;
 │          15/7/1780-29/2/1859
 │   rem 1797 from Falls; 1799 to Falls
 ├─Jeremiah-1 m 14/10/1807 Sarah
 │       Cooper
 │   4/7m/1780-18/5/1872;
 │          23/3/1788-26/8/1865
 │   rem 1808 to Horsham MM
 └─Stephen m 4/4/1807 Lydia Jones
     7/3m/1782-1860;
     rem 1804 to Philadelphia

 ┌─Rebecca 31/10/1783-27/1/1784
 ├─Mary m 12/11m/1806 Solomon C. Jones
 │   11/2m/1785-   ;   30/6/1783-
 ├─Jonathan 12/9m/1786-16/5/1793
─┼─Elizabeth 27/12/1787-7/3m/1859
 ├─Mercy 5/9m/1789-28/9/1826
 ├─Aaron m 17/10/1816 Ann Woolston ──
 │   8/11m/1791-  ; 27/2/1795-
 │   rem 1796 to Falls; ret 1804
 │   rem 1817 to Falls; rem 1840 to Michigan
 ├─Sarah 25/4m/1793-15/11/1821
 ├─Grace 20/4m/1795-29/9/1801
 ├─Moses m 1828 Mercy Comfort ──
 │   10/11m/1797-1/3m/1871;
 │                 24/9/1805-
 └─Josiah-5 m 27/10/1824 Rachel Cad-
           wallader-1 ──
     10/2m/1800-15/12/1852;
            20/8/1802-7/7/1858
     rem 2/1828 from Falls to Middletown
     rem 6/1829 to Falls
```

```
┌─6 children +
├─Ann m 1836 John Wildman
│   11/5m/1815-
├─Mercy m Moses Comfort
│   24/9/1805-10/12m/1881;
│        10/11m/1797-1/3m/1871
│   res Falls

├─Mary Ann-1 unmarried
│   7/9m/1810-8/3m/1868

├─Sarah
│   18/10/1812-6/3m/1815

├─Jesse-1 m 14/8/1845 Elizabeth
│       Thomas
│   9/10m/1814-11/5m/1880;
│          14/11m/1818-6/8m/1868
│   rem to Falls MM

├─Elizabeth m 19/11/1846 Joseph
│       Eastburn
│   3/6m/1816-25/9/1886;
│          18/4/1814-31/10/1891
│   res Buckingham
└─Samuel m(1) 1842 Sarah Stack-
        house-1
     27/4/1818-3/8m/1881;
            13/8/1812-3/7m/1848
     m(2) 1850 **Mercy Ann Stackhouse**
            1824-
     she rem 1854 to Green St. MM


───── 8 children res in Falls




───── 2 children res in Falls


───── 3 children res in Falls

          **Miriam** m 1855 ___ Chappel
          from Salem MM 10/1839
```

Croasdale Family

─Ezra 5/12m/1687-4m/1702

─William-6 m(1) 16/7/1713 Grace
    Harding-2
  19/7/1690- 1781;
        10/11m/1692- 1745
  m(2) 10/5M/1764 Deliverance
    (Bills) Hayhurst-4
  she d. 28/8/1783;
  she m(1) Cuthbert Hayhurst
    15/1/1705-26/12/1753

─Grace unmarried
  6/2m/1692/3-d.y.

─Jeremiah-5 m 20/7m/1720 Grace
    Heaton-6M
  29/8/1694- 1748/9;
      6/8m/1703-23/10/1769?

─Timothy unmarried
  10/2m/1696-

    ┌Mary-1 m(1) 29/3/1745 William Briggs, Jr.
      28/7/1714-   ; 1725-1749
      m(2) 1m/1757 John Blaker
      rem 1758 to Wrightstown
    ─Sarah-1 m 22/3/1740 Robert Lucas
      30/11/1716-   ; 20/2/1719/20(OS)
      rem 9m/1743 to Falls
    ─Ann-1 m 28/8/1742 James Briggs
      28/8/1719-   ; 24/2/1716-1784
      rem 1744 to Wrightstown; ret to Mid 1751
      rem 1757 to Wrightstown
    ─Grace m 22/10/1748 Jonathan Knight
      27/5/1722-7/5/1749; 5/10m/1722-3/1772
      rem 4/1749 to Abington MM
      res: Southampton
    ─George 29/5/1723- d.y.?
    ─John 3/3/1725- 1749
    ─Rebecca m 22/10/1748 Henry Hough
      17/1/1727-1/5m/1773; 25/5/1729-20/12/1805
      rem 1749 to Falls
    ─Rachel m 19/1/1757 Joseph Watson
      17/4/1732-1/3m/1773; 25/5/1729- 1805
      rem 1757 to Falls
    ─Hannah 7/lm/1736-
    └Phebe m 6/1759 Benjamin Watson, (see p. 282)
      28/2/1738-29/10/1815; 14/9/1730-18/10/1796
      rem 1759 to Falls

    ┌Grace m 25/6/1745 John Townsend
      8/9m/1720-23/1/1803;
                 7/11/1724-5/4m/1800
      rem 4/1749 to Abington
    ─Mercy-6 m 25/8/1744 Stephen Comfort-6M
      28/12/1723/4-12/11m/1800; (see pp. 256-7)
      2/6m/1721-27/9/1772
      rem 1754 to Wrightstown; ret 1755
    ─Ezra-6 m(1) 14/4/1749 Sarah Shaw-1
      12/5m/1726-9/3m/1794; 29/4/1729-
      m(2) 20/12/1759 Hannah Scott-1 (b. 1740)
      m(3) 1769 Mary Biles-2
    ─Robert-6 m 15/9/1750 Margery Hayhurst-6
      30/6/1728-9/8m/1780; 15/12/1730-29/6/1783
    ─Ann-6M m 17/9/1748 John Hampton
      15/11/1730/1-28/1/1796;
                17/1/1724-10/9m/1775
      rem 12/1748 to Wrightstown
    ─Eber-1 m(1) 19/5/1757 Anna Shaw-1
      28/1/1733-   ; 16/5/1737-1759
      disciplined (F) but not disowned 3/1758
      dis (D+) 5/1760; rem 1760 to ?
    ─Abijah 5/10m/1735- 1752
    ─Macre-3 m 20/3/1765 Thomas Wilson-6
      -16/8/1777; 19/1/1731-23/7/1803
      he m(1) 21/4/1756 Margaret Bye-1
      from Buckingham to Middletown 5/1772
    └Achsah d. 9/8m/1777

—Anna m 1773 Abraham Knight "of
    Southampton"
    1755-   ; dis (M) 11/1773
┌Joseph-2 m 11m/1780 Rachel Stevenson
    1755-1832; 1757-
    disciplined (W) not disowned 2/1776
    rem 1804 to Horsham MM
 Mary m 1780 __ Simpson
    1757-   ; dis (M) 2/1780
-Benjamin
    dis (F) 5/1806
└Hannah m 1787 Jonathan Croasdale
    12/10m/1765-   ; -1831; dis (M) 12/1787
    she dis (M) 2/1787
┌Ezra (mind impaired)
    12/1m/1770-20/8/1849
-William 12/lm/1773-8/9m/1789
-Grace-6 m 24/9/1803 Asa Knight
    rem 1/1804 to Horsham MM; ret 7/1830
-Sarah m 1801 __ Larue
    dis (M) 5/1801
└Achsah m James Walton
    14/1/1778-13/10/1856;
    rem 8/1795 to Horsham MM

┌Jeremiah-6 m 13/5/1772 **Ann Quinby**-6
    20/4/1751-27/9/1829;
            17/3/1748/9-7/4m/1831
-Abi m 13/12/1770 Evan Townsend
    16/7/1753-
    rem 4/1771 to Abington
-Rachel-1 m(1) 18/12/1777 James Paxson
    7/3m/1756-   ; 12/7m/1749-2/5m/1779
    disciplined (F) but not disowned 3/1779
    m(2) 16/9/1784 Robert Eastburn
    rem 12/1784 to Buckingham MM
-Margery, Jr.-5 m(1) 12/1lm/1778 Daniel
        Livezey
    3/7m/1758-
    rem 3/1779 to Abington; ret 8/1780
    m(2) 1789 Nathan Baker
    rem 3/1819 to Solebury MM
-Macre m 12/4m/1781 Samuel Eastburn
    7/12m/1760-
    rem 5/1781 to Buckingham MM
└Robert-3 m(1) 1786 Tacy Knight
    20/2/1763-15/6/1821; -30/5/1791
    m(2) 25/10/1792 Hannah (Woolston)
        Mitchell [she m(1) 25/10/1784
        Henry Mitchell; she d. 14/9/1793]
    m(3) 11/11/1802 **Ruth Richardson**-1
            25/8/1773-30/9/1854
    rem 2/1835 to Makefield MM
└John dis (W) 6/1776

259

┌**Rachel**-2 m 15/11/1798 Abner Buckman
    13/3/1773-   ;
    rem 1799 to Wrightstown; ret 1815
-Elizabeth 23/12/1774-d. by 1819
-**Ann**-1 m 12/3m/1801 **James Linton**-2
    23/12/1776-   ; 10/12m/1769-1854
    rem 1819 to Stroudsburg; ret 1827 see p.267
-Margery m 22/4/1802 Jacob Twining
    17/1/1779-5/4m/1861;
            28/1/1776-20/9/1863
    rem 1802 to Wrightstown; res. Newtown
-**Robert**-5 m 1824 **Mary R. Rowland**-6
    9/4m/1781-5/8m/1847; -ca.1888
    she rem 1864 to Green St MM; ret 1883
-**Macre**-6 unmarried
    2/211783-3001/1862
    rem 1835 to Makefield; ret 1850
-**Sarah**-1 m 1813 Aaron Phillips
    30/3/1785-   ; - 1858
-**Tabitha** m 1810 William Pickering
    16/12/1786-
    rem 1810 to Buckingham MM
-**Deborah**-1
    2/10m/1788-
    rem 1832 to Wrightstown
-**Aaron** m 1826 Mary Bell
    22/8/1791-
    rem 12/1818 to Stroudsburg
└Martha m 1818 Thomas Hayhurst
    6/lm/1796-
    rem 6/1821 to Frankford MM

┌Jonathan 6/9m/1787-18/4/1793
-Margery-1 25/2/1789-25/4/1823
-James 6/5m/1791-6/9m/1791

┌**Jeremiah Woolston**-6 m 27/17/1825 **Sarah
        Wilson**-3
    14/8/1793- 1873; 9/7m/1799-1/7m/1866

-**Mary R.**-2 m 1828 **Samuel Briggs**
    7/8m/1803-
-Joseph H. b. 8/lm/1806
    rem 1825 to Solebury
-Rachel 20/11/1807-9/l0m/1815
-**Tacy**-1 m 28/3/1833 James Briggs
    28/11/1810-
    rem 1836 to Makefield
└**Robert Maurice** (or Morris)-2 m
        4/3m/1836 **Mercy M. Cadwallader**-1
    6/2m/1812- 1890; 1811- 1896
    rem 1835 to Makefield; ret 1844
    rem 1848 to Falls

Gillam Family

Lucas Gillam m 18/6/1748
        Ann Dungan-2
ca. 1715-

- Susannah-1 m 13/2/1771 Jonathan
  Linton
  -1803; 11/5m/1743-1793
  rem 7/1787 to Sadsbury MM

- Jeremiah m 1777 Margaret ___
  dis (M) 11/1777

- Lucas m Rebecca ___
  dis (W) 4/1778

- Simon-6M m 11/12m/1783 Anna Paxson-6
  24/1/1759-31/8/1839;
      4/7m/1762-ca.1840
  rem 4/1821 to Upper Springfield MM

- Joseph
  dis (left in a disorderly way) 8/1781

- John m 1786 Mary ___
  dis (W,M) 5/1786; reinstated 12/1797
  rem 1798 to NDMM (Phila.)

- Sarah-1 m 11/5m/1780 Euclydus Longshore-1
  -1818; 27/4/1735-14/6/1804
  he m(1) ca. 1760 Susanna Vanhorn ___

- Joshua m 30/12/1790 Anne Taylor
  rem to "Niagara Country" (Canada)
  dis (M+) 9/1791; reinstated 12/1797

- James
  dis (W+) 4/1787

- Thomas m ___
  dis (M,W) 2/1795; rem to Canada

8 LINTON children (see page 267)

Mary m 17/10/1811 Thomas Martin
22/10/1784-6/6/1829;   -ca. 1889
rem 1826 to Upper Springfield, NJ

William-6 m 16/11/1809 Susanna Woolston-6
1/l0m/1786-31/12/1844;
18/11/1787-31/8/1860

Isaac m 11/l0m/1810 Margaret Mitchell
13/4/1788-5/3m/1849;
6/10m/1785-5/2m/1879
disciplined (debt) but not disowned, 3/1822
removed 3/1822 to Springfield MM

Anna (unmarried)
30/10/1794-8/2m/1798

— 6 **LONGSHORE children**
(see page 269)

— 9 LONGSHORE children
(see page 269)

Elizabeth-2 m 27/2/1834 **Joseph Watson**-3
17/9/1810-28/1/1879;
25/8/1805-25/10/1886

Anna-5 m 12/4m/1832 **William Watson Blakey**-5
12/8m/1812-19/3/1876;
22/5/1805-19/11/1879

Harvey-6 m(1) 29/3/1837 **Hannah Hunt**-3
1/7m/1814-10/2m/1891;
1817-25/6/1857
rem 1855 to Cherry St. MM, Phila.
m(2) 1862 Sarah Grubb Caley

Jonathan W.-6 m 12/3m/1840 **Hannah Cadwallader**-5
25/10/1816-30/11/1898; -1891

William m 22/12/1842 **Elizabeth Y. Stackhouse**-1
15/11/1818-9/8m/1892; ca.1818-
rem 6/1853 to Green St. MM

Simon-6M m 15/l0m/1851 **Elizabeth Richardson**-6
24/11/1820-12/1/1889;
ca.1830-21/4/1908

Susanna m 20/3m/1845 **George Justice**
18/4/1823-29/11/1904;
rem 1845 to Falls MM

Hannah-2 m 11/3m/1846 **Lewis R. Appleton**
3/6m/1825-
rem 1846 to Falls; returned 1856

Mary-1 m 27/8/1846 Aaron Winder, MD [non-Q]
25/8/1827-6/llm/1888; 17/10/1821-
retained membership 7/1847

Jenks Family

Thomas Jenks Sr.-6 m 3m/1731
Mercy Wildman-6
1m/1699/1700-4/5m/1797
3/1m/1711/2-26/7/1787
rem 1731 to Buckingham MM;
ret 1734 to Middletown MM

— Mary-2 m 26/10m/1752NS Samuel
  Twining-2
  20/4/1733- ca. 1808; 24/1/1726-
  he dis 8/1766

— John-1 m 1785 Sarah Weir
  1/5m/1736- 1791;
  he dis (F) 6/1780;
  she dis (F+had a child) 2/1794

— Thomas-3 m 1762 Rebecca Richardson-4 —
  9/10/1738-30/5/1799;
  27/1/1742-17/4/1808

— Joseph-1 m(1) 1763 Elizabeth Pierson/
  Pearson-2
  22/12/1743-1/5m/1820;
  m(2) 1770 Mary Ingham-2
  m(3) 1776 Hannah Davis-3
  dis (M) 11/1776

— Elizabeth-6 m 1762 William
  Richardson-6M
  15/3/1746-30/12/1808;
  3/8m/1737-31/8/1813

— Ann-2 m 20/2/1770 Isaac Watson-6
  8/7m/1749-   ; ca. 1746-
  rem 1800 to SDMM

KEY

Numeral after a name indicates
level of meeting activity

1   no committee assignments
2   1 to 5 assignments
3   6 to 10 assignments
4   11 to 15 assignments
5   15 or more assignments
6   15 or more + an office
6M 16 or more + being a
      recorded minister

ABBREVIATIONS:

dis   disowned for an offense other than the ones below
dis (F)   disowned for fornication
dis (M)   disowned for marrying out of unity with Friends
m   married
MM   Monthly Meeting
SDMM   Southern District Monthly Meeting in Philadelphia

- Rachel m 1786 Thomas Story
  23/5/1763-12/2m/1830;
  rem 1787 to Wrightstown
- Mary 12/3m/1765-d.y.
- Joseph R.-2 m(1) 1792 Sarah Watson
  16/9/1767-26/6/1858; 14/4/1767-
  dis (F) 8/1785; reinstated 1/1792
  rem 1797 to Philadelphia
  m(2) *Ann West*
  m(3) 29/2/1844 *Ann Ely*
  -15/6/1854
- Mercy m 1792 Abraham Carlisle
  20/10/1769-19/10/1836;
  rem 1793 to NDMM
- Thomas m(1) 1797 Thomazine
  Trimble
  14/2m/1772-27/2/1828;
  he dis (F,M) 1/1797
  m(2) 1816 Rachel Wilson
  she dis (F,M) 10/1817
- Rebecca m 15/1/1801 *Jonathan Fell*
  3/5m/1775-4/3m/1832;
  31/1/1771-15/7/1829
  rem 1801 to Philadelphia
- Mary, unmarried
  9/7m/1777- 1854
  rem 6/1809 to NDMM
- Phineas m(1) Eliza Murray
  3/9m/1781-6/8m/1851;
  he dis (M) 11/1806
  m(2) Amelia Snyder
- Ruth m 1810 Joseph Dickson
  19/8/1788-16/2/1843;
  rem 6/1809 to NDMM

- Margaret m 12/11m/1783 Samuel
  Gillingham
  6/6/1764-1841; 30/12/1762-1846
  rem 1781 to Buckingham
- William m 1790 **Mary Hutchinson**
  12/8m/1766-5/12m/1818;
  rem 8/1793 to Falls MM
- Elizabeth m 1787 Isaiah Shinn
  21/10/1768-4/12m/1829;
  15/12/1764-25/7/1822
  dis (M) 10/1788

- *Elizabeth-6* m **Joseph Jenks**
  15/7/1793-5/3m/1884;
  12/9m/1792-19/11/1869
- *Watson* m *Julianna Justice*
  22/12/1794-23/3/1855; -1852
  res in Philadelphia (1850 census)
- Sarah, 12/4/1796-20/7/1797

- Hannah West m 2/11m1843 *Stacy Budd Collins*
  -9/9/1885; 19/1/1791-20/6/1873
  rem to New York City
- Elizabeth M. m Rev. Joseph Elsegood
  29/7/1822-29/3/1887;
- William Wallace
  2/11m/1825-20/7/1857
  merchant in Philadelphia (1850 census)
- Simon Snyder, iron founder
- Frederick A., d.y.
- George A., twin, 9/10m/1829-
- Henry L., twin, 9/10m/1829-
- Philip Frederick, MD
  27/2/1832-9/1m/1863

- **Joseph** m 1827 *Elizabeth Jenks-6*
  12/9m/1792-19/11/1869;
  12/9m/1792-19/11/1869
- Rebecca Hutchinson, 30/1/1794-21/4/1797
- **Michael Hutchinson** m(1) 1821 **Mary Earle Ridgeway**
  20/5/1795-16/10/1867; -1846
  rem 7/1837 to Makefield
  m(2) 1848 Mary Canby (d. 23/8/1849)
  m(3) 1851 Ann Higgins (d. 4/8/1854)
  m(4) 1856 **Sarah Leedom**
- Elizabeth Pierson m 1825 **George Yardley**
  14/2/1797-13/12/1884;
  rem to Lower Makefield
- Charles m 1823 *Mary Ann Newbold*
  31/12/1798-5/8m/1823;
- Margery 12/8m/1800-31/1/1802
- Hannah, unmarried 17/6/1802-17/9/1822
- *Mary Palmer* m 1827 Edmund Morris
  25/1/1804-15/2/1875;
- Margaret, unmarried 24/8/1806-20/12/1826
- **William Pearson** m 1837 *Elizabeth Story*
  17/12/1807-17/9/1886;
  6/3m/1807-11/1m/1878
  rem 1829 to Solebury; rem 1844 to Balt.
- *Ann* m 12/10m/1831 **Charles M. Morris**
  26/2/1810-15/4/1870;
  rem to SDMM
- *Susan W.* m 4/4/1838 *Franklin Fell*
  3/6m/1812-4/7m/1838;
  rem 1837 to SDMM

Kirkbride Family

John m(1) 11/1731 Hannah Sykes ——— John dis (F, W) 12/1753
   m(2) 11/1750 Margery Woolston ——— Phineas, 25/2/1754-8/4m/1815
   -6/1753; 3/6m/1721-
   she dis (F) 12/1753

                          ⎡Sarah-6 m 30/6/1763 William Blak-
                           ey-6M (see pages 254-5)
                           31/10/1739-1/10m/1821;
                                19/2/1739-20/6/1822

                          ├Thomas unmarried
                         16/8/1741-23/9/1760?
                         rem to Philadelphia?

Thomas m 31/3/1738 Grace Wool-
       ston-5 ——————————├Hannah m 26/6/1766 William Biles
13/6/1712- 1747;   9/10m/1743-
    11/8m/1715- 1783   dis (M) 2/1767
she rem 1738 to Falls; ret 1754 as
        a widow   ├Jonathan-3 m 23/11/1775 Elizabeth
                                     Willett ———————
                         19/9/1745-3/5m/1804;
                             -20/10/1821

                         └Samuel-2 m 8/5m/1772 Mary Hicks
                       2/7m/1747-3/3/1777;
                           15/1/1753-28/4/1775
                       he disciplined (M) but not disowned,
                       6/1774
                       she joined 3m/1775

The first set of dates under a name is the Kirkbride family member's birth and death; the second set of dates is his or her spouse's birth and death. Bold names are **Hicksite**, italics are *Orthodox*. Other abbreviations include:

dis = disowned; dis (M) = disowned for a marriage offense
m = married
rem = removed [to another meeting]
ret = returned [to Middletown Meeting]

The numeral from 1 to 6 after a name indicates the level of activity in the meeting for business, in terms of committee assignments and offices, with 1 being none and 6 being 16 or more plus an office; 6M indicates 16 or more plus being a recorded minister.

John Paul m 15/10/1817 *Ann Elizabeth Gregg*
15/11/1791-16/11/1841;
28/4/1795-29/4/1878
she rem 1818 to Frankford;
ret 6/1828 with 2 minor children

⌐Samuel 9/11m/1776-

├Grace-1 19/11/1778-1/2m/1844
  rem 4/1813 to Phila.; ret 1825
  rem 2/1826 to Makefield; ret 1830

├Thomas 7/6m/1780-

├Deborah-1 18/2/1782-1/10m/1806

├Sarah-2 30/6/1785-30/9/1840

├Mary-1 6/4m/1787-14/6/1864

├Elizabeth-2 6/4m/1787-18/1/1872
  rem 4/1812 to Falls; ret 12/1824
  rem 2/1826 to Makefield; ret 1830

├Hannah-3 13/4/1789-

├Helena-1 3/1m/1791-1/4m/1857
  rem 1825 to Wrightstown; ret 1835

├Ann-1 8/8/1793-4/2m/1842
  rem 1825 to Wrightstown; ret 1835

├Susanna-1 m 16/12/1828 **John Paxson**
  15/9/1795-9/9/1887;
      1/8m/1801-10/12m/1856
  rem 1812 to Falls; ret 1820
  disciplined (M) but not disowned
  7/1829

└Jonathan-5 m(1) 10m/1829 **Hannah Warner**-2
  1/2m/1802-11/9m/1870;
       ca. 1805-20/2/1856
  m(2) 8/1857 **Lydia Ann Warren**
  he retained membership 2/1858
  rem 1826 to Makefield; ret 6/1830

⌐Joseph 10/8m/1818 – d.y.
├*Richard Maris* m 1849 Ellen von
    Culin [non-Q]
  10/7m/1820-8/4m/1868
  disciplined (M) but not disowned
  1849
├Mary Ann 24/12/1824 – d.y.
└*Harriet Howell*, 14/1/1828-

⌐**Charles W.** m 15/2/1855 **Hannah W. Croasdale**-2
  18/3/1832-10/12m/1873
       28/1/1831-30/12m/1887
  she was called a "lunatic widow" in
  1873

├**Elizabeth W.** 30/7/1834-20/9/1841

├**Lydia** 21/7/1836-1/9m/1836

├**John Blakey** m 17/2/1870 Jane T.
    Roberts
  30/3/1839-6/1923; 10/3/1842-1903

├**Jonathan** m 20/10/1864 **Rachel Croasdale**
  29/6/1840-10/5m/1903;
       4/12m/1839-25/9/1873
  rem 1866 to Falls; ret 1877
  m(2) 1886 [non-Friend]

├**J. Croasdale** 28/12/1841-27/4/1842

└**Thomas** 2/2/1844-

265

Linton Family

―John m 1731 Elizabeth Hayhurst
 -1761; 1/6/1709?- 1795
 rem 1732 to Wrightstown

―Benjamin-4 m(1) 25/3/1726/7 Elizabeth White
 10/6m/1703-25/1/1773;
 9/7m/1705-26/1/1731/2
 m(2) 19/2m/1733 Jane Cowgill
 3/7m/1708-28/10/1791
 members of Falls MM

―Jacob m Elizabeth
 res: Wrightstown

―Joseph-6 m 1726 Mary Blackshaw-2
 21/7/1697-8/11m/1746/7;
 28/2/1705/6-1773
 rem 1738 from Falls to Middletown
 res: Northampton

―5 children plus
―Isaiah m 24/10/1764 Sarah Hirst
 15/11/1739/40-26/1/1775;
 widow rem 7/1799 to Middletown
―William m(1) 30/4/1766 Sarah Penquite
 29/1/1742-1802; -3/1786?
 m(2) 19/3/1788 Mary Janney
 m(3) Letitia (Harvey) Ellicott (she d. 1817)
 res: Newtown

―2 children, res: Falls, plus
―John m Mary Stokes
 26/12/1727-

―5 children plus
―Lucy m 9/11m/1774 Jasper Terry
 11/2m/1734-2/3m/1818; -10/11m/1815
 to Middletown 3/1775 from Falls
 rem 6/1787 to Wrightstown
―Joshua m 16/5/1770 Hannah Hutchinson
 11/11/1737/8-25/3/1807;
 disciplined but not disowned 5/1780
 dis (D+) 5/1788 by Falls; reinstated 9/1806
 she rem 6/1802 to Westland MM
 he rem 4/1807 to Westland, Washington Co.
―Hezekiah m 23/5/1782 Esther Blakey
 23/9/1748- ; 2/7m/1761-
 rem 7/1776 Falls to Middletown
 rem 1783 to Buckingham; 1794 to Sadsbury

―Isaac, 3/10m/1729-
 dis (F) 8/1764
―Elizabeth m 11/5m1758 Thomas Winder
 13/10/1730-24/9/1795;
  25/9/1733-16/12/1785
 rem 1759 to Falls
―Joseph m 12/4m/1759 Elizabeth Winder-1
 1/2m/1736- 1785; 4/6m/1738-
 he dis (W+) 10/1782
 she m(2) 2/4m/1795 David Feaster [non-Q]
 she dis (M+) 7/1795
―Mary m 8/1m/1761 Robert Walker
 18/7/1737-30/1/1790;
  8/4m/1731-22/10/1806
 rem 1762 to Buckingham
―Phebe 26/2/1741- 1784 unmar.
 rem 1765 Wrightstown to Middletown
―Jonathan m 13/2/1771 Susanna Gillam-1
 11/5m/1743-1793; -1803
 disciplined but not disowned 1/1767
 disciplined (W, debt) but not disowned 1787
 rem 5/1787 to Sadsbury MM

┌Laura 22/3/1766-30/9/1828
├Thomas m(1) 1/10m/1796 Mary
│   Cary
│   3/1m/1768- 8/1829; -13/10/1815
│   m(2)13/11/1816 Hannah Wildman
│   9/7m/1793-
├James-2 m 12/3m/1801 **Ann Croas-**
│   **dale**-2
│   10/12m/1769- ; 23/12/1776-
│   rem 1802 Wrightst'n to Middlet'n
│   rem 1819 to Stroudsburg; ret 1827
│   rem 4/1853 to Makefield
├William 13/1/1772-
└Sarah 23/2/1774-

┌John m Mary Briggs
│ 1/4m/1767-21/1/1836; 1773-
└Elizabeth m 16/5/1792 Joseph
   Buckman
   3/12m/1768-16/3/1832;
        30/8/1752NS-
   res: Newtown

└John, dis (W,D) 8/1787

—Joshua Jr.
   rem 7/1798 Falls to Middletown
   rem 12/1802 to Falls;
   rem 5/1802 Falls to Westland MM

┌John m 19/2/1794 Mary Martin
│   15/8/1766-
├Nehemiah d. by 2/1785
├Aaron m 1802 Eunice Greenlaw
│   20/4/1771-
│   rem ca. 1805 to Nova Scotia
│   dis 7/1805 by Falls MM
└Sarah m 23/11/1780 James Martin
   res Falls

—8 children in Sadsbury MM

┌Asa Carey m Sarah Burson
│   1/5m/1797-
├Isaiah, 3/7m/1798-
│   from Abington 8/1829 to Middlet'n
│   rem 2/1850 to Makefield
├Mary, 20/10/1803-
├Silas, 21/6/1806-
└Thomas, 2/1m/1807-13/7/1824

┌William Hurst 23/9/1817-
├Joseph Wildman m 1850 Anna __
│   30/8/1819-
│   rem 7/1849 Falls to Middletown
│   disciplined (F, M) but not disowned
│   6/1850
│   rem 3/1853 to West MM, Ohio; ret
│   6/1855
└Sarah Ann 21/3/1822-

┌**George C**. 2/1m/1802-
├**Lewis C**. 7/7/1804-
├**Maurice P**. 27/1/1807-
├**Robert H**. 17/8/1809-
├**James, Jr**. 4/2m/1812-
│   dis (fraud) 6/1836
├**Ann Croasdale**-1 29/8/1815-
│   rem 1870 to Makefield
├**Deborah C**. m 1846 Mahlon Ridge
│   27/1/1819-
│   disciplined (M) but retained mem-
│   bership 8/1846
└**Jeremiah C**. m 1848 [non-Friend]
     dis (M) 5/1848

┌John m 10/2m/1818 Jane Smith
│   ; 5/7m/1798-
├Mahlon B. m 12/4m/1831 Elizabeth
│   Yardley (she b. 21/7/1807)
├Penquite m(1) 25/4/1833 **Mercy Cad-**
│   **wallader**
│   1808-
│   m(2) Ellen W. Buckman
├Frances m 1/1/1834 David H. Lovett
│   ca.1802-16/8/1834; 20/11/1811-
└Elizabeth m 11/12m/1793 Thomas
    Smith
    ca.1803-19/8/1834 or 20/3/1881;
      23/8/1769-

Longshore Family

Euclydus Longshore-5 m 12m/1715
Alice Stackhouse-5
1692-1764; 1/4m/1699-1741

- Robert m 1740 Ursula Jolly
  13/10/1716-11/1776; 1719-1794
  dis (M) 5/1740
  res Lower Makefield

- Grace 24/2/1719-16/6/1726

- Thomas-1(F) m 10/4m/1742 Johanna
      Vances-1(F)
  13/9/1721- 1777; -1794
  disciplined (F) but not disowned 1744

- Margaret-1 m(1) 16/3 or 5/1741
      Robert Pearson
  21/4/1724-
  disciplined (M) but not disowned
      9/1741
  m(2) John Atkinson
  dis (M) 1762

- Alice m 16/3m/1744 Thomas Lamb
  4/7m/1726-   ; 1721-21/4/1800
  rem 1754 to Fairfax, Va.

- Grace 18/6/1728-11/7m/1731

- Euclydus 4/12m/1729/30-23/10/1732

- Mary 13/8/1732-bur. 4/8/1735

- Euclydus-1 m(1) 1760 Susanna Van-
      Horn
  27/4/1735-14/6/1804;   -ca 1778
  disciplined (M) but not disowned
      10/1761
  m(2)11/5m/1780 Sarah Gillam-1
      -1818
  he requested children of first wife be
      members 7/1782

- Benjamin

─Euclydus, Jr. m Jemima __
  dis 3/1769 for fathering a [bastard] child
─Elizabeth m 23/4/1771 Andrew? Hunter
  dis (M) 1/1772
─Cyrus dis (F, fighting) 7/1774
─Thomas dis (F,M,W) 12/1779
─Margaret m 9m/1776 Thomas Wiley
  dis (M) 6/1777

┌Abner m(2) 21/11/1811 Sarah Powers
│ dis (W) 3/1784
├Asher died young
├Asa died young
├Anna m Garret VanHorn
│ dis (F) 12/1790
├Alice m(1) Isaiah VanHorn
│ dis M 10/1787
│ m(2) ___ Cremer
└Abigail m(1) 1796 ___ Scout
  dis (M) 1/1797
  m(2) Nathan Minor

┌Sarah m 1800 ___ Starr [non-Q]
│ 2m/1781-
│ disciplined (M) but not disowned 1800
├Euclydus m 21/3/1802 Sarah Cox
│ 12m/1781-31/10/1838;
│ rem 1824 to Buckingham, ret 11/1825
├Margaret m 1805 ___ Slack
│ dis (M) 11/1805
├Abraham-2 m(1) 11/3m/1807 **Rhoda Skelton**-2
│ 6/11m/1785-12/1m/1855;
│ ca.1783-27/6/1839
│ m(2) 1841 **Mary White**-2
│ -2/8m/1860
├Mary, d.y.
├Joseph m 1811 Joanna Kelly
│ 24/11/1788-
│ dis (M) 5/1811; rem 1811 to?
├Grace 31/8/1790-
├Rachel m 14/2/1811 Valentine Dickerson
│ 20/3/1792-13/10/1865;
│ dis (M) 9/1811; reinstated 1815
├Thomas Canby m Jane Gaine
│ 21/6/1794-
│ removed 6/1816 to Wrightstown
└James m 1825 Sarah Roberts
  17/10/1797-1861; 1804-
  rem to Wrightstown before 1817

┌**Sarah Ann** m(1) 15/1/1836 Holcombe Walker [non-Friend]
│ 12/26/1807- ; 30/7/1805-25/2/1842
│ disciplined but not disowned 5/1836
│ m(2) Mahlon Kirkbride Taylor
│ rem 1838 to Buckingham, ret 1842;
│ rem 1849 to Makefield
├**Joseph Skelton** MD m 18/2/1836 Julia LaRue [non-Friend]
│ 18/9/1809-5/12m/1879;
│ disciplined (M) but not disowned 10/1737
│ dis 2/1847; reinstated by Phila.YM
│ rem 11/1856 to Green St. MM (Phila.)
├Mary 16/8/1811-27/9/1812 or 1813?
├**Thomas Ellwood** m /1841 **Hannah E. Myers** MD
│ 9/11m/1809-19/8/1898; -1901
│ rem 7/1852 to Green St. MM
├**Carey/Cary** m 13/11/1843 **Matilda Holcombe**-1
│ 1/8m/1814-24/5/1888;
│ 25/4/1811-6/3m/1893
│ disciplined but retained membership 2/1845
├**Isaac S.** m 1845 **Mary Burgess**-2
│ 6/8m/1816-24/5/1888;
│ disciplined (M) but retained membership 9/1845
│ rem 2/1869 to Phila. MM
├John Watson 5/5/1818-1/1 lm/1839
├William 1820-died young
├**Samuel Carey** m(1) Sarah Ann Case
│ 2/11m/1822-
│ m(2) 1853 Rebecca Reynolds
│ disciplined (M) but retained membership 3/1853
│ rem 1855 to Muncy MM (Fishing Creek, Pa.)
├**Elizabeth** m 28/3/1846 **William Burgess**
│ disciplined (M) but retained memb'p
│ 28/4/1825-
│ rem 3/1853 to Muncy MM
└**Anna Mary** MD m 20/7/1854 Lambert Potts
  16/4/1829-29/10/1905;
  disciplined (M) but retained memb'p
  rem 1855 to Makefield; ret 1857

Mitchell Family

John-5 m 19/10/1738 Margaret Stackhouse-5
10/3m/1711-31/7m/1789;
6/6/1714-2/5m/1774

- Richard-5 m 30/10/1765 Sarah Stevenson —
  18/6/1739-16/1/1820;
  30/8/1735-25/8/1810
  he dis (M) 5/1766; reinstated 8/1766
  she joined 10/1775

- John-1 m 1763 Phoebe Randall
  30/4/1741-26/12/1780;
  dis (W) 4/1780

- Henry-2 m 25/10/1782 Hannah Woolston
  7/5m/1743-13/8/1789;
  9/4m/1759-14/9/1793
  he dis (M) 1784; reinstated 4/1787
  she m(2) 25/10/1792 Robert Croasdale

- Sarah-1 m 13/4/1780 Oliver Wilson
  25/9/1745-   ; 17/8/1751(OS)-
  rem 7/1779 from Abington to Middletown;
  rem 1781 to Abington

- Samuel-5 m 12/6m/1774 *Ann Willett*
  21/8/1747-25/12/1826;
  4/8m/1750-11/10m/1831
  disciplined (F,M) but not disowned 4/1775

- Margaret-1 m 14/1/1779 David Wilson
  25/12/1749/50-31/7/1796; 23/8/1754-
  rem 1779 to Wrightstown

- *Pierson*-6 m 15/6/1779 Rebecca Allen-6
  7/9m/1751-4/4/1834;
  26/9/1754-22/7/1815
  rem 3/1780 to Falls (Bristol PM became
      part of Middletown MM in 1788)
  disciplined (W) but not disowned 3/1780

- Amos (unmarried)
  4/2m/1756-3/3/1777

Because of a lack of space in the third generation, several children who died when quite young have been left out.

```
┌Elizabeth-6 (unmarried) 22/9/1766-
├Mary-1 (unmarried) 7/6m/1768-11m/1784
├Margaret m 22/9/1796 John Wilson-1
│   24/7/1770-1821; 16/2/1768-
│   rem 1796 to Buckingham
├Richard, Jr. m Elizabeth Brown
│   27/4/1774-       dis (M) 12/1797
├Sarah-6M m 20/10/1796 Dr. Mahlon Gregg
│   twin 9/12m/1776- ; rem 1836 to Phila.
├Ann-1 m 16/4/1801 John Brown
│   twin 9/12m/1776- ; 1773-
│   rem 1801 to NYC; ret 1803; rem 1811
└John S. m 1810 Margaret Kinsey [non-Q]
    26/8/1781- ; dis (M) 2/1811
┌John unmarried 27/1/1766- 1828
├Joshua m 11/8m/1794 Anna Merrick ─────
│   11/11/1767-1798;   -1798
│   dis (M) 1/1795; reinstated 6/1797
│   rem 1791 to NDMM (Phila.); ret 6/1797;
│   rem 3/1798
├Margaret m Samuel Milnor
│   4/9m/1774- ; rem 1791 to Buckingham
└Amos m Elizabeth Hendricks
    11/1m/1777- ; rem 7/1798 to NDMM
┌John m 17/9/1807 Sarah Hibbs
│   1/11m/1774-      ; 10/10/1786-
│   rem 4/1822 to Wilmington, Del.
├Walter m 15/5m/1799 Hannah Comly-6M ──
│   12?/5m/1776- ; 2/6m/1777-10/8m/1855
│   disciplined but not disowned 7/1815
─   dis (D) 1/1823; rem 7/1849 to Cincinnati
├Deborah unmarried, "special" 24/6/1779-
├Jonathan W. m 24/10/1808? Harriet Milnor
│   29/10/1781- ; 20/7/1786-
│   rem 1806 to Falls; dis 5/1812
├Henry 12/10m/1783-4/9m/1795 or 9/4m/1785
├Margaret m 11/10m/1810 Isaac Gillam
│   5/10m/1785- ; 13/4/1788-24/3/1849
│   rem 1822 to Springfield
├Samuel 15/12/1787-  dis (D) 8/1814
├Gilbert L or S m Letitia Forrest [non-Q]
│   11/3m/1789-   ; dis (M) 3/1811
├Ann 12/10m/1793-288/1794
└Sarah 2/2/1796-22/8/1797
┌┬Gove m 13/10/1803 Rebecca J. Justice
││  27/10/1781-4/5m/1856; 2/1/1782
││  disciplined (F) but not disowned 9/1796
││  rem 1796 to Buckingham, then to Hatboro
│├Joseph 6/11m/1783-27/11/1783
│├John Allen-6 m 24/10/1811 Tacy Stack-
││  house-6
││  31/1/1785-29/9/1863; 24/4/1792-31/5/1867
│├William-6 m 6m/1814 Sarah Paul-5 ─────
││  19/6/1787-13/12/1868;   -6/12nd1860
│└Achsah (unmarried) 18/2/1790-22/10/1825
```

┌Joshua-3 m 15/10/1818 Frances Buckman
│   1797-26/7/1855; 19/6/1795-
│   rem 4/1819 to Falls; ret 5/1830
┌Samuel. Jr. 17/3/1800
│   rem to New Orleans 1822; dis 2/1822
├Joshua C. m Sarah Ann Bosworth
│   25/1/1802-
│   rem 1822 to Wilmington, Del.
├Pierson 17/2/1804-1/10m/1822
│   rem 2/1822 to Philadelphia MM
├Charles Franklin m Elisabeth Ellis
│   18/2/1806- ; 1809-
│   removed to NY 1829
├Mary Elizabeth m 28/2/1844 Austin Hall
│   1/7m/1808-7/1m/1898; 2/12m/1807-1858
│   relinquished memb. 5/1844
├James Comly m Eliza Krosnick
│   22/11/1810-
├Hannah m Abram Brown
│   21/2/1813- ; dis (M) 12/1834
│   (does not want to retain membership)
├Catharine C. m William Hall
│   15/3/1815-
│   dis (M) 1841 (joined "another society")
└2 sons who d.y.

┌Sarah S. m 27/10/1836 Rowland Mather
│   29/8/1812-17/4/1893;
├Isaac Stackhouse 27/8/1814-
├Rebecca m 3m/1850 James W. Newbold
│   18/10/1817-31/10/1862; 6/1m/1823-
├John S.-1 m 13/3/1845 Phebe Gilbert
│   15/7/1820-18/6/1894; 1816-1901
├Pierson-6 m 9/5m/1850 Caroline Burton
│   20/8/1822-1/4m/1904;   -16/5/1890
│   removed to Falls 1850; ret 1/1851
└Gove-1 m 11/3m/1847 Catherine Mather
       Croasdale
    10/2m/1823-17/6/1904;
                26/9/1826-4/12m/1861
    m(2) 14/7/1864 Anna Croasdale
    rem 1867 to Phila

┌Elizabeth A. m 20/7/1852 Jesse Leedom
│   25/3/1815-3/7m/1886;
│   rem 1852 to Makefield
└Joseph Paul m(1) 22/10/1846 Hannah H.
       Mather
    11/6m/1819-30/1/1873; ca.1827-8/1m/1855
    m(2) 16/10/1856 Elizabeth R Mather-3

271

Paxson Family
Part 1

children of William[2] and Mary (Watson)

- William-6 m 25/1m/1740 Anna Marriott-6 ───────
  29/2/1712-29/8/1767; -1/5m/1773

- Mary-5 m 21/10/1732 Joseph Richardson-6 see page 276
  11/11/1713-19/3/1786;
  4/11m/1696/7-16/4/1772

- Thomas-6 m 1737 Ann Paxson-6-
  13/10/1715-7/8m/1790; (page 274)
  8/11m/1718/9-10/2m/1783

- John unmarried
  17/8/1717-

- Henry m 1/2m/1740/1 Martha Shinn
  14/7/1719-15/10/1778;
  22/11/172/3-
  disciplined (M) but not disowned

- James-1 (F 1750) m ca 1756
  Hannah Thornton-1 see page 274
  15/8/1721-21/1/1769;
  10/4m/1733-16/1/1790
  he disciplined (F) but not disowned 1750
  she m(2) 1770 John Knowles

- Deborah m 1742 William Wildman
  23/1/1724- ; 27/12/1722/3-
  disciplined (M) but not disowned,
  7/1743
  he dis (D+) 1/1750/1.
  rem to Virginia

- Martha 23/2/1740/1-12/5m/1742
- William-2 m 18/6/1772 Mary Suber-1 ───
  26/4/1743- 1799; he dis 4/1780
  she joined 4/1772; dis 11/1796
  rem 2/1789 to Bradford MM; ret 12/1792
- Joseph m 25/10/1770 Sarah Rodman ──┐
  25/12/1744/5-11/7m/1793;
  7/8m/1753-7/1m/1828
  she m(2) 16/2m/1809 Joseph Tatnall
  rem 4/1809 to Wilmington MM, Del.
- Phineas m 24/1/1768 Susanna Shaw ───
  18/12/1746/7- ; 5/3m/1750-
  she disciplined (M) but not disowned
  he dis (W) 4/1776
- Thomas m 12/9m/1775 Elizabeth Randall
  31/11/1748/9-20/6/1835;
  12/7m/1752-30/6/1801;
  she joined 8/1800
  he dis (M,F) 5/1776; reinstated 12/1800;
  dis 1824; for children see page 275
- Mahlon m 4/4/1777 Sarah Walker
  17/4/1752-29/9/1832; 1761-8/2m/1832
  disciplined (W) but not disowned 4/1776
  dis (M) 10/1777
- Samuel, 5/5/1754-7/3m/1813
  rem 12/1771 to Wilmington MM, Del.
- Isaac m(1) Elizabeth Hallowell
  9/5m/1756-26/8/1816;
  rem 1771 to Phila.
  m(2) *Elizabeth Shoemaker* (d.10m/1847)
- Joshua-3 m 22/11/1787 Mary Willett-2
  14/7/1758-8/5m/1842;
  3/7m/1765-23/4m/1828
  rem 1808 to Abington MM; see p. 275
- Mary-6 m 25/10/1787 David Landis
  4/7m/1762-18/3/1813; -17/1/1822
- Anna-6 m 12m/1783 **Simon Gillam**-6M
  4/7m/1762-ca 1840;
  24/1/1759-31/8/1839
  rem 1733 to SDMM; ret 12/1781
  rem 4/1821 to Upper Springfield
- Israel m 20/12/1787 Ann Parker
  3/3/1765-4/6m/1809; ca.1771-3/6m/1816
  rem 11/1787 to SDMM (Philadelphia)

Note: The Paxson family chart is divided into two sets of pages; cousins living in Buckingham and Solebury are included only when they were in Middletown Meeting.

┌William m Mary Johnson
│ 27/3/1773- 1841;   dis 1/1798
├Anna m 1796 __ Tomlinson [non-Q]
│ 3/8m/1776-   ;   dis (M) 7/1796
├Samuel 13/10/1781- ; dis (W) 2/1809
└Amos 31/1/1786-

┬Samuel
│ 27/10/1772-12/7m/1773
├Anna-6 m 12/10m/1796 William
│ Richardson, Jr.-6
│ 6/1m/1775-26/9/1863;
│   31/3/1772-5/1m/1832
├John-6 m 12/5m/1802 Sarah
│ Pickering-1 ─────────
│ 17/4/1777-16/11/1850;
│   5/4m/1782-19/8/1867
├William-2 m 1803 *Ann Canby* ─────
│ 26/8/1779-9/3m/1858;
│ rem 12/1794 to NDMM; ret 8/1825
│ rem 1829 to Wilmington, Del.
├*Mary Rodman* m 11/4m/1804 Asa
│ Walmsley
│ 26/12/1781-2/4/1838;
│ rem 8/1804 to Byberry
├Margaret m John Richardson
│ 10/6m/1784-10/3m/1846;
│ rem /1809 to Wilmington, Del.
├Joseph Rodman, unmarried
│ 4/6m/1786-15/1/1838
├Richard S. m 1/4m/1813 Elizabeth
│ Shoemaker ─────────
│ 14/12/1788-24/9/1857;
│   18/2/1792-14/12/1855
│ rem 1804 to Phila.; to Bensalem 1843
└Margery m 10m/1809 *Edward Tatnall*
   28/4/1791-4m/1837;   -13/1/1856
   rem 4/1809 to Brandywine, Del.

┬Charles m 6/1811 Susanna Michener
│ 20/12/1782?-11/1m/1852;
│   20/9/1790-1/3m/1852
└Joseph Shaw m __ [non-Q]
   dis (M,W) 10/1787

─Joseph m ca. 1838 Elizabeth Hunter Gallaher 12/2m/1803-24/9/1867;
─Mary-3 31/10/1804-17/6/1887
─Anna-2 17/10/1806-10/10/1858
─Sarah 6/7m/1808-20/5/1852
─Jonathan-6 m 21/10/1835 Elizabeth
   Knight-6M
   12/8m/1810-1/5m/1876; 16/1/1804-
─Samuel Harrison-4 m 12/5m/1836 Sarah
   Richardson-6
   8/9m/1812-5/11m/1868;
   22/4/1812-3/12m/1903
─Elihu-1 unmarried 2/12m/1814-1/7m/1855
─John R.-1 unmarried 3/lm/1817-19/3/1857
─Margaret m 16/11/1843 Joseph Canby (his
   1st) 19/7/1819-27/10/1861;
─William Henry-2 m 14/4/1858 Sarah P
   Rowlett
   21/12m/1821-29/2/1850; -21/3/1909
─Margery-4 m 1867 Joseph Canby (his 2nd)
   25/3/1826- ;   -11/8m/1875

─Samuel Canby m 7m/1827 Elizabeth Drinker
   3/9m/1804-26/7/1860; res: NYC
─*Frances* 9/3m/1807-28/5/1858
   1825 to 1829 in Middletown
─Anna 16/5/1811-25/5/1811
─Rodman 26/5/1816-25/9/1818

─Joseph Shoemaker m 2/5m/1836 Deborah I.
   Iddings   16/1/1814- ;   dis (M) 1836
   res: San Francisco
─Anna m 13/11/1839 Joshua Pancoast
   29/4/1816-   ;   -23/6/1868
─*Richard, Jr.* m 2/1m/1844 Mary Pickering
   9/10m/1818-3/2/1872; 16/7/1820-
   rem 1844 to WDMM (Phila.)
─Sarah Rodman m 5/6m/1856 *Marmaduke W.*
   Allen
   24/10/1820-1905; 15/3/1821-
   rem 1832 to WDMM
─Charles Henry m Ada Bowen
   26/10/1824-29/2/1884;
   rem 1844 Phila to Middletown;
   rem to San Francisco
─Susan Shoemaker m 19/10/1854 Francis
   Hathaway
   30/7/1826-6/8m/1865; 23-2/1829- res NY
─William Lashbrooke m 20/5/1858 Emily
   Pickering
   30/12/1828-28/5/1871;
─Elizabeth S. m 21/5/1867 Charles Williams
   Pickering
   27/4/1832-   ; 21/7/1824-

Paxson Family
Part 2

children of William[2] and Mary (Watson)

- William-6 m 25/lm/1740 Anna Marriott-6
  29/2/1712-29/8/1767; -1/5m/1773

- Mary-6 m 21/10/1732 Joseph Richardson-6 (see page 276)
  11/11/1713-19/3/1786; -16/4/1772

- Thomas-6 m 1737 Ann Paxson-6
  13/10/1715-7/8m/1790;
  8/11m/1718/9-10/2m/1783

- John unmarried
  17/8/1717-

- Henry m 1740/1 Martha Shinn
  14/7/1719-15/10/1778;
  22/11/17__-

- James-1 (F 1750) m ca 1756 Hannah Thornton-1
  15/8/1721-21/1/1769;
  10/4m/1733-16/1/1790
  she m (2) 1770 John Knowles

- Deborah m 1742 William Wildman
  23/1/1724-   ; 27/12/1722/3-
  rem to Virginia

children of William Jr. and Abigail (Pownall)

- Thomas m 1732 Jane Canby
  20/9/1712- 10m/1782;
  ca. 1710-ca.1819
- 7 siblings, members of Buckingham MM

- 10 children, see page 272
- Thomas m 12/9m/1775 Elizabeth Randall
- Joshua-3 m 22/11/1787 Mary Willett-2

  - Rebecca 24/8/1738-4/11m/1738/9
  - Mary-1 m 23/4/1761 Henry Simmons
    2/1m/1739/40-5/1/1769;
  - Ann-6 m 6m/1759 Joseph Wildman-5
    8/9m/1741-18/12/1806;
    1/12m/1729/30-3/5m/1809
  - Henry 27/8/1743-22/4/1772
  - John-2 12/8m/1745-3/7m/l779
  - Elizabeth 28/7/1747-5/2m/1777
  - James m 12/1777 Rachel Croasdale
    12/6m/1749-2/5m/1779;
    disciplined (M) but not disowned 3/1779
    she m(2) 6/9m/1784 Robert Eastburn
    she rem 1784 to Buckingham
  - Sarah-2 m 1/12m/1785 Robert Drake
    20/6m/1751?-23/4/1796;
  - Thomas-5 m 22/5/1783 Sarah Blakey-6
    4/5m/1753-24/9/1809; 26/3/1763-
    she m(2) 1812 George Walker,
    she rem 1812 to Falls
  - Jane 17/1/1756-27/5/1757
  - Margery-3 m 13/11/1777 John Knight
    28/11/1757-26/1/1841;
    rem 1805 to Horsham
  - Martha 5/5/1760-10/5m/1790
  - William m 10/1784 Elizabeth Walton
    1762-22/3/1799;
    she m(2) 1803 Benjamin Lloyd; rem 1804
  - Joseph 24/5/1758-
    dis (W+) 4/1778
  - Mary unmarried, 18/3/1762-16/1811

  - Rachel-6 m 6m/1764 John Watson, Jr.-6
    6/3m/1744-5/4m/1800;
    12/8m/1736-15/3/1799
  - Jacob m(1) 1769 Lydia Blakey-
    6/11m/1745/6-13/7/1832;
    ca. 1734-3/8m/1772
    in Middletown 1767-1769
    m(2) 13/11/1777 Mary Shaw
    8 or 28/5/1759-17/10/1814
  - Jonathan-6 m 26/6/1771 Rachel Biles-6
    14/11/1748/9-27/7/1797; -31/7/1842
    rem 4/1774 Buckingham to Middletown
    rem 1785 to Abington
  - 4 more siblings

- **Phineas**-3 m 17/4/1817 **Rachel Woolston**-6M
  30/3/1776-7/4m/1850;
  7/9m/1791-5/11m/1860
  he joined 1802; rem 5/1828 to Falls;
  she ret 3/1851 as a widow
  - 3 more children: Sarah, Israel, William
  - **John**-1 m **Sarah** __ 26/12/1780-
    rem 1821 to Frankford; ret 1823
    rem 1826 to Mt. Holly
  - **Isaac**-2 m(1) 24/3/1825 **Sarah Stackhouse**-1
    26/10/1788-24/11/1872;
    28/10/1789-8/1m/1858
    rem 1808 to Falls; ret 6/1823
    m(2) Mary Hamell
  - **Willett** m(1) 13/11/1817 **Sarah Wilson**
    28/3/1790-7/11m/1870;
    9/12m/1786-ca.1808
    rem to Abington; ret 1850
    m(2) 15/8/1849 Sarah Carey-3
  - Joseph m(1) Harriet Lukens
    7/12m/1793-   ; res: Abington
    m(2) Maria T. Shaw
  - Deborah unmarried 26/1/1795- 1873
  - Anna m Anthony Burton
  - 3 more children: Samuel, Ann M., Joshua
  - **Charles** m 4/1m/1844 **Agnes Tyson**
    19/8/1803-2/3m/1880; res: Upper Dublin
  - **Joshua, Jr.**-2 m 8/6m/1848 **Anna W. Ely**-2
    18/10/1805-5/5/1870; 28/1/1824-
    rem 1808 to Abington; ret 1848
    she rem 1871 to Phila. as a widow
  - William L. m 6/4m/1839 Sarah W. Comly
    28/2/1808-12/6/1878;
    29/12/1814-11/4m/1887
  - James 12/9m/1789-
  - **Thomas, Jr.** m 2/6m/1813 Mary Walker
    25/3/1792-
    dis (D+) 5/1811; reinstated 11/1815
    dis (D) 8/1840
  - Joshua m 8/9m/1813 Elizabeth Walker
    29/9/1794-ca. 1836;
    disciplined (F) but not disowned 12/1813
    dis (D) 8/1819
  - Mary, 24/4/1797-
  - Sarah, 5/5/1799-   ; rem 1812 to Falls
  - **John** m 16/12/1828 **Susan Kirkbride**-1
    1/8m/1801-12/12/1856; 15/9/1795-1887
    rem 1812 to Falls; ret 1820

- Samuel 1/5m/1818- d. before 1828
- **Mary W.** 17/1m/1820-
  Elizabeth m 1/1850 **Blakey Bunting**
  28/8/1822- 1876; -1889
- **Thomas** 11/3m/1824-9/1m/1850
- **Lydia Ann**
- **Joshua Woolston**
  27/12/1829-30/1/1842
- **Sarah B.**
  27/5/1833
  rem 1828 to Falls, ret 1851

- Elizabeth 14/7/1814-
- Rachel 26/6/1818-

- John W. m Anna Burton
- David m Ann Evans
- Mary W. m Henry Brooks
- Sarah, unmarried

— 3 children in Abington

— **6 children** in Horsham MM

— Edward Ely 6/5m/1849-2/1m/1864

— 4 children in Abington

Richardson Family

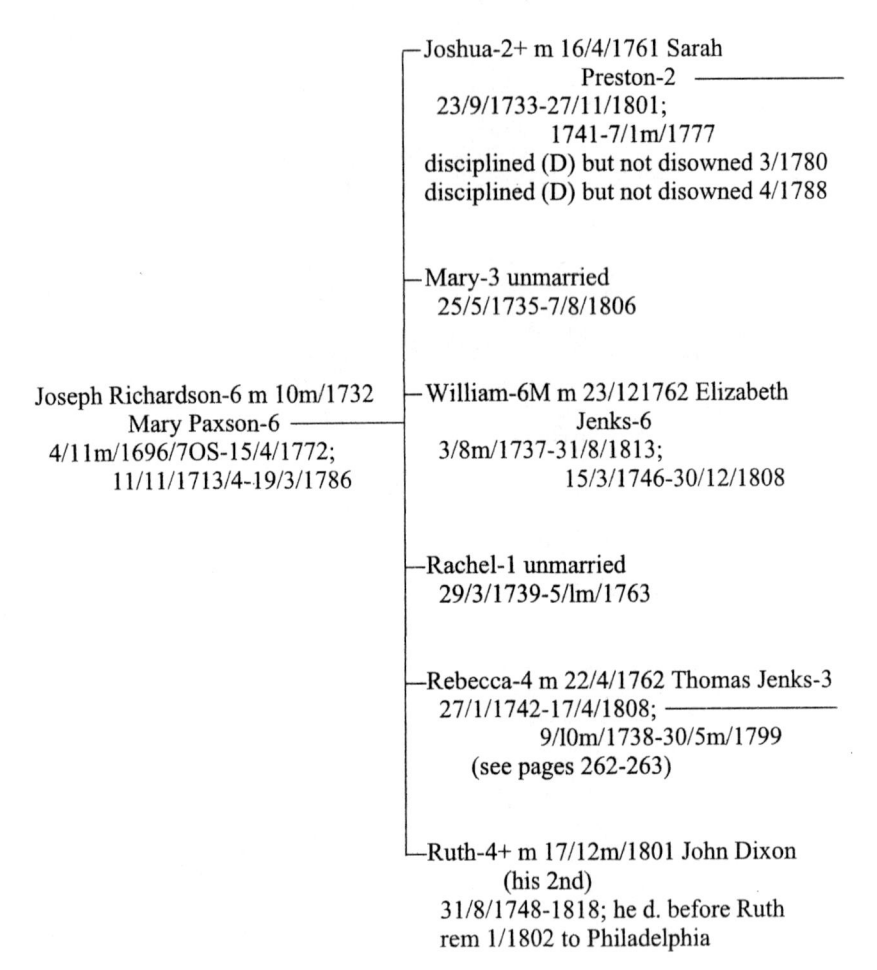

Joseph Richardson-6 m 10m/1732
Mary Paxson-6
4/11m/1696/7OS-15/4/1772;
11/11/1713/4-19/3/1786

- Joshua-2+ m 16/4/1761 Sarah
  Preston-2
  23/9/1733-27/11/1801;
  1741-7/1m/1777
  disciplined (D) but not disowned 3/1780
  disciplined (D) but not disowned 4/1788

- Mary-3 unmarried
  25/5/1735-7/8/1806

- William-6M m 23/121762 Elizabeth
  Jenks-6
  3/8m/1737-31/8/1813;
  15/3/1746-30/12/1808

- Rachel-1 unmarried
  29/3/1739-5/1m/1763

- Rebecca-4 m 22/4/1762 Thomas Jenks-3
  27/1/1742-17/4/1808;
  9/10m/1738-30/5m/1799
  (see pages 262-263)

- Ruth-4+ m 17/12m/1801 John Dixon
  (his 2nd)
  31/8/1748-1818; he d. before Ruth
  rem 1/1802 to Philadelphia

Note: Several other Richardsons who were not descended from Joseph and Mary (Paxson) married into data set families. They are not included here.

┌─Sarah m 13/1/1785 William Allen, Jr.-6M ──────────8 *ALLEN children,* 4 lived, see page 253
│ 4/2m/1762-16/9/1828;   ┌─5 WOOLSTON children, 4 lived, page 289
│   2/8m/1759-8/3m/1837   ├─**Joshua**-6 m(1) 15/6m/1835 **Mary C.**
│ rem 1803 to Falls; ret 1813   │   **Hunt**-1
├─Mary, Jr.-2 m 21/9/1786 Joshua Woolston-5 ─────┤   6/3m/1803-16/5/1874;
│ 19/8/1763-2/1m/1799;   │   10m/1805-18/7/1836
│   19/7/1755-27/12/1821   │   m(2) 15/3/1838 **Mary Knight**-6
│ he m(1) 1777 Mary Stapler (she d. 1782)   │   1812-2/2/1883
│ rem 6/1796 to Falls; ret 5/1804   ├─**Mary Dixon, Jr.**-2 m(1) 11/3m/1830 **Jona-**
│ he m(3) 1801 *Lydia Jordan*-6M   │   **than K. Stackhouse**-3 (page 281)
│ rem 1817 to Falls   │   16/7/1805- ; 28/9/1796-17/8/1842
├─**Jane**-2 unmarried, 22/1m/1766-29/12/1861   │   m(2) 13/9/1849 **Benjamin Borden**
├─**Joseph**-6 m 4m/1802 **Mary Dixon**-6 ───────┤   rem 5/1857 to Gwynedd MM
│ 8/9m/1768-28/8/1826;   ├─**Rachel R.** m 18/10/1832 **Thomas Livezey**
│   19/11/1777-29/5/1834   │   27/7/1808- ; 19/1/1801-
├─**Martha**-1 m 2/3m/1797 Seth Chapman   │   rem 1833 to Gwynedd MM
│ 22/7/1771-   ├─**Sarah**-6 m 12/5m/1836 **Samuel H. Pax-**
│ rem 1797 to Gwynedd; ret 1811   │   **son**-4 (see page 273)
│ rem 1812 to Muncy MM (Fishing Creek, Pa)   │   22/4/1812-3/12m/1903;
└─**Ruth**-1 m 11/11/1802 Robert Croasdale (his │   8/9m/1812-5/11m/1868
           3rd) see page 259 ─────────────────┐ └─John Dixon-1 unmarried
  25/8/1773-30/9/1854;   │   24/1/1815-27/7/1842
           20/2/1763-15/6/1821   └───5 CROASDALE children, (see page 259)
                                                ┌─Sarah Rodman-1 unmar.
┌─**Mercy**-1 m 9/1/1783 Jacob Shoemaker   │   25/7/1797-10/lm/1826
│ 20/4/1764-20/1/1851;   └─**William Rodman**-3+ unmar.
│ rem to NDMM 1/1781; ret 8/1782   6/4m/1801-31/10/1835
│ rem 1783 to Philadelphia
├─**Rachel**-1 m 19/4/1792 David Story   ┌─Mary N. m 20/10/1825 Jacob D. Stroud
│ 21/11/1765-9/11m/1844;   │   20/7/1799-1847; 28/3/1799-
│   20/4/1760-23/2/1832   │   rem 1826 to Stroudsburg
│ rem 1792 to Wrightstown MM   ├─William-1 unmarried, 6/lm/1801-
├─*Ann*-6 unmarried, 12/11m/1767-15/10/1829   ├─*Elizabeth*-2 m *John P. Balderston*
├─*Elizabeth*-6 m 18/11/1802 Josiah Reeve   │   ; 14/9/1802-
│ 31/1/1770-4/1m/1841   │   rem 1829 to NDMM (Phila.)
│ rem 1803 to Upper Evesham, NJ   ├─*Susanna*-1 m 23/10/1828 *Daniel Wills*
├─**William**-5 m 12/10m/1796 **Anna Paxson**-6 ┤ 23/10/1804-3/6m/1861;   -1879
│ 31/3/1772-5/1m/1832;   │   rem 1829 to Burlington
│   6/1m/1775-26/9/1863   ├─*Clayton N.*-1 m Susan Gillam Slack
├─Joseph-3 m 1798 *Rebecca Newbold* ────────────┤ 20/12/1806- ; dis 1831
│ 28/7/1774-2/12m/1814;   ├─*Hannah*-1 m 11/1835 *Josiah H. Newbold*
│ rem 6/1793 to Horsham; ret 9/1795   │   5/11m/1808-1863;
│ she rem 1829 to NDMM (Phila.) as a widow   │   2/11m/1812-23/9/1893
├─*Mary*-6 m(1) 16/3/1797 Marmaduke Watson ─────┤ rem 1829 to NDMM (Phila.)
│ 19/9/1776-30/1/1848;   -1798   ├─Ann unmarried, 28/9/1810-26/11/1812
│ rem 6/1797 to Chesterfield; ret 5/1798   ├─Joseph N. 7/5m/1812-15/11/1812
│ m(2) 11/11/1813 *Samuel Hulme*-6 ────────────┤ Joseph (twin) 4/8m/1813-1/5m/1814
│   15/9/1774-1/8m/1830   ├─*Rebecca, Jr*-1 m **William H. Balder-**
├─Rebecca 13/4/1780-19/9/1791   │   **ston**
├─Hannah-1 28/2/1783-12/9m/1791   │   twin 4/8m/1813-1873;   -1920
└─Thomas-1 m 1818 Abigail Blackwood ─────────┐ │   rem 1829 to NDMM (Phila.)
  16/12/1787-8/2m/1823; -31/3/1822   │ ├─Susanna M. W. m 1817 *Thomas L. Allen*-2
  disc (D) but not disowned 2/1823   │ │   he m(2) 1844 **Sarah Taylor**-1
                                             │ └─2 *HULME children*
                                             └────John B. 1819-1828

Stackhouse Family

Part 1
Children of Thomas and his first wife Grace (Heaton)

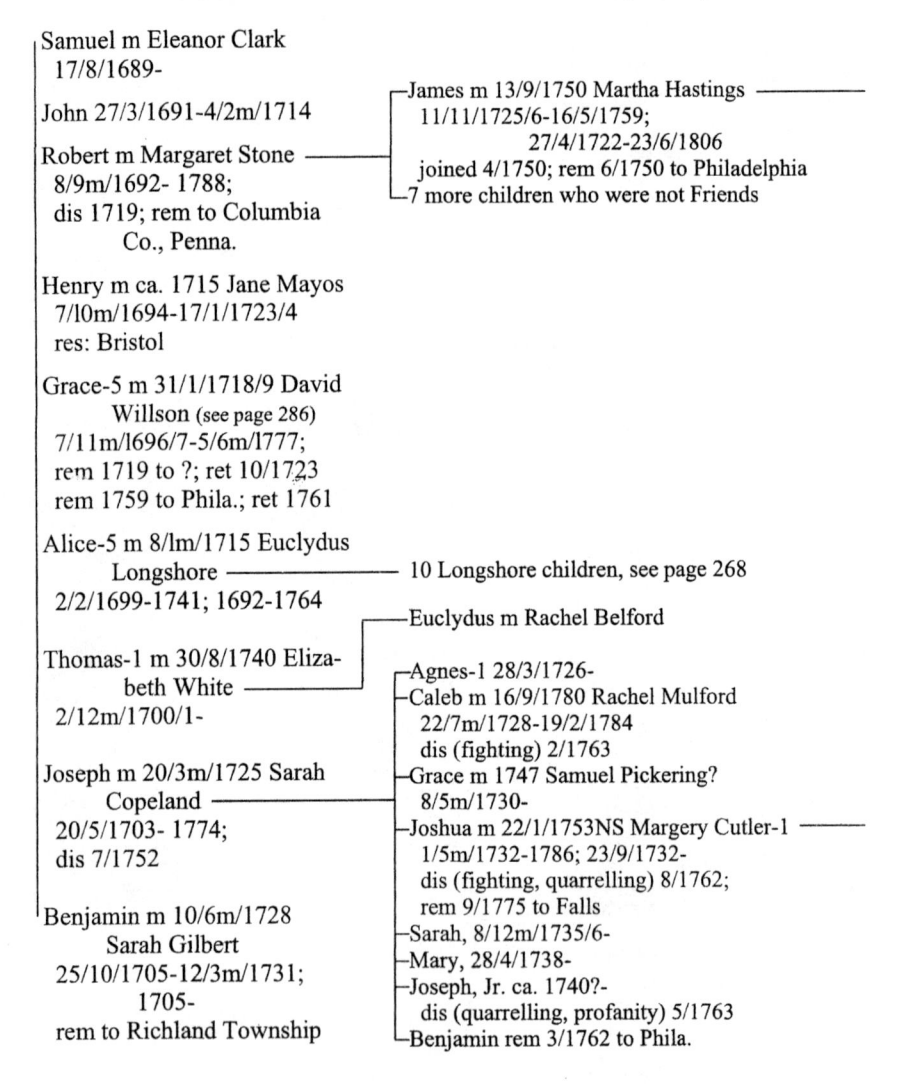

Samuel m Eleanor Clark
17/8/1689-

John 27/3/1691-4/2m/1714

Robert m Margaret Stone ──────
8/9m/1692- 1788;
dis 1719; rem to Columbia
Co., Penna.

 ┌─James m 13/9/1750 Martha Hastings ──────
 │   11/11/1725/6-16/5/1759;
 │   27/4/1722-23/6/1806
 │   joined 4/1750; rem 6/1750 to Philadelphia
 └─7 more children who were not Friends

Henry m ca. 1715 Jane Mayos
7/10m/1694-17/1/1723/4
res: Bristol

Grace-5 m 31/1/1718/9 David
 Willson (see page 286)
 7/11m/1696/7-5/6m/1777;
 rem 1719 to ?; ret 10/1723
 rem 1759 to Phila.; ret 1761

Alice-5 m 8/1m/1715 Euclydus
 Longshore ────────── 10 Longshore children, see page 268
 2/2/1699-1741; 1692-1764

          ─Euclydus m Rachel Belford

Thomas-1 m 30/8/1740 Elizabeth White ──────────
 2/12m/1700/1-

 ┌─Agnes-1 28/3/1726-
 ├─Caleb m 16/9/1780 Rachel Mulford
 │   22/7m/1728-19/2/1784
 │   dis (fighting) 2/1763

Joseph m 20/3m/1725 Sarah
 Copeland ──────────
 20/5/1703- 1774;
 dis 7/1752

 ├─Grace m 1747 Samuel Pickering?
 │   8/5m/1730-
 ├─Joshua m 22/1/1753NS Margery Cutler-1 ──────
 │   1/5m/1732-1786; 23/9/1732;
 │   dis (fighting, quarrelling) 8/1762;
 │   rem 9/1775 to Falls

Benjamin m 10/6m/1728
 Sarah Gilbert
 25/10/1705-12/3m/1731;
 1705-
 rem to Richland Township

 ├─Sarah, 8/12m/1735/6-
 ├─Mary, 28/4/1738-
 ├─Joseph, Jr. ca. 1740?-
 │   dis (quarrelling, profanity) 5/1763
 └─Benjamin rem 3/1762 to Phila.

Note: This family is so large it has been divided into two charts. Many children who were not Friends or did not live in Middletown are omitted.

┌─Hastings m 17/2/1774 Margaret
│   Robbins
│   8/12m/1752-17/1/1800;
│   6/1776 to Middletown from
│   NDMM
│   dis (W+) 9/1779
├─6 more children, res Philadelphia
┘

┌─William m 10/10m/1811 **Ann Allen**
│   7/3m/1790-1826;
│   20/7/1784-5/12m/1833
│   he rem 1809 to Falls;
│   she ret 7/1828 to Middletown as a
│   widow
├─Margery m 1820 Henry Kammerer
│   27/6/1791-
├─John m 27/3/1829 Mary Moon
│   4/1m/1793-24/3/1862;
│   16/12/1803-
│   res New Garden MM
│
├─Mary 2/7m/1794-14/8/1800
│
├─Silas m 11/12m/1817 Mary Skelton
│   4/11m/1795-8/10m/1881;
│   26/5/1796-29/3/1879
│   res New garden MM
│
├─Mercy m 13/8/1822 Isaac Pierce
│   28/4/1798-   ; 22/8/1788-
│
├─David, 17/10/1800-
├─Martha Matilda m 12/9m/1833
│   James Cook
│   (twin) 29/7/1802-ca. 1894;
│   24/9/1811-1876
└─Mary (twin) 29/7/1802-5/1895

┌─David m 6/11m/1789 Martha Mitch-
│   ener
│   29/9/1760-21/1m/1852;
│   15/10/1761-30/10/1842
│   rem 1775 to Falls, ret 9/1792;
│   rem 5/1809 to Falls
├─6 children who lived elsewhere
┘

    ┌─*Sarah* m 1842 *Samuel Comfort*
    │   (his 1st)
    │   13/10/1812-3/7m/1848;
    │   27/4/1818-
    ├─David H. m Sarah Ann Lovett
    │   27/6/1816-17/7/1899;
    │   26/3/1843-1890
    ├─**Elizabeth Y**. m 22/12/1842
    │   **William Gillam**
    │   1818- ; 15/11/1818-9/8m/1892
    │   rem 6/1853 to Green St. MM
    ├─**Mercy Ann** m 1850 *Samuel*
    │   *Comfort* (his 2nd)
    │   1824- ; 27/4/1818-
    └─*Samuel Allen* m 9/6m/1852
         Sarah Allen   -3m/1870

Stackhouse Family, Part 2

Children of Thomas and his second wife Ann (Mayos)

Isaac 11/3m/1712-4/2m/1714
Jacob-1 m 25/3/1732 Hannah
    Watson-2 ─────────
25/8/1713- 1748/9;ca.1718- 1804
Ann m 2m/1736 Charles Plumley
15/5/1715-
Sarah-5 m 19/10/1734 Samuel Cary
6/6/1718-25/5/1808;
Isaac-6 m 29/10/1743 Mary Harding-5 ─────────
5/lm/1720-17/1/1791;
    17/6/1720-4/3m/1782
disciplined but not disowned (for fighting) 11/1791

Children of John and Elizabeth (Pearson/Pierson)

Thomas m Rachel Brown
29/1/1705/6-13/10/1781;
John m 22/8m/1737 Elizabeth Janney
11/3m/1708-23/7/1743; 1714-
disciplined (D +) but not disowned
she m(2) David Wilson, Jr. (p. 286)
Elizabeth-1 m 1738 Thomas Tomlinson
Margaret-5 m 19/10/1738 John
    Mitchell (page 270)
6/8m/1714-2/5m/1774;
    10/3m/1711-31/7m/1789
Samuel, unmarried
16/10/1716-20/7/1742
James 20/1/1718-5/5/1719
Grace m 8/3m/1745 Edward Stevenson
27/7/1720-1780;
rem 9/1745 to Chesterfield MM
James m 13/11/1745/6 Sarah Welsh
10/11m/1717/8-5/3m/1719;
she joined 4/1744; dis 10/1759
he dis (D+) 10/1758
Sarah
21/7/1726-

─ Moses (impaired)
─ Job m 1771 Rebecca ____
    rem 1771 to Falls; she ret 7/1784
    dis (D+) 3/1778; reinstated 10/1778
─ Deborah m ____ Sirrell
─ Mary-1 m 13/5/1762 Joseph Merrick
    rem 1762 to Falls, ret 1793
    rem 1798 to Falls, ret 1805; rem 5/1809
─ Hannah

─ Thomas-2 m 8/5m/1771 Hannah White ─────
    29/7/1744-22/7/1837;
        23/3/1749/50-22/5/1835
    dis (D+) 7/1803
─ Mary m 21/11/1765 Jesse Heston
    5/11m/1745/6-21/9/1800; 25/6/1743-1828
    rem 1766 to Wrightstown
─ Ann m 14/4/1768 John Gilbert
    1/4m/1749-3/1m/1839; 23/5/1743-24/7/1802
    rem 1768 to Abington
─ Jonathan-4 m 14/4/1774 *Grace Comfort*-6 ─────
    31/8/1750-15/4/1805; 5/8m/1755-11m/1827
    disciplined but not disowned 12/1779
─ John-5 m 16/5/1781 Sarah Knight ─────
    11/11/1752NS-12/9m/1828;
        1758-2/6m/1806
    disciplined but not disowned 12/1779
─ Martha m 10/11m/1779 Caleb Gilbert
    13/9/1758-24/6m/1782; 19/9/1754-
    dis (M) 3/1780
─ Isaac-6 m 5/6m/1782 Elizabeth Townsend-5
    8/11/1759-30/1/1835; -23/1/1836
    disciplined but not disowned 12/1779
    disciplined (F) but not disowned 1/1797

─ Lucilla m 16/11/1759 Richard Yardley
    9/4m/1738-
    rem 7m/1764 to Falls
─ Abel m 17/5/1763 Hannah Briese
    4/4/1740-10m/1813;
    dis (M) 9/1763

─ Agnes
─ John
    rem 8/1775 to Falls
─ Sarah m 26/10/1786 Thomas Barwass
    joined 11/1782

⎡Joseph m(1) 1796 Phebe Parry ——————— Thomas P. m 11/11/1819 Abigail Phipps
│ 10/4m/1772-10/10/1806; -3/11m/1801   6/11m/1798-9/9/1842;
│ rem 1796 to Horsham   disciplined (F) but not disowned 1816
│ m(2) Mary Walmsley
⎯Thomas (F) m 1798 Susanna Parry   ⎡Hannah m James West
│ 4/6m/1774-30/4/1848; 23/4/1777-8/4m/1823   ⎯Thomas m 1819 Abigail Phipps
│ disciplined (F) but not disowned 8/1800   from Byberry 1810; to Abington 1820 .
│ rem 11/1800 to Horsham   ⎯**Amos Burriers** -2 m 17/7/1825 **Eliza-**
⎯Isaac m 14/5/1795 Margaret Thornton ———————— **beth Landis**
│ 1775-23/4/1824; -24/12/1847   1800-26/8/1836; 15/1/1800-24/9/1877
│ rem 2/1797 to Horsham   he from Byberry 6/1825;
⎯Mary m 1721 Jesse Knight   rem 12/1835 to Falls; she ret 5/1837
│ 4/4/1783-31/8/1821; 9/12m/1779-1/5m/1829   ⎯Lydia B. m 16/3/1825 Isaac C. Knight
│ rem 1802 to Horsham; ret 6/1804   18/7/1802-4/6m/1835;
│ rem 8/1806 to Horsham   ⎯Benjamin m(1) 1831 Elizabeth Register
⎯Ann m 1805 William Plumly   8/7m/1804-17/11/1873;
    ; 24/10/1777-30/3/1860   m(2) 1838 Mary Phares
  dis (M) 8/1805   24/1/1814-3/5m/1888
⎡Mary-1 m 23/4/1794 Amos Eastburn   ⎯Isaac m Elizabeth Phares
│ 25/1/1775-31/1/1821;   29/1/1806-23/5/1868; -3/3/1883
│ rem 1795 to Buckingham, ret 1811   ⎯Thornton m 1845 Mary H. Twining
⎯Rachel m 19/1/1799 Thomas Worrell   8/9m/1809-30/9/1892;
│ 14/2/1776-18/1/1823; -2/3m/1837   25/12/1814-26/3/1905
│ rem 1797 to Abington, ret 1807   ⎯Margaret m 21/3/1838 James McMullen
│ rem 1811 to Philadelphia   29/1/1814- ; -14/5/1844
⎯Isaac MD, 1/12m/1779- 1807
│ dis (D+) 12/1805
⎯*Mercy*-6 unmarried
│ 24/11/1781-4/lm/1871
⎯*Macre*-5 m 17/11/1808 *John Buckman, Jr.*-5 ——————— *3 children*
│ 3/10m/1784- ;   from Falls 1828
⎯Grace 23/10/1787- 1821
⎯Jonathan m 10/3m/1815 Sarah Simmons   ⎡Joseph m 1858 **Mary Ann Briggs**
  5/l0m/1789-1868; 15/5/1790-15/1/1853   ⎣Elizabeth
— dis (F) 10/1813; she dis (M) 5/1816
−Ann-1 m 19/3m/1801 Jonathan Paul
  28/2/1782-28/4/1855; 17/6/1775-9/2m/1856
—**Margaret**-6 m 12/1825 **Joseph Wilson**-6 (his 2)
  10/7m/1784-3/11m/1859;
                   17/3/1762-1/12m/1840   ⎡**Mary L.** 20/9/1826-1862
−**Mary**-1 23/4/1787-4/l0m/1858   ⎯**Elizabeth** 20/5/1831-1878
  rem 1802 to Horsham; ret 1804; rem 1806   ⎯**David L.** m 29/10/1857 Eliza-
−**Sarah**-1 m 24/3m/1825 **Isaac Paxson**-2   beth Buckman
  28/10/1789-8/1 m/1858; 26/10/1788-24/11/1872 22/9/1833-1888; 18/1/1833-
−**Tacy**-6 m 24/10/1811 **John Allen Mitchell**-6 rem 11/1856 to Green St.
  24/4/1792-31/5/1867; 31/1/1785-29/9/1863   resigned membership 1/1857
−John, Jr. 26/10/1794-29/3/1795   ⎣**Sarah** m William Stephenson
−**Jonathan K**-3 m 3/1830 **Mary D. Richardson**-5 24/8/1835-1883;
  28/9/1796-17/8/1841; 16/7/1805-
  she m(2) 13/9/1849 **Benjamin Borden**
⎡Mary m David Carpenter
│ 3/12m/1783-26/12/1838;   ?___ m 1849 **Rebecca Farquhar**
⎯Thomas, 8/6m/1787-20/9/1787   she came 8/1839 from Carmel MM, Oh.
⎯Evan, 22/7/1788-13/3/1789   she retained membership 12/1849
⎣John T.-1   14/2/1790-27/8/1854   res Bristol

Watson Family

─Mary m 3m/1711 William Paxson (see page 272)
-9m/1760;
4/4/1685-15/10/1733

─Amos m 13/4/1716 Mary Hillborn-2
ca 1690-12/11m/1732/3;
7/10/1694-
rem from Falls to Middletown

    ┌─Thomas m ca. 1742 Martha Neeld ─────
    │ 5/lm/1716/7- 12m/1749;
    │ she m(2) his brother Samuel
    ├─Hannah m 25/3/1742 Jacob Stackhouse
    │ ca 1718-1804; 25/8/1713-3/11m/1748/9
    │ Jacob m(2) 1743 Rachel Winner
    │ dis (M) 1743; res Falls
    ├─Samuel m 1750 Martha (Neeld) Watson ─────
    │ dis 4/1750
    └─Deborah m 18/12/1746/7 John Gregg
       rem 4/1749 to Falls; ret 2/1755
       rem 9/1767 to Kingwood MM

    ┌─Joseph m(1) 19/11/1757 Rachel Croasdale
    │ 25/5/1729- 1805; 17/4/1732-1/3m/1773
    │ rem 1757 to Falls MM
    │ m (2) 12/4m/1775 Deborah Duer
    ├─Benjamin m 21/6/1759 Phebe Croasdale ─────
    │ 1m/1730-18/10/1796; 8/2m/1738-29/10/1815
    │ rem 1759 to Falls
    ├─Ann, Jr. m 26/5/1752 Jonathan Palmer-6
    │ 26/9/1733-7/5m/1806; 20/3/1729-2m/1783
    │ rem to Lower Makefield

─Mark-6 m 1729 Ann Sotcher ─────
ca. 1698-1749;
27/1/1710-18/8/1787
res Oxford Valley, Bucks Co.
she m(2) 1753 James Moon (his 3rd)

    ├─Mark m 8/11m/1761 Mary Davis
    │ 29/6/1735-9/11m/1803; res: Falls
    ├─Amos m 19/9/1764 Phebe Bidgood
    │ 10/11m/1738/9-ca. 1771
    │ rem to Falls, then Abington
    ├─Rebecca m 16/10/1771 Benjamin Gilbert
    │   ; 31/11/1740/1-11/1m/1809
    ├─Deborah m 1767 John Balderston
    │ 23/3/1744-17/4/1794;
    │   15/3/1740-26/4/1821
    │ rem 1768 Falls to Buckingham MM
    └─Isaac-6 m 20/2/1770 Ann Jenks-2
       ca. 1746- ; 8/7m/1749-
       rem 1800 to SDMM (Phila.)

─John, Jr.-6 m 18/9/ 1729 Ruth Blakey-6 ─────
1/2m/1703-1764;
29/3/1699-

    ┌─William 1/12m/1730-d.y.
    ├─Hannah 12/9m/1733-d.y.
    ├─John-6 m 14/11/1764 Rachel Paxson-6 ─────
    │ 12/8m/1736-15/3/1799;
    │   6/3m/1744-5/4m/1800
    └─Ruth, Jr. m 22/4/1766 Oliver Paxson-6M
       12/11m/1740-17/9/1774;
         9/7m/1741-30/10/1817
       rem 6/1766 to Buckingham

    Thomas m19/6/1760 Sarah Woolston ─────
    22/6/1721-31/1/1787; 6/2/1736-14/9/1792
    she rem 1760 to Buckingham MM

- Amos m 5/1772 Elizabeth Davis
  ca. 1743- ; 5/9m/1746-16/5/1775
  she m(2) 1774 William Beal
- John-1 m 14/6/1775 Sarah Hough
  ca.1745-27/4/1815;
  4/2m/1751OS -1816
  - Elizabeth, Jr. m 14/11/1799 William
    Satterthwaite 16/3/1775-6/9m/1859
    rem 1800 to Falls
  - Martha m 7/6/1798 Gabriel Mitchell
    dis (M) 11/1798
    John unmarried
  - Hannah m 1805 Jacob Cox
    -26/6/1868; 1777-21/5/1864
    dis (M) 7/1805
  - Sarah unmarried

- Jacob m Mary Hough
  - Martha m James R. Stackhouse
  - 6 BLAKEY children (see page 255)

- 10 children plus
- **Elizabeth**-6 m 17/10/1792
  William Blakey-6
  5/10m/1766-1/6m/1845;
  29/11/1759-9/10m/1831
  she rem 1/1793 from Falls to
  Middletown

- *Hannah* m 28/4/1791 William
  Newbold
  21/9/1765-5/2m/1831;
  1/3m/1767-17/8/1828
  rem 7/1791 to Upper Springfield
  MM, NJ

- **John**-6 m 19/12/1799 **Lydia
  Blakey**-6
  1/8m/1768-7/lm/1844;
  19/9/1774-22/2/1859

  - **Rachel**-6 twin m 13/3/1845 **James
    Wildman**-3 (page 285)
    26/11/1800-14/8/1878;
    25/9/1800-15/8/1873
  - Sarah-1 twin unmarried
    26/11/1800-19/5/1824
  - **John**-1 twin m 1860 Martha Moon
    27/3/1803-22/10/1883; 21/5/1829-
  - **William B**. MD m(1) 1835 Louisa C.
    Morris
    twin 27/3/1803-16/8/1870;
    rem 3/1835 to Makefield
    m(2) 25/10/1843 **Harriet E. Paxson**
  - **Joseph**-3 m 27/2/1834 **Elizabeth Gillam**-2 (page 261)
    25/8/1805-25/10/1886;
    17/9/1810-28/1/1879
  - **Isaiah P.**-1 unmarried
    26/10/1810-28/4/1873
  - **Mary**-1 unmarried
    6/9m/1812-19 or 9/1m/1835

Marmaduke m 16/3/1797 *Mary
Richardson*-6
-1798; 19/9/1776-30/1/1848
she ret 5/1798 from Chesterfield
she m(2) 11/11/1813 *Samuel
Hulme*-6
he m(1) 10m/1798 Mary Knight

- Sarah m 1792 *Joseph R. Jenks*-2
  14/4/1767-
  16/9/1767-26/6/1858
  rem 1797 to Philadelphia

- Susanna Marmaduke m 19/11/1817
  Thomas L. Allen, MD-2 (page 252)
  ca. 1796-12/8m/1823;
  26/6/1789-3/10m/1856
  he m(2) 5/12m/1844 **Sarah Taylor**-1

Note: Fragments of two other Watson families (Thomas and Marmaduke) are included because they married into data set families.

Wildman Family

William m Mary ___

- Matthew m 24/2/1724 Mary Hayhurst
  11/12m/1678/9-6/2m/1741;
  1703-20/1/1729/30
  - Martin m 1742 Deborah Paxson
    27/12/1722/3- ; 23/1/1723/4-
    she disciplined (M) but not disowned 7/1743
    he disowned (D+) 1m/1750/1
    rem 2/1752 to Virginia
  - James-6 m 21/9/1750 Mary Warner-6
    18/12m/1723/4-14/7/1796;
    28/11/1725/6-23/12/1805
  - Ann m 28/9/1750 Benjamin Hampton
    6/12m/1726-4/9m/1806;
    15/9/1728-17/5/1811
    rem 1749 to Wrightstown
  - Elizabeth 21/4/1728- 1734/5
  - Rachel-1 m 8/9M/1750 James Spicer
    19/1/1729/30-

- John-6 m 1709 Marah (Chapman) Croasdale-6
  2/2/1681-27/3/1739;
  ca.1760-21/7/1747
  - Mercy-6 m 3m/1731 Thomas Jenks-6
    3/1m/1711/2-26/7/1787;
    1/1699/1700-4/5m/1797
    rem 1731 to Buckingham; ret 1734
  - Elizabeth-6 m 3m/1735 John Woolston-6
    30/10/1717/8-1/2m/1800;
    24/2/1708-13/1/1791

- Joseph-6 m(1) 15/9/1709 Rebecca Bunting-1
  23/1/1683-21/1/1739;
  -18/11/1715
  m(2) 1717/8 Sarah Willson-6
  20/6/1695-
  she m(2) 17/8/1751 Jeremiah Dungan
  - Ann 8/10m/1710-bur. 26/10/1710
  - Rachel 30/8/1712-26/11/1712
  - Abigail 10/8m/1714-7/11m/1714
  - Rebecca m 27/3/1741 Jeremiah Cooper
    9/11m/1715/6- ; 30/1/1716-2m/1748/9
    dis (M+) 5/1741
  - Jacob m(1) Mary Walton
    21/10/1718-4/1m/1804;
    m(2) 1742 Sarah ___ (non-Q)
    dis (M) 2/1743; rem to Virginia
  - Mary m(1) 18/8/1744 Thomas Atkinson
    8/8/1720-13/7/1766; 5/6m/1722-5/5/1760
    rem 1745 to Wrightstown
    m(2) 1764 James Moore
    6/3m/1716-1/8m/1809
  - Sarah 13/8/1722-bur. 14/2/1729
  - Rachel m 17/9/1743 Joseph Smith
    17/1/1725/6- ; 1/1/1721-
    he m(2) 4/12m/1760 Phebe Hibbs
    rem 3/1744 to Wrightstown
  - Abigail 2/1m/1727/8-bur. 4/2/1729
  - Joseph-5 m 28/6/1759 Ann Paxson-6
    1/12m/1729/30-3/5m/1809; 8/9m/1741-1806
    disciplined (F) but not disowned 9/1760
  - John-1 m 12m/1757 Mary (Stackhouse) Tomlinson-2
    8/7m/1732- 1784;
    13/5/1739-11/10m/1807
    he dis 1/1756; reinstated 1/1760
    rem 1774 to Wrightstown; ret 3/1777
    disowned (affirmation) 10/1779
  - Isaac 3/9m/1737- bur. 15/7/1739

- James unmarried
  20/1/1685-1714

- Alice m 1719 Henry Nelson
  2/6m/1687-

- Elizabeth m 1720 John Worstall
  19/9/1689-1726;

┌─**James**-5 m 14/11/1793 **Rachel (Wal-**   ┌─**Mary**-4 m 5/4m/1822 Thomas Newbold
│ **ton) Myers**-5   │ 13/5/1795-
│ 5/11m/1754-23/11/1844;   ├─**Rachel**
│   14/4/1758-6/10m/1834   │ 19/2/1799-
│ she m(1) 10/12m/1783 Joseph Myers   ├─**James**-3 m 13/3/1845 **Rachel Watson**-6
├─Solomon-2 m 17/11/1785 **Sarah**   │ 25/9/1800-15/8/1873;
│ **Cary, Jr.**-1   │   26/11/1800-14/8/1878
│ 27/12/1759-29/8/1831;   -1844   └─Hannah 15/4/1802-7/5m/1805
│ rem 6/1789 to Falls; ret 6/1796   ┌─*John* m 1836 *Ann C. Comfort*
│ rem 5/1812 to Falls   │ 18/8/1809- 11/5m/1815-8/8/1887
├─Rachel d.y.   │ rem 9/1811 to Falls
├─Sarah   └─Thomas, 10/12m/1810-22/2/1811
├─Martin m 10/11m/1790 Elizabeth   ┌─John Knight 27/12/1801-15/8/1803
│ Carlisle (b. 19/1/1770)   ├─**Charles** m 17/2m/1830 **Susanna S.**
│ rem 8/1801 to Falls   │ **Albertson**
├─Ann 5/7m/1770-24/9/1771   │ 29/7/1803-29/4/1845;
├─Abigail-2 unmarried   │   15/1/1807-23/4/1863
│ 31/3m/1772-29/9/1810   │ res: Falls; she ret 12/1849
├─Joseph-1 m 11/12m/1799 **Eliza-**   ├─Martha m 29/10/1835 Joel Smedley
│ **beth Baker**-3   │ 11/8m/1805-5/11m/1863;
│ 26/7/1773-   │   4/11m/1799-31/5/1872
│ rem 8/1802 to Falls; ret 6/1805   │ res: Conowingo, Lancaster. Co.
│ rem 9/1810 to Falls; 1829 to Ohio   ├─**Ann** unmarried 7/7/1807-26/12/1863
├─William-1 m 17/10/1810 Elizabeth   │ rem 1863 Byberry to Middletown
│ Miller   ├─Amos 2/8m/1809-27/5/1817
│ -25/3/1814; 3/7m/1791-   ├─Elwood m 23/12/1850 Mary Lloyd
│ rem 7/1812 to Falls   ├─Thomas 3/3/1811-23/12/1860
│ she m(2) 24/4/1816 Elijah Fish   ├─**John**-6 m(1) 15/4/1841 **Abigail Thom-**
├─Elizabeth-1 unmarried   │ **son**-6
│ 3/8m/1778-24/1/1800   │ 10/2m/1813-2/3m/1902;   -23/2/1868
├─Rachel unmarried   │ rem 1840 from Byberry to Middletown
└─Thomas-2 m 1808 Mary Miller-2   │ m(2) 16/3/1871 **Sarah Ann (Taylor)**
   19/12/1785-17/lm/1811;   │ **Warner**
   she rem 5/1811 to Falls   ├─Mary m 2/l0m/1851 Thomas Smedley
┌─Sarah m __ Searle   │ 2/2/1815-3/11m/1876;
│ 24/2/1759-   │   13/12/1797-14/10/1855;
├─Enos-1 unmarried   │ res: Lancaster Co.
│ 20/3/1761-   │ he m(1) 3/5m/1832 Hannah Knight
│ disciplined (W) but not disowned 3/1782   ├─**Edward** m(1) 18/3/1841 **Abi Gilbert**-2
│ rem to Wrightstown   │ 3/3/1817-13/4/1879;   -1856
├─Amos 8/3m/1763-18/8/1764   │ rem to Byberry; ret 6/1850
├─Betsey-1 m 1784 __ Randal (non-Q)   │ m(2) 12/3/1857 **Elizabeth Newbold**-6
│ 23/7/1765-   ├─**Joshua K**. m 28/3/1844 **Hannah John-**
│ dis (M) 11/1784   │ **son**
├─Rachel m 1787 __ Abbot   │ 3/8m/1819-26/2/1867;
│ 27/12/1767-   │ from Byberry 1844; rem 1846 to Byberry
│ dis (M) 10/1787   ├─Jane unmarried
├─**John**-4 m 23/4/1801 **Mary Knight**-3   │ 9/3m/1822-27/3/1858
│ 18/3/1771-21/5/1842;   └─Rachel m 6/6/1861 Hughs Warner (his
│   7/4m/1785-14/1/1861   2nd)
│ disciplined (F) but not disowned   13/3/1824-11/7m/1891;
│ 6/1802   res: Horsham
│ rem 7/1817 to Byberry
└─Joseph 26/7/1773-

GENEALOGY CHARTS OF DATA SET FAMILIES

Wilson Family
aka Willson

David-5 m 31/1/1718/9 Grace Stackhouse-5
29/5/1691-20/5/1768;
7/1 1m/1696/7-6/5m/1777
rem 1719; ret 10m/1723
rem 1759 to Phila.; ret 1760

- Robert m 23/10/1742 Jane Sands
  18/11/1719/20- 1778;
  rem 12/1744 to Falls
- David, Jr. m 21/11/1744/5 Elizabeth Stackhouse
  24/11/1721-
  disciplined (M) but not disowned 10/1745
  rem 2/1750 to Richland MM
- Elizabeth m(1) 2/4m/1742 Joshua Scattergood
  30/11m/1723-16/11/1776;   -11/6m/1752
  rem 12/1742 to Burlington, NJ
  m(2) ___ Baker
- Thomas-6 m 5/1755 Rachel Strickland-2
  31/8/1725-2/7m/1803; -2519/1797
  "of Southampton"
- Grace 16/1/1727/8-
- Jonathan-2 m 4/1759 Sarah Mardon-1
  19/10/1729- 1807; 20/4/1739-13/1/1815
  rem 2/1772 to Abington, ret 1793
  she rem 1807 to Horsham as a widow
- Dinah m 24/4/1755 John Bezer 16/8/1731
  16/8/1731- ; 1731-   rem 1757 to Phila.
- Rachel-3 m 4m/1757 Abraham Harding
  8/10m/1733-13/12/1806; 21/5/1728-27/4/1813
- Asaph m 1/9m/1760 Elizabeth Sands
  27/12/1735/6-
  rem 9/1768 to Abington
- Jesse 15/1/1738/9-

Stephen-6 m 1722 Rebecca Hoge-3
29/12/1694-1761;
-28/11/1760
rem 1741 to Wrightstown;
ret 8/1752 with 3 youngest children

- Isaac m 1744 Sarah Hampton
  2/7m/1723- ; rem 1741 to Wrightstown
- Rebecca, 9/2m/1725- ;
- Stephen, 26/2/1727-1787
- Samuel, 22/12/1729-
- John m Mary __
  rem 1762 from Wrightstown to Middletown
- Francis, rem 3/1764 to Buckingham
- Joseph m 1766 Rachel Sotcher
  disciplined (F) but not disowned 11/1767
  she rem 1773 to Falls as a widow
- William, dis (M) 7/1765

Sarah-6 m 1717/8 Joseph Wildman-6 (his 2nd)
disciplined (M) but not disowned 2/1719
she m(2) 17/8/1751 Jeremiah Dungan

Samuel m Rebecca Canby
res Buckingham MM

- Thomas-6 m(1) 21/4/1756 Margaret Bye-1
  19/1/1731-23/7/1803; 22/1/1737-11/12m/1763
  m(2) 1765 Macre Croasdale-3   -16/8/1777
  rem 5/1772 from Buckingham to Middletown
  m(3) 1779 Sarah Fell-2
- Hannah m 18/1/1786 Robert Kirkbride
  2/5m/1747-16/7/1826;
- Stephen m 25/5/1779 Sarah Blackfan
- Oliver m 13/4/1780 Sarah Mitchell-1
- David m 14/1/1779 Margaret Mitchell-1
- 9 more children

Anthony m 1737 Ann Nelson
she dis 1743
he dis (D) 6/1751

- Thomas m Margaret Knight
- 3 more children

- Amos-1 m ___
  25/8/1756- ___ ; dis (W) 3/1781
- Sarah 15/11/1757
  rem 1800 to Buckingham?
- **Joseph-6** m(1) 26/4/1792 **Mary Blakey-2**
  17/3/1762-1/10m/1840;
  1/8m/1764-21/3/1821
  m (2) 15/12/1825 **Margaret Stackhouse-6** (she d 3/11m/1859)
- Jesse m 11/1790 Amy Parry
  31/12/1766-
  rem 4/1798 to Buckingham
- John-1 m 9/1796 Margaret Mitchell
  16/1/1768- ___ ; 24/7/1770-1821
  dis (F) 12/1791; reinstated 5/1796
- Elizabeth m 11/1809 Isaiah Jones
  30/7/1770-
  rem 1810 to Buckingham
- Rachel 14/4/1776-18/11/1799
  - Hannah m 12/5m/1784 Benjamin Walton
    15/1/1760- 1846; 1760-1826
    rem 1772 to Abington
  - Jonathan 2/2/1762-
    rem 1772 to Abington
  - Jacob m 1786 Rebecca Thomas
    15/6/1764-30/9/1814; -25/11/1842
    rem 1772 to Abington
  - David 6/1/1767-
    rem 1772 to Abington MM
  - Thomas m 1797 Anna Neeld
    20/8/1769-
    rem 5/1799 to Bradford MM
  - Sarah m 27/3m/1794 Jesse Tomlinson
    15/3/1772-
    1/3m/1766-27/10/1821
    rem 7/1794 to Horsham?
  - Rachel 10/1m/1775-
    rem 1807 to Horsham
  - Asa m 10m/1804 Mary Paiste
    3/5m/1778-
    rem 5/1805 to Chester
  - Joshua m 1803 Rachel __
    14/6/1781-26/7/1856; -5/8m/1849
    rem 1772 to Abington; ret 1793
    dis (M) 1803; reinstated 5/1815
    rem 1815 to Abington MM
    - 6 children +
    - Hampton-5 m Ann __
      rem 1807 Falls to Middletown
      rem 1824 to Makefield
  - Benjamin m 1782 Elizabeth Martin
  - Thomas m 1795 Phebe Gilbert
    14/12/1768-

- William 11/12m/1793-30/8/1794
- Thomas 13/11/1796-28/2/1799
- **Sarah-3** m 27/10/1825 **Jeremiah W. Croasdale-6**
  9/7m/1799-1/7m/1866; 14/8/1793-1873
- Rachel 9/2m/1801-7/9m/1823

- Anne m 1787 Jonathan Small
  rem 1808 to Abington
- **Mardon-5** m 1815 **Ann Dewees-2**
  6/1m/1789- ___ ; ca.1783-15/5/1859
  rem 1810 from Byberry to Middletown
  rem 1812 to Upper Evesham
  rem 1817 from Byberry to Middletown
  - 6 more children in Byberry MM

  - Jehu m 8/4m/1840 **Hannah P. Thomas**
    15/7/1816-11/7m/1890;
    rem 1852 to Green St MM
  - Rebecca m 21/3/1839 Benjamin Rush Plumly
    5/1m/1818-
    rem to Chesterfield
  - **William** m 1848 ___
    29/l/1820-
    dis (M) 5/1849
  - Elwood 4/2m/1822-
    rem 1845 to Green St. MM
  - Mary M. m 1/6m/1846 **Edward P. Needles**
    30/4/1824-8/5m/1908;
    rem 8/1847 to Centre MM, New Castle, Del.
  - Sarah P.-2 18/1/1827-
    rem 1866 to Philadelphia
  - Annie Small m 2/5/1850 **George H. Sellers**
    14/10/1828-
    rem 9/1850 to Darby, ret 1854
    rem 4/1859 to Philadelphia
  - Mardon, Jr. 14/7/1831-
    rem 11/1856 to Phila.

- Rachel m 1816 Thomas Jenks
  to Middletown 1807; dis (M) 1817
- Ann, Jr. m 1805 __ Comfort
  in Middletown 1807-1820; dis (M) by Falls 1805
- William B.-2 m Jane __
  rem 7/1842 to Mt. Holly MM, N.J.
- 6 more children

- Joseph, rem from Falls to Middletown 1820

Woolston Family

Jonathan-2 m 19/6/1707 Sarah Pearson
-29/9/1741;   -1730s

- John-6 m 15/3/1735 Elizabeth Wildman-6 —
  24/12/1708-13/1/1791;
        30/11/1717/8-1/2m/1800

- Thomas
  27/4/1709-11/8m/173_

- Jonathan
  8/4m/1711-12/2m/1730

- Hannah
  3/10m/1713-
  rem 1744 to Burl., ret 1760

- Grace-5 m 31/3/1738 Thomas Kirkbride
  11/8m/1715-1783; 13/6/1712-1747
  she rem 1738 to Falls; ret 1754 as widow

- Sarah
  11/10m/1716-15/2/1733

- Elizabeth
  10/8m/1718-

- Samuel-1 m 27/8/1742 Hannah Palmer-2 —
  twin 3/6m/1721-28/3/1798;   -19/1/1795
  rem 4/1761 to Falls, dis 1764

- Margery m 11/9m/1750 John Kirkbride
  twin 3/6m/1721-   ;   -6/6m/1753
  rem 3/1738 to Falls
  dis (F) 12/1753
  he m(1) 11/1731 Hannah Sykes (page 264)

- Jeremiah m 24/4/1753 Elizabeth Palmer —
  11/11/1723-   ; 24/11/1725- 1753
  disciplined but not disowned 6/1744
  rem 4/1749 to Philadelphia

- Mary
  3/4m/1725-1/2m/1729

- Benjamin
  4/2m/1727-

```
─Sarah m 19/6m/1760 Thomas Watson          ─Sarah-1
   6/4m/1736-1792; rem 1760 to Buck ham       rem 1800 to Buckingham, ret 1820?
─Mary m 17/llm/1763 Samuel Smith           ─Elizabeth
   23/l2m/1738/9- ; rem 1764 to Phila.        ca. 1797-
─Elizabeth, Jr.-5 m 14/11/1771 Joseph
      Knight                                ┌Elizabeth m 19/10/1796 Samuel Canby
      24/8/1741-                               27/8/1778-
      rem 1772 to Abington; ret 1775          rem 1796 to Falls
─John-3 m 20/10/1769 Lydia Bye-2           ┤John 17/2/1780-29/10/1784
   22/1/1743/4-8/8/1777;                    └Stephen m(1) 19/12/1804 Jane Lancaster
   she rem 1778 to Buckingham                  21/1/1782-4/8m/1867;    - 1812
─Mercy m 21/4/1768 Thomas Bye                 rem 1796 to Falls
   28/3/1747- ; rem 1768 to Buckingham        m(2)1817 Elizabeth Stockton
─Jonathan-2 m 16/9/1770 Mary Yardley-2
   22/11/1750/1-                            ┌Sarah-1 m 21/6/1821 George Atherton
   rem 8/1783 to Falls; ret 9/1785             2/7m/1787-
   m(2)14/1/1796 Beulah (Cory) Canby-1        rem 1796 to Falls; ret 1804
   she dis (D) but not disowned 5/1798        rem 6/1828 to Gwynedd
     she m(1) Thos. Canby; she d. 25/11/1816 ─Mary 4/12m/1789-10/10/1792
     rem 1799 to Horsham; ret 7/1805        ─Rachel-6M m 4/1817 Phineas Paxson-3
└Joshua-5 m(1) 18/9/1777 Mary Stapler-1       7/9m/1791-5/11m/1860; 3m/1776-4m/1850
   19/7/1755-27/12/1821;    -25/8/1782        rem 1796 to Falls, ret 1804
   m(2) 21/9/1786 Mary Richardson             rem 1828 to Falls; she ret 3/1851 a widow
   19/8/1763-2/1m/1799                      ─Joshua m 16/4/1818 Eliza B. Kelly-1
   rem 6/1796 to Falls; ret 5/1804            12/7m/1793-1/11m/1871; -1871
   m(3)1801 Lydia Jordan-6M                   rem 9/1817 to Falls; 1835 to Makefield
   rem 5/1817 to Falls                      ─Ann m 17/10/1816 Aaron Comfort of Falls
┌Sarah 1/9m/1743-d.y.                         27/2/1795- ; 8/1m/1791-
─Sarah m 1768 Abraham Swain                   rem 1796 to Falls, ret 1804;
   8/8/1745- ; res: Falls                     rem 1817 to Falls
─Elizabeth 16/10/1747-d.y.                  └Joseph 23/10/1797-11/8m/1798
─Jonathan-5 m 18/5/1774 Elizabeth Harvey
   20/3/1749-22/10/1828; 1754-16/5/1819     ┌Lydia m __ Wood
   rem 1761 to Falls, ret 1/1773               26/3/1802-
└Margery-6 m 19/11/1771 William Bunt-         rem 1817 to Falls; 1835 to Makefield
      ing-2                                   dis(M) 6/1838
   8/5m/1757-10/8m/1831; 1746-14/2/1821
   rem 1761 to Falls; ret 1796 from Burl n  ─Mary m 24/3/1795 Giles Satterthwaite
                                               2/1m/1775-
┌Martha, unmar. 25/6/1755                     rem 1795 to Falls
─Sarah, unmar. 18/5/1757                   ─Hannah-1 unmarried
   in Middletown 1771 to 1801                 4/12m/1779-5/1m/1825
─Hannah m(1) 25/10/1784 Henry Mitchell     ─Elizabeth m 19/5/1814 Joseph Satterthwaite
   9/4m/1759-14/9/1793; 1743- 1789            9/1m/1782-4/1870; 18/12/1776-
   ret 1781 to Middletown                     rem 1814 to Falls
   dis 1784; reinstated 1787               ─Sarah 10/4m/1785-24/6/1799
   m(2) 25/10/1792 Robert Croasdale        ─Susanna-6 m 11m/1809 William Gillam-6
─Jeremiah m Sarah Grider                      18/11/1787-31/8/1860;
   15/12/1761-                                1/10m/1786-31/12/1842
   res: Wilmington, Del.                   ─Jonathan, Jr.-6 m 20/9/1821 Ann Bla-
─Benjamin m Jane Henderson                       key-3
   7/6m/1766-                                 9/2m/1791-15/4/1842; 4/1795-27/4/1865
   dis 12/1801; res: Philadelphia          └Samuel 13/9/1793-28/3/1798
└Elizabeth m John Duncan
   8/10m/1767-
```

ABBREVIATIONS

BCHS	Spruance Library of the Bucks County Historical Society, Doylestown, Pennsylvania
Col. Rec.	Pennsylvania *Colonial Records*
FHL	Friends Historical Library, Swarthmore College, Swarthmore, PA.
FHS	Friends Historical Society
HSP	Historical Society of Pennsylvania, Philadelphia, Pennsylvania
MM	Monthly Meeting
MMM	Middletown Monthly Meeting
PA	*Pennsylvania Archives*, followed by series number, as in *PA*2
PM	Preparative Meeting
PMMM	Papers of Middletown Monthly Meeting (housed in FHL)
QCol	Quaker Collection, Haverford College, Haverford, Pennsylvania
QM	Quarterly Meeting
PMHB	*Pennsylvania Magazine of History and Biography*
WMQ	*William and Mary Quarterly*
WRHS	Library of the Western Reserve Historical Society, Cleveland, Ohio
YM	Yearly Meeting

NOTES

Notes for Chapter 1: Introduction

[1] See, for example, Penn, *No Cross, No Crown*, 62-64. See also Paul Buckley's translation into modern English, *Twenty-first Century Penn: Writings On The Faith And Practice Of The People Called Quakers*.

[2] Myles, "'Stranger Friend : John Woolman and 'The Language of the Holy One'" in Heller, ed., *The Tendering Presence*, 45-47.

[3] Marietta, *The Reformation of American Quakerism*, xii-xiii.

[4] Most historians who focus on political or religious history have concentrated on the colonial and Revolutionary periods. See, for example, comment by Hamm, *The Transformation of American Quakerism*, xiv; and, Tolles, *Quakers and the Atlantic Culture*, 19.

[5] Tolles, *Quakers and the Atlantic Culture*, 14-18, 21-22; Larson, *Daughters of Light*; Skidmore, *Weakness in Strength*.

[6] Weber, *From Max Weber: Essays in Sociology*, 285, 291.

[7] Soderlund, *Quakers & Slavery*; Soderlund, "African Americans and Native Americans in John Woolman's World", in Heller, ed., *The Tendering Presence*, 151.

[8] Auping, *Religion and Social Justice: The Case of Christianity and the Abolition of Slavery in America*, 35-36.

[9] Gesell and Ilg, *The Child from Five to Ten*, and several other volumes. These various concepts are advanced for understanding within "modern" western culture. I do not know if they also provide models for human spiritual growth across cultures or for much earlier times.

[10] Wilber, *A Theory of Everything: An Integral Vision for Business, Politics, Science, and Spirituality*; Beck and Cowan, *Spiral Dynamics*. The four areas are self-consciousness, culture and world-view, the brain and physical organism, and social system and environment.

[11] Erikson, *Identity and the Life Cycle*, and *The Life Cycle Completed: A Review*; Fowler, *Stages of Faith: The Psychology of Human Development and the Quest for Meaning*; Peck, *The Different Drum: Community Making and Peace*, 188-200. For an explanation of the stages Quaker ministers went through in their spiritual development, as described in their journals, see Brinton, *Quaker Journals: Varieties of Religious Experience Among Friends*, 4-5. For the experience of female Quaker ministers, see Boulding, "Mapping the Inner Journey of Quaker Women", 81-150.

[12] Wilber defines the "green meme" in present-day terms as aiming for "diversity, multiculturalism, and sensitivity" while he insists it refuses to acknowledge any interior causation, believing only in "scientific materialism", *The Theory of Everything*, 84-88, 123-25.

[13] Peck, *Different Drum*, 190, 192-93; Wilber, *The Theory of Everything*, 9-12.

[14] Brinton, *Quaker Journals*, 25.

[15] See, for example, Arweck and Stringer, eds., *Theorizing Faith: The Insider/Outsider Problem in the Study of Ritual*, especially "Introduction: Theorizing Faith" by Stringer, 1-20; and, Peter Collins, "Connecting Anthropology and Quakerism: Transcending the Insider/Outsider Dichotomy", 77-95.

[16] See, for example, Arweck and Stringer, eds., *Theorizing Faith;* Braude, *Radical Spirits: Spiritualism and Women's Rights in Nineteenth-Century America*. For a popular account, see Anthony Podesta, president of People for the American Way, as quoted in "History textbooks don't make grade in religion study", *The Plain Dealer*, May 26, 1986, 9A.

[17] Friends were willing to absorb quietist ideas from the Roman Catholic Miguel de Molinos (1628-1696), for example. A favorite devotional book for Friends was [Anonymous] *A Guide to True Peace*.

[18] Middletown Meeting records are housed in the Quaker Collection (QCol), Haverford College, and the Friends Historical Library (FHL), Swarthmore College, and most are available at either on microfilm. Four bound volumes of manuscript documents are at FHL. A substantive index of all the Women's Minutes, 1683-1893, prepared by M. Grundy, is available in both libraries. Copies of parts of the records are available in the Spruance Library of the Bucks County Historical Society (BCHS) and in the Pennsylvania Genealogical Society's collection in the Historical Society of Pennsylvania (HSP), as well as on the web.

[19] [Philadelphia Yearly Meeting], *A Collection of Memorials Concerning Divers deceased Ministers and others of the People Called Quakers*, 278; Comly and Comly, eds., *Friends' Miscellany*, 4:76-161.

[20] Lucy Simler has shown in her study of Chester County colonial tax records that the person farming the land was taxed, whether or not he was the owner. Simler, "Tenancy in Colonial Pennsylvania: The Case of Chester County", 542-69. Bucks County tax records are on microfilm at the HSP. Some of the manuscript records are in the BCHS. Some are being posted on the web at rootsweb.com/pub/usgenweb/pa/bucks/. See also McNealy and Waite, comps., *Bucks Co. Tax Records, 1693-1778*. Additional difficulties with tax records are that some individuals were absent in some years; there were not tax records from regular intervals; over the 100 years the currency changed in type and value. Therefore I have used the splendid work of Anne Bezanson and translated amounts into "constant dollars." Bezanson, *Prices and Inflation During the American Revolution, Pennsylvania, 1770-1790*; and Bezanson, Gray, and Hussey, *Wholesale Prices in Philadelphia 1784-1861*. Her work has been used by Cole, *Wholesale Commodity Prices in the United States, 1700-1861*. My use of "constant dollars" is explained in Chapter 2.

[21] Several scholars have studied Bucks County wills, and their findings are helpful for comparative purposes. See for example, Shammas, Salmon, and Dahlin, *Inheritance in America From Colonial Times to the Present*, which includes Bucks County data. For other areas, see, Main, "The Standard of Living in Southern New England, 1640-1773", 124-134, and Carr and Walsh, "The Standard of Living in the Colonial Chesapeake", 135-159.

[22] McNealy, "Bucks County Newspapers and How to Use Them for Research", address to the Bucks County Genealogical Society, May 8, 1986. For a history of Bucks County newspapers in the nineteenth century, see Davis, *The History of Bucks County*, 1:308-24. For a list of the newspapers used in this study, see the Bibliography.

[23] *The Friend*, 1:1.

[24] Buck, *History of Bucks County*; Battle, *History of Bucks County, Pennsylvania*; Davis, *Hist. of Bucks Co.*; Bache, *Historical Sketches of Bristol Borough in the County of Bucks*; Green, *A History of Bristol Borough*; Martindale, *A History of the Townships of Byberry and Moreland in Philadelphia, Pa.*

[25] See Appendix 5 for a chart of each family.

Notes for Chapter 2: Setting the Scene

[1] The standard histories include, among others, Braithwaite, *The Beginnings of Quakerism*, and its companion volume, *The Second Period of Quakerism*; Brayshaw, *The Quakers: Their Story and Message*; Russell, *The History of Quakerism*; Punshon, *Portrait in Grey*; Barbour and Frost, *The Quakers*; Thomas and Thomas, *A History of the Society of Friends in America*. A nearly contemporaneous account is Sewel, *The History of the Rise, Increase, and Progress of the People Called Quakers*. A more radical/Marxist interpretation is Hill, *The World Turned Upside Down*. For American Friends, see Jones, *The Quakers in the American Colonies*.

[2] Brinton, *Quaker Journals*, 48-55. See Barclay's explanations, especially in his Proposition XV, *An Apology for the True Christian Divinity*, 484-503.

[3] Braithwaite, *Second Period*, 636-37; Thomas and Thomas, *History of Friends in America*, 236; Bownas, *A Description of the Qualifications Necessary to a Gospel Minister*; Sykes, *The Quakers: A New Look at Their Place in Society*, Chap. 2, ns. 2, 3, 5. See also Punshon, *Portrait in Grey*, 101, and 120-22, for the differences between Quaker quietism and the continental mysticism of Molinos and Fénelon, among others. For an understanding of quietism as a positive consolidation of a godly way of life that forms the basis for social action as part of the realization of God's kingdom on earth, see Damiano, "'On Earth as It Is in Heaven': Eighteenth-Century Quakerism as Realized Eschatology".

[4] Steere, ed., *Quaker Spirituality: Selected Writings*, 33, 50. For how this worked in practice, see almost any of the eighteenth century Quaker journals, especially those of John Woolman, Daniel Stanton, or David Ferris. For an excellent in-depth study of Woolman, for example, see Heller, ed., *The Tendering Presence*.

[5] Clarkson, *A Portraiture of Quakerism*; Levy, *Quakers and the American Family*, but note the review of Levy by J. William Frost in *Quaker History*, 79:40-42; Taber, *Eye of Faith: A History of Ohio Yearly Meeting, Conservative*; Tolles, *Quakers and the Atlantic Culture*, 117-9; Brinton, *Friends for 300 Years*, 184. It is this family culture, quiet and nurturing, but not self-aggrandizing, that E. Digby Baltzell was unable to see when he compared Boston Brahmins and Philadelphia Quakers. He judged the latter by the former, and found them wanting. If he had been aware of the Quakers' goal of family and inner life, and judged cold New England homes by those standards, the results would have been just as unequal, but in the opposite direction. Baltzell, *Puritan Boston and Quaker Philadelphia*. For reviews of Baltzell supporting this criticism, see Drake, *Friends Journal*, 26:27-28; Laubach, "Philadelphia vs. Boston Beginnings", 29:16-17; Winston, "Did Philadelphia Quakers Really Fail?" 31:14-16.; and Fager, "Review of *Puritan Boston and Quaker Philadelphia: Two Protestant Ethics and the Spirit of Class Authority and Leadership* by E. Digby Baltzell", 1:2-3.

[6] Among the many that could be listed, see Bacon, ed. *"Wilt Thou Go On My Errand?": Journals of Three 18th Century Quaker Women Ministers*; Stoneburner and Stoneburner, eds., *The Influence of Quaker Women on American History: Biographical Studies*; Larson, *Daughters of Light*; Skidmore, ed., *Strength in Weakness: Writings of Eighteenth-Century Quaker Women*. See Skidmore's comment on quietism, *Ibid.*, 6-7.

[7] Steere, *Quaker Spirituality*, 37-39, 41-42. For an explanation of Quaker methods of conducting business meetings, see Sheeran, *Beyond Majority Rule: Voteless Decisions in the Religious Society of Friends*. For the differences between a more secular consensus and faith-based "sense of the meeting", see Morley, "Beyond Censensus: Salvaging Sense of the Meeting".

[8]Frost, *The Quaker Family in Colonial America*, 3-5; Thomas and Thomas, *History of Friends in America*, 173, 176-82.

[9]See Thomas and Thomas, *History of Friends in America*, 177-78. London was slow to establish a women's yearly meeting, Frost, *The Quaker Family in Colonial America*, 5.

[10]Steere, *Quaker Spirituality*, 48-50; Punshon, *Portrait in Grey*, 98-99. For more detailed studies of the establishment of Pennsylvania, see, *inter alia*, Bronner, *William Penn's "Holy Experiment": The Founding of Pennsylvania 1681-1701*; Illick, *Colonial Pennsylvania: A History*; Nash, "The Framing of Government in Pennsylvania: Ideas in Contact with Reality"; Nash, *Quakers and Politics: Pennsylvania 1681-1726*. See also Schwartz, *"A Mixed Multitude": The Struggle for Toleration in Colonial Pennsylvania*.

[11]Levy claims that it was Quaker ideology which chose wheat/mixed farming over tobacco and the quick profits it promised. Levy, *Quakers and the American Family*, 122-23. But in seventeenth-century Maryland early Friends' converts grew tobacco as did their non-Quaker neighbors.

[12]Wyatt-Brown, *Southern Honor: Ethics and Behavior in the Old South*; Isaac, "Evangelical Revolt: The Nature of the Baptists' Challenge to the Traditional Order in Virginia, 1765 to 1775"; Levy, "'Tender Plants': Quaker Farmers and Children in the Delaware Valley, 1681-1735", 177-203; Censer, *North Carolina Planters and Their Children: 1800-1860*; Tolles, *Meeting House and Counting House*.

[13]The standard studies of colonial New England culture include the works of Perry Miller and Edmund S. Morgan. For some of the underlying differences between Puritans and Quakers as reflected in their journals, see Brinton, *Quaker Journals*, 10-11, 15, 19-20, 35, 69, 77.

[14]See Soderlund's sensitive exploration of John Woolman's growing understanding of the interconnections among the Atlantic trading system, European settlement, white greed, and enslavement of both Africans and Native Americans. Because the welfare of Woolman's own family could not be extricated from the Euro-American economic system Woolman felt obligated to remain silent about its injustices. Soderlund, "African and Native Americans in John Woolman's World", in Heller, ed., *The Tendering Presence*, 162.

[15]Davidson, *War Comes to Quaker Pennsylvania*, 167.

[16]Tully, *William Penn's Legacy: Politics and Social Structure in Provincial Pennsylvania*. For other interpretations, see Nash, "The Framing of Government in Pennsylvania: Ideas in Contact with Reality", 183-209; Nash, *Quakers and Politics*; Wendel, "The Keith-Lloyd Alliance: Factional and Coalition Politics in Colonial Pennsylvania", 92:289-305; Lokken, *David Lloyd*; Wellenreuther, "The Political Dilemma of the Quakers in Pennsylvania, 1681-1748", 94:135-72; Hutson, *Pennsylvania Politics 1746-1770*. For a good summary, see Tolles, *Meeting House and Counting House*, 11-28. A thorough institutional history is Shepherd, *History of Proprietary Government in Pennsylvania*. For a biased contemporary account, see Smith, *A Brief View of the Conduct of Pennsylvania, for the Year 1755*. For a view of ethnic/religious disputes, see Schwartz, *Mixed Multitude*, 41 ff.

[17]Tolles, *Meeting House and Counting House*, 11-28.

[18]For a description of the geology of Bucks County, see Murphy and Murphy, *Pennsylvania: A Regional Geography*, 20, 21, 49.

[19]Third month in 1683 was June. Friends used numeric names rather than those derived from pagan traditions. Before 1752 the year began on March 25. So January was Eleventh month of the previous year. For dates between January 1 and March 24 the years were often written with a slash: Twelfth month 1682/3 (meaning February). That usage will be followed here. The numerals will be ordered day/month/year. A lower case "m" will follow the numeral for the month for the first twelve days of the month, to lessen the possibility of confusion. For Friends' acceptance of the

changed calendar, see Falls Men's Minutes for 4/10m/1751, microfilm in QCol. For a chart showing Old Style months and years, see Nickalls' edition of *The Journal of George Fox*, xiii-xiv. For 1691 and 1697 Advices on this subject, see [Philadelphia Yearly Meeting]. *Rules of Discipline of the Yearly Meeting of Friends*, 41.

[20]Davis, *Hist. of Bucks Co.*, 1:159; Michener, *Retrospect of Early Quakerism*, 74-84.

[21]For a fuller description of the care involved in setting off new meetings, see Taber, *Eye of Faith*, 14-17.

[22]Davis, *Hist. of Bucks Co.*, 1:64.

[23]See Davis, *Hist. of Bucks Co.*, vols. 1 and 2 for a description of the early settlers in each township.

[24]For more information on the Keithian Schism, see Butler, "'Gospel Order Improved': The Keithian Schism and the Exercise of Quaker Ministerial Authority in Pennsylvania", 1:431-452; Kirby, *George Keith, 1638-1716*; Frost, *The Keithian Controversy in Early Pennsylvania*. See also, Schwartz, *Mixed Multitude*, 55-58.

[25]There were no membership lists as such. A list has been reconstructed from records of births and deaths, certificates of removal into and from the meeting, marriage records, and individuals named in the men's and women's minutes. In theory that should account for everyone. But the vital statistics are incomplete and therefore unmarried, inactive Friends who did not get into trouble, are probably underrepresented. See Appendix 2 for reconstructed membership list of Middletown Meeting, 1750.

[26]The manuscript tax record is in the BCHS. See also McNealy and Waite, comps., *Bucks County Tax Records 1693-1778*.

[27]Interview with Lucy Simler, August 1986, and Simler, "Tenancy in Colonial Pennsylvania: The Case of Chester County", 546-48.

[28]Bezanson, *Prices and Inflation During the American Revolution, Pennsylvania, 1770-1790;* and Bezanson, Gray, and Hussey, *Wholesale Prices in Philadelphia 1784-1861*. Her work has been used by Cole, *Wholesale Commodity Prices in the United States, 1700-1861*. The specific table used for my calculations here, is in *Wholesale Prices in Philadelphia*, 396.

[29]Some of these data set men were the third generation of their family to live in Middletown; others were the first generation. Of these latter, some were getting up in years, others were new, young arrivals. Age and length of time in Bucks County explain most, but not all, of the difference in wealth.

[30]Thomas Kirkbride's file in the Bucks County Courthouse, for instance, was completely empty. Nicholas Allen (d. 1750) had only an administration paper with amounts paid out, but no indication of what the payments were for. They could be debts or bequests or funeral expenses.

[31]Of course their economic situation could change between 1757 and their death. Real estate which was taxed in 1757 could be devised to children. Surplus wealth could be spent for land or personal goods.

[32]Simler demonstrates that a much higher percentage of rural Chester County inhabitants were artisans than had previously been assumed, and that there was a high degree of integration of non-agricultural with agricultural production throughout the eighteenth century. From 25%-30% of householders combined commercial agriculture with manufacturing. Simler, "Tenancy in Colonial Pennsylvania: The Case of Chester County", 545-46.

[33]Davis, *Hist. of Bucks Co.*, 1:131, 140. The other partners with Mitchell were Jeremiah Langhorne, Stoffel VanSant, John Plumley, and Bartholomew Jacobs. Their names indicate they

were not all English Quakers.

[34] Davis, *History of Bucks Co.*, I:141.

[35] James Stackhouse was disowned for taking strong drink to excess, swearing, neglecting meeting, and removing without a certificate. Middletown Monthly Meeting of Men, Minutes, 10m/1758. Different volumes of the men's and women's minutes have various titles. Citation will be made to the date of the specific meeting rather than to a page and volume number. Dates will be arranged day/month/year, with "m" specifying the month. Hereinafter cited as MMM Men's min. The disownment document is in *Papers of Middletown Monthly Meeting*, 4 bound mms. Vols. 1:234 (FHL). Hereinafter cited as PMMM.

[36] Bockelman, "Local Government in Colonial Pennsylvania", 216-28, gives a clear explanation of the various offices, their duties, and how men were selected for them. Names of the following officials: sheriff, coroner, collector of excise, treasurer, justices of the peace, chief burgess, assemblymen, and a few sporadic others, appear in *Pennsylvania Archives*, 2nd ser., 9:760-784. Hereinafter cited as *PA2*. Some of these, plus other office holders are listed in Battle, *History of Bucks*, 682-84, 689-94, 700-6, 709-11.

[37] Miscellaneous Papers, Bucks County Court of Quarter Sessions, BCHS. Burgesses are listed in Bache, *Historical Sketches of Bristol Borough in the County of Bucks*. Other references are scattered through family histories. A list of 1785 pew holders in St. James Episcopal Church (Bristol) is found in Davis, *History of Bucks* 1:319-20n.

[38] It was the custom then for a woman to drop completely her maiden name when she got married. However, to make family relationships clear, in this book maiden names will be retained within parentheses.

[39] Marietta, *The Reformation of American Quakerism* has made the definitive study of mid-eighteenth century discipline within Philadelphia Yearly Meeting. In order to keep my results uniform with his, I used his computer printout, stored at the QCol. There are a few instances in which I would debate his coding decisions, but here I have followed his data.

Notes for Chapter 3: Tightening the Discipline

[1] Thomas and Thomas, *A History of the Society of Friends in America*, 240-41.

[2] Sykes, *The Quakers*, 166, 170. Because occupations involving an oath (i.e., politics and anything requiring a university degree), or involved with the military or established church, were closed to Friends, and because the early persecutions were especially difficult economically for farmers, British Quakers tended to concentrate in commerce and industry, especially in the newer towns that had fewer regulations.

[3] Myles, "'Stranger Friend': John Woolman and Quaker Dissent", in Heller., ed., *The Tendering Presence*, 45-46.

[4] Tolles, *Meeting House and Counting House*, ix, 109-43, 240-43. Tolles includes a helpful bibliographical essay on studies published before the mid 1940s.

[5] Kobrin, "The Saving Remnant: Intellectual Sources of Change and Decline in Colonial Quakerism, 1690-1810"

[6] See, for example, John Smith's testimony to Philadelphia YM 9m/1764, as reported in Woolman, *The Journal and Major Essays of John Woolman*, Moulton, ed., 139-40; letter from David Ferris to his "cousin" David Ferris, Jr., in Ferris, *Resistance and Obedience to God:*

Memoirs of David Ferris, 1707-1779, Grundy, ed., 89-90.

[7] Mazzenga, "John Churchman and Quaker Reform in Colonial Pennsylvania: A Search for Spiritual Purity", 83:71, 76-77, 86, 95.

[8] Cady, *John Woolman: The Mind of the Quaker Saint*, 7, 86, 91-93. See for example, Chalkley, *The Journal of Thomas Chalkley, to which is annexed a Collection of his Works*, 6, 131-32, 135-36.

[9] Marietta, *The Reformation of American Quakerism*, 73-76. See also, Kenneth L. Carroll, "A Look at the 'Quaker Revival of 1756'", 65:63-80. For more on Friends who travelled in the ministry, see Larson, *Daughters of Light*; and, Skidmore, *Weakness in Strength*.

[10] See, for example, Anthony Benezet's letter to John Smith, 1762, decrying the over-zealous spirit under the influence of which "a kind of hatred was begot against such as would not act agreeable" to it. Brookes, *Benezet*, 245. Thomas Chalkley is an example of someone more concerned with upholding rules than with doing the tough inner work required of deeper spiritual growth. Chalkley, *Journal*. See also Beiswenger, "Thomas Chalkley: Pious Quaker and Businessman". She concluded that Chalkley was a moralist in politics, a first rate pragmatist in business, and a humanist calling for more genuine and responsible individual behavior. But he also "entertained an idealistic view of his own life and personality which prevented him from self-assessment in the same critical spirit as he assessed others' lives. His advocacy of moral conduct stopped short of objectively challenging societal values and norms as the bases for social degradation, particularly where Indians and Black slaves were concerned. Chalkley had the peculiar strengths and weaknesses of the moderate moralist." *Dissertation Abstracts*, Vol. 31, no. 2, 510-A.

[11] Grundy, "Are Outcasts Cast Out?: Disownment, Inheritance, and Participation in Middletown Monthly Meeting", 4:43.

[12] In 1694 Phila. YM warned against marrying a non-Friend. In the *Disciplines* of 1704 and 1712 Phila. YM specified that those who married "out of unity" should be disowned. Tolles, *Meeting House and Counting House,* 119; Marietta, "Egoism and Altruism in Quaker Abolition", 82:8. See also Levy, *Quakers and the American Family*; Frost, *Quaker Families*. Briefly, the correct marriage procedure involved the couple coming before the men's and women's meeting to declare their intentions of marriage. Each meeting then appointed a committee to see if the respective member of the couple was free of other engagements and was "clear" to marry. The financial arrangements of a widow's children would be inspected. The following month the couple reported a second time to each meeting, declaring they continued in their intention. The clearness committees would then report. If the meeting approved, it declared that the couple was free to continue. Another committee, often with the same people, was appointed by each meeting to oversee that the marriage was accomplished "in good order". Usually they married in the next week or two. Within a specially called, unprogrammed "silent" meeting for worship, the couple gave themselves to each other. A written certificate quoting their promises to each other was then read and signed by the couple and by everyone present, as witnesses. The marriage oversight committee reported back the following month, and the certificate was recorded in the meeting's records. See Clarkson, *Portraiture of Quakerism*, 2:2-6; [Philadelphia Yearly Meeting], *Rules of Discipline of the Yearly Meeting of Friends* (1834), 68-77; Philadelphia Yearly Meeting, *Faith and Practice* (rev. 1972), 165-75.

[13] Grundy, "Are Outcasts Cast Out?", 4:43-44.

[14] Marietta, *Reformation*, 31; see 26-31.

[15] Marietta, *Reformation*, 46-55. For the 13 new queries approved by Philadelphia YM, 20-26/9m/1755, see *Friends Intelligencer* 10 (April 7, 1855), 34-5.

[16] Marietta, *Reformation*, Table 1, 6-7; Fig. 4, 49; Fig.7, 56.

[17] Marietta, *Reformation*, 26-7. Marietta explains Chester's comparative scrupulosity in terms of a sub-group of meetings recently settled by strict Irish Quakers, and the early activities of reformer John Churchman. He makes no attempt to explain Bucks Quarter's comparative laxity. Its relative isolation may have played a role. In spite of its proximity to Philadelphia much of Bucks County seemed to be ignored by many of the travelling ministers who crisscrossed the Quaker world, visiting and exhorting, and keeping Friends in close touch with one another. I am struck with how comparatively few visits to Middletown are recorded in journals of eighteenth century Quaker ministers, compared to many other meetings, especially in Chester Quarter.

[18] Data is from Marietta, with some minor changes. His category labelled "incest", which in Middletown involved marriage of first cousins, has been collapsed into "marriage". There are a few other changes where a close reading of the minutes seemed to indicate coding errors or duplications. The big bulge in 1763 was due to 5 cases concerning slavery.

[19] MMM Men's min., 4/12m/1755.

[20] MMM Men's min., 1/1m/1756, 5/8m/1756, 5/1m/1758.

[21] MMM Men's min., 3/3/1757, 2/6m/1757, 5/4m/1759, 5/7m/1759, 7/7m/1757, 2/3m/1758, 6/4m/1758, 3/8m/1758; MMM Women's min., 7/7m/1757, 4/8m/1757. There is a difference in both theory and practice, between Friends' understanding of the "sense of the meeting", often called consensus (which has been co-opted into secular practice), and unanimity. See Morley, *Beyond Censensus: Salvaging Sense of the Meeting*. The frequent use of the word "unanimous" when Middletown Men minuted potentially controversial decisions invites speculation that often decisions did not have full unity.

[22] MMM Men's min., 6/10m/1739, 7/6m/1753, 2/8m/1753, 6/6m/1754, 6/7m/1754; Bucks Quarterly Meeting Men's Minutes, 29/8m/1754. First cousin and sibling exchange marriages were favored in England to facilitate capital concentration. Peter Dobkin Hall, "Family Structure and Economic Organization", in Hareven, ed., *Family and Kin*, 102-3. The same situation was common among wealthy British Quaker families. See, for instance, the genealogical charts in Verily Anderson, *Friends and Relations: Three centuries of Quaker Families*, 11-16.

[23] MMM Men's min., 5/2m/1737, 7/1m/1744-5, 5/10m/1745, 5/8m/1773, 2/9m/1773, 8/11m/1787, 6/12m/1787. MMM Women's min., 2/11m/1745, 6/12m/1745, 6/12m/1787. Later second cousin marriages between Anna Paxson and William Richardson, Jr., (1796) and Lydia Blakey and John Watson (1799) were accepted by the Meeting. *Ibid.*, 8/9m/1796, 10/11m/1796, 7/11m/1799, 9/1m/1800.

[24] MMM Women's min., 4/12m/1755, 4/3m/1756, 3/6m/1756, 5/8m/1756, 4/6m/1767, 7/12m/1769; also many meetings in 1758; 3m/1763. Soderlund, *Quakers & Slavery*, 143, 145-47.

[25] MMM Women's min., 6/12m/1776, 4/12m/1777.

[26] [Philadelphia Yearly Meeting], *A Collection of Memorials Concerning Divers deceased Ministers and others of the People Called Quakers (1787)*, 278-79.

[27] *Friends' Miscellany*, 10:222.

[28] PMMM, 1:180.

[29] For a dissenting view of the prevailing practice of disownment for transgressing marriage procedures unless such acts were condemned for being contrary to Friends' principles, see Anthony Benezet's letter to George Dillwyn, 5m/1781. Benezet acknowledged "it never appeared to me in the criminal light it does to some" and therefore "the least which ought to be said is, that which will imply, that the unity of their Friends is esteemed with them of so much weight, as that

upon their present prospect (tho' they may not see any criminality in the act) they are persuaded they ought rather to have cross'd their inclination than taken such a step." Brookes, *Benezet*, 354-5.

[30] Levy, *Quakers and the American Family*, 138, 311.

[31] Whether poorer Quakers had more difficulty finding Quaker spouses because they were poor isn't proved or disproved by correlating wealth of parents and disciplining of children, even if those disciplined were for breach of marriage process or marrying a non-Friend.

[32] Woolman's Journal and other writings, and his impact on other Friends, demonstrate his remarkable spiritual development.

[33] Lacey, *Quakers and the Use of Power*, 26-7. See also Bownas, *A Description of the Qualifications of a Gospel Minister*. For a description of recent Quaker understanding of "seasoned Friend", see http://www.fgcquaker.org/ library/ministry/seasoned-friend.html.

[34] The grand daughters-in-law were Alice (Fell) Comfort, Sarah (Stevenson) Comfort (clerk and elder), and Ann (Quinby) Croasdale (overseer and elder).

[35] Matthew 18:15-17; See also [Philadelphia Yearly Meeting], *Rules of Discipline of the Yearly Meeting of Friends* (1834), 55; Tolles, *Meeting House and Counting House*, 251-2.

[36] It would be taken to a preparative meeting if there was one; Middletown did not have one until 1788 when it was joined to Bristol, each then became a preparative meeting of the joint Middletown Monthly Meeting. The two preparative meetings met separately to prepare items of business for the monthly meeting.

Notes for Chapter 4: Antislavery

[1] The best study of the abolition of slavery within Philadelphia Yearly Meeting is Soderlund, *Quakers & Slavery*. For a larger context see Nash and Soderlund, *Freedom by Degrees: Emancipation in Pennsylvania and Its Aftermath*. Many others recount in greater or less detail the movement against slavery within the Society of Friends. The standard study has been Drake, *Quakers and Slavery in America*. See also: Carroll, "George Fox and Slavery", 16-25; Jones, *The Quakers in the American Colonies*, 509-21; Frost, *The Quaker Origin of Antislavery*; Davis, *The Problem of Slavery in Western Culture*, especially Chapt. 10, and for the reasons Quakers were more open to change their ideas on slavery, 306-7; Zilversmit, *The First Emancipation: The Abolition of Slavery in the North*, Chapt. 3; James, *A People Among Peoples: Quaker Benevolence in Eighteenth-Century America*, chapter 7; Turner, *The Negro in Pennsylvania: Slavery, Servitude, Freedom, 1639-1861*, 65ff; Jordan, *White Over Black: American Attitudes Toward the Negro, 1550-1812*, 271-76, 282-83. Personal accounts include Brookes, *Friend Anthony Benezet*; Grundy, ed., *Resistance and Obedience to God: Memoirs of David Ferris, 1707-1779*; Woolman, *Journal*. For an overview, see Brown, "Pennsylvania's Antislavery Pioneers, 1688-1776", 59-77; Thomas, *The Attitude of the Society of Friends Towards Slavery in the Seventeenth and Eighteenth Centuries*, 8:263-99; Turner, "Slavery in Colonial Pennsylvania", 141-51; Turner, "The Abolition of Slavery in Pennsylvania", 129-42.

[2] The journals of other Friends, however, give insights into how they enlarged their understanding. See, for example, the letters written by Ferris, in Grundy, ed., *Resistance and Obedience to God: Memoirs of David Ferris, 1707-1779*, 68-84. See also Woolman, *Journal*; and, Brookes, *Benezet*.

[3] Bucks Quarterly Meeting minutes 25/11m/1756 as quoted in Soderlund, *Quakers & Slavery*,

28. As it had done three years earlier, the quarterly meeting deferred to the yearly meeting decision; but this time the yearly meeting had a new instruction.

[4] Philadelphia Yearly Meeting Men's min., 23-29/9m/1758.

[5] Philadelphia Yearly Meeting Men's minutes, 23-29/9m/1758, 30-31; Woolman, *Journal*, 91-97. Woolman described the visit: "We proceeded on the visit in a weighty frame of spirit and went to the houses of the most active members through the county who had Negroes, and through the goodness of the Lord my mind was preserved in resignation in times of trial. And though the work was hard to nature, yet through the strength of that love which is stronger than death, tenderness of heart was often felt amongst us in our visits, and we parted with several families with greater satisfaction than we expected." Woolman, *Journal*, 102.

[6] MMM Men's min., 7/12m/1758.

[7] MMM Men's min., 2/6m/1763.

[8] Bucks County Will file #1662, in the Bucks County Court House, Doylestown, Penna. No constant dollar figure is available for his estate inventory because of the rate of wartime inflation. This does not mean that the men who made the valuation did not know the value of his estate. See also MMM Men's min. for many references to William Croasdale's committee appointments.

[9] MMM Men's min., 4/8m/1763.

[10] MMM Men's min., 1/12m/1763; also 1/9m/1763, 6/10m/1763, 3/11m/1763.

[11] MMM Men's min., 5/1m/1764.

[12] MMM Men's min., 1/3m/1764, 5/4m/1764, 3/5m/1764. See also, James Moon, "An Account of Negroes Set Free", typescript copy in the QCol, 11, 12-13, 16.

[13] MMM Men's min., 7/12m/1769; 6/12m/1770; 5/12m/1771; 3/12m/1772; 2/12m/1773.

[14] MMM Men's min., 1/12m/1774; 5/1m/1775; 3/8m/1775. Additional committees were appointed to deal with other infractions such as being "drowsy in meetings" or neglecting them altogether, and to visit families.

[15] MMM Men's min., 7/12m/1775.

[16] James Moon, "An Account of Negroes Set Free", typescript copy in the QCol.

[17] Meyers, *Quaker Arrivals in Philadelphia*, 77; Samuel Eastburn, "Wm. Paxson Lands Genealogy", Eastburn MSC 51, fol. 35, BCHS; Davis, *History of Bucks*, 1:137; account by Mrs. Joshua Richardson for the DAR in 1954, quoted in the *Delaware Valley Advance*, 22 July 1965, 1B; Eastburn MSC 51, fol. 33, BCHS. For operations of a rural merchant, see Fletcher, *Pennsylvania Agriculture and Country Life 1640-1840*, 276-77. Richardson's stone house and store still stand in Langhorne, see http:hla.buxcom.net/Richardson%20House.htm

[18] MMM Men's min., 5/2m/1744, 7/4m/1744, 7/8m/1755, 2/10m/1755, 4/10m/1759, 6/12m/1759. See also Falls Meeting Men's minutes, 4m/1753, 5m/1753, 1m/1754, 2m/1754, 8m/1755, 9m/1755.

[19] Bucks County Will file #1344 (Will Book 3:268). See also Collections of the Genealogical Society of Pennsylvania, *Bucks County, Pa., Abstracts of Wills 1685-1795*, 285; and, Eastburn MSC 51, fol. 33, BCHS.

[20] Moon, "Account", 2, 11.

[21] MMM Men's min., 2/9m/1779, 3/2m/1780, 8/2m/1787, 10/4m/1788.

[22] Bucks Co. Will file #356.

[23] Bucks Co. Will file #1236.

[24] Bucks Co. Will file #1388; Moon, "Account", 8. In the Marriott family Bible (QCol) Anna is not listed as a sister of the Joyce who married the Quaker abolitionist Anthony Benezet; however, she did sign the Benezet's marriage certificate. Brookes, *Benezet*, 24-25.

[25] Deed Book 1, page 119, BCHS; Moon, "Account", 8-9.

[26] Moon, "Account", 9, 40-1.

[27] It appears that Middletown Monthly Meeting and Bucks Quarterly Meeting, as represented by those appointed to labor with slave owners, were a mix of the two reformist strands identified by Jean Soderlund. As humanitarians, they were concerned that the elderly Matilda be taken care of, while attaining her freedom. But as purists they did not bother visiting the men who were no longer members of the Society. But that is too simple a schema. When other cases are considered, the picture is somewhat clarified, although the records are too incomplete to be really clear. See note 28.

[28] The records of several other manumissions might shed some light on general practice. The account of John Plumley's Negro man named Cudjo, born in Guinea, and estimated to be 100 years old, did not mention how he was to be supported. Joshua Richardson's "antient man" aged about 66 was retained in the Richardson family. The note on Isaac Stackhouse's Ishmael, aged about 56, says "Care towards him Necessary." The case of Ennion Williams of Bristol, however, shows unequivocal concern for the freed slaves. It seems that Ennion had charged a free Black man an exorbitant sum for the freedom of his wife and children. Friends helped Ennion's heirs see their way clear to set up a trust fund to reimburse the man. It looks like where the details are known, Middletown Friends at times may have acquitted themselves humanely, but there are many missing pieces of data.

[29] Davis, *Hist. of Bucks Co.*, 1:134. Thomas Jenks was sued in 1798 because one of Langhorne's slaves, Sarah, had become too old and unable to maintain herself. But this could not have been foreseen by John as an excuse why he did not want to manumit his slave. Bucks County Court of Quarter Sessions, Miscellaneous Papers, Nos. 770, 794, in BCHS.

[30] MMM Men's min., 4/8m/1763, 4/10m/1764.

[31] MMM Men's min., 3/2m/1780 to 1/6m/1780.

[32] Jones, *Genealogy of the Rodman Family*, 7-10, 20, 29-31, 47-52. Sarah Rodman, daughter of John[4] married Joseph Paxson.

[33] Moon, "Account", 16.

[34] MMM Men's min., 5/2/1778.

[35] Moon, "Account", 35; Zilversmit, *First Emancipation*, 82.

[36] Bradley, *Slavery, Propaganda, and the American Revolution*, 81-86.

[37] *Penna. Statutes at Large* 10:67-73 as quoted in "VF Slave Records - Bucks County", 21, in BCHS; Zilversmit, *First Emancipation*, 124-37; Litwack, *North of Slavery: The Negro in the Free States*, 7; Drake, *Quakers and Slavery*, 71-72; Soderlund, *Quakers & Slavery*, 160, 173. On the difference between Quaker and non-Quaker approaches to antislavery, see Frost, *Quaker Origin of Antislavery*, 1-19. For the exchange of arguments between Quakers and the revolutionary generation, see Jordan, *White Over Black*, 290, 292; he found the Quaker arguments were distinct, 342. David Brion Davis claims the Quaker commitment against slavery "came surprisingly late

and coincided with the publication of secular antislavery arguments from jurists, philosophers, moralists, and men of letters." *The Problem of Slavery in the Age of Revolution*, 213. Sydney James also states that between 1737 and 1755 the antislavery campaign began to succeed because of a change in public opinion—a spiritual quickening, political crisis, and new workers in the movement—without any evidence that this "public opinion" actually caused the change among Friends. *A People Among Peoples*, 128. George W. Williams found public opinion fickle, but the "eloquence of Patrick Henry and the logic of Thomas Jefferson went far to enlighten public sentiment" against slavery, until its political power once again grew. *History of the Negro Race in America From 1619 to 1880*, 1:414-5. See Reid, *The Concept of Liberty in the Age of the American Revolution*, 47ff, for why the rhetoric against the "slavery" imposed by British imperialism was understood by most of the revolutionary generation not to mean a protest against chattel slavery. See also Thomas Haskell's "humanitarian sensibility" argument that the "convention" changed to include moral responsibility against slavery. Haskell, "Capitalism and the Origins of the Humanitarian Sensibility, Part 1", 339-61, and "Part 2", 547-66. However, his description of the preconditions for humanitarianism beg the question of cause and effect. He seems to have little understanding of the spiritual motivations of his case study, John Woolman.

[38] Moon, "Account", 11-15, 36; MMM Men's min., 3/12m/1778. There were two Friends named Thomas Wilson, so the minutes differentiate between them by referring to one as "of Southampton".

[39] *Friends' Miscellany*, 8:22-23, 11:377-84.

[40] See, for example, Jordan, *White Over Black*; Litwack, *North of Slavery*; Cadbury, "Negro Membership in the Society of Friends", 151-213; Julye and McDaniel, *Fit for Freedom, Not for Friendship*.

[41] Myles, "'Stranger Friend': John Woolman and Quaker Dissent", in Heller., ed., *The Tendering Presence*, 47 and following.

[42] Litwack, *North of Slavery*, 15.

[43] MMM Men's min., 6/3m/1703. Drake concludes from this that segregated burial was "fairly common" but I have seen no other references to similar overt action by any other meeting. Drake, *Quakers and Slavery*, 16. Perhaps it was not necessary as other meetings kept their cemeteries segregated from the beginning? Paul Cuffe, prosperous African-American sea captain and member of Westport Meeting in Rhode Island was buried (1817) in a far, segregated corner of its graveyard. For instances of the few color-blind burials, see Cadbury, "Negro Membership in the Society of Friends", 160-2. Apparently the Irish Catholic Church in Philadelphia also refused to bury people of African descent in its graveyard, although other Catholic churches there were more color-blind. Litwack, *North of Slavery*, 204n.

[44] MMM Men's min. 2/9m/1738.

[45] For an effort to prove the mildness of Quaker slaveowning, see Turner, "Slavery in Colonial Penna.", 141-51, especially 148-50. However, Lord Acton's admonition holds true for Quakers as well as anyone else: power corrupts and absolute power corrupts absolutely. For an effort to tell the whole story, and revise the pleasant Quaker myths, see Julye and McDaniel, *Fit for Freedom, Not for Friendship*.

[46] Turner, *The Negro in Pennsylvania*, vii, 114, 119, 143.

[47] Blakey, "Journal", 126.

[48] Letter of Oliver Paxson to George Churchman, 16/11/1804. The woman afterwards joined the Baptists but male clergy there did not like her to preach. Oliver and others had a "solid opportunity" with her at a friend's house. *Friends' Miscellany*, 11:387-91. Cadbury, "Negro

Membership", 170-4, 201-2.

[49]Joseph Sturges, as quoted by Litwack, *North of Slavery*, 205. In 1838 the Bucks County Anti Slavery Society deplored the efforts by both political parties to use the cause of African-American votes as a stigma. They castigated the American Colonization Society for promoting prejudice. *B. C. Intelligencer*, 8/8m/1838, 10m/1838.

[50]Litwack, *North of Slavery*, 208; Child, *Isaac T. Hopper: A True Life*.

Notes for Chapter 5: War

[1]A great deal has been written on the Quaker peace testimony. See, for example, Brock, *The Quaker Peace Testimony: 1660 to 1914*; and Paxson, "The Peace Testimony of the Religious Society of Friends". Perhaps the best modern statement is Cronk, *Peace Be with You: A Study of the Spiritual Basis of the Friends Peace Testimony*.

[2]MacMaster, with Horst and Ulle, *Conscience in Crisis: Mennonites and Other Peace Churches in America, 1739-1789*, 214-15. See also Rhys Isaac's observations about the Virginia Baptists in the Revolutionary era, "Evangelical Revolt: The Nature of the Baptists' Challenge to the Traditional Order in Virginia, 1765-1775", 345-68; and, "Preachers and Patriots: Popular Culture and the Revolution in Virginia", 127-56.

[3]Mekeel, *The Relation of the Quakers to the American Revolution*, 16-41.

[4]Mekeel, *The Relation of the Quakers to the American Revolution*, 14-16, 39. See also, Lincoln, *The Revolutionary Movement in Pennsylvania*, 14.

[5]*PA2*, 15:341-345; McNealy, "Justice in Revolt: Bucks County Political Leaders, 1774-1776", 8. There is some debate over the name of the committee. Lincoln differentiates between conservative Committees of Safety and radical Committees of Observation, Inspection, and Correspondence, Lincoln, *Revolutionary Movement in Penna.*, 190n. McNealy notes that the minutes, reprinted in the *PMHB* 15 (1891), 257-290, were inaccurately labelled by William W. H. Davis as "Minutes of the Committee of Safety of Bucks County, 1774-1776", McNealy, "Justice in Revolt", 17-8n. Davis also seems responsible for misnaming them in the *PA2*, 15:341-369. On December 15, 1774 it called itself "Committee of Observation for this County", *Ibid.*, 344.

[6]Mekeel, *Relation of Quakers to the American Revolution*, 72-73, 76. For the increasing conservatism and pro-British slant of wealthy urban Quakers, see, for example, Guenther, "A Crisis of Allegiance: Berks County, Pennsylvania Quakers and the War for Independence", 16-21.

[7]*PA2*, 15:346-49. The quotation is on p. 348.

[8]*PA2*, 15:349-51. Smith was reported as saying "the Measures of Congress had already enslaved America and done more Damage than all the Acts the Parliament ever intended to lay upon us, that the whole was nothing but a scheme of a parcel of hot-headed Presbyterians . . . ."

[9]MacMaster, *Conscience in Crisis*, 27, 214-15, 222-23.

[10]McNealy, "Justice in Revolt", 9.

[11]Mekeel, *Relation of Quakers to the American Revolution*, 162-63; Jones, *Quakers in American Colonies*, 563-64. Philadelphia YM was unable to reach clarity on whether Friends should or should not pay war taxes. Brinton, *Quaker Journals*, 65-66. See Crauderueff, *War Taxes: Experiences of Philadelphia Yearly Meeting Quakers Through the American Revolution*,

21-24; and her "War Taxes: The Experiences of Philadelphia Yearly Meeting Quakers, 1681-1800".

[12] Myles, "'Stranger Friend': John Woolman and Quaker Dissent", in Heller., ed., *The Tendering Presence*, 54. See also Woolman, *Journal*, 84.

[13] Thompson, "Loyalists in Bucks County", 218. For other losses, see the "Journal of Henry Tomlinson of Bensalem", in Buck, *History of Bucks County*, 65. See also Siebert, *The Loyalists of Pennsylvania*, 49. One hundred sixty men who were quartered in Four Lanes' End (the village of Middletown) died of camp fever in the winter of 1776-1777. Holograph memoir of Joshua Richardson. See an account of the archaeological excavation of the graves, Kathy Bocella, "Holding Their Ground on Revolutionary Claim", *Philadelphia Inquirer*, Oct. 4, 1991, B1. There is a summary on the web at http://hla.buxcom.net/burial%20site.htm

[14] For an explanation of the militia system, see Roach, "The Pennsylvania Militia in 1777", 161-230; and [Anonymous] "Bucks County Quakers in the Revolution".

[15] *PA*3, 5:765-84; 6:1-149 has the fines for Bucks County. They are not indexed, and they do not always indicate the township. They are listed under the name of the Captain and/or the company number. There are additional unindexed lists of fines in the Rare Book Room, HSP.

[16] See, for example, the script for a play, "Collecting Militia Fines" telling of the fraudulent seizure of a sheep or fat calf by patriots from a Quaker, in order to eat it themselves. This, however, was published 50 years after the fact. *Bucks County Intelligencer*, 30/1m/1832.

[17] Philadelphia Yearly Meeting, Meeting for Sufferings, Miscellaneous papers, microfilm roll 29Q (1779 #10), and roll 30Q, p. 6, QCol. See also *PA*3, 6:106, 107, 111, 115, 118, 122, 125, 127-30. For another account of depredations and distraints, see Martindale, *A History of the Townships of Byberry and Moreland*, 69-70.

[18] Philadelphia Yearly Meeting, Meeting for Sufferings, Misc. Papers, roll 29Q (1778 #54). Bucks Quarter was remiss in sending in full accounts of its sufferings, so the record is incomplete. Minutes of the Meeting for Sufferings, 16/9/1779, 21/9/1780, 20/9/1781, 15/8/1782, 16/9/1784, 15/9/1785. *Ibid.*, roll 82A.

[19] Philadelphia YM, Meeting for Sufferings, Misc. Papers, 29Q (1779 #24), roll 30Q, 4.

[20] *Friends' Miscellany*, 3:118-9.

[21] *PA*3, 6:44, 46, 50, 105, 106, 111, 118, 121, 122, 127, 128.

[22] Letter from Col. Andrew Boyd, Sadsbury, Chester Co., to Pres. Wharton, *PA*2, VI:432.

[23] MMM Men's min., 3/9m/1761, 5/11m/1761, 2/5m/1776, 6/11m/1800, 4/12m/1800, 7/7/1763, 1/9m/1763, 4/4m/1776, 7/12m/1775; *PA*3, 6:18, 43, 44, 46, 48, 49, 51, 53, 57, 107.

[24] Siebert, *Loyalists in Penna.*, 59-60, 90; Westcott, *Names and Persons who took the Oath of Allegiance to the State of Pennsylvania, Between the Years 1777 and 1789*, xix, xxiv, xxix; Terry A. McNealy said he did not know of any incidents under these provisions. Conversation at BCHS, Feb. 15, 1990.

[25] [Philadelphia Yearly Meeting], *Rules of Discipline of the Yearly Meeting of Friends*, 34. See also Michener, *Retrospect of Early Quakerism*, 287-292.

[26] MMM Men's min., 4/3m/1779, 2/12m/1779, 6/5m/1779, 6/4m/1780, 7/10m/1779. William Paxson does not appear in Westcott's list of those taking the affirmation or oath of allegiance. Westcott, *Names of Persons*, xviii-xix, xxiv, xxix; Siebert, *Loyalists of Penna.*, 59-60.

[27] Crauderueff, *War Taxes*, 19; Hirst, *The Quakers in Peace and War*, 405. James, "The

Impact of the American Revolution on Quaker Ideas about Their Sect", 19:372. For more on the politics of paper money and the requirement to accept it at face value (in Massachusetts) see Smith, *After the Revolution: The Smithsonian History of Everyday Life in the Eighteenth Century*, 37-38; and her dissertation, "The Politics of Price Control in Revolutionary Massachusetts, 1774-1780".

[28] Holograph Memoir of Thomas Watson, Spruance Library, BCHS. For slightly different versions based on John Watson's enlarged and embroidered recollections, see Michener, *Retrospect of Early Quakerism*, 303-6, and Crauderueff, *War Taxes*, 20-21.

[29] Marietta, "Quaker Family Education in Historical Perspective", 63:16. For an assessment of the results of all these disownments on the Society of Friends, see Jones, *Quakers in American Colonies*, 571.

[30] Jack Marietta concluded that in Philadelphia Yearly Meeting as a whole, only 22% of Quakers who were disowned for bearing arms compounded it with some additional breach of the discipline. Marietta, "Quaker Family Education", 16. My point is that *families*, not necessarily individual Friends, had multiple infractions of the discipline.

[31] Falls MM Men's min., 3m/1778, 10m/1778. Job was a member of Bristol PM, which was part of Falls MM until 1788; therefore he was disowned by Falls. Inspite of his disownment, he refused to attend muster days and was fined at least four times. *PA3*, 6:109, 117, 123, 129.

[32] MMM Men's min., 6/3m/1777, 1/5m/77, 5/6m/77. William Rodman was eventually disowned for slaveholding, although his political activity was never really cleared to the Meeting's satisfaction, either. *Ibid.*, 6/3m/1777, 3/4m/1777, 5/2m/1778, 6/5m/1779.

[33] Bucks County Court, Misc. Papers, #656, Spruance Library, BCHS. For Grand Jury lists, see Bucks County Sessions Docket, 1782-1801, Spruance Library. Before 1805 grand juries were chosen by the sheriff on any basis he chose. Stevens, *County Government and Archives in Pennsylvania*, 319.

[34] The proceeds from the sale of the estate, £875, were assigned to the University of Pennsylvania; *PA6*, 12:170, 802; 13:183, 194-6. PMMM 2:422. *Pennsylvania Colonial Records*; 12:547. Hereinafter cited as *Col. Rec.* Ousterhout, "Opponents of the Revolution Whose Pennsylvania Estates Were Confiscated", 30:239; Thompson, "An Introduction to the Loyalists of Bucks County and Some Queries Concerning Them," 7:223; Sabine, *Biographical Sketches of Loyalists of the American Revolution*, 2:155-6; and, Siebert, *Loyalists of Penna.*, 94.

[35] PMMM 2:394. *Col. Rec.* 12:401, 403, 541; *PA2*, 2:226.

[36] Stackhouse, *The Stackhouse Family, Part I: History of the Stackhouse Family from 1086 to 1935*, 88-96. MMM Men's min., 7/10m/1749, 7/4m/1750, 5/5m/1750, 6/6m/1776, 6/5m/1779, 1/7m/1779, 2/9m/1779. Richard K. MacMaster researched the roots of Ontario Friends and their motives for immigrating. In order to acquire larger allotments of land, an immigrant had to testify that he served in the British forces during the "late war". Friends looked askance at members who claimed that privilege. MacMaster concludes that economics rather than politics drove most of the Friends to Ontario. Conversation, Jan. 27, 1989, and correspondence. Some 141 Quakers immigrated from Bucks County to New Brunswick in the fall of 1783 before the British evacuation of New York. In 1784 some 500-600 more went from Pennsylvania. [Anonymous], "'Loyalists' Who Went to Nova Scotia (1783)", 20-21. Mekeel also concludes that more went on economic than on political grounds. Mekeel, *The Relation of the Quakers to the American Revolution*, 319-21.

[37] MMM Men's min., 5/6m/1777, 4/9m/1777, 1/3m/1781, 4/1m/1781.

[38] MMM Men's min., 7/2m/1760, 6/3m/1760, 4/9m/1760, 9/10m/1760.

[39] MMM Men's min., 9/10m/1777, 6/11m/1777, 5/3m/1778, 2/4m/1778, 2/8m/1781,

5/1m/1786, 4/5m/1786, 5/4m/1787, 6/11m/1794, 5/2m/1795, 7/12m/1797, 8/4m/1813; Brey, *A Quaker Saga*, 14-16, 39. Since the British government gave extra supplies to immigrants from the U.S. to Canada who claimed to have rendered "some service" to Britain, there was some incentive to making a claim as a Loyalist. [Anonymous], "'Loyalists' Who Went to Nova Scotia (1783)", 21. See also Lincoln, *The Revolutionary Movement in Pennsylvania*, 14; Mekeel, *The Relation of the Quakers to the American Revolution*, 319-321.

[40]Radbill, "Socioeconomic Background of Nonpacifist Quakers During the American Revolution".

[41]MMM Men's min., 6/2m/1777. The Bucks County Committee of Observation had demanded that all wagons and teams be used to help Washington's retreat across the Delaware on December 8, 1776.

[42]MMM Men's min., 6/1m/1780, 2/3m/1780, 6/4m/1780.

[43]PMMM 2:443; MMM Men's min., 3/9m/1778, 5/11m/1778, 4/7m/1782, 1/8m/1782.

[44]MMM Men's min., 4/4m/7171-4/7m/1771. See also Jones, *Rodman Family*, 28-31, 47-48; Hinshaw, *Encyclopedia of American Quaker Genealogy*, 2:255.

[45]MMM Men's min., 6/3m/1760, 3/4m/1760, 1/5m/1760.

[46]PMMM 3:738 (from the certificate of disownment for Joshua Blakey, Jr., 9/1809).

Notes for Chapter 6: Changing Economic Views

[1]Sykes, *The Quakers*, 166-68, 184-85. For a summary of British Friends and their accommodation to capitalism, see Walvin, *The Quakers: Money and Morals*. For a fictionalized account based on extensive historical research, of the drift to accommodation with the new economic world in Britain, and the weakening of Quaker faith, see Gifford, *The Lost Years*. For Joseph Crosman, an example of a British entrepreneur active in his meeting and local politics, see Musson, *Enterprise in Soap and Chemicals*, 18-21, 33-37, 39, 50-53.

[2]Watts, *The Republic Reborn: War and the Making of Liberal America, 1790-1820*; Sellers, *The Market Revolution: Jacksonian America*; Kobrin, "The Saving Remnant", 228-33, 239.

[3]*Extracts from the Minutes and Advices of the Yearly Meeting of Friends held in London*, 200. George Fox had advised Friends in 1656, "there is danger and temptation to you, of drawing your minds into your business, and clogging them with it, so that we can hardly do any thing to the service of God but there will be crying 'my business, my business'; and so therein ye do not come into the image of God." Sharman, ed., *No More but my Love: Letters of George Fox, 1624-91*, Epistle 131, 53. See also, Bownas, *A Description of the Qualifications Necessary for a Gospel Minister*, 97-98.

[4]See, for example, Michener, *Retrospect of Early Quakerism*, 263-266. For the British Friend Joseph Crosman calling on family and friends for assistance, see Musson, *Enterprise in Soap and Chemicals*, 18-21; for stretching his resources too thin and not ploughing the profits back into his main enterprise, see *Ibid.*, 33-35, 39.

[5]Hansell, ed. *Josiah White: Quaker Entrepreneur*.

[6]Birkel, *A Near Sympathy: The Timeless Quaker Wisdom of John Woolman*, 15-19. See also Woolman's essay, "A Plea for the Poor" in Moulton, ed., *The Journal and Major Essays of John Woolman*. Currently there is a great deal of interest in Woolman. See, for example, Gerald W.

Sazama, "On Woolman's 'Conversations,' Ethics, and Economics", 190-206; Christopher Varga, "'Be Ye Therefore Perfect': Integral Christianity in 'Some Considerations on the Keeping of Negroes'", 207-218; and Michael P. Graves, "'A Perfect Redemption from this Spirit of Oppression': John Woolman's Hopeful World View in 'A Plea for the Poor'", 219-239, all in Heller, ed., *The Tendering Presence: Essays on John Woolman*.

[7] See, for example, Yearly Meeting held for the Provinces of Pennsylvania and New-Jersey, 1722, *The Ancient Testimony of the People Called Quakers*, 43-44, 46; *Rules of Discipline of the Yearly Meeting of Friends* (1834), 136-142; *Christian Advices issued by the Yearly Meeting of Friends held in Philadelphia* (1859), 111-122 (especially 118-19, 120-1). For an example of complications resulting from circulating notes, see *B. C. Intelligencer*, 3/1828. See also Frost, *Quaker Families*, 200-1, 203.

[8] "A Testimony from the Falls' Monthly Meeting in Bucks County, Pennsylvania, concerning our Friend Joseph White", included in John Churchman's memoir, *An Account of the Gospel Labors and Christian Experiences of that Faithful Minister of Christ, John Churchman, late of Nottingham, Pennsylvania*, 314. This can also be found with slightly different wording on ACS microfilm reel 371, pp. 253-54. See also Brinton, *Quaker Journals*, 69-73.

[9] MMM Men's min., 9/2m/1821, 9/3m/1821, 6/4m/1821. Brey, *A Quaker Saga*, 475, 497. For the fall in property values, see Fletcher, *Pennsylvania Agriculture*, 320-21.

[10] MMM Men's min., 9/11m/1823; see notices of the dissolution of his firm, Walton & Paxson, in the *Pennsylvania Correspondent and Farmers Advertiser* 6/25/1822: debts to be paid to Jonathan Walton.

[11] MMM Men's min., 7/5m/1824; *Pa. Correspondent and Farmers Advertiser*, 11/26/1822, 1m/1824.

[12] PMMM 2:350, 393; MMM Men's min., 10/1m/1823, 9/11m/1823, 9/5m/1828; MMM Women's min., 3m/1851. *B. C. Intelligencer*, 16/3/1829.

[13] MMM Men's min., 7/5m/1824; PMMM, 4:885; *Pa. Correspondent and Farmers Advertiser* 11/26/1822, 1/1824.

[14] PMMM 2:350, 393; MMM Men's min., 5/8m/1771, 6/11m/1800, 4/12m/1800; MMM Women's min., 7/8m/1800.

[15] *B. C. Intelligencer*, 27/3/1839.

[16] See, for example, "Christopher Wilson's Warning and Lamentation" written in England 30/6/1759 and published in *Friends' Miscellany* in 1832, 2:394-97. Wilson was "drawn into trading to foreign ports", lost his investment, and felt obligated to hazard more and more in an attempt to recoup his losses. But then he was brought to see that a simple cottage with food and raiment, if it comes with an easy mind, "is preferable to large dealings in trade". "A low station best suits a living minister of Christ;—to eat sparingly, cloath just decently, to have the mind free from cumber, and open to receive every impression of Truth, and free to run when the Lord draws." 394. A letter from his grandfather in New York to James Mott in Philadelphia exemplifies the sort of advice that perhaps meeting elders should have been giving to Friends to avoid conspicuous consumption. Goodman, *Of One Blood: Abolitionism and the Origins of Racial Equality*, 193-95, quoting Anna Hallowell, *James and Lucretia Mott: Life and Letters* (Boston, 1884).

[17] Davis, *Hist. of Bucks Co.*, 1:143; Samuel C. Eastburn, series on local history, "Early Mills", *Delaware Valley Advance*, 20/6/1929. Eastburn, who was born Aug. 2, 1848, says Wilson was hit by the depression of 1837 and he never recovered. I suspect he has the chronology wrong here, although his account of Wilson's motives is likely correct. Eastburn was 24 when Wilson died in 1874. The lawsuit does not appear in the Middletown records because Thomas Jenks was no longer a Friend, having been disowned in 1797 for fornication.

[18] MMM Men's min., 10/3/1848 through 6/4m/1849, 8/2/1850, 6/1851. Michael H. Jenks Papers, MSC 79, Fol. 11, BCHS.

[19] Brown, "Modernization and the Modern Personality in Early America, 1600-1865: A Sketch of a Synthesis", 2: 218-19.

[20] Hammond, *Banks and Politics in America: From the Revolution to the Civil War*, ix. For farmers' need for, but distrust of banks, see Fletcher, *Pennsylvania Agriculture*, 319.

[21] Scott, *Farmers' National Bank of Bucks County, Bristol, Pennsylvania: A Century's Record, 1814-1915*, 7-11; Holdsworth, *History of Banking in Pennsylvania*, 369.

[22] During a visit by Josiah Quincy on his way to Philadelphia, Hulme explained of his sons, "I wished to make them equally attached to each other, and useful members of society . . . I have been rewarded by their good conduct and grateful affection. No one envies another. I have never heard an expression of discontent." Davis, *Hist. of Bucks Co.*, 1:139-40; 3:366; Green, *A History of Bristol Borough*, 254; Hicks, *Journal*, 42. Also, Holdsworth, *History of Banking in Pennsylvania*, 369.

[23] Advice was sought from Nicholas Biddle of the Bank of the United States, who sent Caleb P. Iddings, a competent "gentleman of much experience", who straightened out the bank's affairs. Scott, *Farmers' National Bank*, 30; Holdsworth, *History of Banking in Pennsylvania*, 373-4. For controversy over the move to Bristol, see *Pa. Correspondent and Farmers Advertiser*, 15/3/1824, 19/4/1824, 3/5m/1824.

[24] Holdsworth, *History of Banking in Pennsylvania*, 373; Scott, *Farmers' National Bank*, 32.

[25] Scott, *Farmers' National Bank*, 51.

[26] Hicks, *Journal*, 42. Davis recounts that for "several years Mr. Hulme would not allow a public house to be opened, entertaining travelers at his own dwelling, but when the growth of the village forced him to change his policy, he built a tavern but prohibited a bar." Davis, *Hist. of Bucks Co.*, 1:139.

[27] Blakey, "Journal", 78.

[28] *B. C. Intelligencer, passim.*; *Doylestown Democrat*, 8/7m/1835. For an overview of new agricultural technology, see Fletcher, *Pennsylvania Agriculture*, 91-105.

[29] Barker, "Leadership in Bucks County Agricultural Societies in the Nineteenth Century", in BCHS. There were Friends from other meetings involved in agriculture societies, *Pa. Correspondent and Farmers Advertiser* 22/10/1822, 28/10/1822, 11m/1822, 1m/1823; *B. C. Intelligencer*, see 1844-1850.

[30] Bucks County Will Files #5778, and #7995.

[31] *B. C. Intelligencer*, 5/6m/1832, 13/2/1841, 4/5m/1836, 6/4m/1836, 18/5/1836, 1/2m/1837.

[32] *B. C. Intelligencer*, 4m/1835.

[33] Hicks, *Journal*, 30-31.

[34] Samuel C. Eastburn, *Delaware Valley Advance*, 12/12/1929, 12/26/1929. Joseph Eastburn's wife was Elizabeth (Comfort).

[35] Davis, *Hist. of Bucks Co.*, 2:389.

[36] Davis, *Hist. of Bucks Co.*, 2:389-90; Martindale, *A History of the Townships of Byberry and Moreland*, 199; Pullinger, "Panic and Panacea: Edward Hicks Deplores Over-speculation in the 1830's And the Silkworm Mania That Followed", 1-3. *B. C. Intelligencer*, 10/10m/1838,

24/4/1839. The *Doylestown Democrat* was more cautious than the *B. C. Intelligencer*. In the former, there was a mention of silk raising in Virginia, 17/3/1829; a note that the editor had received samples of silk thread from Berks County, 4/5m/1836; a passing comment that silk and sugar would be the coming things (and noting they both employed females), 19/4/1837; and then finally in the fall of 1939 advertisements for silk and mulberry trees, 9/10m/1839 *passim*. Fletcher noted that the *morus multicaulis* could not survive Pennsylvania winters, *Pennsylvania Agriculture*, 232-35.

[37] Hicks, *Journal*, 122-3. A meeting to promote the cultivation of mulberry trees to raise silkworms was held in Bucks County as early as 4/1828, and the *B. C. Intelligencer* ran an editorial urging folks to try raising a "few thousand" eggs, *Ibid.*, 5/1828.

[38] *B. C. Intelligencer*, 22/4/1840.

[39] *B. C. Intelligencer*, 10/4m/1839.

[40] Blakey, "Journal", 81.

[41] Michael H. Jenks Papers, MSC 79, Fol. 30, BCHS.

Notes for Chapter 7: Evangelicalism

[1] Hamm, *The Transformation of American Quakerism*, 1; Hilton, *The Age of Atonement: The Influence of Evangelicalism on Social and Economic Thought*, 3, 6-8; Russell, *History of Quakerism*, 287-88. See also Appleby, *Inheriting the Revolution*, 197-204.

[2] Hilton, *Age of Atonement*. See also Wallace, *Rockdale*; Holden, *Friends Divided*, 49-50, 54.

[3] For much more detailed studies of the impact of evangelicalism on Quakerism, see Ingle, *Quakers in Conflict: The Hicksite Reformation;* and, Hamm, *Transformation of American Quakerism*. For a shorter summary based on the Gospel of John, as opposed to the Epistle to the Hebrews, that is, a mystical, universal Christianity rather than a ritualistic and priestly religion, see Brinton, *Quaker Journals*, 108-21.

[4] Ingle, *Quakers in Conflict*, 5.

[5] Tallack, *Friendly Sketches in America*, 138.

[6] Evans, *Jonathan Evans and his Time*, 46.

[7] Sykes, *Quakers: A New Look*, 229.

[8] Barbour and Frost, *The Quakers*, 171, 172; Jones, *The Later Periods of Quakerism*, 1:303; Hamm, *Transformation of American Quakerism*, 17-18. See also Kobrin, "The Saving Remnant: Intellectual Sources of Change and Decline in Colonial Quakerism, 1690-1810"; and, Russell, *History of Quakerism*, 284-5.

[9] Barbour & Frost, *The Quakers*, 173-4. The 1820s were a period of vigorous and vociferous periodical publication on religious, moral, and doctrinal topics. Appleby, *Inheriting the Revolution*, 217-218.

[10] Tolles, *Quakers and the Atlantic Culture*, 91, 110, 112-13. For a more psychological explanation of the Great Awakening's appeal to people who had suffered in a diptheria epidemic, an economic depression, and a demographic/family crisis of authority, see Henretta, *The Evolution of American Society, 1700-1815: An Interdisciplinary Analysis*, 131-33.

[11] Tolles, *Quakers and the Atlantic Culture*, 105-6.

[12] Tolles, *Quakers and the Atlantic Culture*, 109. See also, Hamm, *Transformation of American Quakerism*; Gwyn, *Apocalypse of the Word: The Life and Message of George Fox, 1624-1691*, 3, 30-31, 36-37, 41, 63, 72, 119.

[13] Nickalls, ed., *The Journal of George Fox*, 40; see also Barclay, *An Apology for the True Christian Divinity being an Explanation and Vindication of the Principles and Doctrines of the People Called Quakers* (1908), 14-15, 72-97; Grundy, "How Early Friends Understood the Bible", 65-83.

[14] Gwyn, *Apocalypse of the Word*, 95-108, 114-15, 121-25.

[15] Ingle, *Quakers in Conflict*, 9-10; Jacob, *The Shackletons of Ballitore*, 18-20; Jones, *Later Periods of Quakerism*, 1:293-307; Russell, *History of Quakerism*, 293-95; Holden, *Friends Divided*, 51-53, 146. Janney, *History of the Religious Society of Friends . . . to 1828*, 1:16-39; Maxey, "New Light on Hannah Barnard, a Quaker 'Heretic'", 78:61-86. David Kobrin uses the incident to show that Friends were unable to deal with modern thought. On the contrary, I think it illustrates that traditional Friends' reliance on the teaching of the Spirit would allow for continuing revelation; it was only the closed-minded and fearful evangelicalism which could not deal with new ideas challenging traditional Protestant interpretations of the Bible. Kobrin, "Saving Remnant", 292.

[16] Taber, "Toward a Broader Quaker Message", 30:7. See also Hamm, *Transformation of American Quakerism*, 1-2; Gwyn, *Apocalypse of the Word*, 41, 63-67, 97-98, 106-7.

[17] Ingle, *Quakers in Conflict*, 15; Doherty, *The Hicksite Separation: A Sociological Analysis of Religious Schism in Early Nineteenth Century America*.

[18] Blakey, "Journal", 83, 159. See also, Comly, *Journal of the Life and Religious Labours of John Comly, late of Byberry*.

[19] Blakey, "Journal", 85; Hotchkin, *The Bristol Pike*, 366; Faris, *Old Churches and Meeting Houses in and Around Philadelphia*, 238-40.

[20] Green, *History of Bristol Borough*, 79; *B. C. Intelligencer* 17/1m/11831, 8m/1833.

[21] Green, *History of Bristol Borough*, 120-21; Davis, *Hist. of Bucks Co.*, 3:853-54; *Pa. Correspondent and Farmers Advertiser*, 12/1822, 12/1823; *Patriot*, 12/1824; *B. C. Intelligencer*, 12/1827, 10/1830. Bible Society notices appeared regularly in the *Democrat and Farmers' Gazette*, 18/12/1827, 4/11m/1828, and in its successor the *Doylestown Democrat*, 26/10/1830, 4/1m/1831, *passim*.

[22] *B. C. Intelligencer*, 10/8m/1836.

[23] Hamm, *Transformation of American Quakerism*, 24-25. Hamm also found that midwestern Friends were pasting overtly evangelical poems and tracts into their commonplace books. They subscribed to evangelical journals and newspapers. *Ibid.*, 23-24. Unfortunately, this information is unavailable for members of Middletown Meeting for the first quarter of the nineteenth century.

[24] See, for example, *B. C. Intelligencer* 8/1828, 2/1831, 5/3m/1832, 30/4/1832, 18/3/1833, 1/4m/1833, 12/5m/1834, 16/6m/1834, 14/11/1838.

[25] Davis, *Hist. of Bucks Co.*, 1:143; Blankenburg, "A Story of My Branch of the Longshore Family", 6:532ff.

[26] *Pa. Correspondent and Farmers Advertiser* 20/5/1823. *B. C. Intelligencer*, various dates.

[27] Wallace, *Rockdale*.

Notes for Chapter 8: Separation

[1] See especially, Ingle, *Quakers in Conflict*. Other accounts are in, Holden, *Friends Divided*, 54-59; Jones, *Later Periods of Quakerism*, 1:435-487; Russell, *History of Quakerism*, 280-318; Barbour and Frost, *The Quakers*, 171-78. See also an older account, Janney, *An Examination of the Courses which Led to the Separation of the Religious Society of Friends in America*.

[2] Evans, *Jonathan Evans and His Time*, 56ff; Elias Hicks, *Journal of the Life and Religious Labours of Elias Hicks*; Hicks, *Letters of Elias Hicks*.

[3] Frost, "The Origins of the Quaker Crusade Against Slavery: A Review of Recent Literature", 56-58.

[4] Soderlund, *Quakers & Slavery*, 140, 143, 171.

[5] Kobrin, "A Saving Remnant", 191, 206, 251, 258, 287.

[6] Hamm, *Transformation of American Quakerism*, xvi, 172-73. A similar dynamic within the Brethren is analyzed by Carl F. Bowman in his excellent *Brethren Society: The Cultural Transformation of a "Peculiar People"* as the fundamental incompatibility of the founding vision of a people drawn apart in order to make a witness, with the modern desire to be inclusive and embrace diversity. See also, Hamm, *The Quakers in America*, especially Chapter 3.

[7] Doherty, *Hicksite Separation*, 66; Doherty, "Non-Urban Friends and the Hicksite Separation", 445; see also his "Religion and Society: The Hicksite Separation", 63-80.

[8] Peck, *Different Drum*, 194-95.

[9] Appleby, *Inheriting the Revolution*, 204.

[10] This entire section is taken from the MMM Men's min., 11/5m/1827-9/5m/1828; Orthodox Middletown Monthly Meeting Men's minutes, 7/9m/1827-8/2m/1828; MMM Women's min., 6/4m/1827-9/5m/1828; Orthodox Middletown Monthly Meeting Women's min. 7/9m/1827-7/3m/1828. See the Orthodox summary of events in *The Friend*, 3/11m/1827.

[11] For an explanation of Friends' process, see Sheeran, *Beyond Majority Rule*. See also, Gwyn, *Apocalpyse of the Word*, 74.

[12] Extract from the Bucks Quarterly Meeting minutes as recorded in MMM Men's min., 8/6m/1827.

[13] MMM Men's min., 10/8m/1827.

[14] The wording seemed to imply a yearning that somehow the whole still existed, and this was just a large fraction thereof.

[15] MMM (H) Men's min., 9/5m/1828. See also MMM (H) Women's min. of the same date.

[16] Edward Hicks, *Journal*, 127; Samuel C. Eastburn, "1915: Middletown Meeting of Friends Historical Data", p. 3. Samuel C. Eastburn Collection, MSC 51, Fol. 56, BCHS.

[17] MMM (O) Women's min., 7/9m/1827.

[18] Doherty, *Hicksite Separation*, 55-62; Ralph S. Benjamin also assumed that Hicksites had lower or declining occupational status, *The Philadelphia Quakers in the Industrial Age*, 10.

[19] Doherty, *Hicksite Separation*, 56-7. He is not very specific about the dates of the tax records he used, but they seem to have been 1805-10 and 1827 or 1828. I assume his reference to

1872 tax records is a typographical error, "Non-Urban Friends and the Hicksite Separation", 4.

[20]Appleby, *Inheriting the Revolution*, 197-98, 204.

[21]Holden, *Friends Divided*, 148.

[22]Letter fom Eugene Glenn Stackhouse to author, 16 August 1987. It is possible that the poor child was a different David Stackhouse; there were non-Quaker, impoverished Stackhouse families residing in Bristol at that time.

[23]Unpublished memoir, Michael H. Jenks Papers, MSC 79, Fol. 30, BCHS.

[24]It is interesting to note that Woolman's meeting, Mt. Holly, tried to secede from Orthodox Burlington Quarter and join the Hicksite Bucks Quarterly Meeting. Barbour and Frost, *The Quakers*, 176.

[25]Doherty, *Hicksite Separation*, 70; Evans, *Journal of the Life and Religious Services of William Evans*, 103.

[26]Ingle, *Quakers in Conflict*, xiv, 13. This is the same confrontation as that between the Pharisees and Jesus, between the Puritans and seventeenth-century Quakers, between second and fourth levels of faith development. However, what might have been occurring between some Orthodox and some Hicksites, and the theoretical and theological underpinnings thereof, does not at all mean that this was an accurate assessment of all Orthodox and all Hicksites. It was not. Gwyn, *Apocalypse of the Word*, 12, 42-4, 121-2; Peck, *Different Drum*, 188-95.

[27]Bowen, "Quaker Orthodoxy and Jacksonian Democracy"; Russell, *History of Quakerism*, 282-83. For a different interpretation, see Sykes, *The Quakers*, 185. For the British strains (London Yearly Meeting only suffered small splits), see Elizabeth Isichei, *Victorian Quakers;* and, Wilson, "Friends in the Nineteenth Century", 8:353-63, and Wilson, "The Road to Manchester, 1895", 145-62.

[28]Blankenburg, "A Story of My Branch of the Longshore Family", 6:526, 530, 532-34; "Hannah E. Myers Longshore" and "Lucretia Longshore Blankenburg", James, ed., *Notable American Women, 1607-1950*, 2:170-71, 426-28. For more on these two female physicians, see Young, "Quaker Women and Medical Practice in the Nineteenth Century", 302-3.

[29]Ingle, *Quakers in Conflict*, 60-61.

Notes for Chapter 9: Politics, Reform, and Further Accommodation

[1]Barbour and Frost, *The Friends*, 172; Doherty, *Hicksite Separation*, 67-76; Hamm, *Transformation of Am. Quakerism*, 16.

[2][Philadelphia Yearly Meeting], *Rules of Discipline of the Yearly Meeting of Friends*, 33, 103, 144. [Philadelphia Yearly Meeting, Orthodox] *Christian Advices issued by the Yearly Meeting* (1859), 18-20, 76. Also *Book of Discipline of Philadelphia Yearly Meeting* [Hicksite] 1831, 21, 64. See Valentine, "The Disciplines of American Friends" (1828), 22, QCol.

[3]Comly, *Journal*, 53-54.

[4]Kohl, *The Politics of Individualism*, ix, 4, 6, 13, 15-17.

[5]There are several types of data used to determine the political affiliation of various individuals in the second quarter of the nineteenth century. Voting returns by township give a gross picture. Membership in (or attendance at) the wide variety of political clubs and public

meetings was reported in Bucks County newspapers. Each newspaper had a strongly identified political affiliation. In those days people tended to put their marriage and death notices, and usually their real estate or business advertisements only in the newspaper reflecting their political preference. Finally, there are a few memoirs, and some biographies in the late nineteenth-century county histories which mention political affiliation. McNealy, "Bucks County Newspapers and How to Use Them for Research". Although there were as many as six papers at one time in the County, they came and went with alarming rapidity. This study used the *Pennsylvania Democrat and Farmers' Gazette*, (1804-1824), the *Bucks County Patriot and Farmers' Advertizer* (Oct. 4, 1824-Sept. 24, 1827), the *Bucks County Intelligencer and General Advertizer* (Oct. 2, 1827-1851), the *Bucks County Messenger* (scattered issues in 1821), the *Democrat and Farmers' Gazette* (16/1m/1827-12/2m/1831), and the *Doylestown Democrat* (15/3m/1831-1850, *passim*.).

[6]See Snyder, *The Jacksonian Heritage: Pennsylvania Politics 1833-1848*, 22-24. Unfortunately for this study, Snyder did not use any Bucks County or other southeastern Pennsylvania newspapers except for some from Philadelphia. See also Bowen, "Quaker Orthodoxy and Jacksonian Democracy: An Interpretation of the Hicksite Separation", 91-95.

[7]Snyder, *Jacksonian Heritage*, 23. Other labels included "the people versus the faction" and "the People's Ticket", *B. C. Intelligencer* 9/1825, or the "people's candidate" versus the "coalition candidate", *Democrat and Farmers' Gazette*, 14/10m/1828. The pro-Jackson newspaper headlined "down with the faction", *Democrat and Farmers' Gazette*, 9/10m/1927. The pro-Jacksonians also had a fine time razzing their opponents' name changes, *Doylestown Democrat*, 20/5/1834.

[8]Snyder, *Jacksonian Heritage*, 19-21, 131; Klein, *Pennsylvania Politics, 1817-1832*, 58ff; Silbey, *The Transformation of American Politics, 1840-1860*, 7.

[9]Williamson, *American Suffrage: From Property to Democracy, 1760-1860*, 120.

[10]Blankenburg, "A Story of My Branch of the Longshore Family", 6:533-34; *Bucks County Intelligencer* 28/2/1844. An editorial noted later that T. E. L. had sent a "long largely irrelevant response" to correct several inaccuracies in the previously published account. The editor would have printed it except that T. E. L. included a threat that several people would withdraw their subscriptions if it was not printed. *Ibid.*, 20/3/1844. A letter to the editor from "B" in Attleboro defended Longshore's views as "sincere and deeply grounded in conviction"; although on-lookers said "it's what he deserves" and "he ought to go to jail", in fact in court he was "guarded, mild, and courteous"; the "public cries mad dog whenever someone is ahead of the group on a moral issue." *B. C. Intelligencer* 27/3/1844.

[11]Snyder, *Jacksonian Heritage*, 35-48. See *Doylestown Democrat* 20/8m/1833, 1/10m/1833, 7/1m/1834, 21/1m/1834.

[12]Biddle sent an able accountant, Caleb P. Iddlings, to straighten out matters. Scott, *Farmers' National Bank*, 30; Holdsworth, *History of Banking in Penna.*, 373-74. In 1839 Nicholas Biddle retired to his estate in Andalusia, Bensalem Township.

[13]Five years later partisan newspapers were still attacking the federal administration for being against "the banks" (plural). *B. C. Intelligencer* 13/2m/1839.

[14]*B. C. Intelligencer* 5/5m/1834, 2/6m/1834, 2/8m/1834, 11/8m/1834; *Doylestown Democrat*, 25/2m/1834, 23/9m/1834, 7/10m/1834. It is interesting that throughout this period the Farmers' National Bank of Bucks County placed its notices in both newspapers.

[15]Henry Simmons, "Four Journals, 1796-1800"; MMM Men's min. 5/5m/1796, 6/2m/1800. See also Swatzler, *A Friend Among the Senecas*, which is based largely on Simmons's journal. For background, see Russell, *History of Quakerism*, 256-57.

[16]*B. C. Intelligencer*, 1/1830 and others. The *Doylestown Democrat* supported the rights of states over those of Indians, 25/1/1831. It generally approved Jackson's policy, but felt the need to

assure readers that the Indians would be paid and that no force would be used, 15/6/1830.

[17]Smith-Rosenberg, *Disorderly Conduct: Visions of Gender in Victorian America*, 77-164, especially 103, 108. See the snide story of a Quaker bachelor who fell into a ditch, *Doylestown Democrat*, 12/8m/1834. For the jailing of the Philadelphia Quaker draft resister, see *Doyles. Dem.*, 16/7/1833, 23/7/1833; *Bucks County Intelligencer* 17/7/1833.

[18]Snyder, *Jacksonian Heritage*, 96-109.

[19]Snyder, *Jacksonian Heritage*, 105; Litwack, *North of Slavery*, 85. In July 1837 the Pennsylvania Supreme Court, referring to a 1797 case for which there was no documentation, found Blacks were ineligible to vote.*Doylestown Democrat* from 26/7/1837 through 7/2m/1838.

[20]*B. C. Intelligencer* 30/5m/1838, 8/8m/1838, 26/9m/1838, *passim.*; *Doylestown Democrat* from 26/7/1837 through 7/2m/1838. For an example of blatant racism, see the article reprinted from the *New York Evening Star*, in the *B. C. Intelligencer* 30/6/1834.

[21]James, *A People Among Peoples*. For critiques of James's view, see Marietta, *The Reformation of American Quakerism*, 273, 309; and review by Bronner in *Quaker History*, 52 (Spring 1963), 1:41; see also Jorns, *The Quakers as Pioneers in Social Work*; and, Russell, *Quaker History*, 251-52 and ff.

[22]Appleby, *Inheriting the Revolution*, 22; see also 194-238.

[23]Roeber, "J. H. C. Helmuth, Evangelical Charity, and the Public Sphere in Pennsylvania, 1793-1800", 81.

[24]Hamm, *Transformation of American Quakerism*, 22-3, 27.

[25]For more understanding of the Wilburite branch of quietists who split from the Gurneyite Orthodox, see Wilbur, *A Narrative and Exposition of the Late Proceedings of New England Yearly Meeting*; and Taber, *Eye of Faith*, 41-61, 105-163.

[26]While the connection between peace and justice, or "peace, justice, and the integrity of creation" as the World Council of Churches stated it at the end of the twentieth century, seems a late twentieth century understanding, the connections had been pointed out by John Woolman in the eighteenth century. They were there for any nineteenth-century Friend who cared to look.

[27]Kohl, *The Politics of Individualism*, especially chapters 1 and 2.

[28]Tyrrell, *Sobering Up*, 6-7, 104, 110, 125-26.

[29]Lender and Martin, *Drinking in America*, 6, 72, 84. See also Rorabaugh, *The Alcoholic Republic*, 8-9. For comparison, in 1986 Americans averaged .85 gallons of spirits per person; it was estimated that 10% of the drinkers, or 6.5% of the U.S. adult population, accounted for about half the alcohol consumed in the nation. The Cleveland *Plain Dealer*, 25/11m/1989. For a description of the prevalence of alcohol and the cultural pressure to drink, see Appleby, *Inheriting the Revolution*, 205-212.

[30]Lender & Martin, *Drinking in America*, 66-68; Furnes, *The Life and Times of the Late Demon Rum*, 15-16, 38. See also Perrin, "Nothing but Water: The Rise of Temperance and the Emergence of the American Temperance Society".

[31]Elizabeth Levis's article was reprinted from *Friends' Miscellany*, 4:180-82, in the *Doylestown Democrat*, 15/7/1833.

[32]Michener, *A Retrospect of Early Quakerism*, 311-12, 321.

[33]*B. C. Intelligencer* 7/5m/1845, 16/12m/1845.

[34]Furnes, *Demon Rum*, 37-42. The history of the temperance movement is told there and in Rorabaugh, *Alcoholic Republic;* Tyrrell, *Sobering Up;* and, Lender and Martin, *Drinking in America.*

[35]Appleby, *Inheriting the Revolution*, 214-15, 233.

[36]Oliver Paxson to George Churchman, 16/11m/1804, *Friends' Miscellany*, 11:387-91.

[37]*B. C. Intelligencer, inter allia* 2m/1831, 19/3/1831, 4/3m/1833, 12/5m/1834, 6m/1843.

[38]The quotation is from William Goodell of N.Y., reprinted from the *Genius of Temperance*, June 7, in *B. C. Intelligencer*, 1/7m/1833. See also *Democrat and Farmers' Gazette*, 14/10/1828, 27/4m/1830, 22/2m/1831; *Doylestown Democrat*, 25/3m/1834, 27/5/1834, 31/12/1834, 3/6m/1835, 10/8m/1836, 24/5m/1837.

[39]Blankenburg, "Story of My Longshore Family", 532. The following account is from *Modern Chronicles; or, Stoning the Prophet in the Nineteenth Century. An Account of the Persecution of Dr. Joseph S. Longshore, of Bucks County, Pa. on Account of his Labours in the Cause of Temperance,* esp. 6-7, 43-60; MMM Men's min., 9/10m/1846, 8/1m/1847, 5/2m/1847, 8/10m/1847; *B. C. Intelligencer*, 25/11m/1846, 2m/1847.

[40]MMM Men's min. 11/8m/1848, 8/9m/1848.

[41]For a description of the inner work, see Bownas, *A Description of the Qualifications Necessary to a Gospel Minister.*

[42]*Stoning the Prophet*, 14-15. Family historian Jane W. T. Brey recounts that in an earlier generation, as an old man, Lucas Gillam had finally walked out on his daughter-in-law Anna (Paxson) who nagged about his muddy boots and tobacco juice on her imported carpets, and went to live with another daughter-in-law Sarah (Longshore) who was apparently more understanding of his uncouth ways. Brey, *Quaker Saga*, 476. It was Anna's nephew who brought charges against Sarah's nephew, still, perhaps, seen as uncouth and socially unacceptable.

[43]For an understanding of these terms see, for example, Bownas, *A Description of the Qualifications Necessary to a Gospel Minister*; Sheeran, *Beyond Majority Rule.*

[44]There is an interesting parallel from earlier Pennsylvania Quaker history. One of the charges leveled against the Philadelphia Quaker establishment by the ascerbic George Keith in the early 1690s concerned their involvement with slavery. Even after he was disowned and the furor had settled, Friends seemed unwilling to acknowledge the legitimacy of anything he had said. It has been suggested that he put back Quaker antislavery action for a whole generation. For more on George Keith, see references for chapter 2, 295, n. 24.

[45]See Chapter 4; Litwack, *North of Slavery*, 15, 64, 208; Turner, *The Negro in Pennsylvania*, 134, 144-50.

[46]*B. C. Intelligencer* 9/4m/1831, 23/4m/1832, 8/8m/1833, 12/8m/1833, 11/1838. See the mildly favorable colonization stories in the *Doylestown Democrat*, 9/2m/1830, 14/10/1835, 2/5m/1838, 7/11m/1838.

[47]*B. C. Intelligencer* 9/1837, 10/1837, 27/12/1837. The *Doylestown Democrat* was too busy decrying Negro suffrage to notice this debate. For a study of how the Bible has been used on different sides of issues concerning women and slavery, see Swartley, *Slavery Sabbath War and Women.*

[48]*B. C. Intelligencer* 3/1m/1838, 31/1m/1838. By 13/2/1839 the Buckingham Anti Slavery Society had both male and female officers.

[49]*B. C. Intelligencer* 1m/1831, 9/2m/1837, 15/2m/1837, 8/7m/1837, 25/10/1837, 27/12/1837,

17/1m/1838, 20/2/1839, 7/7m/1841. Yards of petitions, sewn into long strips, are stored in the National Archives. They are not sorted or labelled by township so it is difficult to locate which ones were sent from Middletown, Bensalem, or Bristol women and men. For a description of the petitions kept in the National Archives, see Thorne, "Earnest and Solemn Protest: Quaker Anti-Slavery Petitions to Congress, 1831-1865", 47-50. The *B. C. Intelligencer* quoted John Quincy Adams suggesting that the proliferation of antislavery societies weakened the cause, 10/7m/1839. The *Doylestown Democrat* opposed John Quincy Adams and the admission of antislavery petitions to Congress, 25/1/1837, 15/2/1837. For more on petition campaigns, see Sewell, *Ballots for Freedom: Antislavery Politics in the United States*, 7-8, 10-11; Goodman, *Of One Blood*, 228-232; and Jeffrey, *The Great Silent Army of Abolitionism: Ordinary Women in the Antislavery Movement*, 86-93.

[50]*B. C. Intelligencer* 8m/1836, 26/10m/1836, 17/5m/1837, 8/8m/1838, 2m/1839, 8/9m/1847, 25/12m/1849. The *Doylestown Democrat* reported on the Bucks County Abolition Society in order to link it with opposition candidate Joseph Ritner and his gubernatorial campaign, 15/8m/1838, 29/8m/1838.

[51]Gara, "Friends and the Underground Railroad", 3-19; Blockson, *The Underground Railroad in Pennsylvania*, 39, 194-5. Typescript of original manuscript, in possession of Marie Reeder, Gwynedd, Pa. Smedley, "Martha Schofield's Struggle for Social Justice"; also her *Martha Schofield and the Re-Education of the South, 1839-1916*, 4-5, 10-11.

[52]See, for example, Smedley, *History of the Underground Railroad in Chester and the Neighboring Counties of Pennsylvania*, 105, 222; Nash, *Forging Freedom: The Formation of Philadelphia's Black Community, 1720-1840*. The *Doylestown Democrat* described the struggle over a recaptured slave in Hatboro, 28/5/1833, and blamed antislavery people for the riots in New York City, 27/7/1834, and for the burning of "Abolition Hall" in Philadelphia, 23/5/1838.

[53]Turner, *The Negro in Pennsylvania*, 170-90. *Bucks County Intelligencer* 19/7/1837, 4/10m/1837, 11/10m/1837, 25/10/1837, 1/11m/1837, 8/11m/1837, 22/11/1837, 20/12m/1837, 3/1m/1838, 17/1/1838; *Doylestown Democrat*, 26/7, 9/8m, 30/8m, 27/9, 18/10, 1/11m, 22/11, 20/12 all in 1837, 10/1m, 31/1, 7/2m in 1838. The Anti Slavery Society was virtually alone in decrying the stigmatization of abolitionism. *B. C. Intelligencer* 10/10/1838.

[54]Turner, *The Negro in Pennsylvania*, 248.

[55]See, for example, extracts from Baltimore Yearly Meeting, as quoted in *B. C. Intelligencer* 12/21/1842.

[56]Blankenburg, "Story of My Longshore Family", 532.

[57]*B. C. Intelligencer* 23/6/1834, 126m/1849, 26/11/1850, 9m/1836, 5/1834, 5/1836, 12/1834, 8/1837, 1/1842, 1/1848, 8/1844, 6/8m/1845, 27/8/1845, 21/9/1846, 1/9m/1847, 3/9m/1850, 8/10m/1850; *Democrat and Farmers' Gazette*, 18/12/1827. See also Barker, "Leadership in Bucks County Agricultural Societies in the Nineteenth Century".

[58]Little, "Horse Thief Pursuing Companies of Nineteenth-Century Bucks County", 5-18, esp. 11, 14.

[59]Little, "Horse Thief Pursuing Companies", 16-18. This attitude absorbed from the dominant culture is in opposition to the inclusive outreach of early Friends, as well as to a plethora of Quaker stories of Friends dealing creatively and non-violently with dangerous or threatening situations. See, for example, stories transcribed from old sources in Fry, comp., *Victories without Violence*.

[60]For example, the "Misses Vansant" were members of the Fellowship Horse Co., Little, "Horse Thief Pursuing Companies", 7, 16. The only Stackhouse on the roster was Joseph, who was not a Friend because his father had been disowned for marrying a non-Quaker. Most of the

Stackhouse family lived in Bristol township, which was beyond the territory of the Attleborough Company.

Notes for Chapter 10: Data Set, Meetings, and Township in 1850

[1] There are no Middletown Orthodox records of births and deaths in the QCol. or the FHL. There is a fragment of a manuscript listing Bucks County Friends at the time of the Separation, but part of Middletown is missing from it. Bucks Quarterly Meeting Orthodox List of Members, 1827-1829, FHL.

[2] An Orthodox membership list has had to be constructed from references to individuals in the men's and women's minutes, certificates of removal to or from Middletown, disownments or releases from the Hicksite meeting for joining the Orthodox, and the fragment of the 1827 list, all checked against the General Index to the Register of Wills in Bucks County and obituaries in the *B. C. Intelligencer*. See Appendix 4. But there are still 23 names in the Orthodox records which cannot be located in the 1850 census for Pennsylvania or the Register of Wills. The individuals may have died without a will or they may have moved while retaining their membership.

[3] Working backwards from the 9/10m/1858 Hicksite list, checking births, deaths, arrivals, and removals, a list has been constructed as of August 1850 that complements the U.S. census (see Appendix 4).

[4] See Table 20, in Appendix 1. This figure includes those Orthodox who lived in Bristol Borough and Township and parts of Bensalem, who would not have been part of Middletown Meeting in 1750. So the figures are not completely comparable.

[5] Elise Boulding observes that "many women clung to more traditional roles and would not participate in the women s meetings, or carry their share of meeting work." Boulding, "Mapping the Inner Journey of Quaker Women", 98.

[6] MMM Women's min., 5/4m/1839.

[7] The Quakers listing "none" under occupation, with their age, Hicksite or Orthodox affiliation, and value of real estate, were: Samuel Comfort (71, Orthodox, $33,000), Richard Hulme (36, Hicksite, $4,000), Joseph Jenks (57, Hicksite, $0), Elias Livezey (31, Hicksite, $8,000), Abraham Longshore (64, Hicksite, $9,000), Benjamin Mather (64, Hicksite $10,000), [John] Allen Mitchell (64, Hicksite, $10,500), William Mitchell (63, Hicksite, $10,000), Jonathan Thomas (74, Hicksite, $2,500), and John Wildman (36, Hicksite, $2,600).

[8] See for example, Bayard Taylor's novels, *Joseph and his Friend: A Story of Pennsylvania*; in *The Story of Kennett* the author states in the preface that in southeastern Pennsylvania the "conservative influence of Quakers is so powerful that it continued to shape the habits even of communities whose religious sentiment it failed to reach." iv; and *Hannah Thurston, A Story of American Life*, in which, in the introduction, Taylor explains that the real interest of the book lies not on its "slen-der plot, but on the fidelity with which it represents certain types of character and phases of society.", 4. See also, Thomas, *Penelve; or Among the Quakers: An American Story*.

[9] Doherty, *Hicksite Separation*, 55-59, 91-92.

[10] The census gathered a peculiar piece of data, the "aggregate accommodations" of the various churches. The results were surprising. Friends had more than twice as many "accommodations" (presumably seats)—13,200—as the next largest denomination. Presbyterians had 5,570 and Methodists had an even 5,000. Friends had almost 30% of the "aggregate accommodations" for worship in the County. I strongly suspect that with nearly twice the number of meeting houses

after the Separation as before, there were a good many empty benches in Quaker meeting houses. *The Seventh Census of the United States: 1850,* 200-5.

[11]Bucks Quarterly Meeting records. For a demonstration of this method applied to Philadelphia Yearly Meeting for 1760, see Marietta, "A Note on Quaker Membership", 40-43, especially 42. In 1828 it was decided among Orthodox Friends that Bucks Quarter should assume 7% of the yearly meeting budget. That was assessed on the basis of 40% to Falls, 11% to Middletown, 10% to Wrightstown, 30% to Buckingham, and 9% to Solebury. Records of the Minutes of Bucks Quarterly Meeting of the Religious Society of Friends, 29/5/1828, 28/8/1828, QCol.

[12]For a study of some disowned Friends continuing to participate in the Quaker subculture, see Grundy, "Were the Outcasts Cast Out?", 42-43.

[13]*B. C. Intelligencer,* 24/6m/1833. William Goodell, senior editor of the *Genius of Temperance,* spoke June 3, 1833, and wrote to "Br. Hines" June 4. In a review of William R. Wagstaff MD, *A History of the Society of Friends* . . ., the newspaper editor recommended it to "all readers, especially in a community where there are so many Friends, and where their manners and customs have so much influenced society." *B. C. Intelligencer,* 2/4m/1845.

[14]*B. C. Intelligencer,* 6/10m/1828, 5/10m/1836, 9/11m/1848.

[15]Klein, *Pennsylvania Politics, 1817-1832,* 52-56.

[16]*Who Was Who in America 1607-1896,* 1:348, 446; *Dictionary of American Biography,* 2:357-58; *The National Cyclopædia of American Biography,* 17:226-27, B:514. The biography of Lucretia Blankenburg is in James, ed., *Notable American Women,* 1:170-1. Tacy Blakey's husband, John Robbins (1818-27/4/1880) was a member of Congress, 1849-1855, 1875-1877.

[17]*B. C. Intelligencer,* from its beginning through 1850, and Battle, *History of Bucks,* 683-89.

[18]*B. C. Intelligencer,* 10m/1828. In a Senate speech Daniel Webster described Quakers as "Not ambitious, usually, to honor or office, but peaceable and industrious, they desire only the safety of liberty, civil and religious, the security of property, and the protection of honest labor. All they ask of government is, that it be wisely and safely administered." Webster went on to say they can be "excited by a crisis and we have such a crisis now . . . ." Quoted in *B. C. Intelligencer,* 23/6m/1834.

Notes for Chapter 11: Conclusions

[1]Hamm, *Transformation of American Quakerism,* xvi.

[2]Hamm, "The Hicksite Quaker World, 1875-1900", 89:17-41. See also his *Quakers in America.*

Notes for Appendix 1: Demographics of the Data Set and Meeting

[1]The families are: Allen, Blakey, Comfort, Croasdale, Gillam, Jenks, Kirkbride, Linton, Longshore, Mitchell, Paxson, Richardson, Stackhouse, Watson, Wildman, Wilson, and Woolston. Genealogical charts for each family are in Appendix 5.

[2]The census claimed 2,223 but when I counted them I got only 2,122. See the census schedules, microfilm, WRHS, and DeBow, *The Seventh Census of the United States: 1850,* 162.

[3]Wells, "A Demographic Analysis of Some Middle Colony Quaker Families of the Eighteenth Century"; Wells, "Family Size and Fertility Control in Eighteenth-Century America: A Study of Quaker Families", 73-84; Wells, "Quaker Marriage Patterns in a Colonial Perspective", 415-442.

[4]See, for example, Laidig, Schutjer, and Stokes, "Agricultural Variation and Human Fertility in Antebellum Pennsylvania", 195-204; and, Easterlin, "Factors in the Decline of Farm Family Fertility in the United States: Some Preliminary Research Results", 533-45.

[5]These numbers were not derived from family reconstitution, so a higher than average number of unmarried Quaker women, for example, could skew the results. In other words, more study is needed before making a definitive statement.

[6]See, for example, George Fox, *Journal*, 6, 511, 667-8; Margaret Fell Fox, *Womens Speaking Justified: proved and allowed of by the Scriptures*. For a short summary, see Brinton, *Quaker Journals*, 76. For secondary sources, see Cadbury, "George Fox and Women's Liberation", 370-76; Bacon, *As Way Opens: The Story of Quaker Women in America*; Bacon, *Mothers of Feminism: The Story of Quaker Women in America*; Brailsford, *Quaker Women: 1650-1690*; Stoneburner and Stonerburner, eds., *The Influence of Quaker Women on American History*; Dunn, "Saints and Sisters: Congregational and Quaker Women in the Early Colonial Period", 582-601. A good bit of her material is also found in Dunn, "Women of Light," *Women of America: A History*, ed. by Berkin and Norton, 114-33; Bacon, "A Widening Path: Women in Philadelphia Yearly Meeting Move Towards Equality, 1681-1955", 173-99; Barbour, "Quaker Prophetesses and Mothers in Israel".

Notes for Appendix 5: Genealogy Charts of Data Set Families

[1]Before 1752 the British used the Julian calendar in which the year began on March 25. So January was Eleventh month of the previous year. January [Eleventh Month] 1 to March [First Month] 24 are often written with a slash: Twelfth month 1682/3. See page 294, n. 19.

BIBLIOGRAPHY

Primary Sources

Published

Anonymous. *A Guide to True Peace or the Excellency of Inward and Spiritual Prayer, compiled chiefly from the writings of Fénelon, Guyon, and Molinos.* New York: Harper & Brothers in association with Pendle Hill, n.d.

_____. "'Loyalists' Who Went to Nova Scotia (1783)", *Canadian Quaker History* (Winter 1990), 20-21.

_____. *Modern Chronicles; or, Stoning the Prophet in the Nineteenth Century. An Account of the Persecution of Dr. Joseph S. Longshore, of Bucks County, Pa. on Account of his Labours in the Cause of Temperance. Containing a Report of his Trials, both in Church and State. together with the proceedings of public meetings, and the opinions of the press in reference thereto.* No place: Published by his friends, 1849.

Bacon, Margaret Hope, ed. *"Wilt Thou Go On My Errand?": Journals of Three 18th Century Quaker Women Ministers.* Wallingford, Penna.: Pendle Hill Pub-lications, 1994.

Barclay, Robert. *An Apology for the True Christian Divinity being an Explanation and Vindication of the Principles and Doctrines of the People Called Quakers.* Philadelphia: Friends' Book Store, 1908.

Blakey, William. "Journal of William Blakey, late of Middletown, Bucks County, containing some Account of his Religious Exercises, Observations, and Travels," John and Isaac Comly, eds. *Friends' Miscellany: Being a Collection of Essays and Fragments, Biographical, Religious, Epistolary, Narrative, and Historical.* 12 vols. Philadelphia: Printed for the editors by J. Richards, 1833. 4:76-161.

Blankenburg, Lucretia L. "A Story of My Branch of the Longshore Family". *A Collection of Papers Read Before the Bucks County Historical Society.* Published for the Society by the Fackenthal Publications Fund, 1932.

Bownas, Samuel. (ed. by William Taber). *A Description of the Qualifications Necessary to a Gospel Minister: Advice to Ministers and Elders Among the People Called Quakers.* Philadelphia: Pendle Hill Publications and Tract Association of Friends, 1989, from the 1767 edition.

Canby, Edmund. (ed. Carol Hoffacker). "Diaries of Edmund Canby: Quaker Miller, 1822-1848," *Delaware History* 16 (1974-1975). 79-131.

Chalkley, Thomas. *The Journal of Thomas Chalkley, to which is annexed a Collection of his Works.* New York: Samuel Wood, 1808.

Churchman, John. *An Account of the Gospel Labours, and Christian Experiences of a Faithful Minister of Christ, John Churchman, Late of Nottingham, in Pennsylvania.* Philadelphia: Printed by Joseph Crukshank, 1779. Another edition, Philadelphia: for sale at Friends' Book Store, 1862, includes "A Testimony from the Falls' Monthly Meeting in Bucks County, Pennsylvania, concerning our Friend Joseph White". This later edition is on ACS microfilm reel 371.

Clarkson, Thomas. *A Portraiture of Quakerism. Taken from a View of the Education and Discipline, Social Manners, Civil and Political Economy, Religious Principles and Character, of the Society of Friends.* 3 vols. New York: Samuel Stansbury, 1806.

Comly, John. *Journal of the Life and Religious Labours of John Comly, late of Byberry, Pennsylvania.* Philadelphia: published by his children, 1854.

Comly, John and Isaac, eds. *Friends' Miscellany: Being a Collection of Essays and Fragments, Biographical, Religious, Epistolary, Narrative, and Historical.* 12 vols. Philadelphia: Printed for the editors by J. Richards, 1833.

DeGarmo, James M. *The Hicksite Quakers and Their Doctrines.* New York: The Christian Literature Co., 1897.

Evans, William. *Journal of the Life and Religious Services of William Evans, A Minister of the Gospel in the Society of Friends.* 3rd ed. Philadelphia: Friends' Book Store, 1894.

Ferris, David. *Memoirs of the Life of David Ferris, an Approved Minister of the Society of Friends, late of Wilmington in the state of Delaware.* Philadelphia: Merrihew & Thompson's Steam Power Press, 1855. There is a more recent edition, Martha Paxson Grundy, ed. *Resistance and Obedience to God: Memoirs of David Ferris, 1707-1779.* Philadelphia: Friends General Conference, 2001.

Fox, George. (ed. John L. Nickalls). *The Journal of George Fox.* Cambridge: At the University Press, 1952.

_____. (ed. Cecil W. Sharman). *No More but my Love: Letters of George Fox, 1624-91.* London: Quaker Home Service, 1980.

Fox, Margaret Fell. *Womens Speaking Justified: proved and allowed of by the Scriptures, all such as speak by the spirit and power, and how women were the first that preached the tidings of the resurrection . . . .* Amherst, Mass.: Mosher Book & Tract Committee, New England Yearly Meeting, 1980. First printed in 1666.

Friends, Religious Society of. [London Yearly Meeting.] *Extracts from the Minutes and Advices of the Yearly Meeting of Friends held in London, from its first Institution.* 2nd ed. London: W. Phillips, 1802.

_____. Middletown Monthly Meeting, Bucks County, Pennsylvania. "Marriages Authorized by the Middletown Monthly Meeting of Friends, 1685-

1810." *Pennsylvania Archives*. 2nd. Series. Harrisburg: 1896. 9:221-233.

―――――. [Philadelphia Yearly Meeting] *Book of Discipline of Philadelphia Yearly Meeting* [Hicksite]. Philadelphia: 1831.

―――――. [Philadelphia Yearly Meeting]. *Christian Advices issued by the Yearly Meeting of Friends held in Philadelphia* [Orthodox]. Philadelphia: for sale at Friends' Book-Store, 304 Arch St., 1859.

―――――. [Philadelphia Yearly Meeting]. *A Collection of Memorials Concerning Divers deceased Ministers and others of the People Called Quakers, in Pennsylvania, New-Jersey, and Parts adjacent, from nearly the first Settlement thereof to the Year 1787*. Philadelphia: Joseph Crukshank, 1787.

―――――. Philadelphia Yearly Meeting. *Faith and Practice: A Book of Christian Discipline*. rev. 1972. Philadelphia: Philadelphia Yearly Meeting, 1978.

―――――. [Philadelphia Yearly Meeting]. *Memorials Concerning Deceased Friends: Being a Selection from the Records of the Yearly Meeting for Pennsylvania, &c. from the Year 1787 to 1819, Inclusive*. Philadelphia: Solomon W. Conrad, 1821.

―――――. [Philadelphia Yearly Meeting]. *Rules of Discipline of the Yearly Meeting of Friends, for Pennsylvania, New-Jersey, Delaware, and the Eastern Parts of Maryland: Revised and Adopted by the Said Meeting, Held in Philadelphia, by adjournments from the 21st of the fourth month to the 26th of the same, inclusive, 1834* [Orthodox]. Philadelphia: Printed by Joseph Rakestraw, 1834.

―――――. Yearly Meeting held for the Provinces of Pennsylvania and New-Jersey, 1722. *The Ancient Testimony of the People Called Quakers*. Philadelphia: Joseph Crukshank, 1773.

Gopsill's Philadelphia City Directory. Philadelphia: J. Gopsill's Sons, 1867/8.

Grellet, Stephen. (ed. Benjamin Seebohm). *Memoirs of the Life and Gospel Labours of Stephen Grellet*. Philadelphia: Henry Longstreth, 1860.

Healy, Christopher. *Memoir of Christopher Healy, Principally Taken from his own Memoranda*. Philadelphia: Friends' Book Store, 1886.

Hicks, Edward. *Memoirs of Edward Hicks*. Philadelphia: 1851.

Hicks, Elias. *Journal of the Life and Religious Labours of Elias Hicks*. New York: Published by Isaac T. Hopper, 1832.

―――――. *Letters of Elias Hicks. Including also Observations on the Slavery of the Africans and their Descendants, and on the Use of the Produce of their Labor*. Philadelphia: T. Ellwood Chapman, 1861.

Hinshaw, William Wade. *Encyclopedia of American Quaker Genealogy*. 6 vols. Richmond, Ind.: Friends Book and Supply House, Distributors; Ann Arbor, Mich.: Edwards Brothers, Inc., Printers, 1936.

McNealy, Terry A. and Frances Wise Waite, comps. *Bucks Co. Tax Records, 1693-1778*. Doylestown, Pa.: Bucks Co. Genealogical Society, 1982.

Meyers, Albert Cook. *Quaker Arrivals at Philadelphia, 1682-1750; being a list of Certificates of Removal Received at Philadelphia Monthly Meeting of Friends*. Philadelphia: Ferris & Leach, 1902.

Penn, William. *No Cross, No Crown: A Discourse showing the Nature and Discipline of the Holy Cross of Christ, and that the Denial of Self and daily*

Bearing of Christ's Cross is the alone Way to the Rest and Kingdom of God. William Sessions Book Trust. York, Eng.: The Ebor Press, 1981.

_____. Translated into modern English by Paul Buckley. *Twenty-first Century Penn: Writings On The Faith And Practice Of The People Called Quakers.* Richmond, Ind.: Earlham School of Religion, 2003.

Pennsylvania Archives. 9 series. Harrisburg: published by the Commonwealth, 1853-1937.

Pennsylvania Colonial Records. 16 vols. Harrisburg, published by the state, 1837-1851.

Quaker Necrology: Haverford College Library. Boston: G. K. Hall & Co., 1961.

Reckitt, William. *Some Account of the Life and Gospel Labours of William Reckitt late of Lincolnshire in Great-Britain. Also Memoirs of the Life, Religious Experiences, and Gospel Labours of James Gough, late of Dublin, deceased.* Philadelphia: J. Crukshank, 1783.

Roberts, Jonathan. (ed. Philip S. Klein). "Memoirs of a Senator from Pennsylvania: Jonathan Roberts, 1771-1854". *Pennsylvania Magazine of History and Biography* 61 (1937). 446-474.

Sewel, William. *The History of the Rise, Increase, and Progress of the People Called Quakers . . . .* Philadelphia: Friends' Book Store, n.d.

Skidmore, Gil, ed. *Strength in Weakness: Writings of Eighteenth-Century Quaker Women.* The Sacred Literature Series of the International Sacred Literature Trust. Walnut Creek: Rowman & Littlefields Publishers, Inc., 2003.

Smith, William. *A Brief View of the Conduct of Pennsylvania, for the Year 1755 . . . .* London: R. Griffiths, 1756. American Cultural Series, microfilm. Ann Arbor, Mich.: University Microfilms.

Stanton, Daniel. *A Journal of the Life, Travels and Gospel Labours, of a Faithful Minister of Jesus Christ, Daniel Stanton.* Philadelphia: Joseph Crukshank, 1772.

Stevens, Benjamin Franklin. *Facsimiles of Manuscripts in European Archives Relating to America, 1773-1783.* London: Malby & Sons, 1889-1895.

Sutcliffe, Robert. *Travels in Some Parts of North America in the Years 1804, 1805, and 1806.* Philadelphia: Kite, 1812.

Tallack, William. *Friendly Sketches in America.* London: A. W. Bennett, 1861.

Taylor, Bayard. *Hannah Thurston, A Story of American Life.* New York: G. P. Putnam, 1863.

_____. *Joseph and his Friend: A Story of Pennsylvania.* New York: G. P. Putnam & Sons, 1898.

_____. *The Story of Kennett.* New York and London: Putnam, 1866.

Thomas, Richard Henry. *Penelve; or Among the Quakers: An American Story.* London: Healey Brothers, 1898.

United States, Department of Commerce, Bureau of the Census. *Historical Statistics of the United States: Colonial Times to 1970.* Washington, D.C.: U.S. Government Printing Office, 1975.

_____. *The Seventh Census of the United States: 1850.* Washington: Robert Armstrong, Public Printer, 1853.

Wilbur, John. *A Narrative and Exposition of the Late Proceedings of New England Yearly Meeting, with Some of its Subordinate Meetings & their Committees, in Relation to the Doctrinal Controversy now Existing in the Society of Friends:* . . . . New York: Piery & Reed, Printers, 1845.

Woolman, John. (ed. Phillips P. Moulton). *The Journal and Major Essays of John Woolman.* New York: Oxford University Press, 1971.

Periodicals

Bucks County Intelligencer and General Advertizer (Doylestown), 2 October, 1827-1851.
Bucks County Messenger (Doylestown), scattered issues in 1821.
Bucks County Patriot and Farmers' Advertizer (Doylestown), 4 October, 1824-24 September, 1827.
Democrat and Farmers' Gazette (Doylestown), 16 Jan. 1827-12 Feb. 1831.
Doylestown Democrat (Doylestown), 15 Mar. 1831-1850, *passim.*
The Friend (Philadelphia), 1827-1955.
Friends Intelligencer (Philadelphia), 1843-.
Friends Review (Philadelphia), 1848-1894.
Pennsylvania Correspondent and Farmers' Advertizer (Doylestown), 1804-1824.
Publications of the Genealogical Society of Pennsylvania (Philadelphia), vols. 1-15.

Unpublished Materials

"The Booke of Records belonging to the Women's Monthly Meeting in Middletown in Bucks County in Pensilvania, 1683 to [1770]". Succeeding volumes have slightly different titles. FHL.
Bucks County Court of Quarter Sessions. Miscellaneous Papers, Nos. 770, 794. BCHS.
Bucks County Court. Miscellaneous Papers, #656. BCHS.
Bucks County Sessions Docket, 1782-1801. BCHS. (includes Grand Jury lists)
"Bucks County, Manumission of Slaves 1785-1800". BCHS.
Bucks County Will files, in the Bucks County Court House, Doylestown, Penna.
Bucks Quarterly Meeting Orthodox List of Members, 1827-1829. Records of Bucks Quarterly Meeting, deposited at FHL.
Collections of the Genealogical Society of Pennsylvania. *Bucks County, Pa., Abstracts of Wills 1685-1795*. Philadelphia: 1899. Copies at the WRHS.
Cresson, Anne H., compiler. "Records of the Comfort Family." Germantown: typescript, 1902. QCol.
Eastburn, Samuel. Manuscript Collection (MSC) 51. BCHS.
General Index to the Register of Wills in Bucks County. BCHS.
Jenks, Michael H. Papers. Manuscript Collection (MSC) 79. BCHS.
Longshore, Marion H. "A Brief History of Middletown Meeting as gleaned from the Minute Books". Mimeographed pamphlet, n.p., n.d. Author's collec-

tion.

Matlack, T. Chalkley. *Brief Historical Sketches Concerning Friends' Meetings of the Past and Present with Special Reference to Philadelphia Yearly Meeting*. Bound typescript, 1938. QCol.

McNealy, Terry A. "Bucks County Newspapers and How to Use Them for Research". Address to the Bucks County Genealogical Society, May 8, 1986.

Middletown Monthly Meeting records. FHL and QCol.

Moon, James. "An Account of Negroes Set Free", [1776-1780]. Typescript copy in the QCol.

Papers of Middletown Monthly Meeting. 4 bound mms. vols. FHL.

Philadelphia Yearly Meeting, Meeting for Sufferings. Miscellaneous papers. Microfilm rolls 29Q and 30Q. QCol.

"Record of Manumissions of Negroes within the Quarterly Meeting of Bucks. 1776". FHL.

Richardson, Joshua. Holograph memoir in the collection of Marie Reeder, Gwynedd, Penna.

Simmons, Henry. "Four Journals, 1796-1800" [journey to Indian reservations at Oneida, also two letterbooks]. QCol. See also David Swatzler, *A Friend Among the Senecas*, which is based on Simmons's journals.

Smith, C. Arthur, compiler. *Death Notices Copied from the Bucks County Intelligencer, Doylestown, Pa. 1835-1860*. Bound typescript. BCHS.

Valentine, Cloyd Hampton. "The disciplines of American Friends". Typed copy, ca. 1928. QCol.

———. "Summaries of Friendly disciplines". Typescript, ca. 1928. QCol.

"VF Slave Records - Bucks County". BCHS.

Watson, Thomas. "An Account of the Sufferings of Thomas Watson of Bucks County, taken from his own Mouth". Copied from a book of writings entitled "Kaye Papers, 1654-1837" in the possession of Charles J. Holdsworth, J.P., Alderley Edge, near Manchester, England. 1929. QCol.

Secondary Sources

Monographs

American Council of Learned Societies. *Dictionary of American Biography*. Multi-volumes. New York: Charles Scribner's Sons, 1928-1936.

Anderson, J. A. *Navigation of the Upper Delaware*. Read before the Bucks County Historical Society at Doylestown, Pennsylvania, 16 January 1912. Trenton, N. J.: MacCrellish & Quigley, Printers, 1913.

Anderson, Verily. *Friends and Relations: Three centuries of Quaker Families*. London: Hodder and Stoughton, 1980.

Appleby, Joyce. *Inheriting the Revolution: The First Generation of Americans*. Cambridge, Mass.: The Belknap Press of Harvard University Press, 2000.

Arweck, Elisabeth and Martin D. Stringer, eds. *Theorizing Faith: The Insider/Outsider Problem in the Study of Ritual*. Birmingham, UK: University of

Birmingham Press, 2002.
Auping, John. *Religion and Social Justice: The Case of Christianity and the Abolition of Slavery in America.* Mexico, Distrito Federal: Departamento de Ciencias Religiosas, 1994.
Bache, William. *Historical Sketches of Bristol Borough in the County of Bucks, ...* Bristol, Penna.: privately printed, 1853.
Bacon, Margaret Hope. *As Way Opens: The Story of Quaker Women in America.* Richmond, Ind.: Friends United Press, 1980.
_____. *Mothers of Feminism: The Story of Quaker Women in America.* San Francisco: Harper & Row, Publishers, 1986.
Baltzell, E. Digby. *Puritan Boston and Quaker Philadelphia: Two Protestant Ethics and the Spirit of Class Authority and Leadership.* New York: Free Press, 1979.
Barbour, Hugh, and J. William Frost. *The Quakers.* Westport, Conn.: Greenwood Press, 1988.
Bathe, Granville, and Dorothy Bathe. *Oliver Evans: A Chronicle of Early American Engineering.* Philadelphia: The Historical Society of Pennsylvania, 1935.
Battle, J. H. *History of Bucks County, Pennsylvania.* Philadelphia: A. Warner & Co., 1887.
Beck, Don Edward and Christopher C. Cowan. *Spiral Dynamics:* Mastering Values, Leadership, and Change. Oxford and Cambridge, Mass.: Blackwell Business Publishers, 1996.
Benjamin, Ralph S. *The Philadelphia Quakers in the Industrial Age.* Philadelphia: Temple University Press, 1976.
Berkin, Carol R. and Mary Beth Norton, eds. *Women of America: A History.* Boston: Houghton Mifflin Company, 1979.
Bezanson, Anne. *Prices and Inflation During the American Revolution, Pennsylvania, 1770-1790.* Industrial Research Department, Wharton School of Finance and Commerce, University of Pennsylvania, Research Studies 35. Philadelphia: University of Pennsylvania Press, 1951.
Bezanson, Anne, Robert D. Gray, and Miriam Hussey. *Wholesale Prices in Philadelphia 1784-1861.* Industrial Research Department, Wharton School of Finance and Commerce, University of Pennsylvania, Research Studies 29. Philadelphia: University of Pennsylvania Press, 1936.
Bidwell, Percy Wells, and John I. Falconer. *History of Agriculture in the Northern United States, 1620-1860.* Washington, D.C.: Carnegie Institute, 1925.
Birkel, Michael L. *A Near Sympathy: The Timeless Quaker Wisdom of John Woolman.* Richmond, Ind.: Friends United Press, 2003.
Blockson, Charles L. *The Underground Railroad in Pennsylvania.* Jacksonville, N.C.: Flame International, Inc., 1981.
Bowman, Carl F. *Brethren Society: The Cultural Transformation of a "Peculiar People".* Baltimore: The Johns Hopkins University Press, 1995.
Bradley, Patricia. *Slavery, Propaganda, and the American Revolution.* Jackson: University of Mississippi Press, 1998.
Brailsford, Mabel Richmond. *Quaker Women: 1650-1690.* London: Duckworth &

Co., 1815.
Braithwaite, William C. (revised by Henry J. Cadbury). *The Beginnings of Quakerism*. 2nd ed. York, England: William Sessions Ltd., 1981.
──────. (revised by Henry J. Cadbury). *The Second Period of Quakerism*. 2nd ed. York, England: William Sessions Ltd., 1979.
Braude, Ann. *Radical Spirits: Spiritualism and Women's Rights in Nineteenth-Century America*. Boston: Beacon Press, 1989.
Brayshaw, A. Neave. *The Quakers: Their Story and Message*. 3rd ed. London: Bradford & Dickens, 1938.
Brey, Jane W. T. *A Quaker Saga: The Watsons of Strawberryhowe, the Wildmans, and Other Allied Families from England's Northern Counties and Lower Bucks County in Pennsylvania*. Philadelphia: Dorrance & Co., 1967.
Brinton, Howard H. *Friends for 300 Years: The history and beliefs of the Society of Friends since George Fox started the Quaker Movement*. New York: Harper & Bros., 1952; Wallingford, Penna.: Pendle Hill Publications and Philadelphia Yearly Meeting of the Religious Society of Friends, 1964 paperback reprint. There is a newer edition, with an historical update by Margaret Hope Bacon, *Friends for 350 Years*. (2002).
──────. *Quaker Journals: Varieties of Religious Experience Among Friends*. Wallingford, Penna.: Pendle Hill Publications, 1972.
Brock, Peter. *Pacifism in the United States from the Colonial Era to the First World War*. Princeton, N. J.: Princeton University Publications, Columbia University Press, 1968.
──────. *The Quaker Peace Testimony: 1660 to 1914*. York, Eng.: William Sessions Ltd., 1991; Syracuse, N. Y: Syracuse University Press, 1993.
Bronner, Edwin. *William Penn's "Holy Experiment": The Founding of Pennsylvania 1681-1701*. New York: Temple University Press, 1962.
Brookes, George S. *Friend Anthony Benezet*. Philadelphia: University of Pennsylvania Press, 1937.
Brown, Elisabeth Potts, and Susan Mosher Stuard, eds. *Witnesses for Change: Quaker Women Over Three Centuries*. New Brunswick: Rutgers University Press, 1989.
Buck, William J. *History of Bucks County*. Doylestown, Penna.: John S. Brown, 1855.
Cady, Edwin H. *John Woolman: The Mind of the Quaker Saint*. New York: Washington Square Press, 1966.
Cappon, Lester, ed. *Atlas of Early American History, 1760-1790*. Princeton, N. J. Published for the Newberry Library and The Institute of Early American History and Culture by the Princeton University Press, 1976.
Carpenter, W. H., and T. S. Arthur, eds. *History of Pennsylvania from its Earliest Settlement to the Present Times*. Lippincott's Cabinet Histories. Philadelphia: J. B. Lippincott & Co., 1856.
Censer, Jane Turner. *North Carolina Planters and Their Children: 1800-1860*. Baton Rouge: Louisiana State University Press, 1984.

Chambers-Schiller, Lee Virginia. *Liberty, A Better Husband: Single Women in America, The Generations of 1730-1840*. New Haven: Yale University Press, 1984.
Child, L. Maria. *Isaac T. Hopper: A True Life.* first pub. 1852, new ed. Philadelphia: Walter H. Jenkins, 1881.
Clain-Stefanelli, Elvira, and Vladimir Clain-Stefanelli. *Chartered for Progress: Two Centuries of American Banking, A Pictorial Essay*. Washington, D.C.: Acropolis Books, Ltd., 1975.
Cochran, Thomas C. *Pennsylvania: A Bicentennial History*. New York: W. W. Norton & Co., Inc., and Nashville: American Association for State and Local History, 1978.
Cole, Arthur Harrison. *Wholesale Commodity Prices in the United States, 1700-1861*. Cambridge, Mass.: Harvard University Press, 1938.
Committee on Historical Research. *Forges and Furnaces in the Province of Pennsylvania*. Publications of the Pennsylvania Society of the Colonial Dames of America. vol. 3. Philadelphia: Printed for the Society, 1914.
Crary, Catherine S. *The Price of Loyalty: Tory Writings from the Revolutionary Era*. New York: McGraw-Hill Book Company, 1973.
Crauderueff, Elaine. *War Taxes: Experiences of Philadelphia Yearly Meeting Quakers Through the American Revolution*. Pendle Hill Pamphlet no. 286. Wallingford, Penna.: Pendle Hill Publications, 1989.
_____. "War Taxes: The Experiences of Philadelphia Yearly Meeting Quakers, 1681-1800". M.A. thesis, Villanova University, 1988.
Cronk, Sandra. *Peace Be with You: A Study of the Spiritual Basis of the Friends Peace Testimony*. Philadelphia: Tract Association, 1984.
Damiano, Kathryn A. "'On Earth as It Is in Heaven': Eighteenth-Century Quakerism as Realized Eschatology". Ph.D. dissertation for the Union of Experimenting Colleges and Universities, Cincinnati, Ohio, 1988.
Davidson, Robert L. D. *War Comes to Quaker Pennsylvania*. New York: Publications by Columbia University Press for Temple University, 1957.
Davis, David Brion. *The Problem of Slavery in the Age of Revolution: 1770-1823*. Ithaca: Cornell University Press, 1975.
_____. *The Problem of Slavery in Western Culture*. Ithaca, NY: Cornell University Press, 1966.
Davis, William W. H. *The History of Bucks County, Pennsylvania, from the Discovery of the Delaware to the Present Time*. 3 vols. 2nd ed. New York: The Lewis Publishing Company, 1905.
Demos, John. *Past, Present and Personal: The Family and the Life Course in American History*. New York: Oxford University Press, 1986.
Demos, John, and Sarane Spence Boocock, eds. *Turning Points: Historical and Sociological Essays on the Family*. Supplement to *American Journal of Sociology* 84 (1978). Chicago: The University of Chicago Press, 1978.
Doherty, Robert W. *The Hicksite Separation: A Sociological Analysis of Religious Schism in Early Nineteenth Century America*. New Brunswick: Rutgers University Press, 1967.

Douglass, Elisha P. *Rebels and Democrats: The Struggle for Equal Political Rights and Majority Rule During the American Revolution.* Chapel Hill, N.C.: University of North Carolina Press, 1955.

Drake, Thomas E. *Quakers and Slavery in America.* New Haven: Yale University Press, 1950.

Erikson, Erik. *Identity and the Life Cycle, Psychological Issues.* vol. 1 (1959), monograph 1. New York: International University Press, 1959.

_____. *The Life Cycle Completed: A Review.* New York: W. W. Norton & Company, 1982.

Evans, William Bacon. *Jonathan Evans and his Time, 1759-1839: Bi-Centennial Biography.* Boston: The Christopher Publishing House, 1959.

Faris, John T. *Old Churches and Meeting Houses in and Around Philadelphia.* Philadelphia: J. B. Lippincott Company, 1926.

Fletcher, Stevenson W. *Pennsylvania Agriculture and Country Life 1640-1840.* Harrisburg, Pa.: Pennsylvania and Museum Commission, 1950.

Fowler, James W. *Stages of Faith: The Psychology of Human Development and the Quest for Meaning.* San Francisco: Harper & Row, Publishers, 1981.

Frey, Sylvia R., and Marian J. Morton, eds. *New World, New Roles: A Documentary History of Women in Pre-Industrial America.* Westport, Conn.: Greenwood Press, 1986.

Frost, J. William. *The Keithian Controversy in Early Pennsylvania.* Norwood, Penna.: Norwood Editions, 1980.

_____. *The Quaker Family in Colonial America: A Portrait of the Society of Friends.* New York: St. Martin's Press, 1973.

_____. *The Quaker Origin of Antislavery.* Norwood, Penna.: Norwood Editions, 1980.

Frost, J. William and John M. Moore, eds. *Seeking the Light: Essays in Quaker History.* Wallingford & Haverford: Pendle Hill Publications & Friends Historical Association, 1986.

Fry, A. Ruth, compiler. *Victories Without Violence.* London: Peace Book Company, 1939.

Furnes, J. C. *The Life and Times of the Late Demon Rum.* New York: G. P. Putnam's Sons, 1965.

Genealogies of Pennsylvania Families: From the Pennsylvania Genealogical Magazine. Baltimore: Genealogical Publishing Co., Inc., 1982.

George, Carol V. R. *Segregated Sabbaths: Richard Allen and the Emergence of Independent Black Churches, 1760-1840.* New York: Oxford University Press, 1973.

Gesell, Arnold, and Frances L. Ilg. *The Child from Five to Ten.* New York and London: Harper and Brothers Publishers, 1946.

Gifford, Henry. *The Lost Years.* London & Cheddar: Charles Skilton Ltd., 1987.

Goodman, Paul. *Of One Blood: Abolitionism and the Origins of Racial Equality.* Berkeley: University of California Press, 1998.

Gordon, Michael, ed. *The American Family in Social-Historical Perspective.* 2nd. ed. New York: St. Martin's Press, 1978.

Green, Doran. *A History of Bristol Borough* . . . . Camden, N. J.: C. S. Magrath, 1911.
Greene, Evarts B., and Virginia D. Harrington. *American Population before the Federal Census of 1790*. New York: Columbia University Press, 1932.
Greven, Philip J. *The Protestant Temperament: Patterns of Child-Rearing, Religious Experience, and the Self in Early America*. New York: New American Library, 1977.
Gwyn, Douglas. *Apocalypse of the Word: The Life and Message of George Fox, 1624-1691*. Richmond, Ind.: Friends United Press, 1986.
Hamm, Thomas D. *The Quakers in America*. Columbia Contemporary American Religion Series. New York: Columbia University Press, 2003.
_____. *The Transformation of American Quakerism: Orthodox Friends, 1800-1907*. Religion in North America. Bloomington: Indiana University Press, 1988.
Hammond, Bray. *Banks and Politics in America: From the Revolution to the Civil War*. Princeton, N. J.: Princeton University Press, 1957.
Hansell, Norris, ed. *Josiah White: Quaker Entrepreneur*. Easton, Penna.: Canal His-tory and Technology Press, 1992.
Hareven, Tamara K., ed. *Family and Kin in Urban Communities, 1700-1930*. New York: New Viewpoints, A Division of Franklin Watts, 1977.
Hartz, Louis. *Economic Policy and Democratic Thought: Pennsylvania, 1776-1860*. Cambridge: Harvard University Press, 1948.
Harvey, T. Edmund. *Silence and Worship: A Study in Quaker Experience*. London: The Swarthmore Press, Ltd., 1923.
Hawke, David. *In the Midst of a Revolution*. Philadelphia: University of Pennsylvania Press, 1961.
Hazard, Samuel. *Annals of Pennsylvania, from the Discovery of the Delaware, 1609-1682*. Philadelphia: Hazard and Mitchell, 1850.
Heller, Mike, ed. *The Tendering Presence: Essays on John Woolman In Honor of Sterling Olmsted & Phillips P. Moulton*. Wallingford, Penna.: Pendle Hill Publications, 2003.
Henretta, James A. *The Evolution of American Society, 1700-1815: An Interdisciplinary Analysis*. Lexington, Mass.: D. C. Heath and Company, 1973.
Hill, Christopher. *The World Turned Upside Down: Radical Ideas During the English Revolution*. Harmondsworth, England: Penguin Books, Ltd., 1975.
Hilton, Boyd. *The Age of Atonement: The Influence of Evangelicalism on Social and Economic Thought, 1785-1865*. Oxford: Oxford University Press, 1988.
Hirst, Margaret E. *The Quakers in Peace and War: An Account of Their Peace Principles and Practice*. London: The Swarthmore Press, Ltd., 1923.
Holden, David. *Friends Divided: Conflict and Division in the Society of Friends*. Richmond, Ind.: Friends United Press, 1988.
Holdsworth, John Thom. *History of Banking in Pennsylvania*. vols. 1 and 2 of Hon. John S. Fisher, assoc. ed. *Financing An Empire*. Chicago and Philadelphia: The S. J. Clarke Publishing Company, 1928.

Hotchkin, The Rev. S. S. *The Bristol Pike.* Philadelphia: George W. Jacobs & Co., 1893.
Hutson, James H. *Pennsylvania Politics 1746-1770: The Movement for Royal Government and Its Consequences.* Princeton, N.J.: Princeton University Press, 1972.
Illick, Joseph E. *Colonial Pennsylvania: A History.* New York: Charles Scribner's Sons, 1976.
Ingle, H. Larry. *Quakers in Conflict: The Hicksite Reformation.* Knoxville: University of Tennessee Press, 1986.
Isichei, Elizabeth. *Victorian Quakers.* Oxford University Press, 1970.
Jacob, Caroline Nicholson. *The Shackletons of Ballitore.* Philadelphia: Friends General Conference, 1984.
James, Edward T., ed. *Notable American Women, 1607-1950: A Biographical Dictionary.* 3 vols. Cambridge, Mass.: Belknap Press of Harvard University Press, 1971.
James, Sydney V. *A People Among Peoples: Quaker Benevolence in Eighteenth-Century America.* Cambridge, Mass.: Harvard University Press, 1963.
Janney, Samuel M. *An Examination of the Courses which Led to the Separation of the Religious Society of Friends in America, 1827-1828.* Philadelphia: T. Ellwood Zell, 1868.
_____. *History of the Religious Society of Friends, from its Rise to the Year 1828.* 4 vols. Philadelphia: T. E. Zell, 1859-1867.
Jeffrey, Julie Roy. *The Great Silent Army of Abolitionism: Ordinary Women in the Antislavery Movement.* Chapel Hill: University of North Carolina Press, 1998.
Jensen, Joan M. *Loosening the Bonds: Mid-Atlantic Farm Women, 1750-1850.* New Haven: Yale University Press, 1986.
Jones, Charles Henry. *Genealogy of the Rodman Family, 1620 to 1886.* Philadelphia: 1886.
Jones, Douglas Lamar. *Village and Seaport: Migration and Society in Eighteenth-Century Massachusetts.* Hanover, N. H.: Published for Tufts University by University Press of New England, 1981.
Jones, Rufus M. *The Later Periods of Quakerism.* 2 vols. London: Macmillan and Co., Ltd., 1921.
_____. *The Quakers in the American Colonies.* London: Macmillan and Co., Ltd., 1911.
Jordan, Winthrop. *White Over Black: American Attitudes Toward the Negro, 1550-1812.* Chapel Hill: Published for the Institute of Early American History and Culture at Williamsburg, Va., by the University of North Carolina Press, 1968.
Jorns, Auguste. *The Quakers as Pioneers in Social Work.* New York: The Macmillan Co., 1931.
Julye, Vanessa and Donna McDaniel. *Fit for Freedom, Not for Friendship.* [working title] Philadelphia: Quaker Press of Friends General Conference, forthcoming [in 2007?].

Katz, Stanley N. and John M. Murrin, eds. *Colonial America: Essays in Politics and Social Development.* 3rd ed. New York: Alfred A. Knopf, 1983.
Kerber, Linda K. *Women of the Republic: Intellect and Ideology in Revolutionary America.* Chapel Hill: University of North Carolina Press, 1980.
Kirby, Ethyn Williams. *George Keith, 1638-1716.* New York: D. Appleton-Century Company, Inc., 1942.
Klein, Philip Shriver. *Pennsylvania Politics, 1817-1832: A Game Without Rules.* Philadelphia: Historical Society of Pennsylvania, 1940.
Kobrin, David Robert. "The Saving Remnant: Intellectual Sources of Change and Decline in Colonial Quakerism, 1690-1810". Ph.D. dissertation, University of Pennsylvania, 1968.
Kohl, Lawrence Frederick. *The Politics of Individualism: Parties and the American Character in the Jacksonian Era.* New York: Oxford University Press, 1989.
Korbin, Jill, ed. *Child Abuse and Neglect: Cross-Cultural Perspectives.* Berkeley, Calif.: University of California Press, 1981.
Lacey, Paul A. *Quakers and the Use of Power.* Pendle Hill Pamphlet no. 241. Wallingford, Penna.: Pendle Hill Publications, 1982.
Larson, Rebecca. *Daughters of Light: Quaker Women Preaching and Prophesying in the Colonies and Abroad, 1700-1775.* New York: Alfred A. Knopf, 1999.
Leach, Robert J. *Women Ministers: A Quaker Contribution.* Pendle Hill Pamphlet no. 227. Wallingford, Penna.: Pendle Hill Publications, 1979.
Lemon, James T. *The Best Poor Man's Country: A Geographical Study of Early Southern Pennsylvania.* Baltimore: Johns Hopkins University Press, 1972.
Lender, Mark Edward, and James Kirby Martin. *Drinking in America.* rev. ed. New York: The Free Press, 1987.
Levy, Barry. *Quakers and the American Family: British Settlement in the Delaware Valley, 1650-1765.* New York: Oxford University Press, 1988.
Lincoln, Charles H. *The Revolutionary Movement in Pennsylvania, 1760-1776*, Publications of the University of Pennsylvania, Series in History, no. 1. Philadelphia: for the University, 1901.
Litwack, Leon F. *North of Slavery: The Negro in the Free States, 1790-1860.* Chicago: University of Chicago Press, 1961.
Lokken, Roy N. *David Lloyd: Colonial Lawmaker.* Seattle: University of Washington Press, 1959.
MacMaster, Richard K. *Christian Obedience in Revolutionary Times: The Peace Churches and the American Revolution.* Akron, Penna.: Mennonite Central Committee, Peace Section (U.S.), 1976.
MacMaster, Richard K., with Samuel L. Horst and Robert F. Ulle. *Conscience in Crisis: Mennonites and Other Peace Churches in America, 1739-1789, Interpretation and Documents.* Scottdale, Penna.: Herald Press, 1979.
Marietta, Jack D. *The Reformation of American Quakerism, 1748-1783.* Philadelphia: The University of Pennsylvania Press, 1984.
Martindale, Joseph C. (rev. ed. by Albert S. Dudley). *A History of the Townships of Byberry and Moreland in Philadelphia, Pa.,* . . . . Philadelphia: George

W. Jacobs & Co., n.d.

Mathews, Donald G. *Slavery and Methodism: A Chapter in American Morality, 1780-1845.* Princeton, N. J.: Princeton University Press, 1965.

May, Henry F. *Protestant Churches and Industrial America.* New York: Harper & Brothers Publishers, 1949.

McGoldrick, Monica, and Randy Gerson. *Genograms in Family Assessment.* New York: Norton, 1985.

Mekeel, Arthur J. *The Relation of the Quakers to the American Revolution.* Washington, D. C.: University Press of America, 1979.

Meyers, Albert Cook. *Quaker Arrivals in Philadelphia, 1682-1750.* Baltimore: The Genealogical Publishing Co., 1969.

Michener, Ezra. *A Retrospect of Early Quakerism; Being Extracts from the Records of Philadelphia Yearly Meeting and the Meetings Composing it.* Philadelphia: T. Ellwood Zell, 1860.

Moore, John M., ed. *Friends in the Delaware Valley: Philadelphia Yearly Meeting 1681-1981.* Haverford, Penna.: Friends Historical Association, 1981.

Morley, Barry. "Beyond Censensus: Salvaging Sense of the Meeting". Pendle Hill Pamphlet no. 307. Wallingford, Penna.: Pendle Hill Publications, 1993.

Murphy, Raymond E., and Marion Murphy. *Pennsylvania: A Regional Geography.* Harrisburg: Pennsylvania Book Service, 1937.

Musson, A. E. *Enterprise in Soap and Chemicals: Joseph Crosfield & Sons, Limited, 1815-1965.* Manchester: Manchester University Press, 1965.

Nash, Gary. *Forging Freedom: The Formation of Philadelphia's Black Community, 1720-1840.* Cambridge, Mass.: Harvard University Press, 1988.

_____. *Quakers and Politics: Pennsylvania 1681-1726.* Princeton, N. J.: Princeton University Press, 1968.

_____. *Red, White, and Black: The Peoples of Early America.* Englewood Cliffs, N. J.: Prentice-Hall, 1974.

Nash, Gary B. and Jean R. Soderlund. *Freedom by Degrees: Emancipation in Pennsylvania and Its Aftermath.* New York: Oxford University Press, 1991.

National Cyclopædia of American Biography being the History of the United States as Illustrated in the Lives of the Founders, Builders, and Defenders of the Republic, and of the Men and Women who are Doing the Work and Moulding the Thought of the Present Time, The. Multi-volumes. New York: James T. White & Company, 1877-1959.

North, Douglas C. *The Economic Growth of the United States, 1790-1860.* Englewood Cliffs, N. J.: Prentice-Hall, 1961.

Norton, Mary Beth. *Liberty's Daughters: The Revolutionary Experience of American Women, 1750-1800.* Boston: Little, Brown, 1980.

Peck, M. Scott. *The Different Drum: Community Making and Peace.* New York: Simon & Shuster, 1987.

Perrin, Steven Wayne. "Nothing but Water: The Rise of Temperance and the Emergence of the American Temperance Society". Ph.D. dissertation, Southern Illinois University at Carbondale, 1990.

Pratt, David H. *English Quakers and the First Industrial Revolution: A Study of the Quaker Community in Four Industrial Counties—Lancashire, York, Warwick, and Gloucester, 1750-1830*. Peter Mathias, ed. British Economic History: A Garland Series. New York: Garland Publishing, Inc., 1985.

Punshon, John. *Portrait in Grey: A Short History of the Quakers*. London: Quaker Home Service, 1984.

Radbill, Kenneth Alan. "Socioeconomic Background of Nonpacifist Quakers During the American Revolution". Ph.D. Dissertation, the University of Arizona, 1971.

Rasmussen, Wayne D., ed. *Readings in the History of American Agriculture*. Urbana: University of Illinois Press, 1960.

Reid, John Philip. *The Concept of Liberty in the Age of the American Revolution*. Chicago: University of Chicago Press, 1988.

Ritter, Abraham. *Philadelphia and Her Merchants, as Constituted Fifty to Seventy Years Ago, Illustrated by diagrams of the River Front, and Portraits of Some of its Prominent Occupants, Together with Sketches of Character, and Incidents and Anecdotes of the Day*. Philadelphia: Published by the Author, 1860.

Rivinus, Willis M. *Early Taverns of Bucks County*. New Hope, Penna.: 1965.

Rorabaugh, W. J. *The Alcoholic Republic: An American Tradition*. New York: Oxford University Press, 1979.

Russell, Elbert. *The History of Quakerism*. Richmond, Ind.: Friends United Press, 1979.

Sabine, Lorenzo. *Biographical Sketches of Loyalists of the American Revolution with An Historical Essay*. 2 vols. Boston: 1864. Reprinted by Baltimore: Genealogical Publishing Co., Inc., 1979.

Schwartz, Sally. *"A Mixed Multitude": The Struggle for Toleration in Colonial Pennsylvania*. N. Y.: New York University Press, 1987.

Scott, Charles E. *Farmers' National Bank of Bucks County, Bristol, Pennsylvania: A Century's Record, 1814-1915*. Bristol: 1914.

Sellers, Charles. *The Market Revolution: Jacksonian America, 1815-1846*. New York: Oxford University Press, 1991.

Selsam, J. Paul. *The Pennsylvania Constitution of 1776: A Study in Revolutionary Democracy*. Philadelphia: University of Pennsylvania Press, 1936.

Sewell, Richard H. *Ballots for Freedom: Antislavery Politics in the United States, 1837-1860*. New York: Oxford University Press, 1976.

Shammas, Carole, Marylynn Salmon, and Michel Dahlin. *Inheritance in America From Colonial Times to the Present*. New Brunswick, N. J.: Rutgers University Press, 1987.

Sharpless, Isaac. *The Quaker Boy on the Farm and at School*. Philadelphia: The Biddle Press, 1908.

Sheeran, Michael J. *Beyond Majority Rule: Voteless Decisions in the Religious Society of Friends*. Philadelphia: Philadelphia Yearly Meeting of the Religious Society of Friends, 1983.

Shepherd, William Robert. *History of Proprietary Government in Pennsylvania*. Studies in History, Economics and Public Law, Vol. 6. New York: Columbia University, 1896.

Shorter, Edward. *The Making of the Modern Family.* New York: Basic Books, 1975.

Siebert, Wilbur H. *The Loyalists of Pennsylvania.* Contributions in History and Political Science, No. 5. Columbus: Ohio State University, 1920.

Silbey, Joel H. *The Partisan Imperative: The Dynamics of American Politics Before the Civil War.* New York: Oxford University Press, 1985.

_____. *The Transformation of American Politics, 1840-1860.* Englewood Cliffs, N. J.: Prentice-Hall, 1967.

Smedley, Katherine. *Martha Schofield and the Re-Education of the South, 1839-1916.* Studies in Women and Religion, Vol. 24. Lewiston, N. Y.: The Edwin Mellen Press, 1987.

Smedley, R. C. *History of the Underground Railroad in Chester and the Neighboring Counties of Pennsylvania.* (orig. 1883.) New York: Negro Universities Press, reprinted 1968.

Smith, Barbara Clark. *After the Revolution: The Smithsonian History of Everyday Life in the Eighteenth Century.* New York: Pantheon Books [for] National Museum of American History, 1985.

_____. "The Politics of Price Control in Revolutionary Massachusetts, 1774-1780". Ph.D. dissertation, Yale University, 1983.

Smith-Rosenberg, Carroll. *Disorderly Conduct: Visions of Gender in Victorian America.* New York: Alfred A. Knopf, 1985.

Snyder, Charles McCool. *The Jacksonian Heritage: Pennsylvania Politics 1833-1848.* Harrisburg: Pennsylvania Historical and Museum Commission, 1958.

Soderlund, Jean R. *Quakers & Slavery: A Divided Spirit.* Princeton: Princeton University Press, 1985.

Stackhouse, William R. *The Stackhouse Family, Part I: History of the Stackhouse Family from 1086 to 1935.* Marion, S. C.: 1935.

Steere, Douglas V., ed. *Quaker Spirituality: Selected Writings.* New York: Paulist Press, 1984.

Stember, Sol. *The Bicentennial Guide to the American Revolution.* Vol. 2. *The Middle Colonies.* New York: Saturday Review Press/E. P. Dutton & Co., Inc., 1974.

Stevens, Sylvester Kirby. *County Government and Archives in Pennsylvania.* Harrisburg, Pa.: Pennsylvania Historical and Museum Commission, 1947.

Stoneburner, Carol and John Stoneburner, eds. *The Influence of Quaker Women on American History: Biographical Studies.* Studies in Women and Religion, Vol. 21. Lewiston/Queenston: The Edwin Mellon Press, 1986.

Swartley, Willard M. *Slavery Sabbath War and Women: Case Issues in Biblical Interpretation.* Scottdale, Penna.: Herald Press, 1983.

Swatzler, David. *A Friend Among the Senecas: The Quaker Mission to Cornplanter's People.* Mechanicsburg, Pa.: Stackpole Books, 2000.

Sykes, John. *The Quakers: A New Look at Their Place in Society.* Philadelphia: J. B. Lippincott Company, 1959.

Taber, William P., Jr. *Eye of Faith: A History of Ohio Yearly Meeting, Conservative.* Barnesville, Ohio: Representative Meeting of Ohio Yearly Meeting, Religious Society of Friends, 1985.

Taylor, Francis R. *Life of William Savery of Philadelphia 1750-1804.* New York: The Macmillan Company, 1925.

Taylor, George Rogers, ed. *Jackson versus Biddle: The Struggle over the Second Bank of the United States.* Problems in American Civilization. Boston: D. C. Heath and Company, 1949.

Thomas, Allen Clapp. *The Attitude of the Society of Friends Towards Slavery in the Seventeenth and Eighteenth Centuries, Particularly in Relation to its own Members.* American Society of Church History Papers (1897). 8:263-99

Thomas, Allen C., and Richard H. Thomas. *A History of the Society of Friends in America.* American Church History Series. Philadelphia: John C. Winston & Co., 1895.

Tinkcom, Harry Marlin. *The Republicans and Federalists in Pennsylvania 1790-1801: A Study in National Stimulus and Local Response.* Harrisburg: Pennsylvania Historical and Museum Commission, 1950.

Tolles, Frederick B. *Meeting House and Counting House: The Quaker Merchants of Colonial Philadelphia, 1682-1763.* Chapel Hill, N.C.: University of North Carolina Press, 1948. New York: Norton Library paperback, 1963.

_____. *Quakers and the Atlantic Culture.* New York: The Macmillan Company, 1960.

Tully, Alan. *William Penn's Legacy: Politics and Social Structure in Provincial Pennsylvania, 1726-1755.* Baltimore: The Johns Hopkins University Press, 1977.

Turner, Edward Raymond. *The Negro in Pennsylvania: Slavery, Servitude, Freedom, 1639-1861.* Washington, D. C.: The American Historical Association, 1911.

Tyrrell, Ian R. *Sobering Up: From Temperance to Prohibition in Antebellum America, 1800-1860.* Westport, Conn.: Greenwood Press, 1979.

Walker, Joseph E. *Hopewell Village: A Social and Economic History of an Ironmaking Community.* Philadelphia: University of Pennsylvania Press, 1966.

Wallace, Anthony F. C. *Rockdale: The Growth of an American Village in the Early Industrial Revolution. An Account of the coming of the machines, the making of a new way of life in the mill hamlets, the triumph of evangelical capitalists over socialists and infidels, and the transformation of the workers into Christian soldiers in a cotton-manufacturing district in Pennsylvania in the years before and during the Civil War.* New York: Alfred A. Knopf, 1978.

Walvin, James. *The Quakers: Money and Morals.* London: John Murray, 1997.

Watts, Steven. *The Republic Reborn: War and the Making of Liberal America, 1790-1820.* New Studies in American Intellectual and Cultural History. Baltimore, Md.: The Johns Hopkins University Press, 1987.

Weber, Max. Trans. and ed. by H. H. Gerth and C. Wright Mills. *From Max Weber: Essays in Sociology.* New York: A Galaxy Book, 1958.

Wells, Robert Vale. "A Demographic Analysis of Some Middle Colony Quaker Families of the Eighteenth Century." Ph.D. Dissertation, Princeton University, 1969.
Westcott, Thompson. *Names of Persons who took the Oath of Allegiance to the State of Pennsylvania, Between the Years 1777 and 1789, with a History of the "Test Laws" of Pennsylvania.* Philadelphia: John Campbell, 1865.
Who Was Who in America 1607-1896. rev. ed. Chicago: Marquis Who's Who, 1967.
Wilber, Ken. *A Theory of Everything: An Integral Vision for Business, Politics, Science, and Spiritualty.* Boston: Shambhala, 2000.
Willard, Bradford. *Pennsylvania Geology Summarized* . . . . Educational Series, No. 4. Pennsylvania Department of Environmental Resources, Bureau of Topographic and Geologic Survey, 1976.
Williams, George W. *History of the Negro Race in America From 1619 to 1880: Negroes as Slaves, as Soldiers, and as Citizens* . . . . New York: G. P. Putnam's Sons, 1882.
Williamson, Chilton. *American Suffrage: From Property to Democracy, 1760-1860.* Princeton, N. J.: Princeton University Press, 1960.
Woody, Thomas. *Early Quaker Education in Pennsylvania.* Contributions to Education, No. 105. N. Y.: Teachers College, Columbia University, 1920.
Wyatt-Brown, Bertram. *Southern Honor: Ethics and Behavior in the Old South.* New York: Oxford University Press, 1982.
Zilversmit, Arthur. *The First Emancipation: The Abolition of Slavery in the North.* Chicago: University of Chicago Press, 1967.
Zuckerman, Michael, ed. *Friends and Neighbors: Group Life in America's First Plural Society.* Philadelphia: Temple University Press, 1982.

Essays

Anonymous. "Bucks County Quakers in the Revolution", *Pennsyslvania Genealogical Magazine* 24 (1966): 291-99, continued in 25 (1967): 18-31.
Bacon, Margaret Hope. "A Widening Path: Women in Philadelphia Yearly Meeting Move Towards Equality, 1681-1955", *Friends in the Delaware Valley: Philadelphia Yearly Meeting 1681-1981,* ed. by John M. Moore. 173-199. Haverford, Penna.: Friends Historical Association, 1981.
Balderston, Marion. "William Penn's Twenty-three Ships, with Notes on Some of Their Passengers", *Pennsylvania Genealogical Magazine* 23 (1963) 27-67.
Barbour, Hugh. "Quaker Prophetesses and Mothers in Israel" in *Seeking the Light: Essays in Quaker History,* ed. by J. William Frost and John M. Moore. Wallingford & Haverford: Pendle Hill Publications & Friends Historical Association, 1986.
Barker, William Halsey Jr. "Leadership in Bucks County Agricultural Societies in the Nineteenth Century". Senior thesis for B.A., History Department, Princeton University, 1962.

Bausman, R. O., and J. A. Monroe, eds. "James Tilton's Notes on the Agriculture of Delaware in 1788", *Agricultural History* 20 (1946):176-187.

Blankenburg, Lucretia L. "A Story of My Branch of the Longshore Family" in *A Collection of Papers Read Before the Bucks County Historical Society*, 8 vols., Doylestown, Pa.: Published for the Bucks County Historical Society by the Fackenthal Fund, 1932. 6:526-535.

Bocella, Kathy. "Holding Their Ground on Revolutionary Claim", *Philadelphia Inquirer*, Oct. 4, 1991, B1.

Bockelman, Wayne L. "Local Government in Colonial Pennsylvania" in *Town and County: Essays on the Structure of Local Government in the American Colonies.* ed. by Bruce C. Daniels. Middletown, Conn.: Wesleyan University Press, 1978. 216-237.

Bockleman, Wayne L., and Owen S. Ireland. "The Internal Revolution in Pennsylvania: An Ethnic-Religious Interpretation", *Pennsylvania History* 41 (1974):125-159.

Boulding, Elise. "Mapping the Inner Journey of Quaker Women" in *The Influence of Quaker Women on American History*, ed. by Carol and John Stoneburner, Studies in Women and Religion, Vol. 21. Lewiston/Queenston: The Edwin Mellon Press, 1986.

Bowen, David Edward. "Quaker Orthodoxy and Jacksonian Democracy: An Interpretation of the Hicksite Separation". M.A. Thesis, Swarthmore College, 1968.

Bronner, Edwin B. "Review of *A People Among Peoples: Quaker Benevolence in Eighteenth-Century America* by Sydney V. James". *Quaker History* 52 (Spring 1963):41.

Brown, Ira V. "Pennsylvania's Antislavery Pioneers, 1688-1776", *Pennsylvania History* 55 (April 1988):59-77.

Brown, Richard D. "Modernization and the Modern Personality in Early America, 1600-1865: A Sketch of a Synthesis", *Journal of Interdisciplinary History* 2 (winter 1972):201-228.

Buck, William J. "Jeremiah Langhorne", *Pennsylvania Magazine of History and Biography* 7 (1883):67-87.

Butler, Jon. "'Gospel Order Improved': The Keithian Schism and the Exercise of Quaker Ministerial Authority in Pennsylvania", *William and Mary Quarterly*, ser. 3, 31 (July 1974):431-452.

Cadbury, Henry J. "Eighteenth Century Slaves as Advertised by their Masters", *Journal of Negro History* 1 (April 1916):163-216.

———. "George Fox and Women's Liberation", *The Friends Quarterly* 18 (October 1974):370-76.

———. "Negro Membership in the Society of Friends", *Journal of Negro History* 21 (April 1936):151-213.

Carr, Lois Green, and Lorena S. Walsh. "The Standard of Living in the Colonial Chesapeake", *William and Mary Quarterly* 65 (January 1988):135-159.

Carroll, Kenneth L. "A Look at the 'Quaker Revival of 1756'", *Quaker History* 65 (Autumn 1976):63-80.

_____. "George Fox and Slavery", *Quaker History*, 86, no. 2 (Fall 1997):16-25.

Day, A. Bradley. "New York Friends and the Loyalty Oath of 1778", *Quaker History* 57 (Autumn, 1968):112-114.

Doherty, Robert W. "Non-Urban Friends and the Hicksite Separation", *Pennsylvania History* 33 (1966):432-445.

_____. "Religion and Society: The Hicksite Separation of 1827", *American Quarterly* 17 (Spring 1965):63-80.

Drake, Thomas E. "Review of *Puritan Boston and Quaker Philadelphia: Two Protestant Ethics and the Spirit of Class Authority and Leadership*, by E. Digby Baltzell". *Friends Journal* 26 (15 October 1980):27-28.

Dunn, Mary Maples. "Saints and Sisters: Congregational and Quaker Women in the Early Colonial Period", *American Quarterly* 30 (1978):582-601.

_____. "Women of Light", in *Women of America: A History*, ed. by Carol R. Berkin and Mary Beth Norton. Boston: Houghton Mifflin Company, 1979. 114-133.

Eastburn, Samuel C. "Early Mills", Series on local history, *Delaware Valley Advance*, 20 June 1929.

_____. Series on Local History. *Delaware Valley Advance*, 12 and 26 December 1929.

Easterlin, Richard A. "Factors in the Decline of Farm Family Fertility in the United States: Some Preliminary Research Results", in *The American Family in Social-Historical Perspective*, 2nd ed. ed. by Michael Gordon. New York: St. Martin's Press, 1987, 533-45.

Fager, Chuck. "Review of *Puritan Boston and Quaker Philadelphia: Two Protestant Ethics and the Spirit of Class Authority and Leadership* by E. Digby Baltzell", *Friendly Letter* 1 (Eleventh month 1981):2-3.

Forbush, Bliss. "Elias Hicks—Prophet of an Era", *The Bulletin of Friends Historical Association* 38 (Spring 1949).

Frost, J. William. "As the Twig is Bent: Quaker Ideas of Childhood", *Quaker History* 60 (Autumn 1971):67-87.

_____. "The Origins of the Quaker Crusade Against Slavery: A Review of Recent Literature", *Quaker History* 67 (Spring 1978):56-58.

Gara, Larry. "Friends and the Underground Railroad", *Quaker History* 51 (Spring 1962):3-19.

Gibson, George H. "Fullers, Carders, and Manufacturers of Woolen Goods in Delaware", *Delaware History* 12 (April 1966):25-53.

Grundy, Martha Paxson. "Are Outcasts Cast Out?: Disownment, Inheritance, and Participation in Middletown Monthly Meeting", *Mercer Mosaic: The Journal of the Bucks County Historical Society* 4 (Spring 1987):41-44.

_____. "How Early Friends Understood the Bible", *Reclaiming a Resource: Papers of the 1989 Friends Bible Conference*, ed. by Chuck Fager. Falls Church, Va.: Kimo Press, 1990. 65-84.

_____. "The Paxson Brothers of Colonial Pennsylvania: the First Three Generations", *National Genealogical Society Quarterly* 71 (September

1983):193-216.
Guenther, Karen. "A Crisis of Allegiance: Berks County, Pennsylvania Quakers and the War for Independence", *Quaker History* 90, no. 2 (Fall 2001):15-34.
Hall, Peter Dobkin. "Family Structure and Economic Organization: Massachusetts Merchants, 1700-1850", *Family and Kin in Urban Communities, 1700-1930,* ed. by Tamara K. Hareven. New York: New Viewpoints, A Division of Franklin Watts, 1977. 38-61.
Hamm, Thomas D. "The Hicksite Quaker World, 1875-1900", *Quaker History*, 89, no. 2 (Fall 2000), 17-41.
Hareven, Tamara K. "The Family as Process: The Historical Study of the Family Cycle," *Journal of Social History* 7 (1974):322-329.
Haskell, Thomas L. "Capitalism and the Origins of the Humanitarian Sensibility, Part I", *American Historical Review* 90 (April 1985):339-61, and "Part 2", *Ibid.* (July 1985):547-66.
Henretta, James A. "Families and Farms: *Mentalité* in Pre-Industrial America", *William and Mary Quarterly*, 3rd ser., 35 (January 1978):3-32.
Hicks, Sarah W. "The Life and Expatriation of Judge Gilbert Hicks", *Papers*, BCHS, 7:247-255.
Isaac, Rhys. "Evangelical Revolt: The Nature of the Baptists' Challenge to the Traditional Order in Virginia, 1765-1775", *William and Mary Quarterly*, 3rd ser., 31 (October 1974):345-368. This is reprinted in Katz and Murrin, eds. *Colonial America.* 518-540.
_____. "Preachers and Patriots: Popular Culture and the Revolution in Virginia", *The American Revolution, Explorations in the History of Radicalism,* ed. by Alfred F. Young. DeKalb, Ill.: Northern Illinois University Press, 1976. 127-156.
James, Sydney V. "The Impact of the American Revolution on Quaker Ideas about Their Sect", *William and Mary Quarterly,* 3rd ser., 29 (1962):360-382.
_____. "Quaker Meetings and Education in the Eighteenth Century", *Quaker History*, 51 (1962):87-102.
Laidig, Gary L., Wayne A. Schutjer, and C. Shannon Stokes. "Agricultural Variation and Human Fertility in Antebellum Pennsylvania", *Journal of Family History* 6 (summer 1981):195-204.
Laubach, David. "Philadelphia vs. Boston Beginnings," *Friends Journal,* 29 (15 May 1983):16-17.
Levy, Barry J. "'Tender Plants': Quaker Farmers and Children in the Delaware Valley, 1681-1735", *Colonial America: Essays in Politics and Social Development,* ed. by Stanley N. Katz and John M. Murrin. 3rd ed. New York: Alfred A. Knopf, 1983, 177-203.
Lindstrom, Diane. "American Economic Growth before 1840: New Evidence and New Directions," *Journal of Economic History,* 39 (1979):289-301.
Little, Craig B. "Horse Thief Pursuing Companies of Nineteenth-Century Bucks County", *Mercer Mosaic: The Journal of the Bucks County Historical*

Society 3 (January/February 1986):5-18.
Main, Gloria L. "The Standard of Living in Southern New England, 1640-1773". *William and Mary Quarterly* 3rd ser., 45 (January 1988):124-134.
Marietta, Jack. "A Note on Quaker Membership". *Quaker History* 5 (Spring 1970):40-43.
_____. "Egoism and Altruism in Quaker Abolition". *Quaker History*, 82, no. 1 (Spring 1993):1-22.
_____. "Quaker Family Education in Historical Perspective". *Quaker History* 63 (Spring 1974):3-16.
Maxey, David W. "New Light on Hannah Barnard, a Quaker 'Heretic'," *Quaker History,* 78 (Fall 1989):61-86.
McNealy, Terry A. "Justice in Revolt: Bucks County Political Leaders, 1774-1776", *Mercer Mosaic: The Journal of the Bucks County Historical Society* 2 (May/June 1985):7-18.
Merrill, Michael. "Cash is Good to Eat: Self Sufficiency and Exchange in the Rural Economy of the United States", *Radical History Review* 14 (1977): 12-71.
Michel, Jack. "'In a Manner and Fashion Suitable to Their Degree': A Preliminary Investigation of the Material Culture of Early Pennsylvania", Glenn Porter and William H. Mulligan, Jr., eds. *Working Papers from the Regional Economic History Research Center.* 5 (1981).
Molovinsky, Lemuel. "Tax Collecting Problems in Revolutionary Pennsylvania", *Pennsylvania History* 47 (July 1980):253-259.
Nash, Gary B. "The Framing of Government in Pennsylvania: Ideas in Contact with Reality", *William and Mary Quarterly*, 3rd ser., 23 (April 1966): 183-209.
_____. "Slaves and Slaveholders in Colonial Philadelphia", *William and Mary Quarterly*, 3rd ser., 30 (April 1973):222-256.
Norton, Susan L. "Marital Migration in Essex County, Massachusetts, in the Colonial and Early Federal Periods," *Journal of Marriage and the Family* 35 (August 1973):406-418.
Osterud, Nancy, and John Fulton. "Family Limitation and Age at Marriage: Fertility Decline in Sturbridge, Massachusetts, 1730-1850," *Population Studies* 30 (November 1976):481-494.
Ousterhout, Anna M. "Opponents of the Revolution Whose Pennsylvania Estates Were Confiscated", *Pennsylvania Genealogical Magazine* 33 (1978).
Paxson, Thomas D. Jr. "The Peace Testimony of the Religious Society of Friends" in Jeffrey Gros and John D. Rempel, eds., *The Fragmentation of the Church and Its Unity in Peacemaking.* Grand Rapids, Mich.: William B. Eerdmans Publishing Company, 2001, 103-118.
Pullinger, Edna Stover. "Edward Hicks, Newtown Coach Painter, Among Friends". *The Bucks County Historical Society Journal* 2 (Fall 1979):202-224.
_____."Panic and Panacea: Edward Hicks Deplores Overspeculation in the 1830's And the Silkworm Mania That Followed", *George School Bulletin,*

(March 1978). 1-3.
Richardson, Mrs. Joshua. Account for the DAR in 1954, quoted in the *Delaware Valley Advance*, 22 July 1965. 1B.
Rivinus, Willis M. "The Maps & Atlases of Bucks County: American Social History", *The Bucks County Historical Society Journal* 2 (Spring 1979). 159-177.
Roach, Hannah Benner. "The Pennsylvania Militia in 1777", *Pennsylvania Genealogical Magazine* 23 (1964):161-230.
Roeber, A. G. "J. H. C. Helmuth, Evangelical Charity, and the Public Sphere in Pennsylvania, 1793-1800", *Pennsylvania Magazine of History and Biography* 121 (January/April 1997):77-100.
Rothenbery, Winifred B. "The Market and Massachusetts Farmers, 1750-1855", *Journal of Economic History* 41 (June 1981):283-314.
Sachs, William S. "Agricultural Conditions in the Northern Colonies before the Revolution," *Journal of Economic History* 13 (1953):274-290.
Salmon, Marylynn. "Equality or Submersion: Covert Status in Early Pennsylvania." *Women of America: A History*, ed. by Carol R. Berkin and Mary Beth Norton. Boston: Houghton Mifflin Co., 114-133.
Schmidt, Leigh Eric. "'A Church-going People are a Dress-loving People': Clothes, Communication, and Religious Culture in Early America". *Church History* 58 (March 1989):36-51.
Simler, Lucy. "Tenancy in Colonial Pennsylvania: The Case of Chester County", *William and Mary Quarterly*, 3rd ser., 43 (October 1986):542-569.
_____. "The Township: The Community of the Rural Pennsylvanian," *Pennsylvania Magazine of History and Biography* 106 (January, 1982):41-68.
Smedley, Katherine. "Martha Schofield's Struggle for Social Justice", *Friends Journal* 29 (1 May 1983):4-7.
Smith, Daniel Scott. "Family Limitation, Sexual Control, and Domestic Feminism in Victorian America" in *Clio's Consciousness Raised: New Perspectives on the History of Women*, ed. by Mary Hartman and Lois W. Banner. New York: Harper Torchbooks, 1974, 119-136.
Stille, Charles J. "The Attitude of the Quakers in the Provincial Wars," *Pennsylvania Magazine of History and Biography* 10 (1886):294-307.
Taber, William. "Toward a Broader Quaker Message", *Friends Journal* 30 (1 February 1984):6-7.
Thompson, Louis Ely. "An Introduction to the Loyalists of Bucks County and Some Queries Concerning Them," *A Collection of Papers Read Before the Bucks County Historical Society*. 8 vols. Doylestown, Pa.: Published for the Bucks County Historical Society by the Fackenthal Fund, 1937. 7:204-234.
Thorne, Judith Z. "Earnest and Solemn Protest: Quaker Anti-Slavery Petitions to Congress, 1831-1865". *Quaker History*, 88, no. 2 (Fall 1999):47-50.
Tolles, Frederick B. "The New-Light Quakers of Lynn and New Bedford", *New England Quarterly* 32 (Sept. 1959):291-319.

Turner, Edward Raymond. "The Abolition of Slavery in Pennsylvania", *Pennsylvania Magazine of History and Biography* 36 (1912):129-142.

_____. "Slavery in Colonial Pennsylvania," *Pennsylvania Magazine of History and Biography* 35 (1911): 141-151.

Vann, Richard T. "Nurture and Conversion in the Early Quaker Family", *Journal of Marriage and the Family* 31 (1969):639-643.

Wellenreuther, Hermann. "The Political Dilemma of the Quakers in Pennsylvania, 1681-1748", *Pennsylvania Magazine of History and Biography* 94 (1970): 135-72.

Wells, Robert V. "Family History," *Journal of Social History* 9 (1975):11-12.

_____. "Family Size and Fertility Control in Eighteenth-Century America: A Study of Quaker Families", *Population Studies* 25 (March 1971):73-82.

_____. "Quaker Marriage Patterns in a Colonial Perspective", *William and Mary Quarterly*, series 3, 29 (July 1972):415-442.

Wendel, Thomas. "The Keith-Lloyd Alliance: Factional and Coalition Politics in Colonial Pennsylvania", *Pennsylvania Magazine of History and Biography* 92 (1968):289-305.

Wilson, Roger. "Friends in the Nineteenth Century", *The Friends Quarterly*, 8 (23 October 1984):353-63.

_____. "The Road to Manchester, 1895" in *Seeking the Light: Essays in Quaker History in Honor of Edwin B. Bronner*. ed. by J. William Frost and John M. Moore. Wallingford & Haverford, Penna.: Pendle Hill Publications & Friends Historical Association, 1986, 145-62.

Winston, Lindley M. "Did Philadelphia Quakers Really Fail?", *Friends Journal* 31 (15 March 1985):14-16.

Young, Margaret Sery. "Quaker Women and Medical Practice in the Nineteenth Century" in *The Influence of Quaker Women on American History*, ed. by Carol and John Stoneburner. Studies in Women and Religion, Vol. 21. Lewiston/Queenston: The Edwin Mellon Press, 1986.

Index

Abington 99, 100
Abolition 71, 170, 175, 179, 187, 189, 190, 192
    See also Antislavery
Adams, John Quincy 168, 219
Affirmation of allegiance 70, 78, 83, 87, 88, 94, 99, 170, 229
African Americans 19, 58, 69, 72-77, 171, 174, 175, 187, 188, 190, 193, 195, 197, 200, 210, 218, 219
    civil rights 174
    freed 19, 72, 174
    suffrage 174, 175
    See also Negroes, Racism, Slavery, *and* Slaves
Agricultural societies 112, 117, 194
Agriculture
    market farming 3, 109, 128
    subsistence family farming 3, 129
Alcohol 180-182
Allen family 15, 141, 149, 150, 153, 158, 166, 252-53
    Benjamin 151
    David 151
    Elizabeth C. 248
    Emma A. 248
    James W. 243
    Jane 139, 235
    John 33, 142, 144, 153, 184, 185, 235
    Joseph 86, 113, 128, 235
    Joseph W. 168, 171
    Marmaduke 194, 248
    Marmaduke W. 150, 168, 194, 196
    Martha 139, 158, 248
    Mary 235
    Mary (Clothier) 235
    Rachel 139
    Rebecca 235
    Robert J. 248
    Samuel 48, 52, 148, 150-1, 168, 219, 235, 243
    Samuel (1782-1868) 151
    Sarah 48, 139, 148, 235, 243
    Sarah E. 247
    Sarah (Gaskill) 151
    Sarah (Taylor) 150, 245
    Sarah Rodman (Paxson) 150
    Susanna Marmaduke (Watson) 127
    Tacy (Stackhouse) 153
    Thomas L., Dr. 113, 126-128, 139, 142, 145, 150, 153, 158, 168, 171, 188, 189, 191, 211, 248
    William (ca. 1715-1791) 52, 235
    William (1757-1818) 153,
    William (1759-1837) 97, 139, 142, 145, 149, 158, 168, 203
    William, Jr. (1789-1856) 139, 168, 203, 248
Alsop, Mary 235
American Temperance Society 180
Anglican 32
Antislavery 5, 57-73, 90, 131, 160, 188, 228
    See also Abolition
Antislavery petitions 189, 218
Appleby, Joyce 135, 146, 177
Arbuckle, James 235
Ashburn, William 235
Atkinson, Margaret 235
Attleborough 105, 183
Attleborough Protective Company 195, 196, 198
Auping, John 5
Authority 54, 77, 81, 92, 158
Banking 109-11
Bank of the United States as a political issue 167, 171-172, 173
Baptists 24, 31, 85
Barbour, Hugh 122, 327, 338
Barnard, Hannah (Jenkins) 124
Bartholomew, Thomas 235
Baynes, Elizabeth 235
    Janet 235

Baynes, Thomas 235
Beck, Don 6, 327
Bedminster Township 24, 25, 220
Benezet, Anthony 39, 71, 180, 299
Bensalem Township 24, 25, 32, 76, 126, 142, 145, 151, 165, 168, 209, 210, 212, 214, 215, 220
Besanzon, Anne 27, 327
Bettle, Samuel 135
Bible societies 126, 127, 194, 226
Biddle, Nicholas 171
Biles, Ann Mary 46
    Charles 235
Black people *See* African Americans
Blakey, family 15, 51, 147, 148, 158, 254-55
    Achsahanna 245
    Anna 245
    Anna S. 245
    Caroline 245
    Edward H. 245
    Elizabeth 245
    Elizabeth S. 245
    Elizabeth W. 245
    George 245
    Henry C. 245
    Jael (Bickerdike) 50, 235
    James W. 245
    John 142, 144, 245
    Joshua 50, 66, 84, 87, 97, 158, 235
    Letitia 245
    Lydia 235
    Lydia W. 245
    Mary Ann 245
    Paxson 194, 196, 245
    Phebe 234, 245
    Rachel 148
    Sarah 234, 245
    Sarah, Jr. 245
    Sarah L. 245
    Susan G. 245
    Tacy 148
    Thomas 245
    William (1697-1750) 50, 52, 235
    William (1739-1822) 12, 62, 66, 75, 85-86, 97, 111, 117, 125, 126, 144, 158, 159, 164, 235
    William [Jr.] (1759-1831) 97, 142, 144, 168
    William (1811-1862) 196, 210, 219, 245
    William T. 245
    William W[atson] 168, 171, 196, 245
Blankenburg, Lucretia M. (Longshore) 218, 321
    Rudolph 218
Bogan, ___ 89
Book of Discipline 21, 165, 176, 182, 229
Boos, Kasey 211

Borden family 247
Boston Port Bill 78
Bradley, Patricia 71
Braithwaite, William C. 18, 328
Bridgetown 30
Briggs, family 245
    Hannah 235
    John 235
    Margret 235
    Mary 235
    Mary (Croasdale) 235
    Mary (Watson) 235
    William, Jr. 235
Brinton, Howard 6, 9, 328
Bristol Borough 24, 26, 29, 31, 32, 110, 128, 168, 171, 214, 219
Bristol Meeting 23, 24, 137, 138, 212, 243-44
Bristol Township 24, 25, 32, 33, 63, 92, 126, 150, 151, 190, 214, 220
Brown, Richard D. 109, 339
Bryan, George 71
Buckingham Meeting 23, 59, 68, 76, 79, 80, 89, 92, 106, 181, 185, 194, 217
Buckingham Township 24, 25, 183, 190, 220
Buckingham Female Anti Slavery Society 188
Buckman, Abner 247
    Edwin D. 243
    James 243
    John 248
    John, Jr. 148, 203, 205
    John B. 248
    Joshua V. 243
    Macre 248
    Macre (Comfort) 203
    Macre (Stackhouse) 205
    Martha 248
    Mary (Knight) 243
    Mercy 248
    Rebecca E. 243
    Rebecca T. 243
    Susanna 248
Bucks County Agriculture Society 112, 194
Bucks County Anti Slavery Society (male) 188, 189
Bucks County Intelligencer 115, 168, 171, 173, 174, 192, 217, 219
Bucks County Medical Society 194
Bucks County Silk Society 116
Bucks Quarter 24, 42, 65, 70, 180, 194, 216
Bucks Quarterly Meeting 23, 47, 58, 62, 136, 137, 140, 185, 219
Bunting, family 245
    Jeremiah 184, 186
Burgess family 245, 248
Burlington 22, 69, 99

Burr, George 211
Bustleton and Somerton Turnpike Company 108, 114
Bustleton Turnpike Company 113
Byberry Meeting 24, 76, 165, 168, 189, 212
Byberry Township 14, 116, 165, 189
Cadbury, Henry J. 76, 339
Cadwallader family 245
Calvinism 38, 134-135
Camden and Amboy Railroad 69
Canby, family 148, 149
   John P. 245
   Joseph 245
   Joshua C. 113
   Margaret P. 245
   Mary 245
   Mary H. 245
   Sarah 245
Carlile, Hannah 245
   John 235
   Samuel 235
Carter, Martha 245
   Rachel 235
   Sarah 235
   Sarah [Jr.] 235
Cary/Carey, Ann 236
   Bethula 236
   Elizabeth 243
   Hannahmeel 236
   Mary C. 245
   Sampson 235
   Samuel 235, 236
   Sarah 46, 50, 236
   Sarah (Stackhouse) 235
   Thomas (b 7/7/1750) 236
Chalkley, Thomas 40, 299
Chapman, John 80
Charter of Privileges (of 1701) 78, 81
Cherokee Indians 219
   removal of 171-173, 175
Chester County 51, 86, 97, 129, 141, 146, 211
Chester Quarter 42
Child, Maria 74, 329
Churchman, John 40, 322
Clarkson, Thomas 19, 322
Collison, Robert 59, 60, 236, 239
Colonization Society 188, 189
Comfort, family 15, 51, 99, 129, 141, 147-149, 156-158, 166, 226, 256-57
   Aaron 149
   Ann C. 148
   Anna E. 248
   Clara 248
   David 116
   Elizabeth 139, 248
   Elizabeth, Jr. 248
   Elizabeth (James) 203, 205
   Ezra 72, 99, 157, 236
   George 194
   Jeremiah (1750-1780), 99, 236
   Jesse 30, 196, 248
   John 156, 236
   Mary 189
   Mary (Woolman) 156
   Mary Ann 248
   Mercy (Croasdale) 48, 50, 54, 99, 100, 157, 236
   Mercy Ann (Stackhouse) 148
   Miriam 243
   Moses 99, 189
   Moses, Jr. 189
   Rebecca 189
   Robert 99
   Samuel (1778-1860) 112, 113, 139, 142, 143, 145, 157, 189, 203, 205, 207, 211, 212, 219, 248
   Samuel, Jr. (1818-1881) 196, 212, 148, 168, 189, 210, 211, 212, 248
   Samuel F. 248
   Sarah 139
   Sarah (Stackhouse) 148
   Sarah (Stevenson) 145, 157, 203
   Stephen (1720/1-1772) 30, 33, 46, 50, 52, 99, 100, 189, 236, 239
   Stephen, Jr. (1753-1826) 99, 145, 157, 189
Comly family 245
   John 165, 176, 189, 191, 193, 219
Committee of Correspondence 78, 79
Committee of Observation 79-81, 92
Conscription 78, 81, 83
Constant dollars 27, 51, 52, 141, 143, 211, 241
Continental Congress 71, 79, 81
Continental currency 27, 78, 83, 88, 89
Cooper, Hannah 236
Core Creek 30, 68
Cowan, Christopher C. 6, 327
Croasdale, family 15, 100, 147, 258-59
   Abijah 236
   Achsah 236
   Anna 245
   Benjamin 168, 194
   Benjamin R. 245
   Eber 5, 8, 64, 100, 132, 133, 228, 236
   Ezra 52, 100, 168, 171, 236
   Grace 12, 46, 48-50, 54, 72, 88, 164
   Grace (Harding) 236
   Grace (Heaton) 59, 100, 157, 236
   Grace Jr. 100
   Hannah 48, 236, 245
   J. Wilson 196

INDEX

Croasdale, Jeremiah 33, 49, 52, 144, 236
   Jeremiah W. 142, 144, 168, 171, 184, 185, 194, 245
   John 245
   John W. 213
   Jonathan 48
   Macre 236, 245
   Margery (Hayhurst) 48, 54, 100, 236
   Mary R. 245
   Mercy 49
   Phebe 236
   Rachel 236
   Robert 52, 62, 97, 100, 142, 144, 168, 171, 194, 236, 239
   Robert Morris 245
   Ruth 245
   Sarah 245
   William 33, 46, 52, 59, 60, 236
Crockett, Davy 173
Cutler, Benjamin 236, 239
   Elizabeth 236
   Mercy (Bills) 236
Davenport, Joseph 64, 65
Debt 29, 42, 60, 64, 103, 105, 107, 108, 115, 117, 118
Deism 3, 18, 118, 121
Delaware Canal 113
Delaware County 141, 146
Democratic party 166, 167, 169, 174, 190
Disciplinary offenses: affirmation of allegiance 88
   debt 42, 44, 46, 56, 100, 250
   drinking and drunkenness 3, 35, 36, 42, 44, 65, 92, 100, 149, 180-183, 206, 225, 250
   fornication 42, 44, 51, 56, 68, 153, 225, 250
   marriage of first cousins 47, 48
   marriage out of unity 2, 5, 12, 14, 35, 36, 39, 40, 42, 44, 47, 48, 51, 56, 68-70, 92, 95, 97, 98, 106, 108, 132, 148-150, 154, 156, 163, 164, 182, 202, 203, 206, 207, 228, 250
   military activity 44, 90, 91, 93-95, 97, 250
   neglect of meetings for worship 42, 48
   oaths 100
   office holding 82, 99
   quarreling 42, 46
   slander 42, 184
   slave holding 58, 61, 65, 99
Disciplinary procedure 55, 91
Discipline, enforcement of 40-43, 46, 48, 51, 55-56, 82, 140, 161, 206-8
Disownment 8, 47, 51, 55, 68, 82, 90, 91, 97, 104, 182, 185, 192, 201-2, 206, 208, 232-3
   description of process 41, 55, 91, 140, 185
   meaning of 40-41, 86
   partial disownment 59, 70

Distraint of goods 82-87, 92, 96, 98, 224
Doan, Daniel 236
   John 236
   Mary 236
   Sarah 236
   Thomas 236
Doherty, Robert W. 141, 143, 146, 157, 213, 225, 226, 227, 329, 340
Dow Laws (Maine) 181
Downing family 243
Doylestown Democrat 127, 168, 171, 173
Doylestown Insurance Company 114
Doylestown Township 25, 29, 112, 113, 116, 220
Dungan, Jeremiah 236, 239, 242
Dunkers 81
Dunn, Anna (Heaton) 236
Durham Township 25, 26, 29, 63, 220
Dutch Reformed 24, 31
Dutch settlers 24, 57
Eastburn, Aaron 203, 248
   Anna C. 248
   Cyrus 248
   Elizabeth 248
   Franklin 248
   Grace 248
   Joseph 114, 248
   Mary Ann 248
   Mary C. 248
   Mercy 248
   Samuel 59, 107
   Samuel C. 248
   Sarah C. 248
   Sidney 248
Edwards, Mary 236
Enlightenment 3, 4, 7, 118, 122, 160
Episcopalian church 207
Erikson, Erik 6
Evangelical Friends International 133
Evangelicalism 3, 4, 119, 122-125, 128, 129, 134, 135, 177, 192
Evans, Jonathan 121
   William 157
Eyre family 245
Faith development 4-6, 8, 11, 39, 49, 53, 67, 72, 73, 111, 118, 119, 130, 131, 133, 134, 164, 175, 178, 180, 186, 190, 191, 199, 227-229
Falls Meeting 23, 60, 62, 64, 79, 85, 92, 103, 148, 149, 150, 188, 189, 194, 217
Falls Township 24, 25, 32, 105, 189, 220
Farmers National Bank of Bucks County 105, 109, 110, 113, 128, 146, 151, 171, 172, 185
Farming, *see* Agriculture
Federalist party 167
Female Medical College 127, 160, 170

Ferris, David 39, 322
Field. Ann 236
  Benjamin 236
  Benjamin, Jr. 236
  Joseph 239
  Sarah 236
  Stephen 236
  Susanna 236
Fothergill, Samuel 40
Foulke, Thomas 80
Four Lanes' End 63
Fowler, James W. 6, 330
Fox, George 123, 322
Fox, Judge John 174
French Huguenot settlers 24
Freud, Sigmund 6
Friend, The 14
Friends, Religious Society of
  advices 21, 87-88, 103, 104, 107, 108, 165, 169, 172, 178, 185, 199, 215, 216, 221
  elders 20, 39, 42, 48, 52, 64, 81, 98, 99, 121, 135, 136, 138, 157, 159, 161, 186
  marriage 40-41, 202, 227, 299
  marriage clearness committees 60, 108, 203
  ministry 3, 20, 33, 39, 49, 50, 87,121, 132, 176, 226
  organizational structure 19-21, 135-36
  participation in meeting business 33-35, 202-6, 207-8
  queries 21, 42, 48, 49, 117, 137, 138, 140
  reading epistles 59, 137, 140, 227
  reform 38-56, 132-34, 228
  separation of 1827 3, 4, 14, 119, 120, 127, 129, 131-163, 166, 197, 208, 217, 225-28
  theology 1-2, 37, *See* Inward Christ/ Guide/ Light, *and* Light of Christ
  visiting in families 46, 48, 49, 59
  See also Disciplinary Offenses, Disownment, *and* Testimonies
Friends General Conference 228
Friends Intelligencer 14
Friends Review 14
Friends United Meeting 133
Frost, J. William 122, 132, 228, 330, 340
Fugitive Slave Act 190
Galloway, Joseph 96
George III, King 87
German settlers 24, 26, 197
Gesell, Arnold 6, 330
Gilbert family 245
Gillam, family 15, 95, 147, 260-61
  Ann (Dungan) 95, 236
  Anna M. 246
  Anna Rebecca 246
  Elizabeth P. 246

  Elizabeth Y. (Stackhouse) 148, 246
  Hannah 245
  Hannah C. 245
  Harvey 168, 196, 245
  Harvey H. 245
  Isaac 105, 106, 142, 215
  Jonathan 168, 215
  Jonathan W. 113, 194, 196, 245
  Joshua S. 246
  Laura 246
  Lucas 30, 52, 95, 215, 236, 239
  Mary W. 245
  Richard 246
  Simon 95, 104-106, 113, 184, 196, 215, 245
  Susanna 245
  Susannah 236
  William 113, 142, 144, 148, 168, 194, 215, 246
  William Henry 245
Gillingham, Joseph 113
Great Awakening 38, 122, 131
Green Street Monthly Meeting 138, 159
Gregg, Ann (Maris) 203
  John 60, 61
  Patrick 239
Griffith, Abraham 50, 236
  Elizabeth 236
Growden, Lawrence 32
Gurney, Joseph John 126, 177
Gurneyite Friends 14, 177, 178, 228
Gwynedd Meeting 219
Gwynedd Township 24
Hamm, Thomas D. viii-ix, 127, 133, 177, 331, 341
Hammond, Bray 109, 331
Hampton, Ann (Croasdale) 49, 54, 72, 100, 156
  John 49, 100
Harding, Henry 60, 236
  Jane (Scott, Jr.) 236
  John 236
  Mary (Shaw, Jr.) 236
  Thomas 236
Harker, Adam 74, 236
  Grace 236
Harris, George 236
  Mary 236
Harrison, William Henry 181
Hayhurst, Cuthbert 236
  Deliverance (Bills) 236
  Elizabeth 236
  John 236
  Joseph 236
  Margery 236
  Rachel 236
  Rebecca 236

Hayhurst, Ruth 236
   Thomas 236
   William 236
Heaton, Ann (Carver) 236
   Grace (Pearson) 49
   Robert 49, 74
   Robert, Jr. 236
   Susanna 236
Heston, Alice 236
Hibbs, Ann 236
   William 236
Hicks, Edward 111, 114, 116, 117, 125, 140, 159, 193, 219
   Elias 121, 125, 131, 134, 158, 160
   Gilbert 79
   William 219, 248
Hicksite Friends 3, 10, 14, 125, 130-132, 134, 136, 138-161, 163-64, 166, 177, 180, 182, 183, 188-189, 191-92, 196-97, 199, 200, 202-3, 205-6, 208, 211-214, 216-218, 226-27, 231-32, 234, 243-47
Hillborn, Cyrus 06, 107
   Mary 236
   Thomas 106, 107, 236
Hilles family 248
Hilton, Boyd 119, 331
Horsham Meeting 219
Howe, General 94
Huchinson family 243
Hulme, Albert 248
   Elizabeth 248
   George 110
   John 109, 110, 111, 248
   Joseph 105
   Mary 248
   Rachel S. 248
   Rebecca 243
   Samuel 137, 203, 205, 248
   Thomas Canby 207
Hulmeville 30, 109
Hyatt, Mary 236
Ilg, Frances 6
Individualism 7, 167, 177, 178
Industrialization 3, 195, 197
Ingham, Jonathan 80
Ingle, H. Larry 121, 132, 134, 332
Internal improvements 166, 167, 173
Inward Christ/ Guide/ Light 3, 35, 57, 98, 117, 118, 134, 156, 193, 221, 224
Iredell family 243
Isaac, Rhys 22, 341
Ivins family 243, 246
Jackson, Andrew 167, 171-173, 200, 218
James, Sydney 176, 332, 341
Janes, Abigail (Sands) 236

Janney, John L. 211
Jefferson, Thomas 146
Jenks, family 15, 67, 152, 153, 155, 262-63
   Ann 236, 155
   Daniel T. 112, 169
   Elizabeth 228, 236, 248
   Elizabeth (Jenks) 150, 154, 155
   Elizabeth (Story) 150, 155
   Elizabeth Pierson 150, 155
   Howard 196
   John 60, 68, 153, 236
   Joseph 68, 96, 97, 113, 128, 142, 144, 150, 153-155, 168, 196, 236, 248
   Lydia Ann (Martin) 148
   Mary 155, 236, 248
   Mary (Hutchinson) 153, 155
   Mary Ann 139, 155
   Mary, Jr. 139
   Mercy (Wildman) 68, 153, 236
   Michael H. 112, 114, 117, 128, 142, 144, 146, 154, 155, 157, 159, 166, 168, 171, 176, 218
   Phineas 112, 114-116, 127, 168, 187, 188, 194
   Rebecca (Richardson) 68
   Thomas 30, 33, 52, 68, 79, 80, 83, 86, 92, 96-99, 113, 128, 153, 168, 169, 194, 196, 236, 240
   Thomas, Jr. 86, 92, 93, 96-99, 153
   Thomas, Sr. 68, 236
   William 154
   William (d. 1818) 153, 155
   William J. 148
   William P. 248
   William Pierson 150, 155
Jenny, Elizabeth 236
Jolly, Letitia 236
Keithian schism 24
Kirkbride, family 15, 32, 79, 85, 92, 97, 113, 128, 144, 147, 155, 168, 171, 194, 196, 264-65
   Ann Elizabeth 248
   Charles W. 246
   Elizabeth 246
   Hannah 246
   Helena 234, 246
   John Blakey 246
   Jonathan 142, 155, 246
   Jonathan, Jr. 246
   Joseph 79, 85, 128
   Mahlon 32
   Mary 246
   Richard Maris 248
   Thomas 246
Knight family 244, 246

Giles 113
Kobrin, David Robert 38, 133, 333
Kohl, Lawrence 166, 333
Laing family 244
Lamb, Alice (Longshore) 236
    Thomas 236
Langhorne, Jeremiah 68
LaRue, Isaac 211
Latham, Ann 236
Levis/Lewis, Elizabeth 180
Levy, Barry 19, 51, 53, 96, 97, 333, 341
Light of Christ 17, 124 *See also* Inward Christ
Linton, family 15, 147, 191, 192, 266-67
    Ann 246
    Ann C. 246
    Benjamin 30
    Elizabeth 237
    Isaac 236
    James 129, 144, 156, 171, 246
    John 194, 200
    John, Jr. 168
    Jonathan 237
    Joseph 33, 237
    Joseph W. 196, 246
    Joshua 142
    Mahlon B. 127, 128, 168, 189, 190, 194
    Mary 237
    Mary (Blackshaw) 237
    Maurice P. 129
    Penquite 127, 168, 169, 182, 187, 189
    Phebe 237
    Sarah (Hirst) 156
    Thomas 142
Little, Craig B. 195, 341
Litwack, Leon 76, 333
Livezey family 246
    Isaac 185, 246
    Lloyd, John 237
    Susanna (Field) 237
Locke, John 21
London Yearly Meeting 20, 37, 59, 102, 140
Longshore, family 15, 50-51, 122, 147, 160, 191, 192, 200, 215, 228, 268-69
    Abdon B. 194
    Abraham 142, 144, 160, 196, 213, 246
    Alice (Stackhouse) 33, 50, 160, 237
    Anna Mary 129, 160
    Benjamin 237
    Carey 168, 189, 210, 211, 246
    Cyrus 237
    Elizabeth 237
    Ellen 194
    Euclydus[1] (1692-1764) 29, 50, 52, 160, 237, 240
    Euclydus, Jr. 237

Euclydus[2] (1735-1804) 51, 86, 97, 160, 237, 240
Euclydus[3] (1781-1838) 142
Hannah E. (Myers) 129, 160, 246
Isaac 210
James 194
Johanna (Vances) 237
Jolly 190, 194
Joseph S. 116, 127-129, 160, 168, 183, 186, 189-191, 198, 229, 246
Lucretia Mott 218, 246
Margaret 51, 194
Mary W. 246
Rhoda (Skelton) 160
Robert 28, 112, 194, 240
Samuel C. 246
Sarah (Gillam) 51
Thomas 30, 52, 237, 240
Thomas Ellwood 160, 183, 189, 192, 218, 229, 246
William H. 246
William E. Channing 246
Longstreth family 244
Lower Makefield Township 25, 32, 189, 220
Lukens family 244, 247
Makefield Meeting 23, 217
Manumission of slaves 5, 62, 67, 72
Marietta, Jack 2, 40-44, 132, 228, 333, 342
Market capitalism 3, 4, 101, 112, 135
Mather family 246
    Benjamin 137, 246
Mays, John 237
Marriage, Quaker *see* Friends, Religious Society of *and* Disciplinary offenses
Mazzenga, Maria 38
Mennonites 77, 81
Methodist 126, 133, 180, 181, 202, 319
Military activity 80, 81
Mitchell, family 15, 141, 152, 215, 270-1
    Ann 139
    Ann (Willett) 152
    Anna 246
    Caroline 246
    Catherine M. 246
    Elizabeth 246
    Emma 246
    Gove 196, 246
    Hannah (Comly) 138, 153
    Hannah H. 246
    Henry 86, 237
    Isaac S. 246
    John 52, 98, 237, 240
    John Allen (aka J. Allen) 142, 144, 153, 184, 185, 194, 213, 246
    John S. 129, 168, 196, 246

Mitchell, Joseph Paul 196, 246
    Joshua 168, 171, 194, 218
    Margaret (b. 25/12/1749/50) 237
    Margaret (Stackhouse) 237
    Phebe G. 246
    Pierson 139, 142, 145, 152, 158, 196, 246
    Richard 30, 32, 97, 237
    Samuel 86, 97, 237
    Sarah 237
    Sarah P. 246
    Tacy 246
    Tacy Ann 246
    William 142, 144, 194, 213, 246
    William P. 246
Mode, Andrew 237, 240
Monthly and Preparative Meetings *see names of individual meetings*
Moon, Hannah (Price) 237
    James 62, 66, 70, 75, 85, 126, 211, 237, 240, 242
Moravians 81
Morrisville and New Hope Railroad 113
Mott, Lucretia (Coffin) 177
Native Americans 22, 172, 173, 175, 200, 218
    See also Cherokee *and* Oneida
Naylor, Jane 237
    John 237
    Mary 237
Negroes 59, 61, 62, 68, 70, 72, 74, 174, 183
    See also African Americans
Neshaminy Creek 23, 24, 26, 30, 109
Neshaminy Lock Navigation Company 113, 126
Newbold, family 246, 248
    Elizabeth 207
    Emily 207
    John 207
New Garden Meeting 150
New Hope Bridge Company 113
Newspapers 13, 116, 168, 190, 192, 194
Newtown Meeting 23, 24, 116, 168
Newtown Township 24, 25, 30, 79, 89, 106, 112-17, 125, 168, 174, 175, 187, 190, 194, 200, 217, 220
Newtown and Bristol Railroad Company 113
Newtown Female Temperance Society 189
Northampton Township 25, 168, 220
Oblong (New York) Meeting 76
Oneida Indians 172
Orthodox Friends 3, 10, 14, 130, 131, 134-143, 145-164, 166, 177, 178, 180, 182, 188, 189, 191, 192, 196, 197, 200-203, 205-208, 211-214, 217, 218, 225-229, 231, 232, 234, 250
Panic of 1837 110, 115
Parry family 244, 246
Paxson, family 15, 147, 190, 215, 272-5

Paxson, Abraham 194, 198
    Ann 48, 139, 237
    Ann (Canby) 148, 151
    Ann (Paxson) 237
    Anna 151, 244
    Anna, Jr. 66
    Anna (Marriott) 65, 66, 94, 237
    Anna R. 246
    Anna W. 244
    Benjamin 106
    Charles H. 168
    Edward 244
    Edward M. 194
    Elihu 168
    Elizabeth 189, 237, 244
    Elizabeth (Randall) 106
    Elizabeth (Shoemaker) 151
    Frances 148
    Hannah (Thornton) 93
    Henry 237
    Isaac 112, 128, 129, 142, 144, 151, 168, 171, 196, 211, 213, 246
    Israel 171
    James 52, 93, 237, 240
    John 107, 112, 113, 128, 146, 151, 157, 159, 168, 171, 184, 185, 215, 237, 246
    John K. 194
    Jonathan 97, 168, 184, 194, 244
    Joseph 66, 72, 93, 94, 97, 168, 215, 237
    Joshua 244
    Mahlon 66
    Margery 244
    Mary 237, 244
    Mary (Watson) 237
    Mary R. 246
    Mary W. 189
    Oliver 76, 181
    Phineas 66, 87, 94, 105, 106, 189, 191, 237
    Rachel (Croasdale) 54
    Rachel (Woolston) 105, 189, 191
    Richard 168
    Richard S. 151, 152, 211
    Samuel 66
    Samuel H. 168, 196, 215, 246
    Samuel J. 194
    Sarah 244
    Sarah C. 244
    Sarah R. 246
    Sarah S. 246
    Susan K. 246
    Thomas 33, 48, 52, 66, 86, 97, 105, 142, 237, 240
    Willett 244
    William[2] (1685-1733) 63, 65, 237
    William[3] (1712-1767) 27, 29, 30, 32, 33, 52,

65, 94, 215, 237, 240
William[4] (1743-1799) 67, 88, 237
William (1773-1841) 168,
William (1779-1858) 148, 151
William Henry 168, 244
William R. 246
Peck, M. Scott 6-8, 73, 111, 133, 134, 146, 172, 199, 227-229, 334
Penn, Admiral Sir William 21, 27
William 21, 23, 125, 198
Pennsylvania currency 27
Pennsylvanian 218
Philadelphia and Trenton Railroad Company 113
Philadelphia Yearly Meeting 1, 3-5, 23, 37, 39, 42-44, 58, 61, 75, 81, 82, 87, 90, 96, 119, 120, 131, 134, 135, 147, 163, 180, 182, 190, 197, 203, 226, 228
Phillips, Aaron 99
Catherine (Payton) 40
Mercy (Comfort) 99, 157, 203, 205
Pickering, Joseph S. 172
Pierce family 244
Plumley, Ann (Stackhouse) 237
Charles 237
John 237
Plumstead Township 24, 25, 220
Poole, Joseph 237
Rebecca 237
William 237
Praul, John 27, 240
Presbyterians 24, 26, 31, 71, 116, 122, 126, 180, 194, 319
Preston, Jonas 237
Sarah (Carter) 237
"Primitive Christianity" 17
Primitive Friends 150, 228
Primus/Priner, Joseph 65
Purvis, Mary (Townsend) 76
Robert 75, 189
Quakers, *see* Friends, Religious Society of
Quietism 18, 19, 121
Race, John 211
Racism 57, 73-76, 172, 173, 175, 187, 188
Radbill, Kenneth Alan 96, 335
Randall/Randle, Elizabeth 237
George 237
Gilbert 211
John 237
Joseph 237
Mary (Hardin) 237
Rebecca 237
Rebecca, Jr. 237
Rationalism 38, 122, 130, 133, 135, 160, 227
Religion, bias in reporting 8-9
emissary 5, 132-134, 228

exemplary 5, 8, 72, 133, 134, 228
extrinsic 5, 6
intrinsic 5
marginality 73, 83, 224
passionate/indifferent 8, 130, 154, 229
See also Faith development
Religious Society of Friends, *see* Friends, Religious Society of
Revolutionary War *see* War, American Revolution
Rice, Mary 211
Richardson, family 15, 63, 67, 141, 149, 190, 215, 276-7
Ann 139, 141, 203
Anna 246
Anna (Paxson) 149, 191, 200
Clayton N. 142, 145, 168, 169, 196
Edward 247
Elizabeth 139
Elizabeth (Jenks) 64, 67, 149, 153
Hannah 139
Jane 234, 247
Joseph 27, 29, 52, 63-65, 74, 75, 144, 145, 149, 237, 240, 247
Joshua 62-68, 97, 113, 128, 144, 149, 168, 171, 184, 185, 194, 196, 237, 241, 247
Mary 237, 247
Mary (Paxson) 63, 64, 149, 237
Mary J. 247
Rachel 149, 237
Rebecca 139, 237
Rebecca (Newbold) 145, 203
Ruth 149, 237
Sarah (Preston) 64, 65
Susanna 139
William 62, 64-67, 97, 98, 112, 128, 142, 144, 149, 153, 190, 191, 237
William, Jr. 144
William R. 142
Rich family 247
Richland Township 24, 25, 219, 220
Richmond Monthly Meeting in Yorkshire 63
Ritner, Governor Joseph 174
Roberts family 248
Elizabeth 237
Evan 203, 248
Rodman, family 69, 98, 229
Gilbert 70, 99
John 69, 237
Mary 237
Thomas 69, 99
William 60, 61, 88, 92, 93, 99, 237
William, Jr. 70, 99
Rush, Benjamin 181
Sands, John 237

Sands, Mary 237
  Richard 237
  Richard, Jr. 237
  Stephen 237
  William 237
Satterthwaite, family 248
  M. 204
  Pleasant (Mead) 237
  William 237
Scarborough family 247
  John 63, 247
Schofield, Oliver 175, 190, 191
Schwenkfelders 81
Scotch-Irish settlers 24, 26
Scott, Benjamin 237
  Benjamin, Jr. 237
  Jane (Twining) 237
  Thomas 237
Shackleton, Abraham 124
Shaw, George 237
  Gilbert H. 247
  Joseph 237
  Mary 46, 237
Simler, Lucy 26, 343
Simmons, Henry, Jr. 172
  Mary (Paxson) 172
Skepticism 7, 111, 130, 161, 229
Slack, Margaret 211
Slavery 2, 3, 5, 36, 42, 57-59, 61, 63, 68-73, 77, 132, 133, 174, 188-190, 223
Slaves: Davenport, Joseph 64, 65
  James 68
  Joe 64
  Lucia 66, 67
  Matilda 66, 67
  Primus/Priner, Joseph 65
Slaves, purchase of 58, 62, 68, 70, 88
Smith, family 244
  Alexander H. 211
  Joseph 237, 241
  Rachel (Wildman) 237
  Thomas 80-81
Smith-Rosenberg, Carroll 173, 336
Soderlund, Jean 5, 49, 72, 132, 134, 228, 336
Solebury Meeting 217
Solebury Township 24, 25, 190, 220
Southampton Township 24, 25, 168, 171, 220
Speculation 104, 109, 110, 115-18, 153, 215
  merino sheep 115-6
  silk worm industry 115-6
Spicer, James 238
Stackhouse, family 15, 94, 95, 148, 278-81
  Abel 87, 238
  Amos B. 142, 144
  Ann 238

Stackhouse, Ann (Allen) 150
  Benjamin 238
  Caleb 237
  David 151
  David L. 247
  Deborah 238
  Elizabeth 247
  Elizabeth (Janney) 237
  Elizabeth L. 247
  Grace 141
  Grace (Comfort) 88, 99, 145, 148, 157, 205
  Hannah 238
  Hannah (Watson) 238
  Hastings 94, 95
  Isaac 30, 33, 52, 88, 97, 128, 144, 159, 238, 240
  Jacob 238
  James 30, 94, 194, 240, 318
  Job 92, 238
  John 33, 88, 97, 238
  John, Jr. 237
  John W. 113
  Jonathan 88, 97, 99, 145, 148
  Jonathan (b. 31/8/1750) 238
  Jonathan K. 142, 144
  Jonathan P. 168
  Joseph 52, 95, 196, 238, 240
  Joseph, Jr. 238
  Joshua 46, 238
  Lucilla 238
  Macre 148
  Mary 138, 238, 247
  Mary (Harding) 238
  Mary L. 247
  Mercy 139, 148, 205, 234, 248
  Mercy (Comfort) 203
  Moses 238
  Rebecca 244
  Robert 94
  Samuel Allen 148, 248
  Sarah 238, 247
  Sarah (Copeland) 238
  Susanna S. 244
  Thomas 74, 95, 168, 238
  Timothy 32
  William 148
Stamp Act 78
Stanton, Daniel 39
Stapler, Thomas 59, 60, 62, 66
Steere, Douglas V. 18, 336
Stirling, General 89
Stockdale, Sarah (Field, Jr.) 238
  William 238
Stokes, Susannah 238
Swain family 244

Benjamin 110
Sydney, Algernon 21
Sykes, John 121, 336
Taber, William 19, 337, 343
Tayler family 244, 248
Taylor, Bayard 211
Taylor, Zachery 218
Temperance 100, 127, 158, 160, 169, 177, 179-184, 187, 190, 192, 200, 217, 226
   American Temperance Society 180
   Bucks County Society for the Promotion of Temperance 181-82, 183
   Newtown Female Temperance Society 189
   total abstinence 127, 160, 181, 183, 185, 190, 229
   Washingtonian movement 181
Testimonies 2, 17, 18, 39-41, 55-57, 59, 83, 91, 93, 96, 98, 100, 106, 108, 139, 170, 171, 175, 179, 203, 215, 216, 221, 223-225
   economic 18, 102-9, 111
   equality 17, 18,
   hat honor 17
   oaths 18, 59, 87, 100, 165, 169-170, 207
   office holding 2, 70, 92
   peace 2, 18, 78, 82, 83, 86, 90, 91, 118, 120, 173, 179
   plain dress 2, 18, 49
   plain language 2, 17, 49
   slave-holding 2, 57, 59, 63, 65, 70, 73, 149
   tithes 18
Thackray, Isaac 242
   James 46, 238, 240
   Rachel 238
Thomas family 247
   Abel 125
Thompson, John 84, 85
Thornton, Joseph 60, 238
   Margaret 238
Tinicum Township 24, 25, 220
Tolles, Frederick B. 122, 132, 337, 343
Tomlinson, Elizabeth (Stackhouse) 238
   Thomas 238
Tories 79, 93, 96
Townsend, Grace (Croasdale) 72
Townshend Acts 78
Toynbee, Arnold 223
Trevose 32
Tully, Alan 23, 337
Turner, Edward Raymond 75, 337, 344
Twining, Samuel 60, 238
Tyrrell, Ian R. 179, 185, 337
Tyson family 247
Unitarians 3, 10, 122, 159, 202
Upper Makefield Township 25, 80, 220
VanBuren, Martin 218

Walker, Benjamin 238
   George 238, 240
   Joseph 238, 241
   Robert 242
   Sarah (Heaton) 238
Wallace, Anthony 129, 337
Walton family 247
War: American Revolution 2, 4, 12, 18, 27, 38, 51, 70, 71, 73, 77, 90, 91, 95, 96, 99, 101, 102, 104, 105, 116, 118, 120-122, 165, 170, 176, 177, 187, 224, 229
   Civil War (English) 17
   Civil War (U.S.A.) 109, 228
   Great War for Empire (French and Indian) 2, 132, 165, 216
   Mexican 218
   War of 1812 13, 141
   See also Conscription, *and* Military activity
Warner family 244, 247, 248
Warrington Township 24, 25, 220
Warwick Township 24, 25, 220
Watson, family 15, 92, 147, 282-83
   Amos 95, 238
   Ann (Jenks) 218
   Benjamin 242
   Elizabeth 247
   Franklin 247
   Isaiah 247
   John 29, 32, 52, 84, 85, 97, 137, 142, 144, 168, 238, 241, 242, 247
   John, Jr. 196, 248
   Jonathan 194
   Jonathan L. 194
   Joseph 32, 79, 80, 142, 194, 196, 218, 238, 247
   Joseph John 247
   Lydia 247
   Mark (of Falls) 32
   Marmaduke 127, 189, 191
   Martha (Neeld) 238
   Mary (Richardson) 189, 191, 200, 203
   Mary Elizabeth 247
   Reuben 194
   Ruth (Blakey) 238
   Ruth, Jr. 238
   Stacy 196
   Susan G. 247
   Susannah (Woolston) 89
   Thomas 238
   Thomas (of Buckingham) 89, 98, 326
   William 31, 194
   William G. 247
   William H. 168
Weber, Max 5, 132, 228, 337
Wells, Robert 233, 338, 344

Western District Monthly Meeting 152
Wharton family 244
Whig party 167-169, 172, 200
White, Joseph 103
    Josiah 103
Wilber, Ken 6, 199, 227, 338
Wilbur, John 178, 325
Wilburite Friends 14, 228
Wildman, family 15, 147, 284-85
    Abi 247
    Abigail 247
    Abigail T. 247
    Ann (Paxson) 98
    Anna 247
    Benjamin A. 244
    Charles 189, 244
    Edward 196, 247
    Ellwood 244
    Elwood 168
    Hector 247
    James 52, 97, 142, 144, 194, 196, 238, 241, 247
    Jane T. 247
    John 60, 88, 144, 148, 168, 196, 238, 242, 247
    John K. 244
    Joseph 97, 98, 238, 242
    Joshua 168
    Martin 238, 242
    Mary H. 247
    Rachel 238, 246
    Rachel (Walton) Myers 138
    Rachel W. 247
    Sarah (Wilson) 238
    Solomon 97, 144
    Susanna S. (Albertson) 189, 244
Wilkenson, John 80
Williams, Stephen 27, 30, 241
    William 211
Willitt, Augustine 126
Wilmington 66, 271, 273
Wilson, family 15, 147, 286-87
    Ann (Dewees) 108, 247
    Anthony 64, 238
    Asaph 238
    David 30, 33, 48, 52, 64, 238, 241
    Dinah 238
    Elizabeth (Stackhouse) 48, 238
    Grace (Stackhouse) 33, 238
    Hampton 144
    Jesse 238
    John 129
    Jonathan 238
    Joseph 142, 144
    Mardon 107, 108, 113, 114, 128, 137, 142, 144, 146, 157, 159
    Mardon, Jr. 196, 247
    Margaret 247
    Rachel 238
    Rebecca (Hoge) 238
    Samuel 238
    Sarah P. 247
    Sidney 139
    Stephen 29, 46, 52, 129, 238, 241
    Thomas 62, 72, 241
    Thomas (of Southampton) 72, 238
    William 168, 196
    William B. 168, 171
Women, fertility 233
    heads of households 234
    meetings 20, 140
    rights 160
    sexism 193
    status of 2, 18, 234
Woolman, John 18, 39, 53, 59, 73, 99, 103, 156, 157, 161, 189
Woolston, family 15, 147, 148, 198, 288-9
    Ann 211, 247
    Benjamin 238
    Eliza 234, 247
    Elizabeth, Jr. 238
    Elizabeth (Kelly) 189
    Elizabeth (Stockton) 189
    Elizabeth (Wildman) 238
    Hannah (Palmer) 238
    Jeremiah 52, 241
    John 32, 52, 66, 97, 238, 241
    Jonathan 65, 74, 75, 97, 138, 142-144
    Jonathan (b. 22/11/1750/1) 238
    Joshua 97, 109, 112, 113, 171, 188, 191, 194
    Joshua (1755-1821) 148
    Lydia (Jordan) 148
    Mary 238
    Mercy 238
    Samuel 30, 46, 52, 238, 241
    Sarah 238
    Stephen 189
    Thomas L. 194
Worcester v Georgia 172, 173
Worstal, Edward 238
    James 238
    John 238
Worthington family 247
Wright, Charles 241
    Joseph 27, 238, 241
    Rebecca 238
    Thomas 241
Wrightstown 50, 217
Wyatt-Brown, Bertram 22, 338
Yardley, George 150, 263